COADE LONDON
1819

VOLUME ONE

CANADA'S
FIRST
BANK

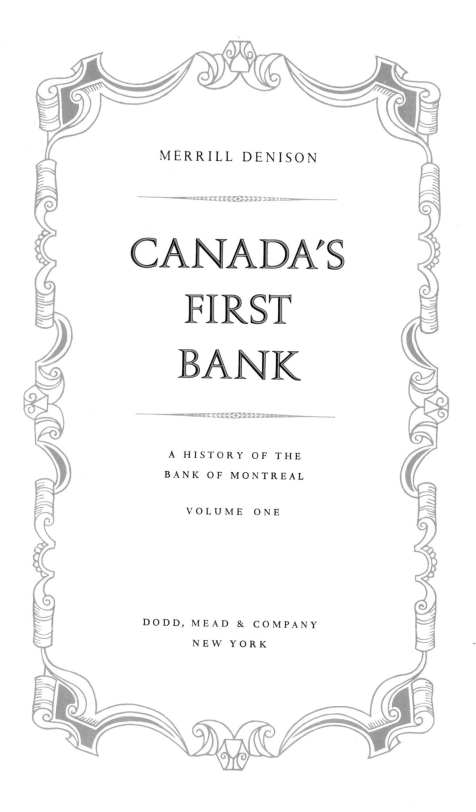

MERRILL DENISON

CANADA'S
FIRST
BANK

A HISTORY OF THE
BANK OF MONTREAL

VOLUME ONE

DODD, MEAD & COMPANY
NEW YORK

L.C. Catalog Card Number: 66-16747

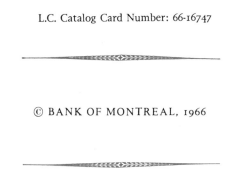

Quotations from the following works appear in this text with the
permission of the publishers:

J. Bartlet Brebner, *Canada: A Modern History*.
Ann Arbor, Michigan: The University of Michigan Press, 1960.

Arthur Bryant, *The Age of Elegance, 1812-1822*.
London: William Collins, Sons & Co., Ltd., 1950.

Bray Hammond, *Banks and Politics in America from
the Revolution to the Civil War*.
Princeton, N.J.: Princeton University Press, 1957.

L. S. Pressnell, *Country Banking in the Industrial Revolution*.
Oxford: The Clarendon Press, 1956.

Dodd, Mead & Company
New York

Printed in Canada by The Southam Printing Company Limited

INTRODUCTION

In 1967 the Bank of Montreal will be observing not only the Centennial of Confederation but also the 150th anniversary of its own founding. The publication, in both English and French, of a comprehensive history of the Bank was, we felt, one of the ways in which we might appropriately celebrate these events.

Most suited to the occasion, it was thought, would be a work that would set the long record of the Bank's activities in an illuminating historical perspective, thus increasing its interest for the general reader. We recognized from the outset that this would be no easy task, and we were therefore very pleased when Merrill Denison agreed to undertake the work. His experience as an industrial historian and his ability to look at Canada in its North American context rather than as a separate economic entity were considered essential to the study of an institution that was international in scope from its earliest days.

The Bank's records and account books dating back to 1817 were made available to Mr. Denison without reservation, and supplementary research was carried on not only across Canada but also in the United States and the United Kingdom. Working with this material, Mr. Denison has brought to light many hitherto neglected aspects of Canadian economic history, and in so doing has provided a fresh insight into the country's development. To give a single example, we believe the crucial part played by John Richardson in his several attempts to start a bank in Canada between 1792 and 1817 has now been fully described for the first time. While rendering a faithful account of the Bank of Montreal as an institution, and of the people who guided its destiny, Mr. Denison has also presented and discussed, vividly and sometimes controversially, the changing economic, political and social environment in which the Bank has conducted its affairs.

To supplement the text, a number of Canadian artists were commissioned to portray scenes from the history of the Bank and of the country. In addition, a selection from existing collections of prints and paintings has been reproduced. We hope that these illustrations will be enjoyed and that, in combination with the text, they will help to stimulate interest in the history of Canada.

Mr. Denison has summed up his own feelings towards our Canadian heritage in these words: "If the facts of the long struggle were more widely understood . . . if there were a deeper appreciation of this historic background, there could be no Canadian inferiority complex; Canadians instead would view themselves proudly in the light of their incredible accomplishments."

In presenting this work as the history of a single institution, we commend it also as a wide-ranging story of Canadian achievement.

Arnold Hart

CHAIRMAN AND PRESIDENT

Montreal,
December 1, 1965.

FOREWORD

For nearly 150 years, successive officers of the Bank of Montreal have been recording the history of their institution in weekly instalments. Written entirely in long-hand, this valuable chronicle is to be found in the Minute, or Resolve, Books of the Board of Directors. Alongside these books in the Bank's archives rest similar records of the several banks that have become part of the corporation through amalgamation: the Bank of British North America, the Molsons Bank, and the Merchants Bank of Canada.

The use of this formidable mass of material, consisting of 108 folio volumes, entailed first its microfilming, and, second, the making of typescript copies for convenient reference. Examination soon indicated that while the Minutes provided an indispensable diary of banking activities and policy decisions, reasons were rarely given and there were few clues to the economic environment in which the management was operating from one decade to another. It was therefore necessary to expand the frame of reference, and research continually revealed new areas of interest that could not be ignored. As a result, this work has become as much a study of a fascinating ecological phenomenon as the biography of a great financial institution. To describe it as definitive would be an error. As an exploratory document, on the other hand, it may serve to open unfamiliar vistas and present the travail of Canada's unfolding in a new perspective.

Every historical writer is, of course, beholden to those who have trod the ground before him and whose special knowledge is his to call upon when needed. This writer is no exception, but if documentation had been supplied for every statement and observation, the book would have taken on the appearance of a cumbersome text. It was therefore decided that there should be no footnotes at all.

Nevertheless, the debt owed to the works of such authorities as the late Dr. Adam Shortt will be apparent to anyone conversant with the literature of Canadian banking. Dr. Shortt's studies in currency and banking have become guideposts to later writers on these subjects, and his series of biographical sketches of Canadian bankers published in the *Journal of The Canadian Bankers' Association* often provide the only information still extant on the lives of Canadians, once eminent, whose stature derived from their leadership in finance, trade, and industry rather than politics.

No less basic for an understanding of contemporary banking in the United States, and of the influences both negative and positive that ricocheted across the border, has been the scholarly assistance rendered personally and through their published works by Mr. Bray Hammond, Dr. Ralph W. Hidy, and Dr. Fritz Redlich. In a different vein, the extraordinary co-operation received from Mr. A. J. H. Richardson calls for special recognition. Early in this project, Mr. Richardson, now with the Historic Sites and Monuments Commission in Ottawa, turned over to the writer his notes for a long-contemplated work on the origins and development of Canadian commercial activity during the eighteenth and early nineteenth centuries. While much of the material lay outside the Bank of Montreal period, it gave the writer an insight into colonial trade and commerce and the dashing men engaged in it that he could never have obtained elsewhere.

Other contributions have been furnished in the same generous spirit: by Mr. S. W. Shelton, Archivist of Glyn, Mills & Co., in London, who supplied microfilms of documents and ledgers, accounts and correspondence pertaining to the role played by that famous institution as London agent of the Bank of Montreal and also, for a period of almost sixty years, as fiscal agent of successive Canadian governments; by Colonel George R. Stevens, whose war-time connections in London unlocked doors ordinarily impossible to open; and by Dr. Craig McIvor of McMaster University and Dr. Kaye Lamb, both of whom made many helpful criticisms of the work in manuscript. From the very commencement of the project, Dr. Lamb, both as a friend and as Dominion Archivist, has given the author much assistance. Not only have the unique resources of the Public Archives at Ottawa been his to call upon, but Dr. Lamb has unfailingly responded to the many demands that were made on his time and scholarly insight.

Many librarians have co-operated beyond the mere use of their facilities, foremost among them the Bank's own librarians, the late Miss Kay Carpenter and her successors, Miss Elaine Harrington and Miss Georgia Phelan, together with their staffs; also Miss Melva Eagleson of the Douglas Memorial Library at Queen's University, Kingston, Miss Marie Baboyant of the Montreal Municipal Library, Miss Beatrice Simon of the Redpath Library at McGill University, and Mrs. Isobel Dobell of McGill's McCord Museum. Major Guy de M. Belleau, Curator of the Royal 22nd Museum at the Citadel in Quebec, was also very helpful in providing and locating material in that city, not only from the Regiment's museum but also from the Provincial and Quebec Municipal Archives.

There are many debts connected directly with the acquisition of biographical and personal material to be acknowledged: to Miss Rosanna Seaborn Todd and Mrs. George Fialkowski for making available diaries kept by their forbears while in the service of the Hudson's Bay Company early in the last century, and also the personal scrap-book of Sir Edward S. Clouston, the Bank's vice-president and general manager from 1890 to 1911; to Messrs. F. W. R. and Donald F. Angus for providing access to the private letter-books of R. B. Angus, the general manager of the Bank from 1869 to 1879 and president from 1910 to 1913; to Mr. and Mrs. F. Alexander Gates of Hamilton, Ontario, for supplying genealogies of the Gates and Bellows families and descriptions of testimonial presentations, still in their possession, made to the Honourable Horatio Gates; to Messrs. Charles and Hazen Porteous for releasing the voluminous business correspondence files of their grandfather, one-time manager of the Port Hope, Ontario, branch of the Bank and later a highly-placed associate of Mackenzie and Mann; and, finally, to Colonel Stephen G. Cantlie who afforded access to a collection of some 135 letters in his possession which had been written by Sir John A. Macdonald to George Stephen (later Lord Mount Stephen) during the building of the main line of the Canadian Pacific Railway between 1881 and 1886.

In the collection and organization of material, the Bank has made possible the employment of a staff of research workers and assistants; among these have been Mabel Tinkiss Good, William E. Greening, Guy Meyler, Patrick F. O'Dwyer, R. H. Hall, Michael S. Addinall, Edgar K. Harding, and Michael G. Huband, the last of whom assisted greatly in the preparation of the final text. The manuscript was typed by Mary Savigny, whose services are also gratefully acknowledged. In addition, the number of the Bank's staff in Montreal, New York, London, and throughout Canada who have responded to calls upon their time has been legion, and two hundred or more of the Bank's pensioners have contributed their personal reminiscences. Special thanks must be given to Messrs. C. W. Harris, J. E. Toten and Munro Brown, the officers of the Bank who have been most intimately connected with the historical project.

Finally, I must also express my deep sense of obligation and gratitude to the Bank of Montreal as represented in the persons of Mr. Arthur C. Jensen, former Chairman of the Board, Mr. G. Arnold Hart, Chairman and President, and Mr. R. D. Mulholland, Vice-President and Chief General Manager, for their unfailing support, and for the extraordinary opportunity that has been given me to work in a relatively unexplored field of Canadian history.

Montreal,
October 15, 1965.

CONTENTS

LIST OF ILLUSTRATIONS

PAINTINGS BY CANADIAN ARTISTS
COMMISSIONED FOR THIS BOOK

A SELECTION OF PAINTINGS,
MAPS, AND DRAWINGS OF THE PERIOD

THE BANK'S FIRST
PERMANENT BUILDING

After operating in rented premises on St. Paul Street for about eighteen months, the Montreal Bank moved into its own building at the northeast corner of St. James and St. François Xavier streets in the spring of 1819. This building—the first in the Canadas to be designed specifically for banking purposes—was on the site of the Bank's present Head Office.

ONE

WITHOUT
FANFARE

Montreal Bank,

23d October, 1817s

T HE B A N K will begin its operations on MONDAY, the 3d of November next.

Bank Hours from 10 o'clock, A M to 3 o'clock P M.

Discount Days, *Tuesdays* and *Fridays*. Bills and Notes for Discount to be sent under cover to the Cashier on the days preceeding

Such was the announcement which preceded the formal opening at ten o'clock in the morning on November 3, 1817, of Canada's first permanent banking institution. Published by order of a newly elected Board of Directors, and inserted by a newly appointed Cashier, the notice duly made its appearance in two of Montreal's contemporary newspapers, the *Herald* and the *Canadian Courant*, on their several days of publication. A copy of the former only has been discovered, but it is most probable that the other insertion was a replica of the resolution adopted by the Board of Directors at a meeting held on October 23. Appearing on an inside page of the *Herald* and flanked by notices of fancy wines and spirits and Mr. Skakel's Classical and Mathematical School for young gentlemen, the modest banking proclamation conveyed no sense of historic import, no suggestion that the event impending could exert a potent influence on Canada's future. Couched in the leanest terms imaginable, the nine-line business card simply took its place in the commercial intelligence of the day as an item of minor importance.

The official opening itself was no more impressive. Although the occasion marked the culmination of twenty-five years of effort to establish a bank in the Province of Lower Canada, no ceremony of any kind was held. No ribbon was cut, no golden key provided. Whether the Bank's first officers, John Gray, the President, and Thomas Turner, the Vice-President, were in attendance is unknown. If they were, Robert Griffin, the Cashier, did not bother to record their presence when he wrote up the Minutes. In fact, he did not even bother to note the opening.

Yet November 3, 1817, can be regarded as one of the significant dates in Canadian history. Except among exponents of the most radical economic and monetary theories, there can be no question as to the value of the contributions made to Canada's development by the banking practices first introduced by the founders of the Bank of Montreal and adopted later by other banks and endorsed by legislative statute. At a time when the small, struggling British North American provinces of Lower and Upper Canada were without a currency of their own, the Montreal Bank, as the Bank of Montreal was originally called, first provided an acceptable and greatly needed circulating medium in the form of bank-notes redeemable in specie, a safe repository for business funds and private savings, a source of commercial loans at established rates of interest, and a reliable instrument for the purchase of foreign bills of exchange and other commercial paper, the price of which had hitherto been subject to chaotic fluctuations. But these are such familiar facts of Canadian economic history that they may be accepted as axiomatic. So may the role played by individual banks and the banking system generally in the slow and often difficult growth of the national economy from its dependence on a few primary staples to the complex industrialism of the present day. What have generally gone unrecognized, however, are the influences exerted by the chartered banks of Canada on other phases of national development.

Students of North American history have noted the striking contrasts presented by westward expansion on the two sides of the common boundary: on the one hand the advance of the frontier was marked by warfare and individual lawlessness, on the other by peaceful occupation and the observance of law and order. Reasons for the difference are of course to be found further back in history, but an added factor can be seen in Canada's highly centralized banking system with its rapid proliferation of branches. South of the international boundary the sheriff and the six-shooter have become the popular symbols of civilization as it advanced westward: in Canada, a fitting substitute would be an unobtrusive man in a dark suit armed only with a black satchel containing cash and deposit slips and other blank forms needed to open a branch bank. Thanks to the great fur-trading companies, the North West Mounted Police and, later, the chartered banks, Canada has never really had a frontier in the American sense of the word. Canada's banks and bankers have, in fact, affected the national mores far beyond the realms of finance, commerce, and material development.

In dealing with the opening of Canada's oldest bank, therefore, we are concerned not only with the birth of a great and venerable Canadian institution, but also with the men who founded it and in so doing set in motion dynamic influences that have helped to mould the Canada we know today: John Richardson, the chief architect of the Canadian commercial state; Horatio Gates, the New England merchant whose Boston and New York connections finally made possible the establishment of Canada's first bank; the belligerent George Moffatt, a director who almost tore the Bank asunder; the scholarly John Fleming who wrote poetry and who left the largest library that had been collected in Canada to that time when he died of cholera in 1832. These commercial giants of another day, along with lesser Forsyths, Ermatingers, Leslies, Platts and Thayers, are now no more than shadows on the pages of Canadian history.

Portraits of many of the founders are extant but biographical data about them are often to be found only in obituary notices that supply no second dimension, much less a third. A few of the original directors took part in the political conflicts of the early nineteenth century, and for that reason appear in the pages of Canadian history, but the majority were business men who left few personal or commercial papers to help bring them back to life.

While the lineaments of once greatly influential figures now elude recapture, the stage on which they played their parts can be readily projected. Few cities on the continent have produced more devoted historians than Montreal, and in their pages, from Dollier de Casson through Stephen Leacock to the contemporary Edgar Andrew Collard, are pictured the sights and activities of every decade for more than three hundred years. For ninety years also, the Antiquarian and Numismatic Society of Montreal has sought to identify the city's historic sites. From these sources, in addition to the Bank's own records, it is known that the Montreal Bank first opened its doors for business in rented premises on St. Paul Street in the block between Vaudreuil and St. Vincent streets in the very heart of the old city.

A block to the south lay the greenish flood of the St. Lawrence River and a short distance to the west, the Place d'Armes, where stood the parish church of Notre Dame and where the gallant Maisonneuve, founder of Ville Marie, had his first encounter with the Iroquois Indians in 1644. No marker records the site of the first bank premises at what was then 32 St. Paul Street, but we know that they were owned by Robert Armour, who, with his partner George Davis, had used them as a general store. The merchandising business, however, had run into financial difficulties, a situation not unknown to Montreal at the time, and the Bank's lease had to be negotiated with the assignees. The rental period was from August 30, 1817, to May 1, 1818, the rent amounting to £150.

The Bank's first premises were strategically located, for, in 1817, St. Paul Street was the principal business thoroughfare of a thriving, fast-growing trading and agricultural community, which numbered about sixteen thousand inhabitants in the town proper and its five suburbs. Newly paved, and lighted by whale-oil lamps installed only two years before, the narrow artery traversed the city from east to west, following a contour now obscured which roughly paralleled the river to the south and marked the foot of a rocky spine along which ran Notre Dame and St. James streets to the north. Lining the street for most of its length stood solid stone structures, many of which owed their presence to the prosperous Vermont trade that had begun in the 1790's and had continued with little abatement during the War of 1812. In such buildings resided most of the town's merchants, who had their shops, counting rooms and warehouses on the street level and dwelling quarters above. Travel memoirs dwell upon the charm of a river view punctuated by numerous church spires, tin roofs glittering in the sun, and ubiquitous fire ladders appended, in accordance with the law, to every gable. Since the entire area within the old city walls comprised no more than ninety acres, it is evident that anyone having business with the Bank would have had a few hundred yards to walk at most.

Even today St. Paul Street retains some of its early nineteenth century architectural quality; hence the appearance of the Bank's first premises can be imagined. In all likelihood, a single doorway on the street level gave access to a vestibule and beyond to an improvised banking chamber, lit by deeply recessed windows which were covered at night with heavy iron shutters. At the rear, according to an 1825 map, was an irregular courtyard surrounded by the gabled walls of other buildings. We know that Mr. Griffin had his living quarters in the Armour house, but of the interior arrangements of the earliest Canadian banking chamber we know very little. The Directors' Minutes contain references to "the counter" and, along it, railings behind which the staff worked in protective isolation. The month being November and the Canadian climate being what it was and is, we can be sure that some means of heating was provided—fireplaces, probably, and perhaps one or more of the prefabricated, knockdown cast-iron stoves manufactured at the Forges du St. Maurice near Three Rivers, in French days one of the largest iron works in North America. We can picture also the high book-keeping desks later to be romanticized by Charles Dickens, and upon them quill pens, ink dusting powder and the pristine sheepskin-bound ledgers just procured from Nickless & McDonnell, Stationers and Bookbinders, "opposite the Courthouse."

About one aspect of the opening morning we can be certain: the staff of seven, being paid employees, were in their places—the Cashier, Robert Griffin, a man of standing in the community and brother of the Bank's first notary, Henry Griffin; Henry B. Stone, the first teller, on loan from the Bank's mercantile friends in Boston; James Jackson, the second teller; Henry Dupuy, the accountant, who had just returned by a devious route from Hartford, Connecticut, where he had been sent on a somewhat delicate mission; Benjamin Holmes, the discount clerk, who later, as Cashier, was to prove a source of both strength and weakness; Allan McDonell, the second bookkeeper, and Alexander McNiven, the porter.

Of these seven employees Stone was to leave his mark on the history of American banking, and Holmes on that of Canada. Little can be learned about the others beyond their names and the details of their employment.

BANKING BEGINS
AT 32 ST. PAUL STREET

Winter was tossing its first snow about under cold grey skies when, on November 3, 1817, Canada's first bank quietly opened its doors onto Montreal's main street. Twenty-five years of effort had preceded this occasion, and yet it appears to have fallen on the populace with no more weight than the snowflakes they were brushing from their coats.

The men who founded the Montreal Bank, however, were not disturbed by this apparent neglect. To them the Bank was not an experiment; as progressive merchant-traders, they saw banking as a vital necessity to the proper conduct of their business and an inevitable adjunct to Canadian development.

Montreal at this time was the centre of the country's commerce and St. Paul Street was the hub of the city's activity. The location of the Bank, at the corner of Vaudreuil Street, was no more than a few paces from the headquarters of most of the country's mercantile houses. The spire of Bonsecours Church, a familiar landmark to sailors, can be seen at the far end of St. Paul Street, much as it appears today.

Many of the merchants lived above their places of business, but not so John Gray, the first president of the Montreal Bank, who had a good five miles to travel in his coach from his residence in the village of St. Catherines. We see him here as he would have arrived any Tuesday or Friday during those first weeks to preside over the consideration of discounts.

Painting by Lorne Bouchard, R.C.A.

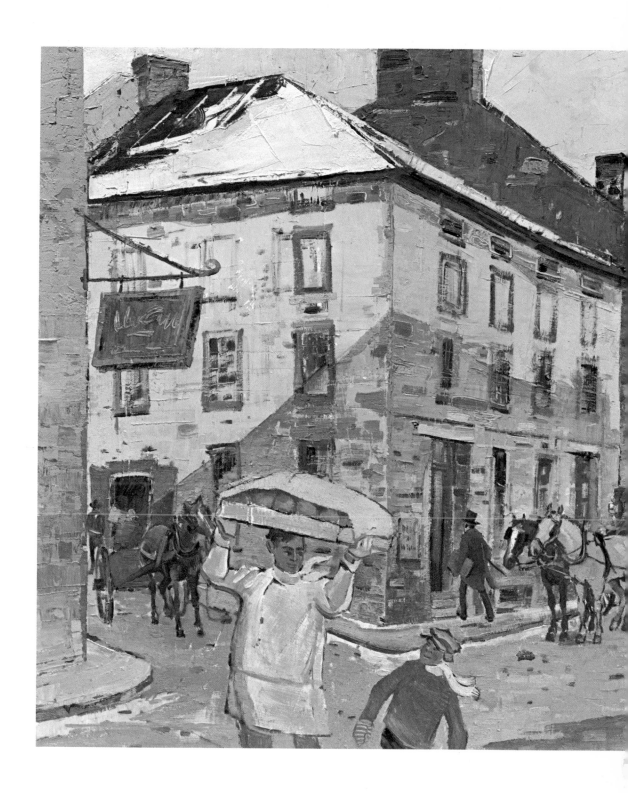

Although members of the staff were chosen from amongst a number of applicants, it is probable that the only one with any banking experience was Stone, who had served with the Manufacturers and Mechanics Bank of Boston. The others were likely schooled in the art of double-entry book-keeping but, whatever their other qualifications or experience, the mere fact that they numbered seven must have impressed the Montreal business and mercantile fraternity with the serious purpose of the founders of Canada's long-awaited, pioneer financial institution.

That several persons were so impressed is attested by the next day's Minutes of the Board. In Robert Griffin's flowing script is a brief notation to the effect that "several discounts were offered, some of which were agreed to." The first deposit ledger, one of the few early books of account that have been preserved, bears witness to other encouraging activities on the opening day In it are recorded the names of persons who called to open accounts and make deposits.

Some of the names are still well-known in Montreal today, others are long since forgotten. In either case, they are significant. In a community in which commercial enterprise was cordially distrusted by a large segment of the population, the first depositors of the Montreal Bank not only had faith in the usefulness of the institution and the integrity of its directors, but were instrumental in starting a chain reaction of far-reaching consequences. With funds on deposit, it was possible for the first time in Canada to transfer money by cheque.

The payee, upon presentation of the cheque at the Bank, would receive bank-notes in return, which represented the Montreal Bank's promise to pay the bearer, on demand, the face value of the note in gold or silver coins. In the beginning, the Bank's promises to pay would have been based very largely on the *bona fides* of the directors, all of whom were known to be men of substance with established business reputations. Bank-notes were by no means a novelty in Lower and Upper Canada, of course; preceding them had been the Army Bills issued during the War of 1812, and American bank-notes circulated freely, especially in Montreal and along the Vermont border. In the minds of French Canadians, however, there lingered a deep distrust of paper money, an inheritance from the card money of the Ancien Régime and from the worthless Continental currency introduced by the American Army during its invasion of the Province of Quebec in 1775. The prejudice was soon to be seized upon in an attempt to undermine the Bank, but the

MONTREAL — 1803

Montreal was 161 years old and had a population of more than 9,000 when this print was published on March 1, 1803.

The hill at the far right, on top of which sits the Citadel with its Union Jack, was levelled about 1820 to provide fill for a nearby pond and to extend the Champ de Mars parade ground. The military supplies and munitions were then moved to St. Helen's Island, where this picture was painted.

At the foot of Citadel Hill can be seen Bonsecours Church, in which mass is still regularly celebrated. Next to it is the large stone residence of Sir John Johnson, who succeeded his father, Sir William, as Superintendent of Indian Affairs. This building later became the famous Mansion House Hotel.

To the left of Mount Royal, which rises 700 feet above the river, the spire of the Parish Church of Ville Marie marks the site of Place d'Armes, home of the Bank of Montreal since 1819.

prompt acceptance, from 1817, of its notes as currency in Canadian commercial circles and the adjacent American states, reveals the need that then existed.

Taken all in all, when the Cashier secured the Bank's premises at the close of the first day's business, the staff could feel that they had participated in a successful opening. In the light of Montreal's commercial prospects in the late autumn of 1817, there was no apparent reason why it should have been otherwise. During the preceding decade and a half, the city had enjoyed an expanding trade with both the nearby state of Vermont and the rapidly growing settlements of Upper Canada and during the recently concluded War of 1812 had experienced such burgeoning prosperity as to make sorely stricken New Englanders sardonically envious. In Boston it was even said that Montreal should erect a monument to President Madison in gratitude for the benefits it, and it alone, had reaped from the abortive conflict. The city allowed the debt to go unrecognized, but in 1817, despite deplorable harvests in Lower Canada for several years, every prospect seemed to confirm the truth of the contention.

That year Montreal burst its bounds, both literally and figuratively. The old fortification walls, finally demolished at the end of fifteen years of dilatory effort, no longer hid the splendid view of the St. Lawrence nor of the new suburbs creeping northwestward toward Mount Royal's wooded slopes. The "Little River," named for St. Martin, still drained the mountain's eastern flank and wandered through James McGill's farm where McGill University now stands, but on either side of the stream could be seen new streets and houses, evidences of a building boom. Just as significant in point of growth were the new steamboat wharf near the foot of the Hay Market, the new foundry below St. Mary's Current, and Montreal's newest hostelry, the luxurious Mansion House Hotel on Victor Street, near the present Bonsecours Market.

These and many other signs of progress were largely the result of the prosperity brought about by the Napoleonic Wars and the War of 1812. Begun in 1793, with only a brief period of peace, the last of the great English-French conflicts had created a strong demand for colonial products and, after Napoleon's blockade of the Baltic in 1806, produced a preferential market for colonial timber and other naval supplies. For its part, the War of 1812 had made Montreal the staging depot for British reinforcements and

FATHER OF CANADIAN BANKING

John Richardson, born in Scotland in 1755, died in Montreal
in 1831 after forty-four years spent in Canada. He had run the
gamut from privateer to parliamentarian during his busy life,
but his overriding interest was in the development of Canadian
commerce, for which he fought continuously in the legislature.

Without doubt, Richardson's greatest achievement was the
foundation of a bank which became the model for the Canadian
banking system. Based on his knowledge of American banking,
it was a giant step in the commercial evolution of his adopted
country.

the supply base for the military forces in Lower and Upper Canada. Despite a state of war, the important trade with Vermont and northern New York continued with only a little interruption, while that with Upper Canada expanded enormously to meet military needs.

Together, the long-established fur trade and the commerce of Lake Champlain and Upper Canada had made Montreal one of the fastest-growing cities on the continent with far from unrealistic hopes, once canals could be built around the rapids of the St. Lawrence, of rivalling Boston, New York, and Philadelphia. Begun by De Casson at the close of the seventeenth century, the St. Lawrence canals had become by 1817 a source of agitation in the legislatures of Lower and Upper Canada. With canals, Montreal merchants could envision a day when the city would become both the port and the metropolis for the interior of the continent as it had earlier become the entrepôt of a fur trade that embraced a territory extending from the Ohio River to the prairies and westward to the Pacific Ocean.

Considering the commercial prospects, it seems surprising that the founders of the Montreal Bank should have launched their enterprise without fanfare or ceremony of any kind. What is the explanation? A stereotyped reply would be that John Richardson and his associates were "hard-headed business men" and "rugged, dour Scots to boot," phrases that frequently recur in the literature of the northwest fur trade. Thus doubly inhibited, it would hardly have been in character for them to squander money on needless self-aggrandizement or indulge in festive self-congratulation.

Of their hard-headed business qualities there can be no question. Without exception, those associated in the founding of the Montreal Bank were all successful merchants at a time when success in business demanded shrewd judgement and solid foreign connections. But, long-established legend to the contrary, less than half of the original directors had Scottish antecedents and those who had were long since adapted to their New World environment. It is also doubtful if dourness was a characteristic of the city or the time, the legendary Scottish temperament notwithstanding.

According to its own historians and to travellers of the period, early nineteenth-century Montreal was noted for the exuberant quality of its social life. In addition to the famed Beaver Club of the North West Company traders, whose ritual gatherings assumed saturnalian overtones, there were such social organizations as the Bachelor Barons, the Assembly, and innumerable sporting clubs dedicated to the delights of the four seasons; even at far-away Michilimackinac Island, the advance base of the fur trade, there existed a "Hunt" whose members sported silver buttons, procured from London, on their dinner coats. All such social organizations drew their membership from the commercial elite of the community, government circles, and the British regiments garrisoned in the town, and all, according to the social historian E. Z. Massicotte, contributed to the gaiety of life with a seemingly endless succession of balls, assemblies, theatrical offerings, and gargantuan feasts. Private entertaining, though formal and restrained, was also on a lavish scale. Every noteworthy event was seized upon as the cause for a celebration, whether it was the arrival of a Governor, the break-up of ice on the St. Lawrence in the spring, or the launching of a new Molson steamboat.

In spite of such social customs, there appear to have been good reasons for the Bank's quiet inauguration. The facts are that the banking venture at its outset must have been clouded with uncertainty and anxiety. As has been pointed out above, a quarter of a century of frustrated efforts had gone into its creation and when the decision was made in May, 1817, to form a private joint-stock banking corporation or partnership, Canadian support was somewhat less than enthusiastic. Only a handful of subscriptions were obtained in Quebec City and Upper Canada, while French-Canadian business men in Montreal, with a few exceptions, and even such prominent leaders in the English community as John Molson and Thomas Torrance, abstained from association with the enterprise. Had it not been for Horatio Gates, who was able to place almost half of the stock in New York City, Boston, and other New England centres, it is possible that the first bank might have died at birth. In addition to the difficulty encountered in raising a capital of £250,000 ($1,000,000) in Canada, there was widespread criticism in Lower Canada of banking generally and of bank-note circulation in particular. If these factors alone were not enough to suggest that the Bank's operations should begin unostentatiously, there were others. At the time of the Bank's foundation, the bitter struggle between the Canadian North West Company and the English Hudson's Bay Company was entering its final phase, which turned Montreal into two camps of angry and resentful partisans. And on the Bank's first directorate, in addition to three or more New Englanders who appear to have represented the American stock interest, were men who owed their financial and personal allegiance to opposite warring factions. It was in the presence of such tensions that the Montreal Bank finally opened its doors for business. With an unpredictable future, the only prudent policy was to proceed with circumspection.

Fortunately for the country and for those more intimately connected with Canada's first bank, the institution was successful from the very beginning, so markedly in fact that the directors were able to declare an initial dividend of three per cent in five months' time. However, to understand the problems that were involved, and the steps that were taken to overcome them, it is essential that they be placed in their historical context.

TWO

THE EARLY
ENVIRONMENT

THE EARLY ENVIRONMENT

I.

As Dr. Adam Shortt, Canada's pioneer historian of banking, observed more than half a century ago, "Banking facilities do not burst upon the business community as a quite new and undeveloped service: they simply afford an easier, more effective and generally less costly manner of rendering services which are already performed in more or less primitive fashions." The point is that as human inventions banks are organic rather than mechanical phenomena and as such must be studied in relation to the social environment that produced them, "social environment" meaning the entire ecological complex arising out of geographic, economic, commercial, and political conditions—the seed bed, soil and climate necessary to germination, growth and change. The story of any bank, therefore, is both a story of men and ideas and of all the influences impinging on them at a specific place and time in history. Approached in these terms, the history of the Bank of Montreal falls into two separate but intimately associated divisions, one dealing with the origins and evolution of Canadian trade and commerce, and the other with the men who finally provided the entrepreneurial leadership to make the Bank a reality.

The commercial history of Canada has yet to be written. A considerable body of literature has appeared, but it is fragmentary in character and is confined largely to economic developments that took place within the boundaries of Canada as it exists today. In consequence, there have been excluded from examination areas now in the United States which played important roles in moulding the Canadian economy – notably Vermont, the region south and west of the Great Lakes, and northern New York State above the rapids of the St. Lawrence. Even a cursory study of the trade between Canada and Vermont up to the War of 1812 and after leads to the conclusion that it played a more important role in making Montreal the commercial capital of the St. Lawrence system than did the fur trade with other parts of Canada. As for the region south and west of the Great Lakes – Ohio, Michigan, Indiana, Wisconsin, Illinois, Missouri, Minnesota, and the Dakotas – from this area rather than the romanticized northwest came the main support of the Canadian fur trade during the first thirty or forty years of British occupation; and northern New York furnished the pioneer settlers of Upper Canada for many years with the supplies needed for their survival. Of even greater significance to the history of the Bank of Montreal is the fact that two of its principal founders, John Richardson and Horatio Gates, began their business careers beyond the international boundary: Richardson in New York and the American midwest, Gates in New England and Vermont.

2.

When the French explorer Samuel de Champlain met the Algonquin Indians on the future site of Montreal at the beginning of the seventeenth century, the red men bartered their beaver pelts and other furs for the Frenchman's beads, ironware and gaily coloured cloth. Two hundred years later, most of the inhabitants of the provinces of Lower and Upper Canada were conducting their trade in much the same primitive manner.

By that time the City of Quebec had become an important seaport, Montreal was the entrepôt of a trading area that embraced a large part of North America, and the United Empire Loyalists had established their pioneer settlements on the Niagara Peninsula, the Bay of Quinte, and along the north shore of the St. Lawrence River. Along ancient travel routes that had existed since the ice age passed the manufactured goods of England and products of West Indian distillation.

Lacking adequate supplies of currency, the Canadian colonists had no other means of trading since they were largely dependent for specie on the monetary imports of the British government to pay the troops, support the commissariat, and buy presents for the Indians. The extent of such imports has yet to be verified, but it seems certain that they were the main support of the colonial economy until well into the nineteenth century. Whatever its volume, the hard money so introduced quickly disappeared from circulation. Some found its way into the savings of the people, but by far the larger part gravitated into the hands of merchants who used it to buy bills of exchange on London or to pay for goods bought in the United States.

In the villages, the millers still ground the farmers' grain on shares or, doubling as general storekeepers, traded tea, tobacco, ironware, and lengths of English goods in exchange for timber, staves, potash, hides, furs, wheat, pork, beef, or anything else the settler could offer in exchange. When a storekeeper had accumulated a sufficient quantity of staples to make a load, it was drawn, usually in winter time when the ground was frozen, to an up-country merchant or factor to pay for imported commodities and manufactured articles that had been obtained on credit several months before. And in his own good time and turn, the up-country merchant, located in York, Niagara, or Amherstburg, would ship his staples down the Lakes to Kingston to be rafted for delivery to a mercantile house in Montreal, to pay for the goods obtained on credit over a somewhat greater interval. Stored in warehouses on Montreal's St. Paul Street or in the Lower Town of Quebec, the staples would remain there until they became part of the cargo of a sailing vessel bound for London, Bristol, or some other English port where they would be consigned to the mercantile export-import house that had begun the trading cycle on credit as long as eighteen months to two years earlier.

The general anatomy of this "Canada Trade" was determined soon after the Seven Years' War by groups of English mercantile interests that accompanied the victorious British fleet as naval contractors to the siege of Quebec in 1759, and by a separate group of Scottish-American traders who had established themselves at Albany and Schenectady during the war. Whether as "Quebec merchants" or "Schenectady traders," the composition of the several groups was much the same. Founded by merchant-adventurers and welded strongly together by regional, clan, and family ties, they were able to take over and organize most of the commerce of the country.

This commerce became more complicated as it developed. Even before the fur trade had been reorganized, Quebec merchants were trading with markets other than London. West Indian products, particularly rum and molasses, were exchanged for Canadian fish and staves, and after the American Revolution a brisk trade developed with Vermont. To facilitate such commercial activities and transfer funds from England, drafts and bills of exchange were used, while in the towns, particularly those in which British troops were garrisoned, cash or hard money in the form of coins of heterogeneous origin, inscrutable vintage, and debatable value circulated, until such time as they were drained off to pay for the excess of imports over exports.

The inadequacies, inconveniences and difficulties of such a commercial system are difficult to visualize today. For the English mercantile house, it involved great risks and tied up capital for lengthy periods; for the Canadian importer it made trading highly speculative since he had to buy his goods at English prices and pay in Canadian staples, the value of which continually fluctuated between the time of shipment and the date of eventual delivery. As for the Canadian inhabitants, the system required them to pay the highest prices for the manufactured goods they needed, while forcing them to accept the lowest price for the farm and forest products they had to barter in exchange. For it was the unfortunate settlers, trappers, and Indians, both as primary producers and ultimate consumers, who had to bear all the costs of the far-flung trading operation, both coming and going, and provide the profits into the bargain.

The reasons for these conditions were embedded in the mercantile philosophy of the seventeenth and eighteenth centuries, according to which colonies were producers of raw materials for the mother country and consumers of her manufactured products. Trade with other countries was prohibited and all commerce had to be carried under the flag of the mother country. Colonial interests were thus made wholly subservient to those of the parent nation. Elaborate superstructures of trade and navigation laws were enacted and navies maintained to enforce them. In consequence, colonial economies everywhere suffered from two crippling disabilities: unfavourable trade balances, since the revenue from exports rarely equalled the

MONTREAL—1815

This is a section of a map produced by Joseph Bouchette, Surveyor General for British North America, two years before the Bank was founded and while the old fortification wall, which had protected the settlement since 1722, was in process of demolition.

The position of the wall is shown on the map by the dotted line running parallel to, and just below, the "Little River" and thence at right angles to the St. Lawrence.

20

Its elevation along the waterfront can be seen in the print of Montreal on page 9.

It is interesting to observe the direction indicated by the magnetic-north sign at the lower right-hand corner of the map in relation to St. Paul, Notre Dame and St. James streets, which have long been regarded as running east and west rather than north and south. Map references as late as 1825 make note of the north end of St. Paul Street, but for the last hundred years the street has been known as St. Paul Street East or West.

cost of imports; and a chronic shortage of currency, since any specie that found its way into a colony for the military chest or civil establishment was quickly and inevitably drawn off to redress the unfavourable trade balance.

3.

The story of currency and exchange in New France requires but brief mention here. From its inception the colony suffered from the lack of an adequate circulating medium. Specie in the form of French coinage was sent over from France by the government to pay the expenses of the colony and by devout individuals to support the religious orders. A third source was the illicit sale of furs to the Dutch and, later, English traders at Albany, payment being made mostly in debased coins of diverse origin – Spanish, Portuguese, English, German, Austrian and Dutch – which circulated in the British American colonies because of their trade with the West Indies. The introduction of this money into New France soon brought Gresham's law into operation. French louis d'or, écus, and silver livres were shipped to France or hoarded by thrifty people, while only debased coinage remained in circulation. Various edicts raised the value of French coins by one-third in the hope of keeping them in the province and in circulation. Two monetary standards were thus created, *monnaie du pays* (the colonial standard) and *monnaie de France* or *livres tournois*. The great Intendant, Talon, proposed another solution – the creation of a Canadian coinage. The proposal was not accepted. Since one of the most sovereign of all sovereign powers is the right to coin money and control the currency, it was hardly reasonable to expect that this power would be delegated to a colonial dependency which had never paid its way.

An empirical solution was stumbled on by the Intendant Jacques de Meulles in 1685 when the French pay ship failed to reach the Quebec roadstead before winter closed the port. With payments totalling thousands of livres to meet, and with his personal resources exhausted, he did what many another harassed debtor has done; he issued IOU's. This was accomplished by cutting playing cards into four and signing the pieces in denominations of four francs, forty sols and fifteen sols to conform to a soldier's monthly pay. Card money and other forms of paper currency were resorted to intermittently from 1685 to 1760, by which year the value of the various certificates, card money, bills of exchange and ordinances outstanding was estimated to be 83,000,000 livres. Greatly depreciated at the end of the Seven Years' War, about half of this paper money was eventually redeemed by the French government at an average rate of fifty-nine per cent of its face value.

Except in the tenacious memories of some 65,000 French Canadians, paper currency of all kinds dropped out of circulation, yet the monetary problems under British rule were largely a repetition of what had gone before but more complicated and vexatious. Although sterling was the legal money of account, there followed the introduction of American specie into Canada, mostly the Spanish or Mexican silver dollars which formed the currency of the colonies. Some of this money was imported to pay the troops and for other official accounts, and some was brought in by the Quebec merchants and the traders who settled in Montreal with the intention of engaging in the fur trade. Whatever the source, the new currency, though generally debased by sweating or clipping, circulated freely in Canada along with the coinage of the French regime as the latter returned to circulation from hoarded savings amounting, it was later estimated, to around five million dollars.

By this time, the late 1760's, the following coins were circulating in the province: in gold, the Portuguese Johannes and moidore, the German Carolin, the British guinea, the French louis d'or and the French and Spanish pistole; in silver, the Seville, Mexican or pillar dollar (the Pirates' famous piece of eight), the French crown, pièce, pistareen and ninepenny piece, and the British shilling. Complicating the currency situation further were the discrepancies in American ratings. Despite an ordinance of Queen Anne's reign, each of the overseas colonies had placed its own value on its local currency. Thus, in 1760, Massachusetts rated the Spanish dollar at five shillings and New York at eight shillings. Since most of the specie in Quebec City came from Massachusetts by way of Halifax, and that in Montreal from New York, commercial transactions between the two cities had to be conducted on a basis of haggle and compromise.

The currency dispute was finally settled in favour of Quebec in 1777 and the value of the Spanish dollar legally established at the Halifax rate of five shillings, or four dollars to the pound. The familiar suffix "cy" to indicate "Halifax currency" differentiated this monetary standard from sterling and from "York currency," which was retained by Upper Canada until 1796. Although sterling remained the money of account in both provinces, thereafter the Spanish silver dollar became the basic unit of Canadian currency, a position it retained until the adoption of the decimal system by the legislature of the Province of Canada in 1858.

As was pointed out above, the unsatisfactory condition of the currency was simply, from the Canadian point of view, a reflection of the weakness inherent in the mercantile system. Several factors were responsible, among them the post-war boom that developed soon after the Capitulation, the rapid increase in population that ensued, and the more favourable climate for commercial activity that succeeded British occupancy. So far as can be determined, prosperity was stimulated initially by the infusions into the economy of specie brought in to pay for the army and navy, by the local consumption made possible by the savings of the French Canadians, and lastly by the revival of the fur trade toward the end of the 1760's. A brief recession ensued until 1776-77, when reinforcements brought by Burgoyne from England raised the army strength to around ten thousand. After the close of the War of American Independence came the beginnings of the Vermont trade, the settlement of Upper Canada, and the rapid expansion of the southwest and northwest fur trades. As long, however, as the Imperial Government remained apathetic to currency reform, and the colonial administration lacked the authority to undertake effective measures, Canadian commerce was beset by a strange paradox: no matter how prosperous the country became, there was no relief from the currency shortage. The greater the prosperity, the greater was the demand for imports; the greater the demand for imports, the greater was the drain on the specie supply to meet foreign accounts. Whether in prosperity or depression, therefore, domestic transactions could be carried on only with the greatest difficulty and against seemingly insurmountable obstacles.

4.

It would be wrong to assume that the several British governors from Murray to Simcoe were not keenly sensible of the currency problem or that they did not make as honest an effort to find a solution as had the French governors and intendants before them. Nevertheless, it was left to private initiative to take the first adequate steps toward the improvement of the haphazard system that existed. This was to be accomplished by the establishment of a private bank of deposit, note issue and discount in Montreal. The proposal first appeared in the semi-official Quebec *Gazette* on August 9, 1792:

> The undersigned having experienced great inconvenience in Canada from the deficiency of specie, or some other medium to represent the increasing circulation of the country, as well as from the variety of the

money now current; and knowing the frequent loss and general difficulty and trouble attending receipts and payments, have formed the resolution of establishing a bank at Montreal, under the name of the Canada Banking Company. ⁄

The establishment of banks has found favour in most intelligent commercial countries, and from the experience of ages, there does not now exist a doubt of their utility and the consequent increase of the trade and industries of the countries, wherever they have been promoted and wisely conducted. The operations of the present establishment will be confined solely to the business usually done by the most respectable banking houses in other countries, and the parties interested are restricted by agreement from using any part of the funds appropriated to this concern for any other purpose whatever, and are jointly and severally responsible for the faithful performance of their engagements. ⁄ The business proposed by the Canada Banking Company and usually done by similar establishments is,

to receive deposits of cash,
to issue notes in exchange for such deposits,
to discount bills and notes of hand, and
to facilitate business by keeping cash accounts with those who choose
to employ the medium of the bank in their receipts and payments.

It is proposed also to extend the operations of the bank to every part of the two provinces where an agent may be judged necessary, and it is presumed that the institution will be particularly beneficial to the commerce of, and intercourse with, the upper province.

The concerned hope that the public will judge with candor of the motives for this establishment, and of the credit and respectability of the parties; and they beg leave to add that they are determined to conduct every part of the business with the punctuality necessary to promote the credit and success of the undertaking, and with due regard to the convenience and safety of the public.

(Signed) Phyn, Ellice & Inglis
Todd, McGill & Co.
Forsyth, Richardson & Co.

Dated in London, 31st March, 1792.

Several features of the prospectus attract attention. First, the general tone, particularly its sweeping assumptions. At a time when banking was in poor repute in England, the promoters of the proposed company seem to have credited the Canadian business community with a largely non-existent knowledge of banking principles and practices. Certainly, no previous discussion of the subject has been discovered; it appears, instead, that the new bank was to spring, like Venus, full grown from the waves. A second interesting point is the proposal to establish branches at a time when branch banking was unknown in the Old Country outside Scotland, where business conditions were much different and where the system had yet to prove an unqualified success. It was not until the founding of the National Bank of Scotland in 1824, in fact, that the modern Scottish system of a few large banks with numerous branches came into being. The third point is the similarity between this proposal and others made subsequently in Canada: the Canada Banking Company was in fact the direct predecessor of the Bank of Montreal. Lastly, who were the three signers of the document—Phyn, Ellice & Inglis; Todd, McGill & Co.; Forsyth, Richardson & Co.—and why should they, rather than others of the Canadian commercial group, have taken the initiative in launching such an enterprise?

The 1792 decision to form a banking company in Montreal was undoubtedly influenced by the passage of the Canada or Constitutional Act the previous year by the British parliament, creating the provinces of Lower and Upper Canada, each with its own representative assembly and legislative and executive councils. Superseding the unfortunate Quebec Act of 1774, the new constitution marked an important advance in Canada's political development and for the first time gave promise to the increasingly powerful commercial group of a voice in the government of the country. Even more influential in the creation of a Canadian bank, perhaps, was the establishment, by Act of Congress on February 25, 1791, of the Bank of the United States.

Now known as the First Bank of the United States, to differentiate it from its successor, the American institution was founded primarily through the efforts of the new Secretary of the Treasury, Alexander Hamilton, who was possessed of a profound knowledge of English, Scottish, and European banking practices. Designed to serve American fiscal, financial, and commercial needs, it included branches in several state capitals and commercial centres, but whether their introduction was based on Scottish practice or was an

CANADA'S FIRST HEAVY
INDUSTRY

Iron ore was known to exist in the vicinity of Three Rivers as early as 1670, but more than half a century elapsed before efforts were made to utilize this valuable resource.

After several years of organization, the first Canadian iron was produced in 1732, and the Forges du St. Maurice went into regular operation about six years later. In 1744 the first of the famous knockdown, cast-iron St. Maurice stoves were offered for sale at 100 louis each, and by mid century 120 men were employed in Canada's first heavy industry. The iron produced was described as being equal or superior in quality to that of England or Sweden, especially in its resistance to the rigorous Canadian climate.

After several rapid transfers of the rights under British suzerainty, the forges were acquired in 1793 by a group from Quebec led by Matthew Bell, later a member of parliament and also of the Quebec Board of the Bank of Montreal. Bell controlled the industry until 1846, when it was sold at auction.

Here, Matthew Bell is seen showing his wares to prospective purchasers both from the army and from civilian life. In the background can be seen the forges themselves with their huge bellows run by water-wheels in a sluice.

In the early 1800's, the forges were working seven months a year and employing 300 men in four daily shifts. By 1830, annual production stood at £30,000, representing mainly the stoves, lye kettles and cannon pictured here. Products of the forges also included all manner of lumbering apparatus, from peaveys to portable forges.

The fires were finally extinguished in 1883, and it is said that at that time they were the oldest active furnaces on the American continent.

Painting by Douglas Johnson

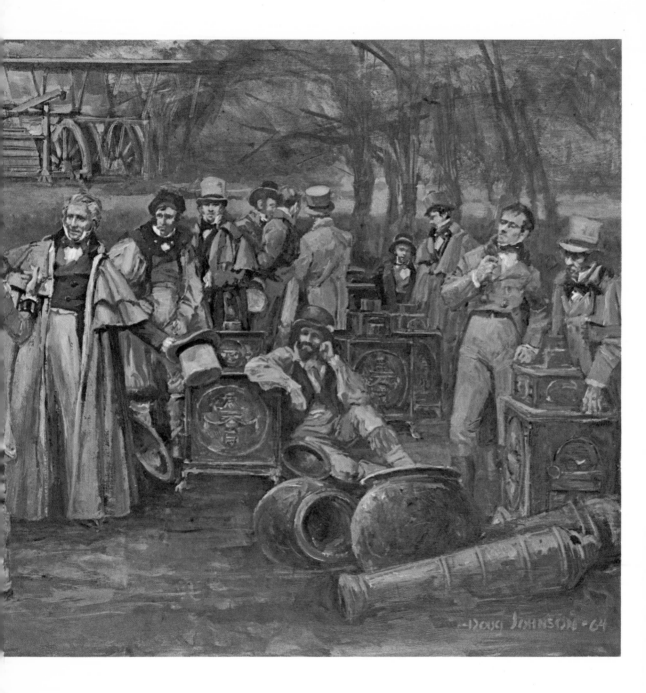

indigenous and necessary invention is open to argument. However, study of Hamilton's writings and of other American literature of that period on the subject reveals that the Canadian prospectus could have been taken almost verbatim from American financial pamphlets or from any one of several similar banking proposals then current across the border. This fact, along with subsequent developments in the history of banking in Canada, leads to the conclusion that the Canada Banking Company drew its inspiration directly from American sources.

The reason for the American influence is to be found in the external communications of Montreal during the last quarter of the eighteenth century. By the early 1790's, those between the Canadian city and New York and Boston had become sufficiently improved to permit, for that time, relatively easy intercourse. Roads leading southward were much better than in other parts of Canada and it was from New York and Boston, rather than from the Old Country directly, that Canadians received the journals and newspapers that kept them in touch with the outside world. Even during the open season of navigation it was often quicker to send letters overseas from Montreal by the southern route than directly via the Gulf of St. Lawrence. Be it remembered, too, that many of Montreal's merchants had come from the American colonies. Whatever the views of English-speaking Montrealers on the relative virtues of monarchical and republican institutions, their social outlook was American as were their business habits and attitudes, and even after the Revolution, the majority kept unbroken their personal and commercial ties beyond the border.

An equally potent influence can be found in the background of the principals and in the source of their financial strength: the firms of Phyn, Ellice & Inglis and Forsyth, Richardson & Co. were bound together by family ties in a typical mercantile alliance of the period, and Todd, McGill & Co. had been their associates for almost thirty years in numerous trading ventures. By 1792 this combination had become, both commercially and politically, one of the strongest, if not the strongest, of the groups doing business in Canada. Unlike most of their competitors their interests extended far beyond the fur trade to include ocean and interior forwarding, government contracting, general trading on both sides of the Canadian-American boundary, and extensive land holdings in Canada, the United States, and the West Indies. The financing and management of these widespread operations involved many of the functions of private banking. With such experience, the members of the group would be the first to see the advantages that a bank could bring to themselves and to the Canadian community.

5.

The story of this group has its beginnings in the then Province of New York during the closing years of the Seven Years' War. That conflict began as a dispute between Virginia and New France over their respective claims to the Ohio territory lying west of the Allegheny Mountains and south of the Great Lakes, and it was for this rich area that the American colonies fought their French and Indian War, rather than for the scattered settlements along the St. Lawrence. On September 10, 1760, two days after the articles of surrender were signed, General Murray sent his redoubtable Major Robert Rogers up the St. Lawrence to take over Detroit, Michilimackinac, and other French posts in the interior. The posts were quickly serviced by traders operating from Schenectady rather than Canadian bases, because the American town was outside the area of military occupation and was near the headquarters of Sir William Johnson, Superintendent of Indian Affairs and chief dispenser of government trading patronage. Licences were more easily procurable there than in Canada, and communications with the outside world via New York were more economical and efficient than those via Quebec and the St. Lawrence.

The bulk of the western trade began, however, to shift to the St. Lawrence–Ottawa axis in 1769, when American merchants formed an embargo against British goods in protest against certain import tariffs imposed by the Townshend Acts of 1767, and the refusal of mercantile groups in Canada to join the embargo made Quebec the only available supply port. This windfall lasted only one year, as the Acts were repealed in 1770, but it stimulated the exodus of experienced traders from Schenectady to Montreal which had begun in 1768 when jurisdiction over the Indian Reserve was transferred to the several provinces, making trading licences more easily procurable in Canada. Shortly after, the American Revolution eliminated the strategic advantages of Schenectady.

The growth of the Phyn-Ellice complex, described in detail in Appendix D, began with the arrival in Schenectady of John Duncan. So successful were his early business ventures that, during the 1760's, his Scottish mentor, George Phyn, sent one of his own sons, James Phyn, and Alexander Ellice, a nephew, to join Duncan. In 1767 they bought out Duncan, and the firm became known as Phyn & Ellice. At this time the firm not only acted as a supply agent for western trading posts, but also had secured several government contracts which involved the partners in commercial paper, government drafts, bills of exchange and other facets of banking. Under the new management the business was initially consolidated and expanded, but was soon beset with the same troubles as afflicted the other Schenectady traders. In order to combat the increased Canadian competition, James Phyn, in 1774, opened a London office to further the interests of his own company and any other desirous of obtaining the benefits of his experienced services. John Richardson, a grandson of George Phyn, was subsequently sent out from Scotland to bolster the staff in Schenectady.

The London venture was immediately successful and enabled the company to profit handsomely from an exchange situation which involved selling London drafts in New York drawn on James Phyn and transmitting the proceeds to him through Isaac Todd, the firm's representative in Montreal where sterling bills could be bought more cheaply than in New York. However, other business in Schenectady was severely hampered by the Quebec Act of 1774 which extended the boundaries of the province to include the territory claimed earlier by New France and prohibited importation except through the customs office at St. Johns, twenty miles southeast of Montreal. The American Revolution in 1775 caused the firm to split up, some partners returning to England, others, like John Richardson, gravitating to New York to look after the company interests there. A year later an office was opened in Montreal and subsequently run by Robert Ellice and a cousin, John Forsyth. The next decade saw the rapid expansion and diversification of the business. New York and London concerns helped supply the British forces in New York and Philadelphia during the Revolution and extended mercantile operations to other parts of the Atlantic seaboard and the West Indies, while the Montreal outlet increased the firm's interest in the fur trade and contracted with the British government to outfit the United Empire Loyalist refugees in Canada.

However, the Montreal firm greatly over-extended itself in the American middle west at a time when the fur trade was shifting to the northwest. As a result, John Richardson was ordered from New York to straighten out the company's affairs and ended up, in 1790, being given a partnership in the Montreal office which subsequently became Forsyth, Richardson & Co. With his extensive business experience and close connections in New York, he became the first Canadian merchant to engage simultaneously in different commercial activities, and to perceive the enormous obstacles to their prosecution arising from the state of the currency and exchange and from the survival of French commercial law and practice. It was the former circumstance that led Richardson to formulate the idea of establishing a bank in Canada. He visited England in the summer of 1791 and while there appeared before the House of Commons to give his views on the projected division of Canada into two separate provinces; during the same visit he discussed with his London associates the proposal to found a banking company in Canada on the same principles as those of Alexander Hamilton with which Richardson was already familiar.

6.

That the promoters of the Canada Banking Company were serious in their intentions is borne out by the list of arrivals at Quebec in the spring of 1792, as published in the Quebec *Gazette*. Among these were Mr. John Forsyth, of Forsyth, Richardson & Co., Mr. and Mrs. Edward Ellice, and Mr. George Phyn Jr. of Phyn, Ellice & Inglis, as the London firm was now called. Later in the summer the Ellices and Phyn continued their journey to New York, to look after the firm's interests there in the hands of William Constable, a brother-in-law of James Phyn. Their main object in coming to North America, however, was to assist in the launching of the banking enterprise. Significantly, they sailed in the *Eweretta*, one of a series of ships of the same or like name to be owned by James Phyn.

Whether because of political obstruction or commercial rivalry, the banking mission proved unsuccessful. The Canada Banking Company's notice appeared in a few issues of the *Gazette*, but there is no record that a charter was applied for and none of any effort to sell shares. There is evidence, however, that the company did function briefly as a private bank of deposit and issue in Montreal, possibly in the same premises on St. Paul Street in which the Montreal Bank opened for business twenty-five years later.

Two varieties of Canada Banking Company notes have been preserved in private Canadian and American numismatic collections. One has the denomination of five shillings and is dated August 10, 1792; the other has a blank space for the denomination and is undated except for the numerals "179-" and is unsigned. The latter variety shows the notes as authorized by the three firms: Phyn, Ellice & Inglis, Todd, McGill & Co., and Forsyth, Richardson

& Co. All bear the same decoration, a small engraving depicting a beaver gnawing at the roots of a tree, with a sailing ship – no doubt the gallant *Eweretta* – appearing in the background.

The failure to establish a bank in Canada in 1792 has many puzzling aspects, since such an enterprise was presumably as desirable then as it was to prove a quarter of a century later. A bank of issue would have solved many of the vexatious problems connected with the currency and exchange, and its other facilities would have stimulated trade and commerce. Furthermore, with such impressive backing as that provided by Phyn-Ellice there could hardly have been any question of the integrity of the promoters. So numerous were the proffered advantages, in fact, that they should have led to serious discussion of the project in business and governmental circles. Yet no record of any such debate has been discovered.

Later writers explain the failure on the grounds that the Canadian economy was still too primitive to support such an institution. Along the chain of correspondencies that extended from the parent export-import house in England to the merchants in the trading centres of Upper Canada, each in turn performed such banking services as the provision of credit, the making of collections, and the acceptance of deposits, while the general storekeeper did business by a system of barter in which currency was redundant. With such arrangements, there would have been little need for such a novel and little-understood institution as a bank, located several hundred miles away in another province.

In other words, the failure of the Canada Banking Company has been attributed to the fact that the French Canadians did not want it and the English Canadians did not need it. While this conclusion is valid as far as it goes, it disregards a most important factor – the struggle for control of the fur trade.

Until 1779, the fur trade had been largely confined to the territory southwest of Michilimackinac Island, the staging and collection base for an operation that covered a large part of what is now the United States, and had been supplied principally by the Phyn-Ellice group because of its superior capital resources, experience, and organization. From 1775 or even earlier, however, independent and often irresponsible traders had been operating in the northwest beyond the head of Lake Superior and in the territory between Lake Erie and the Ohio River. In the southwest, particularly, competition had given way to strife, the old trading patterns had been disrupted, and the future of the trade jeopardized by the corruption of the Indian with cheap cut rum from Quebec and the West Indies. Driven by the necessity to eliminate cutthroat competition and debauchery, to apportion trading areas and engage in co-operative marketing, far-sighted traders at Michilimackinac negotiated, between 1779 and 1792, a succession of agreements designed to save the trade by division and regulation. The division of the trade into separate sectors, southwest and northwest, led to bitter rivalries and to the rise of Simon McTavish, first as the organizing genius of the northwest fur trade and then as its autocrat. An owner of a two-sixteenths share under the 1779 agreement which brought the North West Company into being, McTavish, on the reconstitution of the company in 1784, was largely responsible for the division of the trade into its separate sectors. Three years later, in 1787, he became the senior partner and in association with B. and J. Frobisher obtained an exclusive supply contract with the North West Company which provided for a five-per-cent commission on all trade imports, four per cent for overhead expenses, and six per cent on all other advances.

While statistics of the fur trade are notoriously unreliable, it appears that the Canadian export value of the trade about this time was around £200,000, of which fifty per cent was produced by the southwest and less than forty per cent by the northwest, the balance coming from the Lower St. Lawrence. These ratios changed so rapidly under the suzerainty of McTavish that profits divided amongst the Nor'Westers rose from £39,000 in 1787 to £53,000 in 1793, a year that saw five Nor'West sailing vessels on the Upper Lakes, large expenditures to improve the road between Lake Ontario and Georgian Bay, and the purchase of seigneuries near Montreal by four of the nine North West partners.

When a new agreement was signed in 1787, Robert Ellice & Co., with Todd, McGill & Co., became the leaders of the southwest group which, several years later, broke away to form the XY Company under the leadership of Forsyth, Richardson & Co. and Sir Alexander Mackenzie. About the same time, Phyn-Ellice, acting through Robert Ellice & Co., obtained the United Empire Loyalist contract and were able to help finance McTavish, Frobisher & Co.'s North West Company contracts, securing a fifty-per-cent share of the profitable supply business. So able, however, was Simon McTavish's conduct of the North West Company's affairs, that in 1792 he secured a revised contract to ship and market all NorthWest Company furs in London and to handle all of the company's accounts. Also in 1792 we find him in London, engaging unsuccessfully in negotiations with the Hudson's Bay Company to import trade goods via the Bay, and forming a partnership with John Fraser, a cousin experienced in the Canada Trade, to handle the London business of McTavish, Frobisher & Co.

While the relation of the rival groups at this juncture remains confused, the available evidence strongly suggests that one of the reasons for McTavish's trip to London was to arrange for his own financing at the very time when Phyn, Ellice & Inglis and their Canadian associates were planning to establish a bank in Canada. In view of these and subsequent events, it is obvious that the ambitious chief of the Nor'Westers, along with his numerous partners, had good reason to withhold support from an enterprise promoted by their most formidable rivals to serve ends which were largely extraneous to the fur trade and from which that trade could reap few benefits.

So far as the literature of Canadian banking is concerned, little or nothing more is heard about the subject until 1807, when merchants in Quebec and Montreal launched a movement for the establishment of a bank in Lower Canada.

7.

The quarter century from 1792 to 1817 is one of the most interesting periods in Canadian history, for that was the time when the twig was bent and the shape and vigour of its future growth determined.

The period witnessed the spectacular population growth of Lower Canada; the settlement of Upper Canada; the conflicts between the two over customs revenues; and the polarization of the bitterly opposed French and English factions, the first steeped in seventeenth-century tradition, the second in industrial materialism. Less than fifteen years after the publication of Adam Smith's *Wealth of Nations*, John Richardson and the men he drew around him were converts to laissez-faire and in touch with progressive developments elsewhere, while the French party that opposed them was still living in a world of mediaeval ecclesiasticism. In both provinces, the formative period nurtured demands for representative government and brought a promise of national consciousness.

These political developments are generally familiar in broad outline, while those related to changes in the economy are virtually unknown. The country's economic development is usually pictured as having been brought about by

BUSINESS BY BARTER

When the Bank was founded in 1817, Indians were still trading with merchants in Montreal as they had in the days of the French regime, sixty years before. Here, in the Market Square, trade in furs and fabrics is being conducted by barter, which was still the order of the day for most transactions when Canadian banking began.

Although the great bulk of fur-trading in Canada moved westward with the exploits of Hudson's Bay and North West traders, there was considerable trapping in the area around Montreal until well into the nineteenth century.

In the early days, before settlement spread and the large companies penetrated the wilderness, Montreal was the scene of great fur fairs every summer. Buyers from as far away as New York City would attend, probably combining the lengthy trip with a visit to the base of the American fur trade near Albany.

the combined efforts of the fur traders, the activities of the habitants along the St. Lawrence, immigration, and the land-clearing, pioneering efforts of the Loyalist settlers of Upper Canada. While accurate in part, the resulting picture is somewhat oversimplified.

As indicated earlier, the most important single factor in maintaining the Canadian economy for several decades after the British Conquest was the large sums of money sent from England to pay the army, purchase presents for the Indians, support the civil list, supply the United Empire Loyalists with the tools of mere existence, and construct military communications and defences. Expenditures on these and other accounts established a domestic market, provided local employment, and became the principal provincial source of specie with which to pay for imports. While all early statistics must be accepted with reservation, it is unlikely that the gross export value of the fur trade even at its peak about the end of the eighteenth century ever exceeded £275,000. Yet in 1800, a year in which the army strength numbered 3,700 of all ranks, the pay of the military establishment amounted to £260,000, and an estimate for 1801 puts the cost of stores for the local garrisons at £600,000, indicating a possible total of £900,000 per annum. A further example of substantial Imperial expenditures in Canada at this time is the figure of $30,000,000 that has been given as the over-all cost to the British government of transferring the United Empire Loyalists to the Canadas, the Maritimes, and England.

Next to the subventions of the mother country, the mainstay of the primitive economy came from the fur trade. Its principal expenditures were made in England for trade goods and its not overly generous wages in Canada were paid, as far as was possible, in kind. The truly important contributions of the trade to the country's development lay not in the value of the trade *per se* but in the opening of internal trade routes and the extension of territorial claims to the Arctic and Pacific oceans. The export value of fur remained fairly constant after 1790, while the other products of the forest and the soil steadily increased until, by the end of the decade, the value of both these classes of staples exceeded that of the more romantic export. In human terms there was no comparison, of course, the fur trade representing little more than short-sighted exploitation, the other activities, settlement and material progress.

As beneficial to the early Canadian economy as any of the foregoing stimuli were those provided by events in Europe and the United States. Encompassing the years from 1793 to 1814, the French Revolutionary and Napoleonic Wars established a high-price demand for Canada's natural and cultivated exports. Simultaneously, but only partly due to war's exigencies, the rapid expansion of the English textile industry gave rise to an insatiable demand for potash. Obtained by leaching the ashes of burned maple, beech and other hardwoods, pot and pearl ashes were used in bleaching, and ordinarily provided the pioneer settler with his first cash crop.

Equally important to Canada's early economic evolution were concurrent developments in the United States that included the successful establishment of an indigenous American banking system at a time when that of England had been disrupted by war-time financing; the population movement which peopled Vermont, New York, and Ohio; and the prolonged duel between Britain and her former American colonies over maritime commerce. The most significant single stimulus to Canada's early commercial expansion, however, was the geographic relationship between the St. Lawrence and Champlain valleys. Because the latter drained northward and was surrounded by mountains on the east, south, and west, the only outlet for the bulky pioneer products of the region was down the Richelieu River to the St. Lawrence and thence to the open sea.

8.

For nearly half a century—from 1777 to 1822—the natural ties between Montreal and the Lake Champlain littoral were so strong that neither Britain's mercantilist policies, American embargoes, Loyalist prejudices, nor even war, could put them asunder. The traffic in natural products originating south of the 45th parallel and the return trade in English manufactured goods—plus war-time demand in Britain—made Montreal the commercial capital of the St. Lawrence trading system and one of the fastest-growing cities on the continent.

The geographic affinity of the two regions becomes apparent very early in the history of New France: during the seventeenth century French *coureurs de bois* traded their furs in Albany for cash, to the confusion of the French colonial currency, and 'English visitors' came north to the great fur fairs held in Montreal. Following the Seven Years' War, fortnightly summer mails were established between Quebec and New York City via Montreal, and in its edition of March 30, 1769, the Quebec *Gazette* reported with considerable excitement the improvement of the road from Skene's Borough at the head of Lake Champlain to Fort Edward on Lake George as greatly beneficial to persons having business in the colonies. The same item notes that a fortnightly packet-boat service "from St. Johns in the Government of Quebec to Skene's Borough" made possible a safe and speedy passage from one end of Lake Champlain to the other.

Communications were also consolidated by Montcalm's army, then by Burgoyne's, each plodding onward with their lumbering artillery trains and heavy baggage wagons to eventual defeat. In 1778, also, Washington ordered one General Bayley to cut a road "from your house [in Newbury, Vt.] into Canada." Extended in 1785 toward the Canadian line at Newport, the Hazen-Bayley Road later became part of a proposed route surveyed by the Boston and Montreal Turnpike Company, chartered by Vermont in 1805 to build a road across Vermont "in the most direct course from Boston to Montreal." Even earlier, in the 1790's, stage-coaches were already operating between Montreal and Boston, and before the outbreak of the War of 1812 such services were available between Montreal and Burlington, Bennington and Albany. In contrast, the first stage-coach service between Montreal, Kingston and York in Upper Canada did not begin until 1817 and then ran only during the winter months. Improvement of communications inevitably led to settlement, and settlement to the export of commodities by the only route possible –down the Richelieu.

The nature of this trade is set forth in the 1784 commercial treaty negotiations between Vermont and the government at Quebec, when the imposition of the British Trade and Navigation Acts had closed the border to all legal commercial traffic. Claiming an independent status, Vermont contended that the Acts should not apply to her and both the government and the commercial interests of Quebec City and of Montreal agreed. In consequence Lord Dorchester decided in 1787 to regulate the Vermont trade according to his own judgement, but subject to the approval of the Legislative Council. Schedules issued in that and subsequent years include such pioneer products as mast and ship timber, staves, pot and pearl ashes, agricultural products of all kinds – flour, leather, horses, hogs, cattle – and in addition more exotic items such as tobacco, rum, tea, Indian goods, cuprous ore (for tanning furs), pig iron, and specie. In return, the southward flow consisted largely of furs and English manufactured imports: farming and lumbering tools, dress goods, textiles, and articles not yet produced in the United States.

Following the Jefferson embargo of 1808 and until after the War of 1812, many imports were unobtainable from other sources and smuggling became both habitual and praiseworthy.

Smuggling rose indeed to fabulous proportions, and statistics of the Vermont trade are almost impossible to find. Furthermore, most American products, after entering the stream of Canadian commerce, lost their identity to take advantage of Imperial preferences. Nevertheless, the growth of the trade and its importance are attested to by political and other developments at this time. In the first category are Vermont's negotiations for a commercial treaty at Quebec in 1784 and at London in 1796, and the customs dispute between Lower and Upper Canada in 1797 over duties on American imports; in the second, such phenomena as the growth of Montreal after 1791 and the increase in Vermont's population, which doubled between 1790 and 1800 and reached 215,000 midway in the next decade. The population of Upper Canada was then about 70,000 and of Lower Canada, 250,000. Support can also be deduced from a land boom at Missisquoi Bay in the 1780's, the storied efforts of American revenue officers against smuggling after 1808, the records of Lake Champlain steamboat traffic, and even shipments overland of fresh cod and oysters to Montreal in the 1790's by enterprising Boston fish dealers.

The monetary value of the trade between Lower Canada and Vermont and between Upper Canada and New York and the western territories can probably never be precisely determined. Sufficient data are available, however, to indicate its relative proportions. The average annual value of Canada's exports to Britain for the five-year period ending 1805, for example, was estimated at £757,000 sterling, of which furs made up £263,000, leaving a balance in round figures of £500,000. Imports from the United States in 1797, on the other hand, largely destined for export to Britain, were in excess of £300,000, or more than three-fifths the value of the other exports.

After 1808, however, the proportionate value of the trade between Canada and the States grew abnormally as the result of two events: the Napoleonic blockade of the Baltic which forced Britain to turn to her transatlantic colonies for timber, and the Jefferson embargo on trade with Britain. Shut off from the sea, first by presidential proclamation and then by British sea power, Vermont flooded the Canadian market with her natural products while New England and New York turned to Montreal for the articles they could no longer obtain through their own ports. This situation prevailed throughout the War of 1812 and gave rise to such familiar Vermont place-names as "Smugglers' Notch" in the Green Mountains and "the Old Smugglers' Route" across the Hero Islands at the foot of Lake Champlain.

By means of the Vermont trade, Canada, assisted by her bills from Britain in payment of the military, civil, and Indian accounts, was able to support her own unfavourable merchandise balance with the mother country. As between the United States and Canada the trade balance was against Canada, as between the United States and Britain, against the United States, but the over-all balance between Canada and Britain (including the government account and re-exports from Vermont) was against Britain. As a consequence, the supply of London bills in Canada was often greater than the domestic demand, making them procurable at a discount, while in Boston, New York, and other American cities the same paper was in short supply and therefore brought a premium. There naturally developed an active business in British exchange between Montreal and New York which introduced considerable quantities of American currency into Canada, including a great number of light and debased foreign coins. However, this currency was quickly returned to the United States to pay for imports; domestic drafts were unacceptable because there was no market for them south of the border, and the individual transactions were too small to permit direct transfers of the large English bills. On balance these operations did not augment the meagre supply of currency circulating in the provinces, but the increased trade added to the difficulties of day-to-day business and further aggravated the need for long-term credits already seriously extended by geographic distances and natural obstacles to transportation.

These monetary complexities and confusions, which progressively confounded Canadian commercial dealings, goaded the business leaders of the country into a further effort to forge an instrument which could alleviate such problems.

THREE

A GENTLEMEN'S
AGREEMENT

A GENTLEMEN'S AGREEMENT

I.

The second attempt to establish a bank in Canada was initiated in 1807 by the same interests that had failed fifteen years earlier. There was, however, a marked difference in approach. In 1792, a successful firm of London mercantile bankers, in association with a Canadian subsidiary and its affiliate, simply announced their intention to engage in the banking business in Canada. In the second instance, the effort was launched by the publication in the Quebec *Gazette* of March 5, 1807, of an open invitation for the inhabitants to attend a meeting the following day "to consult on the proper measures to be taken for the establishment of a bank in this province." A similar notice appeared in the Montreal *Herald* and other papers. The more expansive gesture was dictated by the changes wrought during fifteen years of economic, commercial, and political change within Canada itself.

The most striking economic change is seen in the decline of the fur trade as a principal support of the economy and its replacement by diversified production. As in Vermont, the westward migration from the seaboard states brought a new wave of settlers to Upper Canada to hasten the growth of trading centres, the opening of roads, and the establishment of saw and grist mills, distilleries, smithies and general stores in small convenient clusters. Stimulated both by increased American trade as settlements grew south of the Great Lakes, and by the continuance of war-time demand in Britain, the economy had altered and expanded. As in the interior province, Lower Canada had witnessed an astonishing growth in population, and had seen Montreal become the commercial capital of a far-flung hinterland.

In 1794, Jay's Treaty had caused the withdrawal of the British garrisons from the American posts held since the Treaty of Paris; this brought about the concentration of Canadian fur-trading interests in the Northwest Territories and their extension to the upper reaches of the Columbia River. Notwithstanding a decline in relative value, the fur trade continued to produce substantial revenues after 1804, when the warring factions representing the original North West Company, led by McTavish, McGillivrays & Co., and the XY or New North West Company, led by Sir Alexander Mackenzie and Forsyth, Richardson & Co., were reunited after five years of ruinous competition. Old business rivalries and differences had been reconciled, and the trade itself had been changed from a loose alliance of swashbuckling wintering partners and their mercantile providers into a highly centralized operation under William McGillivray, in which, however, Sir Alexander Mackenzie, Forsyth-Richardson, the McGills, and the relatively new firm of Parker, Gerrard & Ogilvy, all retained an interest. In addition to such changes, a second generation of Scottish clerks and apprentices had appeared, and from south of the border had come such energetic merchant-traders as Abel Bellows, Horatio Gates, Charles Bancroft, George Platt, Zabdiel Thayer and others. Most of them were engaged in the Vermont trade and many would later participate in the founding of the Bank of Montreal.

In a growing commercial community of widening interests, it is easy to understand why John Richardson would have seen the need for widespread support in establishing a bank. In the fifteen years since the abortive launching of the Canada Banking Company he had grown greatly in political experience. Elected a member for Montreal East in the first provincial legislature of 1792, Richardson had immediately become the leader of the English commercial party, and in his maiden speech in the House had won the undying enmity of the French-Canadian majority by his vigorous opposition to the use of French as an official language. During his incumbency he revealed his interest in economic problems by introducing a bill to establish the relative values of gold coins current in the province, and by giving strong support to an act for the construction of the Lachine Canal. Despite Richardson's refusal to stand for re-election in 1796, he remained one of the most forceful leaders of the English faction and one of the most effective advocates of economic and civic progress. Persuaded that his presence was sorely needed in the legislature, he again stood for election in August, 1804, and was returned for Montreal West. Later the same year he was appointed a member of the Executive Council.

No records of bank meetings in Quebec and Montreal have been preserved, nor were any reported in the journals of the day. That the manoeuvre for public support was successful is borne out by the signing in 1807 of a petition by "divers inhabitants of Quebec and Montreal." It was placed in the hands of the Montreal members of parliament for presentation to Thomas Dunn, President of the Government and interim administrator in the absence of the Governor, and to the Legislative Council and the House of Assembly. The petition, however, was found to be unacceptable in that it prayed only for the establishment of a bank without specifying by whom or under what conditions. For this reason and because of the approaching close of the session, it was withheld until February, 1808, when it was presented by John Richardson in amended form. The revised petition, requesting an Act of Incorporation, states:

> That the Commerce and Agriculture of this Province, labour under many inconveniences, and discouragements from the quantity of Specie in circulation, being greatly inadequate to its necessities and increasing population, from thence enterprise and industry languish, and the natural advantages arising from a fertile soil, large and navigable Rivers, and most valuable and extensive Fisheries, in the Rivers, Bays and Gulph of the *St. Lawrence*, remain almost dormant and unimproved.
>
> The petitioners therefore beg leave to represent to the House, that in the present situation of the Province, nothing could have so great and immediate tendency to advance the commerce, agriculture, wealth and prosperity of the Province, as the establishment of a Bank. Time and experience have incontestibly proved the utility and security of Banks. They have been a safe and convenient substitute for gold and silver, and

have increased the industry and wealth of every country in which they have been established.

The petitioners therefore most humbly pray, that they may be incorporated into a body politic, by the name of the *Bank of Canada*, to be established in the Cities of *Quebec* and *Montreal*, with all the privileges and immunities usually granted to such corporations; and subject to such limitations and restrictions as the House in its wisdom may think best.

The original petition was again presented and both were referred to a committee of seven – Messrs. Richardson, Bedard, Blackwood, Mure, Berthelot, Perrault, and Taschereau – which reported back to the House on March 4, 1808, as follows:

To prove the allegations of the petitions, a Member informed the Committee that the balance of trade between this Province and the *United States* by Inland Navigation, being greatly against us, a constant drain of *Specie* from this Country is thereby occasioned, which can be replaced only by importations *thereof* from *Great Britain*, or by sending down Sterling Bills to the *States*, and bringing back their proceeds in Gold and Silver coin. That the former has not yet been resorted to, excepting by government, and is not likely to be attempted by individuals, and the latter (bringing money from the *States*) is attended with considerable loss, expense, and great risk.

That *Specie* is very sensibly decreasing in this Province, and some safe substitute would be greatly desirable and tend to facilitate the trade of the Province, particularly the export trade, which is often cramped by the heavy loss on Bills of Exchange, consequent upon the disproportion between the amount of them for sale, and the circulating coin.

He therefore was of opinion, that the institution of a Bank would have a tendency to remove, at least in part, the inconveniences at present felt from the scarcity of a circulating medium, and be otherwise beneficial to the Province.

That such institutions had been useful in other countries, and although there might be difficulties here to encounter, in a matter so new to the bulk of the Inhabitants, yet that he thought it would finally surmount those difficulties, and at all events merited a fair trial.

Although couched in somewhat different language, the similarity between the petition of 1808 and the prospectus of 1792 is rather striking. Both set forth the same facts with respect to the confused condition of the currency and to the difficulties encountered in making foreign payments; both refer to the proven utility and safety of banks in other countries; and both represent banking as an institution dedicated to the public weal rather than to private gain. A comparison of the two documents clears up a point that has long remained obscure: the actual authorship of the proposal, dated London, March 31, 1792, to form the Canada Banking Company. It is now abundantly clear that John Richardson was the author of both and that it was he, and probably he alone, who provided the entrepreneurial impetus for the introduction of banking in Canada.

The petition and committee report succinctly outline the problems faced by Lower Canada owing to the insufficiency of currency for both domestic purposes and foreign payments. That the establishment of a bank would increase the amount of specie, plate, and bullion in the province might at first seem impossible; however, there were indirect ways in which this could be effected. The issuing and acceptance of bank-notes would release some of the specie employed in domestic business for use in international transactions where it was most needed. At the same time, if those people who had been hoarding precious metals could be induced to exchange them for notes, deposits, or stock, there would result an additional increase in the available supply of specie. Furthermore it would be situated in a large central depot rather than in scattered caches, thus enabling its more effective allocation. Since it was later proposed that the bank be able to issue notes up to three times the value of the specie in its coffers, domestic intercourse would profit even more by an outright expansion of financial credit. On the other hand, the bank would also ameliorate the foreign exchange position by acting as a trustworthy and efficient intermediary for the consolidation of payments on an organized basis. The claims set forth as to the safety and utility of banks, and their beneficial effects on trade and commerce, were to be proved entirely valid.

Letters in the press, however, held that the issuance of bank-note currency could only lead to an increase in the widespread counterfeiting then notoriously prevalent along the Vermont border, where gangs of accomplished engravers were busily engaged in producing facsimiles of the notes of all the known – and even unknown – banks in the United States. Such practices, if

MEETING PLACE—1807-8

From the first attempt in 1792 to start a bank, James McGill had been a close ally of John Richardson. In preparation for the second attempt in 1808, McGill's home on Notre Dame Street, shown here, is believed to have served as a meeting place for the planners of the project.

Adjacent to the house on the east is the Château de Ramezay, whose west gate can be observed in the picture. Both buildings were erected in the early eighteenth century; only the Château de Ramezay, now a museum, remains.

On his death in 1813, James McGill bequeathed part of his estate for the purpose of founding a college. As well as £10,000 in cash, this bequest included "Burnside," his 46-acre farm at the foot of Mount Royal, which became the site of McGill University.

introduced into Canada, it was maintained, would make the French Canadians an easy prey to Yankee rogues and forgers and so render paper currency worthless. Another correspondent averred that memories of "the French King's paper" would frustrate any further effort to circulate bank-note currency in lieu of metallic counters, and still others feared that the creation of a bank would automatically lead to the creation of a money-monopoly whereby a few wealthy, and hence detested, merchants would further enslave an already captive and helpless people.

Instead of being based on concrete examples procurable one or two hundred miles away in the United States, opposition to the banking proposal relied on abstract generalities inspired mainly by fear of change in any form. But the support of the five French-Canadian merchants and professional men on the seven-man legislative committee ensured that the matter would not be allowed to die. In consequence, a bill to incorporate a bank in Lower Canada was introduced in the House of Assembly by John Richardson on April 12, 1808. Following a remarkably well-informed dissertation by its sponsor, the measure passed the first reading and four hundred copies were ordered printed for the study and consideration of the members of the legislature.

2.

So great, apparently, was public interest in the proposed banking legislation that on May 2, 1808, the Quebec *Mercury* reprinted Richardson's speech in full, and the Quebec *Gazette*, in its issue of September 1, advertised for sale at its new printing office and at the establishments of Messrs. Neilson and Ménéclier in Montreal, reprints of both the bill and speech. Nothing is known respecting the distribution of the reprint, nor has a single copy of the item come to light. Original copies of both the bill and the issue of the Quebec *Mercury* containing Richardson's speech are preserved, however, in the Public Archives of Canada.

After alluding to the fact that the bank bill could not be considered in the current session of the House because of the approach of prorogation, the speaker explained in brilliant synthesis the origin and evolution of money as a medium of exchange and showed why the combined scarcity, durability, utility, and portability of gold and silver had made them the preferred media of exchange and standards of value throughout the world. There followed a brief summary of the evolution of paper currency from its beginnings in the form of deposit receipts for gold and silver to its gradual acceptance as a circulating medium in lieu of the bulky precious metals. Given the state of the Canadian economy, with its deficiency of gold and silver, Richardson must have been sorely tempted to advocate the formation of a land or country bank.

Such institutions had sprung up in certain areas of Britain where there was both a lack of specie and a need for credit. Seeing this, a wealthy landholder, either by himself or in partnership with others, would found a bank, the notes of which would be backed not by specie, which was unobtainable, but by the landed property owned by the partners. Naturally such banks were willing to take property mortgages as security for loans. As long as land was sufficiently scarce for it to maintain a constant or rising value, such a system was adequate. However, Richardson knew that land in Canada, except in a few established centres, was virtually valueless, and even in Quebec and Montreal the value of land could easily deteriorate, bringing about a disastrous depreciation of the bank-notes and collateral assets. The alternative, which Richardson wisely chose, in spite of Canada's deficiency of specie, was a specie or money bank, which, through sale of stock, would acquire gold and coin in its vaults. It would then be empowered to issue bank-notes up to a predetermined multiple of the value of specie in its coffers. Its loans would be primarily commercial credits of short duration, secured by readily salable merchandise or merely the credit-worthiness of the borrower or co-signer, thus putting the institution in the class of what today is known as a commercial bank. It was thought that short loans of this type would enable the bank to maintain a liquid position at all times. While this theory would be valid under most circumstances, a sudden severe depression could make collateral merchandise as worthless as the land on which the bank would not lend. However, the commercial loan principle has proved the safer in practice.

Referring to Adam Smith as having written upon the subject of political economy "with an intelligence and profundity of observation beyond any other person," Richardson quoted him to support the contention that "Bank-notes, issued by people of undoubted credit, payable upon demand, in gold and silver, without any condition . . . become in every respect as a circulating medium, equal to gold and silver."

Richardson then engaged in a simple and very lucid comparison of private or joint-stock banks and corporate banks. In private banking, he explained, each of the proprietors was liable for the debts of the whole, while in corporate banking each stockholder was liable only for the amount of his stock. "At first view," the speaker pointed out, "it will strike the uninformed in such questions that private banks are safer for the public, and Corporate Banks safer for the stockholder." Admitting that corporate banks were undoubtedly safer for the stockholder, in that each one could only be held liable for the amount of his investment save under exceptional circumstances, Richardson argued that they also offered security for the public which private banks could never ensure for the reason that the latter were under no legal obligation to confine their operations to the business of banking, being free to use their funds for speculation as they might see fit, while corporate banks were under legal limitations, in the provisions of their charters, to restrict their operations to banking business only. Citing the issuance of bank-notes – the creation of paper currency – as one of the primary functions of a bank, Richardson then explained how this became the principal source of profits to the stockholders but with less prospect of immediate advantage to themselves than to the commercial community and the public at large. Emphasizing the public interest, he had this to say:

> Time only can beget confidence in new undertakings, and I am not sanguine in the hope of immediate benefit to the Stockholders, from the contemplated Bank – it may require some years to convince the bulk of the community in this province, that they can safely take Bank-notes; and until such conviction arises, the business will be a losing one; but that should not deter the proprietors from perseverance even under a lengthy disappointment. It will, from local circumstances, require great caution in the Directors at the outset, and probably for some years; but in the end, success must ensue unless the people of this province be composed of other materials than mankind are in other countries, which none can have the folly to believe.

The speech is found to answer every question that could reasonably be asked by any unprejudiced person with respect to the operations of the proposed bank, its organization, share capital, stockholders' liability, bank-note circulation, and counterfeiting – punishable by death "without benefit of clergy" – and in conclusion, Richardson explained the technical provisions of the charter in these words:

> The stock is not to exceed £250,000 currency, unless the government of the province see fit to take an interest therein, in which case it may be

£50,000 more. This stock is to consist of shares of £25 each. There are to be 24 Directors who are to choose out of their number a President and Vice President, whereof half are to be for Quebec and half for Montreal, at which cities the two superior branches of the Bank are to be held, with a power of erecting offices of deposit and discount, in other parts of Canada when found advisable. If government take an interest they are to appoint two Directors. The Dividends are to be paid half yearly. A deposit of ten per cent is to be paid down, for each share on subscribing, which will be forfeited if the first instalment thereafter of ten per cent be not paid in due season. The shares are put at a low rate, that they may be more generally diffused over the provinces. Foreigners may hold shares, but cannot be Directors. They may, however, vote at general meetings by proxy, if the proxy be one of His Majesty's subjects.

The votes are endeavoured to be established upon such a scale of proportion as shall exclude an over bearing preponderance in those who shall hold a large interest in the concern, and yet assure to property therein, that influence which it ought to possess in every well regulated institution.

It is proposed that there shall be no other corporate Bank in Canada during the continuance of the contemplated one, but there is a power of revocation thereof, under certain limitations, and formalities, if found to be hurtful in practice. The stock of the Bank may be increased when requisite, and its notes are proposed to be receivable in payment of duties imposed or to be imposed by the Provincial Legislature.

The bill contained some forty-one sections and subsections and provided much the same powers as those embraced in the Canada Banking Company proposal of 1792, namely, to receive deposits in cash, to issue bank-notes in exchange for such deposits, to discount bills and notes of hand, and to facilitate business by keeping cash accounts for those who wished to use the bank services for their receipts and deposits. The new institution, however, was to be known as "The Bank of Lower-Canada," and in view of its corporate character, the bill contained elaborate safeguards as to stockholders' voting rights and privileges, personal liability, note issue, and public responsibility. The bank's total indebtedness was not to exceed three times the paid-up capital; it could hold only such real estate as was necessary to the conduct of its banking business but could hold mortgages on real property where these were acquired for debts contracted in the ordinary course of business, and was required to furnish the government on demand sworn statements of the capital stock, debts due the bank, and deposits and notes in circulation. One of the provisions of the proposed charter, referred to by Richardson in his summation, but without precedent in English or Scottish banking, was that enabling the government to become a stockholder to the extent of one-sixth of the total share capital of £300,000.

As we have already noted, both the bill and the speech which introduced it in the House of Assembly of Lower Canada on April 12, 1808, constitute a remarkable historical record. Not only do they form an outline for the Canadian banking system as it later developed; but when taken in conjunction with the proposal of 1792, they indubitably establish John Richardson as the father of Canadian banking in the same sense that Alexander Hamilton is known as the father of American banking. Experience has amply borne witness to the soundness of Richardson's judgement.

3.

Few beliefs have been more tenaciously held than that which attributes the origins of the Canadian banking system directly to eighteenth-century Scottish banking philosophy and practice. So widespread in fact has been this popular assumption that it is now almost a part of the national folklore along with the legends of the fur trade and the Mounties.

It was not until the 1890's that the first serious study of Canadian banking was undertaken; prior to that date, therefore, there is nothing to show when or by whom the misconception was promulgated. This work, *The Canadian Banking System*, was written by Dr. Roeliff Morton Breckenridge, sometime Seligman Fellow in Economics at Columbia College. As an American, Breckenridge could have had no reason to distort the facts as he found them, and concluded, though on hearsay evidence, it would seem, that Scotland had provided the immediate model for Canadian banking. To drive home his point, he stated that out of the 144 charter members of the Bank of Montreal, at least ninety had Scottish names. The first stock register of the Montreal Bank, however, shows that the original subscribers to that institution numbered 289, and that no fewer than 121 were residents of New York, Boston, Middletown, Conn., and other towns in New England. Among the remaining 168 subscribers, most of whom were residents of Montreal, Scottish names were, as already remarked, in the minority.

Had Breckenridge had access to the archives of the Bank of Montreal, and not merely to the 1822 charter, he must have discovered the facts set forth above. In any case, he was severely criticized by Adam Shortt, author of "The Early History of Canadian Banking"; and later, in a revised edition, Breckenridge recognized the American origin of Canadian banking and at the same time acknowledged his debt to Shortt.

While there were certain similarities between eighteenth-century Scottish banking and that which developed in Canada, these seem to have been largely coincidental. The Canadian system derived directly neither from Scotland nor from England but from the United States. There, by 1808, banking based on specie capital and mercantile credit had been in successful operation for many years and had proved its worth by profitable operations which had been of immense value in promoting prosperity and stabilizing financial conditions in the Republic. It was to this system, developed largely by Alexander Hamilton, that John Richardson turned for the model of the Canada Banking Company, the Bank of Lower-Canada, and finally the Bank of Montreal.

It was only natural, and even inevitable, that Canadian banking should have been cast in a mould furnished by New rather than Old World experience, the one being germane and contiguous, the other remote and irrelevant. At the beginning of the nineteenth century, the economies of Canada and the United States were inextricably conjoined, particularly along the lines of pioneering endeavour, and Canadian merchants doing business across the border were much more numerous than those engaged in the transatlantic trade, still centred largely in Quebec. In addition, Montreal was then the metropolitan centre for most of the trade of Vermont and northwestern New York and, until the completion of the Erie Canal, of the American states and territories abutting on the Great Lakes. The ties with New England, both commercial and cultural, were much stronger than is commonly recognized. The subscription books of the Boston *Gazette* for 1816-17, for example, list more than a hundred Montreal subscribers, and almost as many in Three Rivers and Quebec combined. While this was at a somewhat later date, there is no reason to believe that conditions following the War of 1812 were in any way different in Lower Canada from what they had been before it.

With an informed knowledge of the affairs of the neighbouring republic through business dealings, frequent travel to and fro, and familiarity with American newspapers and periodicals, it is not surprising that Canadian men of affairs should have been impressed by the striking changes brought about in the fortunes of the United States by the financial policies of Alexander Hamilton.

Moreover, John Richardson, as an employee of an important English mercantile house in New York which somehow survived the Revolution, had been a resident of that city during the period of the great monetary, financial, and fiscal discussions which led to the founding of the Bank of North America in 1781 and the Bank of New York and the Massachusetts Bank (Boston) in 1784. Furthermore, after leaving the American metropolis in 1784, he would unquestionably have retained his contacts with William Constable, with whom he had served in the New York office of Phyn, Ellice & Inglis and who continued as the firm's New York agent after the Revolution, becoming in 1791 a director of the Bank of New York. It is clear, therefore, that John Richardson had a first-hand knowledge of Hamilton's banking principles.

4.

As early as 1780, Alexander Hamilton had urged the establishment of a "national" bank. Hamilton envisaged a great federally chartered trading and banking corporation under private management but with government participation and partial government control, which would unite the moneyed classes of the country in the support of government credit, and manage the currency on sound banking principles. He proposed a commercial bank based on specie capital but embracing certain practices of land banking such as lending on mortgages. In 1781, upon the continued urging of Hamilton and others, Morris, the Superintendent of Finance of the Continental Congress, proposed the establishment of the Bank of North America with a share capital of $400,000 payable in gold and silver. Its function was to lend money to the government in anticipation of its revenues and for the stabilization of the near-worthless Continental paper currency issued during the Revolution, while enabling its subscribers to circulate their capital for the benefit of commerce and industry. The Bank of North America opened on January 6, 1782, but vacated its federal charter in 1785. It continued under state charter as a local bank until 1929, when it merged with another Pennsylvania financial institution.

The first American bank to maintain convertibility at all times was enormously successful in its purpose. It strengthened the finances of the United States at a moment when the future of the Republic seemed doomed by its inability to purchase necessities, and proved the solid worth of Hamilton's

BEAVER CLUB MEMBERS
HONOUR
LORD DALHOUSIE

Montreal in the late eighteenth and early nineteenth centuries was the epitome of gay social life. Contributing to this, perhaps more than any other factor, was the Beaver Club, famous since 1785 for its gourmet gatherings.

When the members invited Lord Dalhousie, the Governor General, to be guest of honour on May 14, 1824, the Beaver Club was holding its fortnightly dinners in the newly rebuilt Mansion House Hotel (later the Masonic Hall) which was situated on St. Paul Street where the Bonsecours Market building now stands. The hotel was the last word in elegance; indeed, it was said to compare favourably with any in England.

Here we see Lord Dalhousie chatting over sherry before the dinner, which was attended by some fifty members and presided over by John Finlay, with Alexander Mackenzie acting as vice-president.

Meetings of the club generally lasted well into the small hours of the morning. While the viceregal nature of this occasion may have curbed the frivolities of members somewhat, it was probably the most memorable in the club's history. Each member in attendance was presented by his lordship with a silver snuff-box.

The Beaver Club had been organized, nearly forty years before, by nineteen North West traders who were then going regularly into "le pays d'en haut" to find their fortune in furs among the Indians. An indispensable condition of membership was at least one winter's sojourn in the Indian country, where the chief commodity the traders sought was the pelt of the beaver.

Several of the men connected with the Bank of Montreal, including John Richardson and his partner, John Forsyth, were members of the club, and at one period George Moffatt served as secretary.

Painting by Bruce Johnson

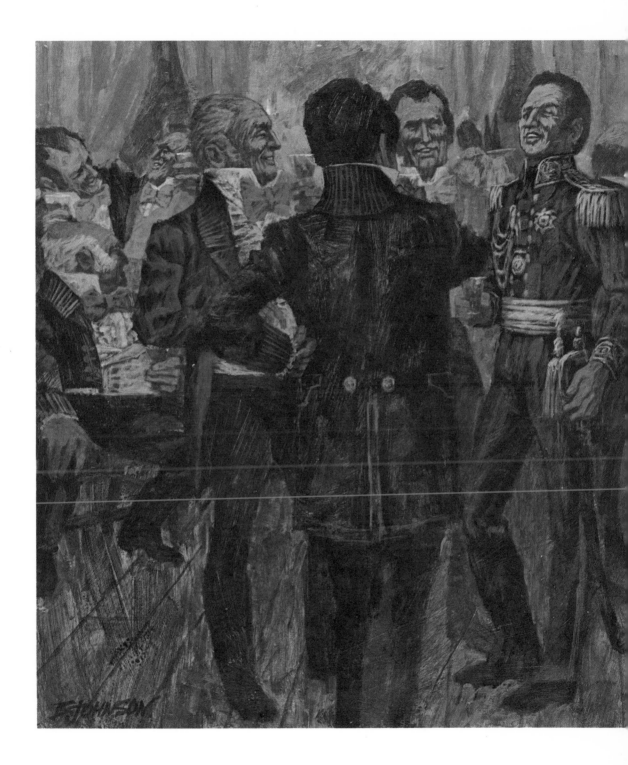

theories. But the bank was located in Philadelphia, with government financing its principal responsibility. In consequence, it did little or nothing to alleviate the commercial stagnation which had been brought about in other centres by the disappearance of a trustworthy medium of exchange and lack of commercial credit. There resulted in the several states a public demand for local banking facilities which in turn provoked much the same controversy as that which agitated public opinion in Canada more than twenty years later. Despite fears of the untried and unknown among the generality of the population, there were established in 1784 the Bank of New York and the Massachusetts Bank, the first under articles of association, the second by state charter embodying identical principles.

The author of the articles of the Bank of New York was Alexander Hamilton, whose views had changed significantly from those expressed in letters to Robert Morris in 1780 and 1781. By 1784 he had become implacably opposed to land banking, even to the extent of barring loans secured by land mortgages, and was instead a determined advocate of genuine specie banking as practised by the Bank of England and the leading banks of Europe.

Since the articles of association of the Bank of New York, 1784, the charter of the Massachusetts Bank, and the proposal for the Canada Banking Company, 1792, are virtually identical, it is certain that they had a common source, either Hamilton's matured convictions on the subject of banking or a meeting of minds among the group of individual merchant-traders of New York, London, and Montreal to whom we have already been introduced. In each case, the public nature and responsibilities of banking are referred to, and in each, the experience of other countries as to the stability of banks is stressed, the phraseology often being identical. In all three instances, also, the design called for the establishment of banks of limited share capital, based on gold and silver coin, plate, or bullion, with prescribed powers as to the issue of bank-notes and other public safeguards.

Judged from either a private or public point of view, both the Bank of New York and the Massachusetts Bank were immediately successful. Both paid dividends from the outset and both established their utility for the promotion of trade and commerce by marshalling the capital resources of their subscribers, making the combined capital available to commercial borrowers in the form of bank-notes or bank credit transferable on order, and serving as repositories for state funds. Despite the deflation of the Continental paper currency, notes of the two banks rapidly became acceptable for the payment of private and public debt. On the other hand, the more serious charges brought against banking failed to materialize: specie did not fly the country, nor was there any orgy of speculation and overtrading as had been predicted. Managed with rigid conservatism and integrity, both institutions proved the utility of banks to the public interest and welfare and became the model for the establishment of state banks elsewhere. Both, however, were separate local institutions with no community of interest, and they could contribute little to solve the grave financial problems which faced the United States upon the adoption of the Constitution in 1789.

5.

In September 1789, when Congress established the Treasury Department, Washington promptly appointed Alexander Hamilton as its first Secretary. In order to assist his many reforms, Hamilton proposed, as the principal instrument of his fiscal policies, the creation of a bank, founded under a national charter, which would bear much the same relation to the United States government as had the Bank of England to the English government for almost a hundred years. Specifically, the bank would be the financial agent of the government, which would hold shares in it, but it would be managed by directors elected from among the private shareholders.

Indicative of the confusion with respect to banks and banking theory then current, Hamilton thought it necessary to examine in detail every feature of his proposal. He stressed particularly the need for a much greater capital than had been used by the Bank of North America, and the advantages of private ownership and management. Only by such means, he insisted, could the banks help further the growth of trade and commerce, and at the same time be of assistance to the government whose fiscal strength depended so largely on their prosperity. Were the institution to be made simply another engine of government, or to be controlled or managed by it, the affairs of the bank would be conducted in accordance with government policy instead of the proven banking principles required for its success. On the other hand, government participation was held to be essential to ensure stability, promote confidence at home and abroad, and manage both interstate and foreign transactions. Despite its advocacy of private ownership and management, the report also stressed the need to limit voting rights, lest a few large shareholders gain control, and to rotate directors, lest a small clique perpetuate itself indefinitely. Contrasting bank-note currency redeemable in specie with the emission of United States government currency of an inconvertible nature, Hamilton pointed out that the latter alternative was "so certain of being abused that the wisdom of the government will be shown in never trusting itself with the use of so seducing and dangerous an expedient."

In spite of violent criticism and opposition, the First Bank of the United States was chartered by Congress in February, 1791, and began operation soon after. The Act of Incorporation created a corporate body with a share capital of $10,000,000 divided into 25,000 shares of $400 each, payable partly in specie and partly in government stock. Two million dollars were to be subscribed by the United States, in exchange for which the government would receive advances of a comparable amount; these would be repaid in ten annual instalments at six per cent interest—an arrangement similar to that made between the British government and the Bank of England in 1694. Stockholders, whether private or corporate, with the exception of the government, were limited to one thousand shares each, and voting rights thereon diminished progressively: one share, one vote; three shares, two votes; five shares, three votes; and so forth. Only stockholders resident in the United States could vote, in person or by proxy, and the charter was to continue until March 4, 1811.

The bank was restricted from holding real estate in excess of that required for its own accommodation but could acquire mortgages as additional security for undischarged debts previously contracted. Later to become a principal article of faith in Canadian banking, this provision was to prove the most contentious of all those proposed by Hamilton, and provoked a controversy which later rocked American banking to its foundations. The liability of stockholders was limited to the amount of their stock, but directors were personally liable for all debts which exceeded capital plus deposits, unless notice of absence or dissent had been given the President of the United States. A similar provision, carried to Canadian banking, later became the focal point of a schism in the Bank of Montreal directorate.

The bank was enjoined from mercantile speculation of any kind and limits were placed on loans to the federal and state governments; no loans were to be made to a foreign power or state without previous authorization by Congress. The bank could sell that part of the public debt acquired through stock subscription but could not purchase government securities. Notes of the bank, payable in gold and silver on demand, were to be "receivable in all payments to the United States"; interest on discounts was limited to six per

cent; permission was granted to open offices of discount and deposit any-
where in the United States, and no other bank was to be incorporated by the
United States during the life of the charter. The head office of the bank was
located in Philadelphia and it was not until it had begun operation that the
directors decided to open branches in New York, Boston, and other commercial and financial centres. It would appear, therefore, that branch banking,
later to become a distinctive feature of the Canadian system, was an indigenous and necessary invention, wholly unrelated to Scottish precedent.

The First Bank of the United States (1791-1811) was a pronounced success,
and fully justified Hamilton's most sanguine claims. Even greater than the
profits to the stockholders, which amounted to over $16,000,000 in dividends
by 1811, were the public benefits gained by the stabilization of the currency
and the establishment of the credit of the United States. The example which
it set was equally beneficial, as future banks were forced to conform to its
high standards and the emphasis on convertibility which it carried over from
the Bank of North America. In conjunction with fiscal policies that imposed
heavy excise taxes for internal revenue purposes, the bank, in an extraordinarily short interval, had so strengthened and invigorated the entire American economy that henceforth no difficulty was experienced in securing from
Europe the capital required for its continuing expansion. However, this very
fact proved its undoing. In 1809, when Gallatin, then Secretary of the Treasury, recommended that the charter be renewed, it was disclosed that no less
than 18,000 of the 25,000 shares were held by foreigners. The remaining 7,000
shares, owned in the United States, controlled the institution, but this fact
availed little and the bank went out of business in 1811.

The charges levelled against the First Bank of the United States by Jefferson,
Madison, and other agrarian theorists were valid in part. It controlled foreign
and domestic exchange, it was the collection and payments agent of the government, and it was able to dictate the discount practices throughout the
country. Its principal function, moreover, was to serve the needs of the federal
government rather than strengthen the commercial, manufacturing, and agricultural energies unleashed at the close of the long struggle for independence.
In contrast with England, however, where the central bank had an exclusive
charter and other banking operations were confined to partnerships of not
more than six proprietors, every American state could adopt any banking
laws and charter any kind of bank it chose. In consequence, as early as 1792,
state charters, in addition to those already granted the Bank of New York and

the Massachusetts Bank, were obtained by the Essex Bank in Salem, the Union Bank in Boston, the Bank of Providence, the Bank of Albany, the Hartford Bank in Connecticut, and the Maryland Bank in Baltimore. All of these institutions adhered closely to the banking practices already established by the Bank of North America and the First Bank of the United States. Each was chartered by its respective state, and each was a commercial bank of discount and deposit, empowered to issue its own notes redeemable in specie, accept customers' deposits, discount short-term commercial paper, and buy and sell domestic and foreign exchange.

Despite the sound intentions of their banking principles and their excellent management, the early American banks were exposed to a storm of criticism that mounted during the 1790's and early 1800's. It is not difficult to understand the reason. Lack of competition gave these first banks a monopolistic character in communities where wealth was largely inherited or mercantile, and established merchants could secure accommodation far more easily than the small business man and tradesman or the growing class of manufacturers who were anxious to establish local industry. In the small market towns and the rural communities appended to them, there were as yet no banking facilities whatever.

Following Jefferson's defeat of the Federalist party in 1800, however, came a surge of state banking legislation designed to undermine monopolistic control of credit and with it a marked increase in the number of chartered city banks and a rapid proliferation of country and private banking. The first of these groups operated as money banks, with specie capital, the second as land banks, with capital made up of real or personal estates. The frequency of such names as "Manufacturers and Mechanics" and "Farmers and Mechanics" in the titles of the city banks of the early 1800's shows that they were founded to serve the credit needs of separate segments of the community, as the country banks were created to provide rural credits unobtainable from any other source. With the rapid extension of the American frontier following 1800 there was a great increase in the number of the latter institutions, so much so that by 1808, when the effort was made to charter the Bank of Lower-Canada, there was hardly a market town in Massachusetts, New Hampshire or Vermont without a private country bank, whose notes circulated widely and in areas remote from the place of issue.

That these developments went unobserved in Lower Canada is inconceivable. Yet no documents relating to them have been brought to light, except a

TRAVEL FOR TRADE

Transportation was still very largely by water when the Bank began business. Although sailing ships had been used on the inland waters for well over a century, and steamboats had begun to appear on the St. Lawrence and Ottawa rivers, the birch-bark canoe remained the most common mode of travel for the colonial traders, as well as for the Indians, because of the ease with which it could be portaged around the rapids and other natural barriers to be found on most routes before the construction of canals.

Here, a crew of intrepid canoeists navigate the Lachine Rapids, with merchants and government officials as passengers. Such canoes, especially those used by the fur-trading companies, were often tremendous – sometimes running to forty feet in length, six in width, and two in depth, and capable of carrying a load of more than four tons.

few letters to the press viewing with alarm the activities of counterfeiters along the Vermont border; otherwise, a veil of complete obscurity clouds this important phase of Canadian-American relations. Nevertheless, the intimate nature of these relations is established both by later evidence of association between the Montreal banking group and like-minded groups in Boston, Hartford, and New York, and in the proposed charter of the Bank of Lower-Canada. With the alterations imposed by the absence of a public debt in the Canadian province, the necessary changes respecting citizenship, and a new clause respecting stockholders' liability, the Canadian charter was a direct replica of that of the First Bank of the United States.

6.

The second attempt to establish a bank in Lower Canada was no more successful than the first, for even more inscrutable reasons. Even the precise fate of the bill for incorporation is uncertain. Having been dropped in the legislative hopper, it appears never to have emerged, but whether it died a natural or unnatural death remains unknown. Thereafter, and until the War of 1812 was ended, the plans to found a bank in Montreal and Quebec remained quiescent. Why John Richardson and the group around him suddenly abandoned their well-formulated plans to found an institution so badly needed in the province seems puzzling. The mystery deepens when their wide knowledge of American precedent and experience is understood. They had already established close connections with bankers across the border and had numerous examples to draw on of successful banking operations pursued without benefit of charter. A decade later, in fact, they were to have recourse to the same articles of association that Hamilton had used in founding the Bank of New York. Why, then, did they not continue to pursue their objective in 1808?

The accepted historical explanation is largely political. The years 1807 to 1811, which marked the administration of Sir James Craig, were unhappy ones for everyone concerned, including Craig himself. He was largely responsible for the emergence of French-Canadian nationalism as a political force, and at the same time he succeeded in alienating many of his councillors among the English commercial group.

There was re-enacted the classic feud between the colonial administrator and the members of the Assembly which expressed itself in a bitter struggle for control of the purse, and over the method of taxation for the purposes of government and local improvements. As agrarians, the French Canadians were opposed to land taxes, and as fledgeling parliamentarians they resented an administration whose conduct became more insufferable as it grew more autocratic. Craig resolved the inevitable impasse by dismissing the Assembly and calling for elections, only to find himself opposed by an even more recalcitrant Assembly. The situation prevailed until his recall in 1811, by which time war with the United States was accepted as a probability. It must also be remembered that there still lingered in the minds of the French Canadians, who were in a majority in the Assembly, a distrust of paper currency as epitomized by card money and hence a dislike of any form of banking.

In such an atmosphere of dissension and conflict, with its numerous cross-currents of political and economic interests, it is easy to understand why the bank bill of 1808 should have fallen by the wayside. However, the political climate alone could hardly have persuaded so powerful a group as Forsyth-Richardson and their associates to abandon a scheme which they regarded as so necessary and beneficial.

During the period under review, the major impacts on the Canadian economy were produced by the weakening of the English war-time market that accompanied Napoleon's great European victories; England's adoption of colonial timber preferences when supplies from the Baltic were no longer available; and President Jefferson's embargo on trade with Britain and her colonies. The weakening of the British war-time market reduced drastically the exports of Canada's two principal staples, wheat and fur. From 399,168 bushels in 1808, wheat shipments declined to 97,553 bushels in 1811, and fur cargoes out of Hudson Bay fell from a value of £38,400 in 1800 to a mere £8,700 in 1809, after which the company passed its dividends until 1814. On the other hand, the granting of bounties on colonial timber proved a boon, establishing Canada's third great staple trade.

As shown in an earlier chapter, the effects of the various embargoes and non-intercourse proclamations on the Canadian economy are impossible to determine with any pretence of accuracy. Whether trade declined or increased in volume or value is unknown. Vermont smuggling legends indicate the latter, as does the deterioration of the specie situation in Canada. The evidence points to the fact that there was insufficient capital available at this time to found a bank, not only among the entrepreneurial banking group but in the business community as a whole. This possibility is borne out by the contemporary involvement of Forsyth-Richardson and McTavish-McGillivrays in one of the final acts in the great drama of the fur trade: the formation of the Southwest Company with John Jacob Astor in 1811. Equal amounts of capital were subscribed by the Canadian and American interests, and this venture may have temporarily precluded other investments. The refusal of Congress to extend the charter of the First Bank of the United States in 1811 may also have made pursuit of a similar institution in Canada unpropitious.

News of the American declaration of war on June 12, 1812, was conveyed to the Governor at Quebec by John Richardson who had received the intelligence from business friends across the border. The inaction that had overcome the Canadian economy was dissipated by the infusion of men and money from Great Britain, and the thirty months of war brought greater prosperity to Canada and the Maritime Provinces than they had ever experienced. Montreal, as the staging base for reinforcements moving up the St. Lawrence, and with little or no threat to its security from neutralist New England, grew rapidly in both wealth and stature. From a banking point of view, however, the most important by-product of the war was the introduction of a novel form of currency by Great Britain to pay her war-time needs.

Under ordinary circumstances, specie would have been procured through the medium of treasury bills. There were, however, insufficient supplies of specie in the colony, and to avoid the cost and risk at sea of importing coin from Great Britain, recourse was had to a managed paper currency for the payment of men and supplies. This took the form of Army Bills, which were made legal tender and were first issued in denominations of $25 to $400 bearing six-per-cent interest and redeemable on demand in bills on England and Quebec. The original issue, made in 1812, was for 1,000,000 Spanish dollars; additional issues were authorized, bringing the total to $6,000,000 of which $250,000 were in denominations of from $1 to $20 to facilitate everyday business transactions. The smaller notes were redeemable in specie on demand and bore no interest.

The success of the military paper currency had a marked effect on Canadian monetary psychology and the public attitude toward banks and banking. For the first time in colonial experience, the people of the two provinces were provided with a satisfactory circulating medium in sufficient quantities to meet all their daily needs. Backed by the Imperial Government, and attractive as an investment, the larger bills were readily accepted by merchants and military contractors and, toward the end of the war, by the devious processes of exchange, they became a magnet which attracted large quantities of specie from the United States, where English bills commanded high premiums. The smaller bills, on the other hand, found their way to all strata of society, with the result that the old barter business was broken up; farmers bought and sold for cash instead of store credit, and in the process enjoyed their first modicum of financial independence and economic self-respect.

The abundance of the circulating medium, coupled with its convenience and manifest advantages, led the public, and even many of its mercantile leaders, to conclude that the paper had induced the prosperity. In point of fact, the main cause of affluence was the indirect stimulus to consumption, production, and exports brought about by the war itself, over and above the increased military expenditures. In any case, the approaching redemption of the Army Bills, and their consequent disappearance from circulation, fostered demands for a satisfactory substitute. In a colonial context, the only possibility seemed to lie in the provision of banking facilities and the creation of a bank-note currency. Thanks to the Army Bills experience and the successful proliferation of banking in the neighbouring states, the next proposal to found a bank in Canada received a greater public acceptance than any of those preceding. In the legislature it met the same frustrations and confusions that had beset its predecessors.

On February 8, 1815, Austin (or Augustin) Cuvillier, a leading Quebec merchant, moved that the House resolve itself into a committee "to consider the expediency of establishing a bank in this Province." The motion was brought up four more times in February but was then apparently dropped until the next session when the same sponsor, on February 7, 1816, introduced a petition of divers merchants and other inhabitants of Montreal for the incorporation of a banking company, but without specifying its name or character. The petition was referred to a committee of five, headed by Mr. Cuvillier, which sat on February 8 and heard several witnesses, among them Messrs. Woolsey (later President of the Quebec Bank), Stewart, Mure, Symes, Grant, and Lymburner. All represented leading mercantile interests, all were in favour of a bank's incorporation. Emphasized were the need to provide a circulating medium, the stimulus to commerce and agriculture that would ensue, and the proven value of banks in other countries. It was proposed that a bank would augment and sustain the supply of specie in the country. It was also asserted that were a bank to be founded "on the most liberal principles" but "under wise and permanent limitations" it would immediately induce the inhabitants to provide the capital by becoming shareholders.

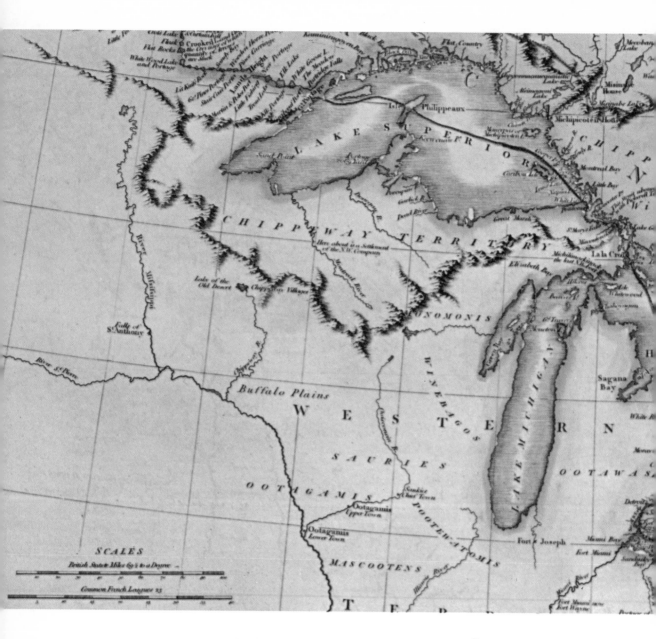

UPPER AND LOWER CANADA—1807

Prepared by John Cary, Engraver, this was described as a "new map of Upper and
Lower Canada" when it was issued in 1807.

An unusual feature of Mr. Cary's map is the information supplied in appropriate
places: for instance, that trout and pickerel abound in the strait east of Lake
Superior; that, south of Lake Ontario, "the Niagara falls down a stupendous

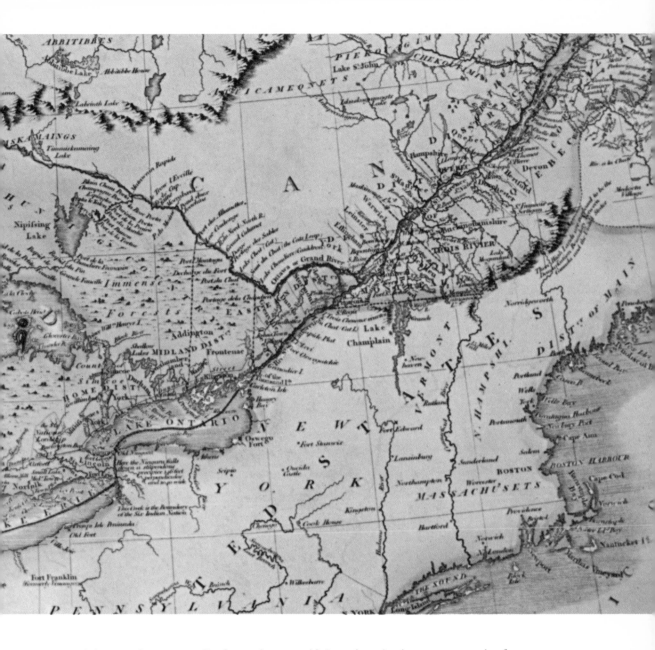

precipice 146 feet perpendicular and 1040 wide"; and again, in an area south of Lake Superior, that "Here about is a Settlement of the N. W. Company."

Another interesting feature is the route shown from Montreal to the head of the lakes—specifically to "Gt. Portage" or Grand Portage, the site of the North West Company's western headquarters before removal to Fort William some forty-five miles to the northeast.

The committee reported back to the House on February 14 and on the same day a bill to incorporate a bank in Lower Canada was presented and read for the first time. It was given its second reading on February 19, when a new committee of five was named to examine persons, papers, and records. Although no copy of the bill of 1816 has come to light, the differences between it and its predecessor were unquestionably of a minor nature, and could only have referred to the name and to government participation. This second committee reported back to the House on February 23, with no recommendations for amendments, and it was ordered that the bill come before a Committee of the Whole on February 27. As in 1808, however, the bill fell victim to prorogation, announced on February 26 by a new administrator, Sir Gordon Drummond, for an old cause: to forestall the impeachment of Judges Sewell and Monk by the French-Canadian majority in the Assembly.

Nothing daunted, Cuvillier again submitted the bill for incorporation on January 31, 1817, at the next session of the legislature. Once again the familiar ritual was repeated. The bill was given its second reading, February 5, referred to a committee, and one hundred copies ordered printed in French and English. This time it reached the stage of being discussed in Committee of the Whole, but again the legislature was prorogued, again by a new governor, Sir John Coape Sherbrooke, and again to forestall impeachment. By this time, however, the sands of patience had run out, and after twenty-five years of recurrent effort the group John Richardson had brought about him decided with dramatic suddenness to proceed without benefit of charter, as had the Bank of New York in 1784. An additional irritant to the group, no doubt, was the fact that while their own attempts to get a charter were constantly obstructed by the indifference of the governor and the actions of the Assembly, a bill to charter the Second Bank of the United States was passed in Congress in 1816, an event which inspired the merchants of Kingston to revive an earlier movement to charter a similar institution in Upper Canada. The legislature having risen on March 15, 1817, discussions were held and committees named, culminating in a general invitation to the public to examine the proposed Articles of Association of the Montreal Bank at the Court House on May 19. No serious criticism being received, the Articles were officially adopted that same day and subsequently published in English in the Montreal *Herald* on May 22 and in French in *Le Spectateur Canadien* on May 26. The long interval of gestation had ended and the period of growth begun.

FOUR

THE MEN
AND THEIR
PRINCIPLES

THE MEN
AND THEIR PRINCIPLES

I.

No records have been preserved of the preliminary discussions which culmi-nated in the decision to establish a commercial bank in Montreal without benefit of incorporation. In interpreting this pivotal phase in the history of the Bank of Montreal it therefore becomes necessary to have recourse to deduction based in certain instances on newly discovered facts, in others on the logic of inevitability, and in still others on reasonable assumptions. The Montreal *Herald*, in its issue carrying the Articles of Association, also printed a congratulatory editorial – a most unusual departure for journals of the day – which the Quebec *Gazette* reprinted on May 29, 1817:

> "In the first page of this paper the articles of the Montreal Bank Asso-ciation are laid before the public. Such an establishment has always been a favorite with this journal, and we cannot but congratulate the com-munity on the prospect of a wonderful change for the better in the agri-cultural and mechanical pursuits of this province. The articles of this

most laudable association, so far as we are able to judge from practical experience in our younger years, and from much reading, are drawn up with great judgment and wisdom, and seem extremely well calculated for our local position. We forebear making any remarks on the subject for the present, further than that we wish the establishment the utmost success in all its bearings."

Le Spectateur Canadien also published an editorial in its issue of May 31 lauding the founding of the Bank and pointing to the great economic benefits which had been derived from such institutions in Europe and especially in the United States, calling banks the channels from which life and vigour are communicated to the various classes of society. With its issues of June 14 and July 26 the *Spectateur* also published special supplements in which the Articles of Association were once more translated into French. The discussions which led to the "Montreal Bank Association" must certainly have been begun many months before the public advertisement of its formation. For example, the Quebec *Telegraph* in its issues of February 8 and 15, 1817, reprinted in French some excerpts from Richardson's speech of 1808.

There can be no question that John Richardson provided the imagination and purpose that finally brought the Bank of Montreal into being. From the beginning, he had the support of his English associates, the Phyn-Ellice-Inglis group, and of his partner and first cousin, John Forsyth. At various times, many persons prominent in the commercial world were associated with him in his endeavour. Nevertheless, the Bank of Montreal was as uniquely John Richardson's creation as the Bank of England was William Paterson's and the Bank of the United States was Alexander Hamilton's. Each had his indispensable associates but in each instance the dynamic impulse was provided by a single individual. In the case of Richardson, the question now arises: why was the accomplishment so long denied him? Or, to put it another way, what new factors were present in 1817 making for success that had not been present earlier? Were they political, economic, or personal?

The first of these possibilities can be summarily dismissed. There had been no substantial change in the political climate of Lower Canada between 1808 and 1817, nor would there be until the Rebellion of 1837 and the Durham Report which it provoked. With respect to the second possibility, there had, of course, been important economic changes. The War of 1812 brought unprecedented prosperity to all the Canadian provinces, and toward its close the first marked influx of immigration from the British Isles began, while that from the United States to Upper Canada was resumed immediately on its cessation. The effect was to widen the base of the Canadian economy and at the same time make it more complicated. As a result, the public attitude toward banking became more favourable as the need for banking facilities became more imperative. Furthermore the use and redemption of the Army Bills had demonstrated the safety, convenience and other advantages of notes or bills as circulating media, and at the same time had broken down some of the old prejudices and fear of paper money. With the inability, or unwillingness, of the colonial government to supply a substitute currency on their withdrawal, the idea of a bank of issue to fill the vacuum became more acceptable. Yet, alone, the economic factors do not provide a satisfactory explanation for the protracted stalemate. Had the founding of the Bank been related solely to the disappearance of the Army Bills, it should have begun business in 1815, when it was announced that all Bills would be redeemed for cash, no new ones issued, and no further interest paid. The answer to the enigma would seem to rest therefore on the personal or human factor – on someone among the several persons who agreed to engage in the business of banking under the name or style of The Montreal Bank and in the manner set forth in the twenty-five articles of association.

The signers were nine in number: John Richardson, George Garden, George Moffatt, Robert Armour, James Leslie, Horatio Gates, John C. Bush, Austin Cuvillier and Thomas A. Turner. Ordinarily referred to simply as "Montreal merchants," the group actually included representatives of many different interests then present on the Montreal commercial stage; however, it was by no means wholly representative.

John Richardson was appointed to the Legislative Council in 1816; otherwise his connections have already been sufficiently established. George Garden and George Moffatt were two of Montreal's leading merchants, the first as head of Maitland, Garden & Auldjo, the other as one of the partners of Gerrard, Gillespie, Moffatt & Co., successor to Parker, Gerrard & Ogilvy, the Michilimackinac traders. This firm Moffatt later controlled. Peculiar interest attaches to the inclusion of representatives of these two firms, the one allied with the North West Company, the other the Canadian agents for Lord Selkirk and the Hudson's Bay Company, then engaged with the Nor'Westers in the final throes of the struggle for control of the northwest fur trade. The bitterness of the dispute divided Montreal society into two opposed factions for several

years and haunted the Bank during its first difficult decade of operations, causing acute embarrassment and internal strife.

Austin Cuvillier, who was a member of the Legislative Assembly, was a
well-to-do importer with French-Canadian connections; James Leslie, a retired
army officer and the son of Wolfe's Assistant Quartermaster-General at
Quebec, a socially prominent and popular business man; Robert Armour, a
publisher and bookseller; and Horatio Gates, a New Englander engaged successfully in the Vermont trade. Little is known about the origins of Thomas
Turner or J. C. Bush, but there is reason to believe that they represented
American commercial or financial interests.

Austin Cuvillier, as the only French Canadian in the original group of nine
associates, and as its only representative in the Legislative Assembly, played
a significant role in the formation of the Montreal Bank. He was a friend
and supporter of Papineau, despite his close links with the English-Canadian
community in Montreal, and thus enjoyed the unique distinction of commanding the respect of both parties in the Assembly. While his combination
of financial and legislative talents was excelled only by that of John Richardson himself, his sophisticated impartiality provided a very necessary antidote
to the offensive racialism of the latter. It was Cuvillier who introduced the
bank bill in 1815 and in subsequent years, and as Adam Shortt has observed,
"The ultimate successful outcome was evidently due almost entirely to the
persistence and tactful handling of the measure by Mr. Cuvillier."

Of these nine men, Cuvillier, Garden, Gates, Leslie and Moffatt would later
serve as directors of the Bank of Montreal and two, Garden and Gates, as
officers, the first as vice-president, the second as president on two occasions.
Of those five directors, however, only two retained an active connection with
the Bank after the first decade: the stormy petrel of early nineteenth-century
Canadian business and politics, George Moffatt, and the former New Englander, Horatio Gates. At a later, critical period, Moffatt exercised an important influence on the conduct of the Bank's affairs; he also became one of the
most forthright political figures of his generation in Canada. However, he does
not appear to have played a decisive role at the time of the Bank's formation.
It is to Gates, therefore, that we must turn for a solution of the enigma.

2.

When Horatio Gates died in 1834 at the age of fifty-six, Montreal went into
mourning, flags flew at half mast all day, and minute-guns boomed from St.

Helen's Island. The funeral cortege was the largest Montreal had ever seen, and the newspapers devoted columns to eulogies of the great man and his inspiring career. As Adam Shortt remarks in his biographical monograph on Gates, one theme recurs in all the obituaries. It is to the effect that whoever may be forgotten in the years to come, the memory of Horatio Gates will be treasured as that of one of the most notable men in the country, whose career will be an inspiration to youth and a comfort to age. Today, Horatio Gates is almost as shadowy a figure on the Canadian historical scene as George Phyn, the legendary Laird of the Corse of Monellie. Beyond the fact that Gates was born in Barre, Massachusetts, little is known of his early life.

The first significant clue to Gates's career turns up in the genealogy of the Bellows family, a famous Massachusetts dynasty that played a leading role in the industrialization of New England. There we find that one Horatio Gates was a partner of the firm of Bellows & Gates which was doing business in Montreal around 1802, the senior member being Abel Bellows of Walpole, Massachusetts. This firm was probably the largest engaged in the Quebec-Vermont-New England trade, yet the first Canadian reference to it discovered is in a petition to the Crown published in the Quebec *Gazette* under date of 1810. This is rather significant. The commercial practice of the day was to advertise goods as they arrived by ship: teas from China, wines from Madeira, spices from the Islands, cottons from India, brocades from Italy, ironware from England, rum from the Indies, tobacco from Virginia – every issue of the Quebec *Gazette*, Montreal *Herald*, and other newspapers, contains columns of such eagerly awaited intelligence, displayed over the names of the leading import houses of the day. The absence of similar Bellows & Gates announcements suggests that the firm was engaged wholly in the Vermont trade, which would require no local advertising since most goods were for re-export. As will be seen, this deduction is supported by the extent of Horatio Gates's international banking affiliations and connections.

The 1810 reference to Bellows & Gates sheds some light on the character of the partnership and the ambitious scope of its operations. At the time, the port of Montreal was frequently so crowded that vessels had to anchor off shore for days and sometimes a week or more before they could find a berth to discharge their cargoes – this after they had been towed up St. Mary's Current between St. Helen's Island and the city by teams of as many as forty oxen. To improve the situation, Bellows & Gates petitioned the Crown for the

THE FOUNDERS –
A DREAM TAKES SHAPE

Canada's banking system was essentially the idea of one man – the Honourable John Richardson. It was an idea he had cherished and promoted for a quarter of a century.

We see Richardson here – centre of the group in the foreground – with business associates who have gathered to give written confirmation to his dream. The affixing of their signatures to the Articles of Association of the Montreal Bank in June 1817 followed the publication of the Articles in the English and French press during the previous month.

These nine men of vision were business leaders of Montreal. While most of them were native sons of Britain who had come to Canada at an early age to seek fortune, if not fame, two had come from the United States and one was born in Quebec City. They were a solid, determined group.

Seen with Richardson are two of the most colourful and influential characters in the early life of the Bank: on his left, the Honourable Horatio Gates; on his right, George Moffatt (later the Honourable). Gates, a native of Massachusetts, settled in Montreal at an early age and, despite numerous clashes with the customs authorities, founded what came to be one of the largest mercantile houses in British North America. Moffatt, the youngest of the founders, was not yet thirty when he put his signature to the Articles. Born in England, he had come to Canada at the age of thirteen. A few years later he was a North-West trader, and at the age of twenty-four he formed his own business partnership. Before many more years, he was head of Gillespie, Moffatt & Co.

Austin Cuvillier, the only Canadian-born member of the group, had been elected in 1814 to the legislature of Lower Canada, where he served with distinction for twenty years, being noted for his outstanding grasp of economic affairs.

Painting by Will Davies

grant of water lots adjacent to their property "below the current." The petition was dated at Montreal March 7, 1810, and was referred to a Committee of the Council at Quebec on April 26. It provoked an uproar in shipping and mercantile circles. Although Trinity House had been established on the venerable British model in 1805 to regulate and improve navigation on the St. Lawrence River, few improvements had been undertaken because of the unwillingness of the French-Canadian majority in the Assembly to vote appropriations. There were no navigation aids down-river from Montreal, nor any wharfage facilities of any kind in the pool above the Current, now one of the largest harbours in the world.

The petition of Bellows & Gates for water lots on which "to build a wharf and Store Houses for the Accommodation of ships and the advancement of Commerce" would, if granted, have given the proprietors a virtual monopoly of wharfage facilities in Montreal, as well as control of the harbour approaches. In consequence, it was countered by the petitions of other property owners in the locality, praying for the same privileges, and finally by one bearing the signatures of 102 mercantile firms and individuals of Montreal, praying that the beach property be reserved for the public. As a result of this protest, the riparian rights from the foot of the rapids to the cove above them were granted to the Wardens of Trinity House in trust for the public. It was due in part at least to the initiative of the two American expatriates that official attention was drawn to the navigational shortcomings of the St. Lawrence and that increased appropriations were afterwards made for their improvement. Appropriately enough, Horatio Gates was appointed a Warden of Trinity House in 1827.

Following his one brief public appearance on the Canadian scene, Abel Bellows disappeared until 1817, when he became one of the original subscribers to the stock of the Montreal Bank. It was no doubt due to his influence and connections that eighty persons in the Boston area, including eleven members of the Bellows family, subscribed to no less than 1,565 of the original issue of 5,000 shares. Forty-one other persons residing in New England and New York bought an additional 795 shares, making the total American subscription 2,360 shares out of a total of 5,000, or 47.2 per cent.

The name of Horatio Gates continued to appear frequently in the local press in connection with internal improvements, more particularly roads between Montreal and the American border to connect with the old Hazen-

Bayley road, by then in the hands of the Boston and Montreal Turnpike Company. One of the most interesting phases of his career took place during the War of 1812 when the rather bizarre logistics of the conflict made him, an American, a contractor for the British Army, smuggling food and other essentials from neutral Vermont to supply the British garrison at Montreal, and driving cattle from northwestern New York across the St. Lawrence to feed the British forces in Upper Canada. Gates and his associates paid for these items with British gold and British bills of exchange which, despite the condition of warfare, were accepted without reservation. As a result of these activities, Gates became one of the most controversial figures in Lower Canada.

Still an American citizen, Horatio Gates in February 1813 petitioned the Governor General, Sir George Prevost, to be allowed to remain in Canada and become a British subject. The petition was referred to a committee of the Executive Council consisting of Hon. James McGill, Hon. John Richardson, and Hon. Chief Justice Monk, but, despite impressive letters of support, it was refused on the grounds of Gates's earlier vacillations. Notwithstanding the committee's unfavourable recommendation, Gates was allowed to remain in Canada "to continue his mercantile pursuits." He was also permitted to take an oath of allegiance to His Majesty King George III which, however, absolved him from taking up arms against the United States.

The nature of these mercantile pursuits is revealed in a petition filed by Horatio Gates for the immediate return to him of a shipment of hides imported by him from the United States on consignment for the British military forces. While a condition of war existed between the United States and Great Britain at the time, and while American troops were stationed at Plattsburg, New York, there appear to have been none on the Vermont side of the border, New England having remained neutral throughout the conflict. As a result, commercial intercourse continued not only along the mountainous border extending eastward from Lake Champlain but on the lake itself and the Richelieu River. The hides in question had been passed by the customs official at St. Johns but seized in Quebec on the ground that they were contraband, the country being in a state of war. In a legal opinion, Solicitor-General Sewell held that this was not the case and that the goods should be returned to Mr. Gates forthwith. Coupled with the opinion was the recommendation that Messrs. Forsyth, Richardson & Co. and McTavish, McGillivrays & Co. be permitted to export to the United States certain "Returns of Furs" in their possession. Both petitions were granted.

There is, also, a letter from Horatio Gates to Thomas McCord, the customs official at St. Johns, which sheds further light on the somewhat unconventional conduct of the War of 1812. In it is set forth the desire of Mr. John Bellows and other Gentlemen of Boston (the former described by Gates as his old partner) to take out 300 to 400 packages of goods of such kind as "are allowed to go out" and for which cash had been received in Montreal "a long time ago." A request was made that Bellows "be allowed to come to Montreal or even St. Johns for the sole purpose of superintending the transfer of the goods." There is no record of Mr. McCord's response but there is no reason to believe that it was other than favourable.

It is obvious that Horatio Gates provided an essential link between Lower Canada and the United States during the War of 1812, not only as an army contractor but as the expediter of much of the trans-border commerce from which Montreal profited so greatly. His activities were to prove invaluable to the Bank during its early years. At the time of the Bank's opening, Gates was the Montreal agent of the New York private banking house of Prime, Ward & Sands, which in turn was the American correspondent of Baring Brothers of London, England. Other New York and Hartford banking connections have come to light only recently. In the possession of his descendants in Hamilton, Ontario, are a silver jug and tray presented to him by the Phenix Bank of New York; two goblets belonging to the set are said to have been stolen in 1857. The tray bears the signature of a well-known silversmith, L. Richard of New York, and the inscription: "The Phenix Bank of New York to Horatio Gates, Esq." The Phenix Bank was established in 1812 and enjoyed a profitable existence for twenty years at least. In Knowlton, Quebec, there is preserved another Phenix presentation, identical except for the inscription, which reads: "The Phenix Bank of New York to Charles Bancroft, Esq." Bancroft is believed to have come to Montreal in 1815 at the age of twenty-seven. He became a partner in the firm of Gates & Nephew, and in 1817 married Gates's niece, Mary Ann Jones, at Barre, Massachusetts.

Some close connection evidently existed between Horatio Gates and the Phenix Bank, but no records have survived. It is probable, however, that Gates rendered the bank a valuable service in Canada by buying for it the silver dollars so greatly in demand by the Americans engaged in the China Trade, and forwarding them to Boston or New York. This being the case,

PLACE D'ARMES—EARLY 1800'S

This is the historic centre of Montreal as it appeared shortly before the Bank's establishment.

At the left is the Parish Church of Ville Marie. A new church built slightly to the south and east in 1829 eventually superseded the old church depicted here. Today, the Parish Church of Notre Dame, occupying the south side of Place d'Armes, is still the greatest in capacity of any church in Canada. There are, in fact, very few churches in the world that can seat more people.

On the right of the picture is the north side of the square running into St. James Street. On the left side of that street is the tavern of Richard Dillon, who painted this picture in 1807 and called it "French Square." It was in Dillon's Tavern that the members of the Beaver Club held many of the convivial meetings for which they were famous.

79

Gates would have come to know Charles Bancroft through his dealings with the Phenix Bank and become so impressed with the young man's abilities that he invited him to join him in business in Montreal.

A bank of the same name in Hartford, Conn., but spelled Phoenix, also bears an interesting early relationship to the Montreal Bank, as will be seen below, but once again it has been impossible to discover when or by whom the connection was established, although the inference is that it was Gates and Bancroft, singly or in combination.

Space limitations preclude a more detailed examination of this hitherto unexplored segment of early Canadian trade and commerce. Obviously, it is one that presents a challenge to interpretations of Canadian economic history. For the purposes of this history, however, enough facts about Horatio Gates have been established to make clear the crucial role that only he could have played in the establishment of the Montreal Bank. What we do not know and never will know in all probability is whether it was Richardson who sought out Gates or Gates who volunteered to co-operate with Richardson.

3.

As published on May 22, 1817, and several times thereafter, the Articles of Association of the Montreal Bank contained substantially the same provisions as the bank bill introduced by John Richardson in the legislature of Lower Canada in 1808. The unwavering devotion to the principle that the notes of the proposed bank should be backed by gold and silver in the vaults calls for comment. It would seem that the temptation to engage in land banking, in which note issues were based on land holdings and personal credit (and loans made on mortgages as security) must have been even greater in 1817 than a decade earlier. The many land banks founded in the United States after the close of the War of 1812 had yet to undergo the test of a major depression. This would not occur until 1825. There was yet no reason on the basis of the seemingly successful American experience, therefore, to suppose that the one system was necessarily better than the other.

The Montreal group, through their London associates, were cognizant of the failures of many private English and Scottish banks during the two decades of warfare which had just come to an end. From this knowledge they could draw two lessons. At all times the bank should strive to maintain the convertibility of its note issue, and it should never engage, as did the unrestricted private banks of the time, in speculative ventures, but should lend only to well-established commercial enterprises and for only a short period of time. Unfortunately there is no prescribable ratio of notes to specie or degree of risk which will be valid under all circumstances; such decisions must continually be made by the men on the spot. In retrospect, one can only be impressed by the rock-ribbed conservatism of the early Canadian bankers, whose foothold, from the beginning, seems to have been "tenon'd and mortised in granite."

Whether their conservatism, inspired and supported by their unquestionable integrity, was to prove wholly advantageous to Canada's growth and development became a question which engaged Canadian opinion for many decades. While providing admirable security for shareholders, depositors, and note-holders alike, it seemed to the skeptically minded of successive generations that the commercial branch banking system that rapidly became established in Canada offered an explanation, in part at least, for the tardy development of the country as compared with that of its neighbour to the south. The "sound" money advocates could brush aside such heresies by pointing to the deplorable and continuous record of bank failures that later characterized American financial history; the heretics, on the other hand, could claim that private banking had been able to provide what passed for money in the market place and was capable of bringing about the exchange of goods and services which were translated into enduring physical assets in the form of houses, roads, bridges, churches, jails, and schools, before financial stringency in a multitude of cases brought about collapse. No doubt many shareholders, depositors, and note-holders suffered at this juncture, but before such recurrent disasters struck, a way had been found to release constructive energies for the promotion of a material progress which, for some reason or another, and despite her abundant natural resources, did not exist in Canada. Whether on balance the social gains outweighed the individual losses in communities served by private banks is difficult to assess. In many frontier towns, however, banks were established on a private basis solely because the legislature for some capricious reason refused to grant them a charter. Such banks operated under sound principles and later either received their charters or were absorbed by a chartered bank when it expanded into that region.

The Articles of Association adopted in 1817 differed in some details from those of the proposed Act of Incorporation of 1808. Provision for government participation was omitted, the capital was reduced to £250,000, and the form of presentation was changed to conform with the altered character of the institution. The number of clauses also was reduced, from forty-four to twenty-five. In all important respects, however, the revised articles adhered closely to the banking principles first embraced in 1792 and reaffirmed in 1808, which is to say, those originally adopted by Alexander Hamilton.

In common with the proposed charter of 1808, the Articles of Association announced in 1817 comprise most of the essential principles of the Canadian banking system which have been retained to this day. Because of their interest and historical significance the Articles will be found in Appendix A as they appeared in the first official record book of the Montreal Bank, each page signed at the bottom by the nine co-partners and every correction bearing their initials; here, the more important clauses need only be briefly indicated.

They provided for a capital of £250,000 Halifax currency ($1,000,000), divided into 5,000 shares of £50 each, and limited, initially, to twenty shares per stockholder, payable in gold or silver coin, current in the province. Provision was made to open a subscription book under the superintendence of the nine original co-partners and shares were made payable, five per cent on subscription, ten per cent following the election of directors, and thereafter at the rate of ten per cent as required by vote of the directors. The first election of directors was to take place when £5,000 had actually been paid in, but no bank bills were to be issued or notes discounted until the sum of £25,000 in bullion, specie, or plate was actually in the vaults. Thereafter the directors, thirteen in number, were to be elected annually at a stockholders' meeting to be held on the first Monday in June, and during their tenure of office were to appoint a president and vice-president from among their number, who were to be responsible, with the approval of the directors, for the conduct of the Bank's affairs. To help them in this important task the directors were empowered to employ such skilled assistance as they might deem necessary, provided all officers, clerks, and servants furnished acceptable sureties and were satisfactorily bonded.

Provision was made for the infusion of new blood by requiring that four new directors be elected each year, and for the removal of directors for such causes as absenteeism and maladministration. Curiously enough, no citizenship qualifications were demanded of directors, as has been implied by Shortt, Breckenridge, and other writers. The only reference, contained in the ninth article, required that directors hold ten shares of stock and be actual residents of Montreal for the year before election, two years at any time

previously, and four years elsewhere in the province. The absence of citizenship qualifications marked a radical departure from American practice of the
day which was unyielding on this point and, in the case of the First Bank of
the United States, even denied to foreign shareholders the right to vote by
proxy. No doubt the proviso was dropped from the Montreal association to
make possible representation of the heavy American stock interest that may
have already been secured. If so, the result was accomplished only after considerable patriotic circumlocution, as the clause itself reveals:

> NINTH. None but a stockholder, actually resident in the City of Mont-
> real and holding at least ten shares in the Capital Stock and being a na-
> tural born subject of His Majesty, or a subject of His Majesty naturalized
> by Act of the British Parliament, or a subject of His Majesty having be-
> come such by the conquest and cession of this Province, *or any person
> who shall have resided seven years in the Province*, and in any of the
> above cases, who shall have resided three years in this City, one of
> which shall have immediately preceded the day of election, shall be
> capable of being elected or chosen a Director of the said Bank, or shall
> serve as such. [Italics supplied.]

Directors were to receive no emoluments except as specifically voted by the
shareholders, but the president and vice-president might be rewarded for unusual services rendered on the Bank's behalf. No specific reference was made
to branches and no residence or citizenship limitations were placed on voting
by proxy.

Other articles provided for the restrictions on voting noted in the 1808
charter: one share, one vote; three shares, two votes; and so on at a decreasing ratio to one hundred shares, which gave their owner twenty votes, the
maximum that could be cast by one shareholder. The procedures for calling
special stockholders' meetings, payment of dividends, and the protection of
individual customers' accounts from unauthorized inquiry or examination
were also provided, the last-mentioned being an almost mandatory assurance
to suspicious customers in the early days of banking everywhere.

The heart and core of the co-operative agreement, however, is contained
in the twenty-second article, which contains these crucial words:

> The said Company shall not directly or indirectly deal in anything,
> excepting bills of exchange, gold or silver bullion, or in the sale of goods
> really and truly pledged for money lent. . . .

The acquisition of land except for the Bank's own needs was similarly prohibited, as were mortgage loans on real estate, although such collateral could be accepted to support delinquent loans. The debt of the Bank, whether by bond, bill, note, or other contract, could not exceed treble the sum of the capital stock actually paid. In case of excess, the directors were to be held individually and severally responsible. Stockholders' liability was limited to the amount of their investment. The agreement was to run until the first day of January, 1838, but provision was made for its dissolution before that date. Actually, the Articles of Association remained in force until May 18, 1822, the day royal assent was given to the bill incorporating the Bank of Montreal as a limited-liability chartered bank. During the five intervening years Canada's first successful bank operated on no stronger legal sanctions than a gentlemen's agreement embodying principles which were to provide the mould for future Canadian banking.

4.

In conformity with the Articles of Association and concurrently with their publication on May 22, 1817, the public was notified through the press that a book of subscriptions would be opened on the following June 23, from 12 to 2 o'clock, and would continue open at the same time and place every lawful day following until the Capital Stock should have been subscribed, or an election of directors have taken place. The notice was inserted "by order of the Committee," dated at Montreal, May 19, 1817, and bore the signature of John Richardson as chairman.

In accordance with the notice, the Book of Subscription was opened at the Court House on Monday, June 23, under the supervision of a committee of seven chosen to accept subscriptions and receive deposits: Garden, Moffatt, Turner, Cuvillier, Leslie, Gates, and Bush. Less than two weeks later, on July 4, these gentlemen were able to announce that subscriptions totalling £100,000 had been received and a five-per-cent deposit paid. With £5,000 in gold and silver in hand, it now became mandatory to call a meeting of shareholders to elect directors. Only one paper has yielded a copy of the pursuant notice, *Le Spectateur Canadien*, which printed it in its issue of July 5, 1817, and three times thereafter. The meeting was duly held and was recorded by a secretary pro tem. whose name is unknown. Written with a quill pen, in India ink which is little faded, the entry became the first of many thousands in a newly acquired and handsomely bound "Resolve Book," as the Directors'

Minute Book was first called. This book is the first of a series of such volumes in which the Directors' Minutes of the Bank of Montreal have been recorded for nearly 150 years.

The first Minute reads:

At a general Meeting of Stockholders to elect Directors for the Montreal Bank, pursuant to a public advertisement of the Committee acting heretofore that Five thousand pounds had actually been paid in to them in Gold & Silver as Deposits, and fixing this Day the 7th of August for the general Election of Directors, agreeable to the articles of association, did by a Majority of Votes elect the following Persons to serve as Directors until the first Monday in June, 1818. – viz.

John Gray Esq.	Fredk. Willm. Ermatinger Esq.
John Forsyth Esq.	John McTavish Esq.
George Garden Esq.	Austin Cuvillier Esq.
George Moffatt Esq.	James Leslie Esq.
Horatio Gates Esq.	Hiram Nichols Esq.
Thomas A. Turner Esq.	George Platt Esq.
	Zabdiel Thayer Esq.

We have already met some of these gentlemen; others have still to be introduced. Some have been found impossible to identify beyond a brief association with the first Canadian banking institution. No contemporary references, for example, have been found to either Hiram Nichols or Zabdiel Thayer. The mere fact that they have remained unknown, plus the unmistakable New England flavour of their names, suggests that they represented Boston and New York interests, as did Horatio Gates. The assumption is strengthened by the fact that among the Boston subscribers was one Edwin Thayer, possibly a brother of Zabdiel. All that is known of Nichols is that he was a partner in the Montreal firm of Nichols and Sanford. Another American on the Board of Directors was George Platt, who came to Montreal prior to 1807 to deal in hardware and become a machinist. He is best known because of a most interesting early Canadian technological document: the statement rendered by him to John Molson for machining engine parts for Canada's first steamboat, the *Accommodation*, launched in 1809. Of the other new directors, the names of Ermatinger and McTavish were well known in Montreal; the first, of Swiss origin, dates back to 1764; the other, to 1774 and the famous Simon McTavish of the North West Company.

Whether John McTavish was a relative of Simon is unknown, nor has it been possible to identify Frederick W. Ermatinger beyond the fact that he was Sheriff of Montreal for seventeen years and was connected, through relatives, with the fur trade. John Gray, on the other hand, was a member of a well-known professional family. One of his brothers was Jonathan, the foremost English-speaking notary of the day, and another, E. W., was for some time also Sheriff of Montreal. John Gray himself was a successful North West trader living in retirement in the village of St. Catherines, now Outremont. Among the slate of directors elected, one name is conspicuously absent— John Richardson. The explanation could be that he was already planning to sail for London in late September to spend the winter there; the other, that having launched the enterprise so dear to his heart he was willing to have other men shoulder the responsibility of its management. In any case, he was assured of a permanent proxy in the person of his partner, John Forsyth.

It is clear from the complexion of the Board that it was the intention of the steering committee to secure as widespread a representation of commercial interests as possible. This view was borne out on August 9 when the newly elected directors held their first meeting and elected John Gray as president and Thomas A. Turner as vice-president, to serve until the annual stockholders' meeting to be held the first Monday in June, 1818. As a retired, and retiring, fur trader with a first-hand knowledge of the business, John Gray was apparently acceptable to both Hudson's Bay and North West Company interests; Thomas Turner, for his part, although a partner of Allison, Turner & Co., one of the foremost wholesalers of the period, does not appear to have been identified with any particular trading interest and was therefore also acceptable to the group as a whole.

With the election of officers and directors, the Montreal Bank was at last in business. Before its doors could be opened to the public, however, several things had yet to be accomplished. Temporary banking quarters had first to be acquired, a competent staff hired in a community where double-entry bookkeeping was still somewhat of a novelty, and bank-notes designed, engraved, and printed. Even more important, a further call for ten per cent had to be made on the subscribers since no notes could be issued or bills discounted until £25,000 in coin, that is to say £20,000 more, was actually in the vault where it could be handled and counted. There is the probability also that

THE FIRST MINUTE OF CANADA'S FIRST BANK

This entry, on the first page of the Montreal Bank's "Resolve Book No. 1," records the election of the first directors, men who were obviously too practical to be superstitious about joining a board having thirteen members.

Although John Richardson, "the father of Canadian banking," apparently chose not to be included, his dream was now clearly realized.

Among these thirteen men there was not only a strong representation of the Canadian commercial community, but also an important group from the United States with sufficient business experience there to give the Bank's operation far more than local significance. They made Canada's first bank an internationally-minded organism from the start.

difficulty was found in raising the necessary capital in Canada initially and it was for this reason that investors had to be sought in the United States. For example, it was not until September 19, 1817, that the last undisposed shares of the Bank had been taken up. Notices were sent out to the newspapers to inform the public of this fact because, by then, demand was such that the shares were commanding a premium. It is possible, also, that the officers and directors, as yet unschooled in the practical day-by-day conduct of a bank, may have had to assimilate that rather necessary knowledge. In any case, these and possibly other considerations were to delay the actual opening until the third day of November, 1817.

FIVE

THE PROMISE
REALIZED

THE PROMISE REALIZED

I.

On January 17, 1815, W. Gray, the publisher of the Montreal *Herald*, then the leading English newspaper in the city, was inspired to include this editorial comment in his journal:

> Lower Canada never was more prosperous, nor more happy, and were it not for the sufferings of our fellow subjects in various parts of Upper Canada, we might pronounce British North America as the most favoured portion of the British foreign dominions.

In effect, said Mr. Gray, "We never had it so good"; but by early spring, less than two months later, the economic climate had so worsened that he struck this dour note in the *Herald*'s issue of March 4:

> Now that we are in possession of the treaty of Peace with the United States of America, we may be permitted to give our opinion of its im-

mediate merits. Everybody knows that the war was sought and provoked by the American government. Its objects were the assistance of Bonaparte, to paralyze and eventually to ruin the British Empire. The termination of the war has already had a wonderful effect upon our markets. Many articles have fallen 50 per cent. The Vermontese pour in plenty on us. Persons who had hoarded wheat many months and had frequently been offered 15s per bushel, now beg to sell it at 7s 6d! Who can pity such men? Beef of good quality is 4d per lb. Fowls from 2s to 3s per pair – Turkeys once 15s now 7s 6d. Such are the blessings of Peace. Men who wallowed in wealth by government contracts, and profitable speculations will repine and complain at Peace; and for our part we do not join them. We congratulate those having fixed incomes. . . .

The above excerpts, depicting the general deterioration of the Canadian economy that set in following the "American War," would go far to account for the inability of the promoters of the Montreal Bank to place much more than fifty per cent of their stock in Canada. Apart from the reluctance of those who held specie to part with it, the business depression that followed the lush profits of the war years was hardly of such a nature as to foster speculation in the shares of an untried enterprise. The net revenues collected by Lower Canada, for example, declined from an 1814 peak of £144,961 to a low of £56,332 in 1818; while in Upper Canada customs dues received from the lower province fell from £39,250 in 1815 to £17,984 in 1819, a reduction of almost sixty per cent. More evidence of the depressed conditions is found in the files of the Montreal *Herald* and other papers for the same years. Notices of bankruptcies, forced sales of merchandise, and mortgage foreclosures were frequent, and even as early as 1817 settlers in the Eastern Townships were giving up the struggle and moving westward to Upper Canada and Pennsylvania.

The causes of the malaise were complex. Among them were the vagaries of nature; the post-war years were remarkable for cold, wet springs, summer droughts, and August hurricanes. Farmers who had grown accustomed to selling locally at war-time prices all the produce they could raise, and to finding ready employment for themselves and their teams, were reduced to subsistence living, while wheat and flour had to be imported from the neighbouring states. The reduced purchasing-power of the largest sector of the community had its repercussions of course along the entire trading chain that extended from the up-country merchants to the wholesale houses in Montreal, with attendant difficulties in making payments and collecting debts on goods contracted for at inflated prices. In a predominantly agricultural economy, successive crop failures alone would have caused widespread distress, but the Canadian provinces were also exposed to other influences beyond their control. These gravely compounded their difficulties. Paramount among them was the return of peace to Europe and America. Overseas demand for wheat, flour, and other export staples collapsed, large numbers of British troops were repatriated or pensioned off in Canada with land and meagre stipends, and, accelerating the speed of the descending spiral, the reapplication of the Trade and Navigation Acts to all the British North American provinces disrupted established trade with the United States, as did the introduction of American protective tariffs. Finally, as Canada's foreign-exchange position weakened with the loss of her export markets and continued importation from the States, the southward flow of hard money across the border was accelerated.

The conditions outlined can explain sufficiently the original Canadian share participation in the Montreal Bank. In fact, so unfavourable do they seem to have been that no organized effort was made to dispose of stock in Canada outside Montreal. Only twelve subscribers are listed as living elsewhere in Lower Canada, including four in Quebec and two in Three Rivers, and a mere eleven in the entire upper province, among them the Reverend John Strachan, later to become Bishop of Toronto. Glasgow provided three subscribers, none of whom is otherwise identifiable, and London five, listed as Alexander Alljo (sic), Inglis, Ellice & Co., Simon McGillivray, William Maitland, and William Northgate & Co. The five firms or individuals with a London address are recognized as having interests in the Canada Trade and hence in any effort to facilitate it. No such generalization is possible with respect to the 135 Montreal residents who became the initial owners of 2,158 shares in the new enterprise, in contrast with those 121 across the border, who owned 2,360 shares.

As would be expected, the subscription list includes all who signed the Articles of Association, along with those who were elected directors on August 7. With the names of these individuals are coupled in many instances those of firms and relatives. Thus, Forsyth, Richardson & Co., Hon. John Richardson, John Forsyth, and George Forsyth each subscribed for twenty shares of stock, the maximum initial allotment for any one subscriber, while the Gates interest was represented by Horatio Gates & Nephew, Horatio Gates, Charles Bancroft, and Gates's wife, Clarissa. The names of several women appear in the list of subscribers, including Marie-Claire Cuvillier, who conducted a successful commission business under the name of M. C. Cuvillier & Co., and along with them were many prominent commercial names of the day. While the names of many of the original Montreal subscribers can be found in Doige's *Directory of Montreal* (1819), the first "Who's Who" of any kind in Canada, there remain those of a greater number who now defy explanation, except in so far as they were willing to venture, in most cases, the not insignificant sum of £250 ($1,000). In spite of the coverage given the Bank in both French and English newspapers, many prominent citizens did not see fit at the time to lend their support to an enterprise which, by bringing immediate relief to the chronically chaotic currency and exchange conditions prevailing in the provinces, was to prove of national importance.

It can only be concluded that those men of means who held back had good reasons for not participating, since they were undoubtedly aware of the way in which banks in the United States had been rewarding their share-holders with large dividends. The lack of support at home forced the founders to turn to the Americans for capital. In view of the Canadian reaction and the large number of banks already existing in the United States (260 in 1816), the success of the mission must be considered little short of spectacular, and the reasons for it bear investigation.

2.

During the period under review, conditions south of the border were in some respects similar to those to the north but there were also dramatic contrasts. In Canada, the cessation of hostilities sharply reduced the transfusions of currency from the mother country into the economic bloodstream. Concurrently, the readjustment to peace in Britain after twenty years of almost continuous war greatly lessened the demand for colonial products. The loss of these stimuli, as we have seen, was reflected in a progressive commercial stagnation which reduced most forms of economic activity by more than fifty per cent. In the United States, the ending of Mr. Madison's War had an opposite effect. Notwithstanding a national debt larger than that caused by the War of Independence, a newly depreciated currency, deranged business conditions, and the virtual disappearance of its maritime commerce, the Republic responded to peace with an outburst of commercial and industrial activity that was rapidly to make it the commercial rival of the European nations and draw to it the European capital essential to its development and expansion.

No longer land-bound by a British blockade, mercantile interests from New England to Chesapeake Bay introduced the era of shipbuilding that was within a single generation to make America the world's foremost maritime trader. Simultaneously, the restless migration westward, that was to populate half a continent, was resumed, and along the Connecticut and other New England rivers, new industries based on water power sprang up as southern planters embarked on a mighty expansion of cotton-growing to satisfy the demands of industrialized Britain. Formidable difficulties were encountered and overcome by decisive action. As in Hamilton's day, the national debt was funded by establishing the Second Bank of the United States (the First had perished in 1811), and met by the sale of public land and the resumption of heavy excise taxes on wines and spirits. To protect the interests of an infant manufacturing industry, tariffs higher than any advocated by Hamilton were imposed. The effect of these and other actions, coupled with seemingly illimitable resources, produced a spirit of daring and adventure in the United States and a willingness to engage in venturesome speculations which was largely lacking to the north, where colonial dependency, in the mercantile scheme of things, made a state of war the only possible blessing.

Especially germane to this discussion is the American experience with banking as an effective mechanism to marshal collective capital resources, make them available for productive purposes and, at the same time, provide a circulating medium which both simplified and facilitated commerce. Beginning with Thomas Paine's Pennsylvania Bank, which, although little more than a loan association, preceded the Bank of North America, these institutions proved so successful in practice that by 1816 there were two hundred and sixty banks in the country with a capital of more than eighty million dollars. From 1811, when the First Bank of the United States was closed, to 1816, when its successor was established, the absence of any strong banking leadership led to excess issues of paper currency and concomitant inflation, but, generally speaking, American banks performed the function for which they were intended: to serve agriculture and promote the commerce and industry of the nation. As in the case of the First Bank of the United States, whose profits attracted the large European investment which led to its undoing, most of the early banks paid dividends from their inception, in some cases as

RURAL LIFE IN
THE CANADIAN COLONIES
– 1820's

When a settler first arrived in Canada he was given a "location ticket" roughly describing the situation of his land, to which he proceeded and camped in a tent until the surveyor arrived and the boundaries were marked out. The next step was the clearing of a small plot and the construction of a cabin to house himself and his family during the first winter.

While the snow covered the ground, more land was cleared. A good rate for an industrious man was an acre a week, but no more than ten acres were usually cleared in a single year. The main problem was disposal of the green wood. Some of it was saved for building or split for fences, but most of it had to be laboriously burnt. Where possible, the ashes were collected for sale and export.

As a rule, the tree stumps were still in the ground when the first crops were sown, but they took up a great deal of space and eventually had to be chopped, burnt or pulled out by ox and chain. As soon as he could, the settler would begin work on a larger and more comfortable log cabin. Each log was notched and fitted, without nails, and the chinks were caulked with moss, chips of wood, and clay. A cabin would usually be eighteen by twenty feet, the whole comprising a single room with a fireplace at one end.

Many of the major tasks were accomplished by the holding of "bees"; neighbours for miles around would contribute their efforts in return for liberal servings of whisky and a hearty meal – an undertaking that required several days of preparation. The pioneers, whose life was hard, lonely and dull, welcomed such occasions, which would often include a dance that lasted till dawn.

Painting by William Kurelek

high as twenty per cent. There were no failures until 1809 and relatively few thereafter until the panic of 1818, when the effects of depression in England swept the United States and brought to a temporary halt the proliferation of banking institutions.

Founded originally by wealthy mercantile families and cliques in the principal coastal cities, under charters granted by the individual states, the first banks gave rise to a phenomenon known as "bancomania," so great was the enthusiasm for their stock for investment or speculation. Although dividends soon levelled off to between six and eight per cent (so that reserves might sensibly be accumulated), the enthusiasm remained unabated on the granting of additional charters to the other commercial and manufacturing groups referred to in a previous chapter. Despite the constriction of commerce caused by the Jefferson and Madison embargoes and by the war-time dislocation that followed, banks continued to flourish and multiply whether based on specie, land, or a combination of the two.

It is therefore easy to understand why wealthy individuals in Massachusetts, Connecticut, and New York should have readily subscribed to the stock of the new bank to be formed in Montreal. For most commercial purposes the Canadian metropolis appeared as nothing other than a northward extension of New England. They knew it well, for they had been profitably engaged in trade there for a quarter of a century or more. They also knew and trusted its leading business men, who, except for the matter of national allegiance, were in no way different from themselves. On the basis of their own experience they had every reason to believe that a properly managed bank would succeed in Canada and give rise to other advantages as well. Before the development of the clearing-house system, it was the practice to place bank-notes in circulation as far distant from the place of redemption as possible. A Montreal bank could serve that purpose and in addition become a source of the specie, particularly silver, which was in such great demand for the rapidly expanding East Indies and China trades.

Since the early business of the Montreal Bank was to be largely in foreign exchange, the possibility exists that it was the intention from the beginning to give it an international rather than a merely local or provincial complexion. If this conjecture is correct, it would explain the almost equal stock distribution between Canadian and American shareholders as satisfactorily as our earlier assumption that sufficient capital could not be raised in Canada. If the facts could be determined, they would probably reveal a multiplicity of incentives, both impersonal and personal, but they could in no way lessen the extent of American interest in Canadian enterprise even at this early date.

As we know, the American interest in the Montreal Bank stemmed largely from the activities and connections of Horatio Gates. It is possible also that Inglis, Ellice & Co. were helpful, either indirectly through Richardson and Gates, or directly through the London banking house of Baring Brothers, via the latter's New York agents, Prime, Ward & Sands. It is clear, however, that Gates acted as the principal financial ambassador, drawing in such men as John Bellows, the brother of his old business partner, who at this time was President of the recently established Manufacturers and Mechanics Bank of Boston, an institution formed to help finance the establishment of manufacturing in New England. It was John Bellows who furnished the Montreal Bank with its first professional banker, Henry Stone. The latter returned to Boston after a six-month sojourn in Montreal to become one of the leading bankers in New England, where, first as Cashier of the Eagle Bank and later as President of the Suffolk Bank, he was one of the founders of the first clearing-house system in the United States.

In addition to the impressive allegiance of the Bellows clan, two or more members of other prominent families subscribed to a maximum allotment of the Canadian stock, among them representatives of the Appleton, Goddard, Dana, Dwight, Hale, Lawrence, and Otis families. All the names were important in the contemporary manufacturing, banking, and political history of Massachusetts, and most of them were intimately connected with the establishment and early development of the American textile industry. Three of the subscribers, Nathan Appleton, his brother William, and their cousin William Cochran, established the first power textile plant in the state, and later were mainly instrumental in founding the Suffolk Bank.

It is apparent from the foregoing that the seventy-four Bostonians who subscribed to Montreal Bank stock, along with six more in nearby Walpole, Massachusetts, provide a representative cross-section of established wealth, family, position, and entrepreneurial activity in the New England capital. The Connecticut association is more difficult to explain. Twenty subscribers were secured in the state, all of them residing in Middletown, a city near the mouth of the Connecticut River. In the days of sailing vessels this was the outport of Hartford, the state capital, and was engaged largely in the China and Indies Trades. It would appear probable therefore that interest in the

Montreal Bank was stimulated by the need for silver in conducting those trades. Unlike the Bostonians, most of the subscribers appear to have had mercantile rather than manufacturing interests, but like the former, they were persons prominent in the business and political life of their state. Interestingly enough, one of them, a China Trader named Thomas McDonough, had commanded the American fleet on Lake Champlain which in 1814 defeated the British under George Dowie.

Although nothing more has been discovered about Gates's New York banking connections than is suggested by the service of plate from the Phenix Bank, it is obvious that those connections led to the twenty New York subscriptions. No less than seven were obtained from the firm of Prime, Ward & Sands alone. Another New York subscriber, Benjamin Franklin Butler, was later Attorney General of the United States for fifteen years, and still another, Phillip Hone, served one term as mayor of New York. Other familiar names were those of Henry Brevoort, father and son.

Summing up, it would appear that the prestige of the Montreal Bank in influential American financial and banking circles, even before it opened its doors for business, was definitely higher than in Canada.

3.

Today, Boston and Hartford and New York are an hour or so away from Montreal by air; in the summer and autumn of 1817, they were from three to five days distant by ferry, stage-coach, and steamboat. Coaches left the Hay Market in Montreal several times weekly for the south by way of Lachine, La Prairie, and St. Johns on the Richelieu River, where connections were made with steamboats on Lake Champlain; or the traveller could proceed by road to Lake George, Saratoga, and Albany down the west shore of the lake or to St. Albans, Burlington, Rutland, and Bennington down the east. Journeying by steamboat, the traveller could count on reaching Whitehall in ten hours, whence he could proceed by stage or other conveyance to Albany, where Robert Fulton's line of commodious Hudson River steamers were available to take him to New York. John Molson, returning post-haste from meetings with Fulton in September, 1810, covered the 425-mile journey in four days.

For the time, travel between Montreal and New York was both comfortable and speedy, as diaries of the day attest, and in marked contrast with that

TRADE ROUTE VITAL TO CANADA

In this water-colour by Lieutenant Hamilton, of the 71st Regiment, we see a peaceful, pastoral stretch of the Richelieu River, which flows north from Lake Champlain to the St. Lawrence.

The history of the Richelieu has, however, been far from peaceful, as can be judged from the number of forts dotted along its shores. Champlain ascended the river to attack the Iroquois in 1609, and later it was the scene of frequent encounters between French and English. In 1775 the Americans used it successfully, but in 1814 they were turned back a few miles north of the border.

During quiet interludes the surface was rippled by vessels of various sorts transporting pioneer products from New England and northern New York to Montreal for sale and shipment to England. Not all this trade went through customs, but, legal or illegal, it laid the foundations of Montreal as a commercial metropolis.

between Montreal and Kingston, Upper Canada, which in 1817 required a week or more, although a line of stages had been opened from Montreal to Utica by way of Prescott and Ogdensburg the year before. Strangely enough, almost nothing can be discovered regarding the pattern of communications between Montreal and Boston. As we have seen, they had become sufficiently well-established before 1800 to permit shipments of frozen fish and oysters overland between the two places, and by 1817 several roads had been opened between the Connecticut River and Lake Champlain, but which of these was ordinarily followed remains in doubt. However, from stage-coach advertisements in contemporary Vermont journals, it seems that most of the through travel was from Bennington eastward across the Berkshires to Deerfield, Fitchburg, and finally Boston.

How many times during the summer and autumn months of 1817 such journeys were made by one or more of the directors of Canada's first bank cannot be ascertained, but the record suggests that travel to Boston, Hartford, or New York was almost continuous, with one or more directors or members of the Bank's staff always on the road. Meanwhile, in Montreal, the Board attacked the numerous problems of organization with confidence and dispatch.

Two days after the election of directors on August 7, the meeting was held in the office of Thomas A. Turner at which John Gray and Turner were elected President and Vice-President respectively for the ensuing year, and the two officers together with Ermatinger and Gates were named a committee of four to report on a suitable location for the Bank's operations. No such location having been found by the time of the next meeting, on August 15, it was resolved that advertisements should be placed in the three local newspapers, French and English, inviting "proposals for leasing a Building fit for the Establishment in the central part of the City for a Term of Years." At the same meeting, a decision was made to begin modestly with a staff of four. Notice to this effect was also incorporated in the advertisement, inviting interested persons to submit their applications for the positions open. A large number of responses were received and dealt with at two successive meetings of the Board. On August 20 the directors decided to accept the offer of F. W. Ermatinger of the dwelling on St. Paul Street belonging to Robert Armour, one of the nine original signers of the Articles of Association. The building was currently under receivership and Ermatinger, the Sheriff of Montreal, was one of the assignees, together with George Moffatt and R. Pattinson. A proviso that the lessors "do put the vault into a state of security" was undoubtedly prompted by the crime wave then rampant in the city, and the fact that the same premises seem to have been broken into by two armed robbers earlier in the year.

Meeting in its new offices for the first time on August 23, the Board appointed Robert Griffin, Cashier, at a salary of £300 with the use of the house on St. Paul Street as his living quarters; Henry B. Stone, first (paying) teller, at a salary of £300; Henry Dupuy, accountant, at £250; and James Jackson, second (receiving) teller, at £250. Sureties ranging from £1,000 to £2,000, and signed by two guarantors, were required from the appointees. The inclusion of the name of H. B. Stone at this relatively early date suggests that arrangements for his leave of absence from the Manufacturers and Mechanics Bank in Boston had been made some time previously. The salaries and requirements as to securities were in line with American banking practice of the day. On August 29, Robert Griffin signed the Directors' Minutes for the first time, after noting a resolution to call on the shareholders for the first instalment of ten per cent.

Peculiar interest attaches to the next meeting, held on September 5. That day resolutions were passed to import a rolling press from England, and give notice in the *Herald, Courant,* and *Spectateur* of a shareholders' meeting to be held on October 20 for the purpose of preparing an application to the provincial legislature for incorporation. It was resolved also "that an officer of the Bank should be sent to Hartford in Connecticut, to bring up all the Plates & Bills that have been executed for the Bank, and also a quantity of blank paper." Chosen to discharge this task was Henry Dupuy, the accountant, who recalled his experience in a letter written more than fifty years later. Found among a heterogeneous collection of old papers some years ago, it is now in the Bank's archives and is the only personal document relating to the early history of the institution known to exist.

Henry Dupuy was for many years manager of the branch of the Bank of Montreal in Kingston, where his letter, dated June 4, 1868, was written several years after his retirement. Addressed to F. Franklin, Esq., in answer to an inquiry made by the latter, it recalls the formation of the Bank and the appointment of officers, before continuing as follows:

> As the accountant I was ordered to proceed to New York for the purpose of looking into the method of keeping books according to the system of the United States Bank, Mr. Catlin being the celebrated cashier

in those days. Inspected the books, etc., but found nothing unusual in their system.

I then proceeded to Hartford, Conn., to the celebrated engraver Reid (at that time) who was engaged to engrave the bank-notes in a very ordinary style. Many young men were occupied in the work of engraving and it struck me that forgeries some day or other would occur, and after two or three years my suspicions were confirmed, the plates were then removed and engraved on steel using the die the most difficult to imitate.

I remained in New York and Hartford until the bank-notes and plates were ready and according to strict instructions took my departure for Canada by way of Utica so as to avoid the duties and other obstacles which might have occurred at the Custom House by way of Lake Champlain, landed at Prescott by way of Utica to avoid all obstructions and remained in that town nearly two days for a conveyance to Montreal by stage, as steamboats were not to be seen in those days.

One can only conjecture as to the obstacles that might have been encountered at the custom house at St. Johns, but there is reason to believe that at least one of the directors of the Bank may have held the establishment in low esteem. Returning to La Prairie from St. Johns by calèche late at night after a visit to the customs the previous February, John Forsyth, the senior partner of Forsyth, Richardson & Co., had been challenged by a party of the 19th Light Dragoons deployed to prevent smuggling, and when he refused to stop had been fired upon and wounded in the arm.

The Dupuy letter continues in interesting detail for several pages and will be referred to again in later contexts. Here it will suffice to note that even before his return the Board decided to issue the bank-notes entrusted to his care as soon as he should have reached Montreal by the circuitous route decided on. At the same meeting a resolution was adopted to have the paper still in Hartford struck off by Abner Reed (Dupuy's 'Reid') of East Windsor, Connecticut, under the supervision of George Beach, the Cashier at the Phoenix Bank of Hartford. Beach was later to be paid generously for his services in connection with the engraving and printing of the notes. John Richardson, due shortly to depart for England, was also instructed to procure for the Bank a set of plates in London and have them struck off on "the best bank paper," having as its watermark "the Montreal Bank," similar to the watermark on Bank of England notes. These, together with "a rolling press of the best construction," were to be shipped to Montreal by the first vessel in spring. One of the plates and some of the notes from Hartford have been preserved in the Bank's museum and are in denominations of one, five, ten, twenty, and one hundred dollars. Evidently, difficulties were encountered with the English order, for the Bank appears to have resorted to a local firm, Leney & Rollinson, to procure further plates. Counterfeiting was so widespread in those days that the Bank had always to keep an extra set of plates ready so that a whole issue could be changed the moment fraudulent bills were detected. For this reason also the designs on the early notes vary widely, from a heraldic "Britannia" to a simple engraving of the first bank building on Place d'Armes. More significant than the vignettes on the face of the notes, however, was the fact that the first paper currency issued in Canada should have been in dollars, showing the Spanish and American influence, rather than in pounds, the money of account.

Even at this early stage, when the official opening was still a month away, the directors revised their modest estimate of the Bank's personnel requirements. Early in October, Alexander McNiven began his duties as porter, and Benjamin Holmes and Allan McDonell were added to the clerical staff, the first as discount clerk, the other as second bookkeeper, at salaries of £200 and £150 respectively. With Holmes's appointment began one of the most interesting and most influential careers in the early history of Canadian banking. Several other events during October reflected a spirit of optimism. On the tenth, the Board received an offer from John Molson, brewer and steamboat proprietor, to erect on property belonging to him in the centre of the city a bank building which he would lease for a term of twenty-one years at a rental on the value of the land and building of eight per cent for the first year and six per cent thereafter. The proposal seems somewhat curious in view of the fact that Molson had not yet become a stockholder. It was for this reason perhaps that the Board *unanimously* rejected the offer (underlined in the original); instead, Gates, Garden, and Cuvillier were appointed a committee to purchase a suitable site at a cost of not more than £3,000 on which the Bank would erect its own building. The other outstanding events of October, 1817, were the general meeting advertised for the twentieth, the adoption of by-laws for the conduct of the banking business, and the decision reached at the end of the month to call on the shareholders for the payment of the second instalment of ten per cent, payable January 10, 1818.

The petition "For the incorporation of the Bank of Montreal" (*sic*) is preserved in the *State Papers, Lower Canada, 1792-1841*. It is an interesting document for several reasons. In the preamble once again occur references to the public utility of banks and the economic benefits to be derived therefrom, which have been referred to earlier in these pages. Of interest also are the signatures appended to the petition which had been drawn up by the Bank's newly appointed solicitor, James Stuart. While many share-holders signed for themselves, the majority were represented by various directors. It therefore becomes possible to obtain a clearer picture of the com-mercial mosaic of early nineteenth-century Montreal. For example, John Forsyth signed for himself and for Forsyth, Richardson & Co., Inglis, Ellice & Co., John Richardson, and William Allan, the firm's correspondent in York, Upper Canada; James Leslie for himself and wife, and for John McNaught and Donald Taylor, both of Glasgow; Blackwood and François Larocque for them-selves and for Peter Guérout, Laurent Le Roux, W. E. Ord and Joseph Larocque (with the Cuvilliers, the principal French-Canadian shareholders); George Garden for Maitland, Garden & Auldjo; and George Moffatt and John McTavish for their associates in Gerrard-Gillespie and McTavish-McGillivrays respec-tively. Horatio Gates signed for all the Boston subscribers, and for most of those in Hartford, as well as for Prime, Ward & Sands in New York. Other New York subscribers, however, were proxied by John C. Bush and Thomas A. Turner, reinforcing our previous assumption that these gentlemen represented American interests.

During a second meeting held at six o'clock on the afternoon of the next day, the shareholders heard read and voted to adopt the by-laws for the management of the Bank and the conduct of its affairs, which had been drawn up by a committee appointed for the purpose on September 26. So far as can be determined, none of these gentlemen had any previous experience in banking, except for Gates and possibly Turner. Yet the forty-two clauses con-tained in the table of "Rules and Regulations" provide in precise detail for the management of the Bank, the division of responsibilities among the several officers and employees, and the disciplines to be imposed. The code is of such interest as to call for inclusion in its entirety as Appendix B; here it will suffice to note some of its highlights.

The first clause stipulates the banking hours and holidays. The next four clauses concern the seal of the corporation and the transfer of stock, and empower the Bank to receive cash deposits and also ingots of gold, bars of silver, wrought plate, and other valuable articles of small bulk for safe keeping. The sixth and seventh clauses govern the conduct of board meetings

BOSTON — 1837

Boston, long the commercial capital of New England, furnished a large proportion of the original American subscriptions to the capital stock of the Montreal Bank. Indeed, Boston subscribers were outnumbered only by those of Montreal.

Pictured here is State Street leading up to State House, the former home of the British and State governors, but used as the city hall from 1830 to 1840. State House was also "the popular pulpit," and from its balcony the Declaration of Independence was read to the people gathered in the street below. Also the scene of the Boston Massacre, State Street subsequently became the address of many banks and insurance houses, and its sidewalks were used as the merchants' exchange.

Many of the Montreal Bank's early dealings in foreign exchange were with Boston merchants and bankers engaged extensively in foreign trade, especially with the East Indies.

and provide for the daily attendance at the Bank of the president or vice-president together with one director, chosen as director of the week, to manage the affairs of the Bank during recesses of the Board. The next two clauses establish Tuesdays and Fridays as discount days and bar from discount any note receiving the negative votes of two directors, all decisions of the Board being made by ballot. In the eleventh and twelfth clauses is found the essence of the commercial nature and stability of Canadian banking: the one provides for sixty-day discounts unless by unanimous vote the directors present should grant an extension; the other, for a payment of at least ten per cent when discounts were extended. The shortness of the term was intended to ensure liquidity, and made the discounts attractive only to those engaged in commerce with a relatively rapid turnover.

One of the most interesting and, as it later turned out, controversial provisions in the Rules and Regulations is contained in the fourteenth clause, which states *inter alia* that all persons doing business with the Bank should "subscribe to the sixth clause of the fundamental articles of this association." This article limited the liability of the shareholders to the amount of the stock owned by them and explicitly outlawed any recourse against the separate property of any present or future member of the company. Additional clauses governed the manner of collections, limited credit advances to £10,000 unless collateral security was furnished, instituted the weekly inspection of the vaults by the president or vice-president, and charged the cashier with the routine conduct of the business and supervision of the activities of employees. The duties of each employee are set forth in explicit detail, even to those of the messenger and the porter. The first was charged with the daily collection of monies owing to the Bank on all notes of hand, bills of exchange, bonds, and obligations, while the second was required, in addition to keeping the bank house and appurtenances clean and in good order, to make the fires, light the lamps, and deliver the keys to the president or vice-president after securing the premises at night. He would be expected "to have the same again at the Bank timely in the morning if required."

The Rules and Regulations having been unanimously adopted by the shareholders and circulated among those directly charged with their observance, the Montreal Bank was at last ready to offer its services to the public. Notices to this effect were inserted in the local newspapers and at ten o'clock on the morning of Monday, November 3, 1817, the doors of the Montreal Bank were officially opened in the manner already related in the first chapter.

SIX

INITIAL

EXPANSION

INITIAL EXPANSION

I.

When the Montreal Bank commenced business in November 1817, it had a tiny paid-up capital of $150,000. Seventy-five years later, it had become a giant among banks, with the largest capital of any in North America. In the course of the intervening decades, its assets had grown from $150,000 to $54,000,000 (360 times), while Canada's population had grown only ten times and its foreign trade less than twenty-five times.

It is with this projection in mind that the story of the Bank can best be told. Unlike its famous counterparts, the Bank of England and the two Banks of the United States, it was never a central bank and never directly a financial instrument of government nor a part of the national fiscal apparatus. Yet the history of the Bank of Montreal is more intimately interwoven with that of the country of its origin than any of the other three. From the day of its opening it cast over Canadian affairs a shadow greater than itself, a shadow that steadily lengthened as the years advanced. Initially the enhanced stature was gained from the services the Bank could immediately offer: a stable and trustworthy medium of exchange in the form of bank-note currency, filling a vacuum that had existed, except for the brief Army Bill interval, throughout the history of the colony; but a more potent influence stemmed from the enlightened self-interest of the Bank's directors.

As advocates of economic progress, the principal shareholders and directors of the Montreal Bank were also the leaders of an English-speaking party which strove for urgently needed internal improvements. The party further advocated the introduction of land taxes to pay for such improvements, the revenues obtained from modest customs duties and excise taxes having proved totally inadequate. The demand for land taxation provoked the implacable opposition of the French-Canadian majority in the Assembly. The clash of the two interests led to a generation of political cleavage in Lower Canada in which the Bank of Montreal became both the instrument and symbol of one of the irreconcilable factions.

In a sense both were fighting a battle for survival, the French Canadians for their culture and political identity, the English-speaking commercial group for its economic future. To understand the social and political outlook of the latter it is necessary to know something of the situation in which it found itself at the time the Montreal Bank began business.

Figuratively speaking, the United States turned its back on Canada in 1778, when George Washington abandoned a plan to use the Hazen-Bayley Road to mount a second offensive against Quebec. The independent position of the remaining British North American provinces was thus tacitly accepted and the self-proclaimed republic of Vermont permitted to occupy a neutralist position, conclude an armistice with the Government of Quebec, and even consider, sincerely or insincerely, remaining a British province. While the peace of 1783 made Vermont politically American, its geography kept it commercially Canadian. Despite the endeavours of both the British and American governments, the trade between Vermont and Quebec persisted until the War of 1812 and even continued during the conflict. The very persistence of the trade, however, tended to obscure the full significance of the 34-year-old American decision to let Canada go her own way. So long as the Vermont trade continued to add to Montreal's commercial strength, and so long as the settlements in Upper Canada remained small and isolated, the interdependence of the two economies made the separateness of the two countries an entirely political concept. So Montreal's merchants were able to nurture the dream of a commercial empire that would be based on the city and by means of the lordly St. Lawrence draw into its orbit the rapidly expanding export trade of the American middle west.

A rude awakening came as an aftermath of the War of 1812 in America and of the Napoleonic Wars in Europe, when British manufacturers began dumping large quantities of goods in the United States at depressed prices. Demands for protection arose immediately from the infant industries established in New England during the war years, with the result that the United States shortly adopted a policy of economic nationalism and, with it, protective tariffs. As another expression of exuberant nationalism a series of great public works was undertaken, among them the Erie Canal across New York State to join the Atlantic Ocean and the Great Lakes, and, as a feeder, the Whitehall Canal from the head of Lake Champlain to join that waterway and the Hudson River. With the completion of the latter it was plain that the Vermont-Quebec trade would diminish to the point where the only traffic moving northward would be that seeking to take advantage of the now threatened British colonial preferences. But the Erie Canal project was even more menacing to the dream of the Commercial Empire of the St. Lawrence. With its completion as a navigable waterway from Buffalo to Albany and thence down the Hudson to the sea, traffic originating in the Great Lakes littoral would be diverted from the St. Lawrence, together with most of that of Upper Canada, were a projected connecting link from Oswego southward via the old Stanwix portage route to be completed. In this extremity, the only hope of saving the commercial potential of the St. Lawrence lay in the construction of canals around the rapids up-river from Montreal and the use of this improved waterway by the traffic of the American middle west to take advantage of the preferential colonial tariffs.

Against this background of American rejection, and a large measure of British misunderstanding and indifference, the early nineteenth century political struggle in Lower Canada becomes intelligible. On the one hand, a French-Canadian coalition of able parliamentarians, shrewd notaries, and dedicated clericals fought stubbornly to maintain the *status quo*; on the other a group of English-speaking commercial interests sought with every resource within its power to promote internal improvements that would enable Canada to overcome the natural and imposed obstacles blocking its development. In the conflict that ensued, the French Canadians obstructed all improvements under the compulsion of ethnic hegemony, while the English strove by submissions to London to break the legislative deadlock, and, when this failed,

KEY ECONOMIC FACTOR

Part of an early program of public works in the United States was the building of the seven-million-dollar Erie Canal from Albany to Lake Erie. Providing as it did a navigable waterway four feet deep between the Great Lakes and the Atlantic via the Hudson River, it dealt a serious blow to the commerce of the St. Lawrence system.

In the year of its opening, 1825, the Canadians completed their own Lachine Canal around the rapids at Montreal. However, the Erie drained off much valuable traffic that might otherwise have reached Montreal; in the first year of its operation more than 13,000 vessels were locked through it, and in 1830 its annual toll receipts exceeded a million dollars.

It was not until after the union of Upper and Lower Canada that Canadians were able to start improving their own waterway to make it competitive with the American route.

proposed a reunion of the provinces that would strengthen the position of the English-speaking minority in the Canadas and so enable them to make their policies effective.

It was against this backdrop of economic cross-purposes, political dissensions, and racial antagonisms that the drama of the Bank of Montreal was initially enacted.

2.

As the annual rings of a tree provide a record of past growth, so the annual statements of a corporation provide a similar record in terms of its assets, liabilities, dividend payments and capital accumulation. Tree rings, however, are at best a very general index of the environmental influences to which any given specimen has been exposed. So with a corporation: while the annual statements may provide a record of growth, they do not necessarily indicate whether or not that growth took place in a favourable or unfavourable economic climate. Missing is any clue as to the capacity of management to profit by changes in the economic climate or combat adverse circumstances. This is strikingly apparent as one studies the early records of the Montreal Bank. Although annual statements were not published during the period when the Bank operated without a charter, sufficient data have been assembled from the early ledgers and from later legislative publications to present an anomalous picture of immediate success under generally unpropitious conditions.

One of these conditions has been described above. Vanished were the days when pioneer settlements astride the 45th parallel or on opposite shores of the St. Lawrence could traffic freely with one another. In future, Canadian exports of domestic produce and manufactured goods from Britain would have to scale an American tariff wall that would become more formidable as the years advanced. Worsening the commercial climate were conditions overseas that had been largely responsible for the introduction of protective tariffs by the United States. In England, the combined effects of industrial revolution and peace after two decades of almost uninterrupted war had ushered in a period of economic chaos, social unrest and political upheaval destined to last for more than a generation, while in Europe, the same conditions had precipitated disturbances that were to lead to widespread revolution in less than twenty years. In these circumstances, the Canadian provinces found themselves in serious economic straits.

There were, of course, compensations, otherwise the provinces of British North America could never have overcome the handicaps that beset them. These compensations took a variety of forms. Throughout the British Isles, and later throughout many European countries, the very economic conditions that had temporarily curtailed the demand for Canadian wheat, potash, timber, and other products, soon led to the great European exodus that helped populate Canada and the United States alike during the nineteenth century. In Canada the strength of the British garrison was maintained to guard against the fancied threat of an American invasion, to the benefit of the colonies' stock of specie, and in the United States, more particularly New England, the rapid expansion of trade with China and the Indies created a demand for silver that placed specie and exchange on London at a premium.

It was under such circumstances that the Montreal Bank began business as a joint-stock company without the legal sanction of a charter and, except for the public avowals of its founders, without formal control or supervision of any kind during the first five years of its existence. The early conduct of the Bank's affairs thus appears phenomenal, not so much with respect to profits, which were modest, but because it firmly established the Canadian banking system at a time when English banking was in a state of grave dislocation and American banking was subject to adventuresome and even wild experiment. In England, the system based on the Bank of England and an unlimited number of land banks had produced a succession of costly failures. In the United States, despite the establishment of the Second Bank of the United States, the demand for capital to develop an exploding economy had given rise to a multiplicity of dubious banking experiments that would continue to plague the country for nearly a hundred years. In Canada, on the other hand, a banking system was inaugurated that has survived with relatively minor changes down to the present day without experiencing a single major crisis.

The strength of the Canadian banking system appears to have been drawn from three sources: its foundation on those tenets of specie and commercial banking which held convertibility and liquidity to be indispensable; the conservatism of its founders, in whom, as the economy expanded and the need for banking facilities grew greater, entrepreneurial ability and managerial integrity of a high order were happily combined; and, lastly, the restricted arena in which the Bank experienced its early growth. At the time of its birth, for example, the entire population of the Canadas was only 430,000. Of this number only 16,000 lived in Montreal, which was connected with Quebec and the seas beyond by the St. Lawrence and with the south by well-developed communications but was still virtually cut off from the 95,000 inhabitants of the upper and more productive province by the rapids of the St. Lawrence. But if the large-scale business opportunities present across the border were absent, so were the temptations to experiment and change that were, perhaps, their inevitable corollary.

The restricted character of the Canadian setting is reflected in early books of accounts of the Montreal Bank and in the Directors' "Resolve Books," now in the Head Office archives of the Bank of Montreal. The account books reveal a story of negligible resources and modest day-by-day commercial transactions. Lacking the journals that accompanied them, the early ledgers often baffle interpretation. It is difficult, for example, to establish the extent of the deposits, commercial loans or discounts, and note issues of the Bank's early operations. Nevertheless, the Montreal Bank was able to provide hitherto unavailable services to the community, and this fact, supported by careful management and supervision, seems to have ensured the success of the enterprise from the beginning. Before many months had passed, sufficient business had developed to make profitable the use of additional capital. A call for £25,000 was therefore made on the shareholders, to be paid by May 1, 1818, and a second call (the fourth instalment) in the same amount to be paid by November 5. In addition to these decisions to increase the paid-up capital, the directors voted on April 28 to declare an initial dividend of three per cent, payable June 1. Before the year was out, yet another £25,000 was called up and a second dividend, this time of 4½ per cent, was declared. The following year, 1819, shareholders were called on for a further £50,000, making the paid-up capital £187,500 (or, counting by the Halifax rate, $750,000); dividends totalling 6½ per cent were declared, and a rest fund was established out of undistributed profits. The initial entry shows that these reserves amounted to £1,042 at the end of 1819. The record of the three succeeding years, or until the Bank finally received its charter in 1822, continues the story of modest growth. In 1820, with paid-up capital established at £187,500, a dividend of 6½ per cent was declared, and the Rest increased to almost double. A drop in earnings in 1821 reduced the Rest by almost a third and the dividend rate to 6 per cent, but the following year there was a general enlivening of the Canadian economy, in response to restored overseas demand, and an increase in the Bank's business that almost doubled the deposits, bank-notes in circulation, and discounts or commercial loans. In 1821, for example, the

FIRST BANKING HOUSE
BUILT IN CANADA

In the early spring of 1819, the Montreal Bank was getting ready to move into its new quarters on St. James Street. Commissioned at the beginning of 1818, the first building in Canada designed specifically as a bank was then nearing completion, and the more commodious offices were eagerly anticipated by the staff of eight and the thirteen directors.

As pictured here, the stonework has all been done, and the carpenters, having finished most of the interior furnishings and put the windows in, are working on the roof over the Doric portico. In the foreground John Richardson, the eldest of the Bank's founders, and James Leslie, one of the youngest of the current directors, are scrutinizing the final touches.

Of special interest to Richardson are the terra-cotta plaques he ordered from Coade of London and is now seeing for the first time. Depicting Agriculture, Arts and Crafts, Commerce, and Navigation, they are being mounted on the facade of the banking house where, greatly admired, they were to remain for more than half a century.

The Bank used the sturdy stone edifice for nearly thirty years before erecting next to it the larger domed building which is still used as the Main Office in Montreal. When the Bank moved in 1847, the building pictured here was occupied by the Banque du Peuple. It was demolished in the 1870's to make way for the Montreal general post office, and the plaques were installed over the entrances of the postal building.

Years later, because of the sentimental attachment, the plaques were returned to the Bank by a special order-in-council of the federal government, passed in 1935, and were held against the time they could be utilized.

When the new Head Office building was opened in 1960 on the site of the original office of 1819, these relics found an appropriate setting in the north wall of the passageway linking the new building and the old domed structure of 1847.

Painting by Henry Simpkins, A.R.C.A.

first year for which a statement of discounts is available, the total reached £699,969, and a year later it was £1,120,649.

The explanation is to be found in the semi-weekly "resolves" of the directors. The data they afford fall into several categories, among which are the routine management of the Bank's affairs, its extensive dealings in foreign exchange both in New York and London, the establishment of branch banking, and the repatriation of stock ownership. These, and such related topics as the political dissensions of the first five years, will be explored separately below.

3.

Although the early American banks, unlike the joint-stock banks of England, received their charters as quasi-public utilities which would serve the public interest, the early history of American banking is replete with examples of indifference to the public weal. The same charges were to be laid before many years had passed against the directors and management of the Montreal Bank, but with different results. In the United States, the public clamour against special privilege and favouritism in the granting of loans and discounts to directors and their associates led to a proliferation of bank charters. As the frontier moved rapidly westward, there was added the creation of bank credit based on land or in some cases nothing more substantial than handsomely engraved promises issued by ephemeral banks to pay on demand in specie which they did not possess. Canada was spared the worst of these excesses by her very smallness: that there was neither an excessive demand for capital nor the opportunity to use it profitably can be deduced from the entries in the early ledgers which show that the Bank's funds were never fully tapped.

Charges of socially undesirable monopolistic practices, although substantially justified, as will be seen, in the case of the Bank of Upper Canada and the Family Compact, were largely political in motivation where the Bank of Montreal was concerned. Nevertheless, it is easy enough to understand why such accusations were forthcoming. As in New England, the first Canadian bank was established by men engaged in mercantile pursuits and was intended primarily to pool their collective capital, make it available for use on satisfactory security, and simplify the problems of exchange in the days of the sailing ship by sea and atrocious roads by land. Despite protestations of public utility, banks were profit-making institutions run primarily for the benefit of the shareholders and it seems only natural that the proprietors should have used their own capital to their own advantage. It was not surprising, however, in a

community in which the nature of banking operations was but poorly understood, that charges of monopoly and favouritism should take the form of
vitriolic polemics against the Bank of Montreal and all those connected with
it. To such attacks, John Richardson and Edward Ellice replied over pseudo-
nyms with polemics just as vitriolic but more gracefully composed.

Even had a legislative inquiry conducted by the Bank's political enemies
not exonerated the directors and management of charges of using the Bank's
funds to their exclusive advantage, the early account books would have done
so. Ledger No. 1, for example, contains the accounts of some 350 customers
for the years 1817 to 1820, of which not more than a third were sufficiently
active to extend over five or more folio pages. The system of bookkeeping is
primitive and the accounts are lacking in detail, making the whole record
rather cryptic to the modern observer. However, among the entries are found
the names of the well-known firms with which many of the directors were
connected—Forsyth, Richardson; A. Cuvillier; Horatio Gates & Nephew; Maitland, Garden & Auldjo, etc.—but these by no means accounted for all the
loans, and the names of several directors never appear as borrowers. It is
apparent in view of the evidence that favouritism in granting discounts was
not a common practice at this point in the Bank's career, whatever may have
developed later.

The most vivid impression received from scanning the columns of faded
entries, made in India ink that was freshly ground with mortar and pestle
every morning, is the small and even minuscule nature of the day-by-day
banking transactions. Four thousand pounds, sixteen shillings and threepence,
Halifax currency – the entry immediately arrests the eye, so enormous does
it seem in contrast with the multitude of lesser entries which fill the DR and
CR sides of the ledger pages, all of which were inscribed with exultant
flourishes, as if each entry was a matter for celebration. In fact it is somewhat
amazing to discover how meagre was the scope of Canadian commercial
enterprise toward the close of the second decade of the nineteenth century.
(At a time when the exports from New Orleans had attained an annual value of
$40,000,000, those of Lower Canada were less than one-twelfth as large.) The
explanation is to be found in Ledger No. 1. There it is seen that the balances in
the Bank's largest and most active customer accounts seldom exceeded
£10,000 and that relatively small amounts of capital were used over and
over again in pursuit of mercantile adventures. Compared to the magnificent
dreams of commercial empire, the reality is seen to have been somewhat

insubstantial. One must conclude that the Bank's resources were adequate to finance all legitimate enterprises and that there would have been no need for the directors to discriminate on a personal basis. The fact that the Bank never approached its prescribed discount limit detracts further from the validity of any accusations of favouritism.

Yet from the very beginning the confident conduct of the Bank's affairs belies the modest nature of the early operations. Whether the President, John Gray, or the Vice-President, Thomas A. Turner, or some of the more energetic directors, such as Horatio Gates, George Garden, and James Leslie, were endowed with a prophetic vision of future greatness or were simply determined to make a success of their undertakings are unfathomable questions; the fact is that they did so with the utmost vigour, assurance, and dispatch. Affirming those attributes are several of the actions already noted: the decision to enlarge the staff, bring H. B. Stone from Boston, and order notes engraved in Hartford before the doors were opened and the succession of capital levies made soon afterwards. Even more indicative of determined purpose was the rapidity with which exchange dealings were undertaken, notes put in circulation, foreign correspondencies secured, agencies established (the genesis of Canadian branch banking), and a new banking house approved.

4.

Having summarily rejected on October 10, 1817, the offer of John Molson to construct a bank building at his own expense, the Board resolved at the same meeting that "a piece of Ground should be purchased and a building erected thereon from the funds of the Bank, for the more convenient carrying on of the Business." Appointed as a committee to act on the resolution, Gates, Garden, and Cuvillier, with the President serving *ex officio*, reported early in December that a plot of ground on St. James Street owned by James McDouall could be secured for £2,500. Its purchase was recommended. The site, two blocks north and five blocks west of the rented premises on St. Paul Street and overlooking the historic Place d'Armes, was in every way desirable, but the Board cannily countered by offering McDouall £2,000. The purchase was concluded before the year was out for the even lower price of £1,875. A bill of sale, registered on February 8, 1818, describes the property as being bounded by St. James Street, the extension of the line of St. François Xavier Street, Fortification Lane (lately created by the removal of the old city wall) and the establishment of Mr. Dillon, a well-known hotel and restaurant keeper of the day. A second committee, consisting of Gray, Gates, and Platt, together with Thomas Torrance, later to become a member of the Board, was appointed to procure plans and specifications for a structure to be built on the newly acquired land. The situation was to become to Canada what Lombard Street was to England and Wall Street would become to the United States. Today it is occupied by a new Head Office building of the Bank of Montreal, and St. James Street remains one of the world's great financial thoroughfares.

The plans of the first bank building have disappeared and the name of the architect is uncertain, although it was probably he who established the architectural idiom that gave commercial Montreal its Georgian character throughout the nineteenth century. It could have been George Platt, whose mechanical skill had produced a working engine for the *Accommodation*, or Thomas Torrance, who was no doubt appointed to the building committee because he was then engaged in the construction of an elaborate stone mansion on the mountain slope above the town. It seems more likely, however, that a professional architect had been brought over from the Old Country, possibly by George Garden, to design the new counting house which Maitland, Garden & Auldjo were then building on St. Paul Street and to which the Bank's building committee frequently referred. Whoever the architect may have been, it is clear from the austere Georgian character of his design that he was possessed of a Glasgow, Belfast or Dublin background, and that he, or the building committee, drew inspiration from one of those sources rather than from across the border, where the classical revival housed the Second Bank of the United States in a replica of the Greek Parthenon. When one recalls the strong American ties of the Bank's directors, it is interesting to note that they turned their backs on the fashionable aesthetic of the Republic in favour of a more simple and more appropriate solution to their own architectural problems.

Although the architect's plans are no longer extant, the specifications of the building have been preserved. Discovered recently in Montreal's Judicial Archives, where some ten million notarized documents are filed, is the contract between Andrew White, described as a "carpenter and joiner," and the committee acting in the name of "the Persons carrying on the Banking business at Montreal." It provided for "the erection of a good Substantial stone Building or House with a Stable, Ice House and privy with a good stone wall all around the said Lot." Dated January 23, 1818, the document describes the lot as measuring 129 feet in front and 100 feet in depth, and specifies the wall surrounding it be twelve feet high and two feet thick, and that it should have iron gates. The stable, ice house, and privy were also to be built of stone, and were provided as essential appurtenances for the operation of the Bank and the comfort and convenience of the cashier, who would make his residence on the premises, as well as for the officers and directors, such as John Gray, who lived outside the town and would need stabling for their horses.

That the prototype of Canada's first banking house existed elsewhere can hardly be questioned, yet a study of the contract signed by Andrew White of the first part, and John Gray and others of the second part, reveals a high degree of knowledge of banking needs on the part of men hitherto regarded as tyros. Required was a counting house, seventy-four feet in length, forty-eight feet in depth and fifty-five feet high in front, embellished with a stoop and Doric portico of four columns and pilasters, to be built of the best quality grey stone obtainable, "hammer dressed . . . as in the front of Messrs. Maitland, Garden and Auldjo's New House in Saint Paul Street . . . to be furnished, made, done, completed, executed and performed by the said Andrew White in the most substantial workmanlike manner possible." The structure was to comprise four storeys: the first, below ground level, vaulted; the second, sixteen feet high, enclosing the main banking chamber and directors' offices; the third, the cashier's living quarters; and the fourth, the garret. A handsome staircase with a cherry handrail and wrought-iron banisters led from floor to floor, and the roof, which, like the stone facing, was to conform to that on Maitland, Garden & Auldjo's building, appears to have been constructed with cedar joists and pine planks finished off with tin, with lead gutters and flashings. At the core of the establishment were the book and money vaults, each with four-foot, ironbound stone walls, iron doors, and overhead tackle to raise and lower bullion. Chimneys at either end and provision for stovepipe holes in every room suggest that the whole would be heated by both fireplaces and stoves. References to handsome stucco cornices, carved ceilings, marble fireplace mantels, six-panel doors, and sashes "glazed and hung in the best English manner" suggest that the interior was also in the Georgian tradition. The floors were to be of the best native material available – two-and-a-half-inch clear pine plank, six to seven inches wide, with joints hidden. The fireplaces in the directors' rooms were to be faced with marble slabs, but "plain cut stone with hardwood borders around the hearth" sufficed for those in the drawing-room and parlour above.

Curiously enough, the original contract contains no mention of an architectural detail which has long been regarded as the most distinguished feature of the building: four terracotta tablets set in the facade above the windows to the banking chamber. Executed in high relief and representing "Agriculture," "Navigation," "Arts and Crafts," and "Commerce," they bear the signature, "Coade, London, 1819". The Coade factory was founded in 1769 and soon became famous for its special clay formula and firing process which gave its products astounding durability. This is attested to by the Bank plaques, which are in remarkable condition after having withstood the punishment of more than half a century of Canadian winters before being moved inside when the banking house was demolished in the 1870's to make way for a new Montreal general post office. In 1960, the four panels were incorporated in the passageway that joins the two present banking structures, the one built in 1847, the other in 1960.

The Coade family enhanced the reputation of their factory in its early years by employing such gifted sculptors as John Bacon and John Flaxman, whose works adorn St. Paul's Cathedral and Westminster Abbey. Some Coade catalogues and etchings are still extant in the British Museum, but these fail to establish conclusively who actually designed the plaques. For many years the work was attributed to John Flaxman, but on further investigation it would now appear more likely that John Bacon drew the original figures, although he died some years before they were cast into terracotta for the Bank. Some of the Coade account books have also come to light and they reveal that it was none other than John Richardson who negotiated the purchase of the plaques for the Montreal Bank early in 1819.

The new building, begun in the spring of 1818 at a projected cost of £5,550, was completed a year later at an additional expense of £3,250, entailed no doubt by changes and improvements as the work progressed. That contractors in 1818 did not take the same precautions as their descendants of today is evidenced by a story in the *Spectateur* of September 5, 1818, which relates how Mr. Uniacke, the Attorney General of Lower Canada, fell into the foundation excavation of the Bank's ice house and remained there for an hour before his cries brought help. As on the occasion of the Bank's opening, some seventeen months before, the occupancy of Canada's first bank building was not fêted by the owners. In the press, however, the Bank was praised for its elegant building, "which for solidity, for beauty and convenience equals, we may say, surpasses any structure of the kind on this continent."

A curious item appears in F. W. Terrill's *Chronology of Montreal*, a volume which contains a business and commercial directory of the city from 1752 to the date of publication, 1893. The item states that the first bank building was destroyed by fire in 1820 and rebuilt at a cost of £11,000. Although no mention of the episode is found in the Directors' Minutes, the Montreal historian, Alfred Sandham, notes that a fire did occur in the Place d'Armes on November 10, 1820, when a bolt of lightning struck the spire of the Parish Church of Notre Dame, but he makes no reference to any damage to the Bank.

5.

The business transferred to the new banking house in time for the second annual meeting of the shareholders on June 7, 1819, was different in character from that begun two years before. Then, American support had been required to launch the enterprise; by 1819 conditions had so altered that the Montreal Bank stood firmly on its own feet. Connections with leading banking houses in New York and London had been established, agencies in Quebec City and several points in Upper Canada provided, and a considerable portion of the American-owned shares repatriated. Signs of growing strength are found in a resolution passed at the first annual meeting to increase the Cashier's salary to £500, and a year later another to remunerate the President, John Gray, Esq., in the sum of £500 "for his hitherto great attention to the interests of the Bank." Thomas A. Turner and Zabdiel Thayer, both of whom appear to have represented the American interest, had retired as directors and had been succeeded by David David, a successful Montreal merchant, and Charles Bancroft, the nephew and business partner of Horatio Gates. In 1818 George Garden had succeeded Turner as vice-president, an office he was to hold for four years except during a three-months' absence in England in 1819, when Bancroft took his place.

The Bank's initial growth appears to have resulted from several factors, among them an informed foreign-exchange operation, an increased use of its services locally, especially by the government at Quebec, and a gradual improvement of business conditions in England. On the other hand, many of the Bank's Boston shareholders found themselves in difficulties in 1818 when a crisis in American financial circles was precipitated by disclosures of wanton mismanagement of the Second Bank of the United States. Only large importations of specie from England saved the situation, and in the meantime some Boston shareholders of the Montreal Bank suffered losses which restricted their China and Indies trading. This state of affairs resulted in the sale of stock

KINGSTON—MAIN STREET SOUTH

Within eight months of its founding in Montreal in November 1817, the Montreal Bank established at Kingston the first banking office to be opened in Upper Canada. The agent in charge was Thomas Markland, who was later involved with the "pretended" Bank of Upper Canada and who, as early as 1813, had been issuing his own paper money to facilitate his business dealings with merchants in Lower Canada.

The history of Kingston itself began in 1783, when the old site of Cataraqui was surveyed in preparation for its settlement by United Empire Loyalists. In 1818, when the first Montreal Bank notes started circulating among the 3,000 inhabitants, Kingston was still a garrison town and served as a trans-shipment port between the Great Lakes and the St. Lawrence. Stage-coach service to Montreal had been established the year before.

by many of the American shareholders and its purchase by John Richardson, George Moffatt, Horatio Gates, Samuel Gerrard, and other influential Montrealers. While never a director, John Richardson affirmed his enduring faith in his creation by becoming its largest shareholder.

The Bank's first profits came from dealings in specie and foreign exchange, both English and American. The first transaction took place as soon as the paid-in capital reached £37,500, when the Board resolved to invest £20,000 in government exchange (government drafts on London) and H. B. Stone was sent express to Quebec with £2,000 sterling as a deposit. The journey was not only successful but made with considerable dispatch. Stone left by steamboat for Quebec September 23, 1817, and on the 3rd of October £10,000 exchange on London was sold at a premium of four per cent. Five days later, one Simon Greene of Boston offered to buy £20,000 exchange at two per cent premium and was allotted £13,500 of the London draft bills. No other dealings in foreign exchange occurred until December 30, when the Board resolved to send 100,000 Spanish dollars to Boston in the care of Thomas Turner. Early in January 1818, the sum was increased to $130,000 and this was then packed into sixty-five kegs, each weighing about a hundred pounds. A special interest attaches to the transaction in view of the character of transportation at the time and the condition of the roads; however, the shipment from Montreal to Boston seems to have been undertaken as a routine matter without any special safeguards. Since the Vice-President was to accompany the shipment, no insurance was provided, and when he left Montreal around January 13 he also took with him $20,000 in small bank-notes to put into circulation in Boston. So great was the demand for specie in Canada, however, that on February 6 we find a letter being sent to Turner in Boston with instructions "to bring up with him all the specie he can procure, [and] to take in preference American Dollars and Half Dollars." At the same time John Bellows, President of the Manufacturers and Mechanics Bank in Boston, offered to buy the remainder of the Spanish dollars held by the Bank at a two-per-cent premium. Thus a further $60,000 in coin was shipped, at buyer's risk, to be paid for in American silver.

Even before this date, the Montreal Bank had opened an account with the New York branch of the Second Bank of the United States as a result of a proposal of one of its American shareholders, John Hinsdale of Middletown, Connecticut. Having disposed of four hundred shares of Montreal Bank stock in that place, Hinsdale suggested that instalments due on them be made payable to the Montreal Bank's credit in the New York bank. The same privilege was extended to Prime, Ward & Sands and other New York subscribers, and to those in Boston, where instalments were to be paid by New York drafts drawn by the Manufacturers and Mechanics Bank. These arrangements led to further business and on February 13, 1818, the Board resolved to lend the New York branch of the Second Bank of the United States "such sums of money in gold as the Montreal Bank can conveniently spare," at one-half of one per cent commission and six per cent interest secured by bills on London.

With the establishment of a New York account, the Montreal Bank next appointed as its agents there Prime, Ward & Sands, for whom Horatio Gates had acted as agent in Montreal, and who were also New York agents for the House of Baring of London, whose financial involvements in the United States had already become extensive. On the recommendation of Baring Brothers and after considerable correspondence, the Montreal Bank appointed as its London agents the private banking house of Thomas Wilson & Co. There was thus established early in 1818 the intricate apparatus for transferring funds and making payments between Canada, New York, Boston, and London which has continued to the present day.

The anatomy of the trade in specie and bills of exchange was extremely complex even at this early date. Spanish dollars appeared in Montreal as a result of Canadian sales of staves and cod to the Caribbean islands and Mexico. Received by the Montreal Bank in return for stock, notes, or deposits, these silver coins were shipped to Boston where they were used in the trade with China and the East Indies, while the Bank brought back American dollars and half dollars with which they bought Treasury drafts on London. The government at Quebec needed whatever acceptable coin it could get to pay its soldiers and other military expenses because it was too costly and risky to ship sterling specie out from England, and even when this had been tried, the British silver soon recrossed the Atlantic in payment for imports. The excess bills of exchange on London, not needed to finance Canadian imports of British goods or Canadian investments in Britain, were then sold by the agents of the Montreal Bank in New York, and used to service American debts to Britain. In return, the Bank received American dollars and the process began all over again, the Bank usually making a profit on each transaction and certainly over the whole circle. From looking at this operation, we once again get an indication of the magnitude of British military expenditures in Canada at this time. The government drafts sent over to pay for the garrison not only played a major role in financing Canada's trade deficit with Britain but also provided the means whereby a large part of the American account with Britain was settled.

Thus, specie shipments seem to have been almost continuously on the road between Montreal and Boston or New York, while other shipments were moving to and from Quebec, in summer a pleasant steamboat trip but in winter a wearisome three-day journey by calèche or sleigh. In some instances the transfers of coin, bullion, and bills of exchange were made under the auspices of one of the directors but more generally under those of one of the banking staff. Among the latter, Benjamin Holmes, the discount clerk, was by far the greatest traveller. From 1819 to 1821 he made several journeys to New York to deliver or procure specie in amounts as large as $100,000, yet on one occasion only does the record suggest that there may have been risks involved. Taking down a shipment of gold and bringing up another of silver in 1821, Holmes was empowered, "*if necessary*, to engage at Albany a person, whose fidelity can be relied on, to accompany him to Whitehall, as an additional safeguard." On the other hand, a bank employee on his way to Upper Canada in July 1819 with a shipment of bank-notes had his trunk broken into and a packet containing $8,000 in five-dollar bills stolen. A reward of £250 was offered, but no information turned up until two years later when an attempt was made by an up-country physician to circulate the bills. The directors decided to prosecute, but so discreetly was the matter noted in the Minutes that neither the name of the thief nor the outcome of the action was recorded.

With the exception of this single incident, nothing more can be discovered regarding these nerve-racking responsibilities, nor are there any descriptions of the trials and tribulations suffered by the Bank's couriers on their three to four days' journey to New York, Boston or the upper province. However, the reminiscent letter written by Henry Dupuy, in which he recalls his Hartford journey, also contains a vivid description of an adventure that may have been typical of many others. It belongs to the next decade, but conditions of travel between Montreal and Upper Canada were poorer in 1832 than they had been for many years past between Montreal and the south.

About 1832 the Rideau Canal was constructed under the superintendence of Colonel By of the Royal Engineers, and in the course of a short time a large quantity of specie would accumulate at the Kingston Branch

HENRY DUPUY'S JOURNEY

Henry Dupuy's memoir is virtually the only account left to us of the experiences of a junior officer during the early days of Canadian banking. One must not suppose, however, that the troubles he encountered on his trip from Kingston to Montreal, depicted here, were of an exceptional nature; similar situations must have faced many of his contemporaries at a time when the banks had to be quite self-sufficient and their employees were counted on to perform tasks now taken care of by the other service industries.

The list of duties for which the messenger and porter were made responsible in the first by-laws of the Montreal Bank is itself an indication of the range of services expected from all members of the staff. These two positions were often held by one man who, in addition to clerical work, had to make deliveries and collections, clean the banking house, act as guard, light the lamps and make the fires. Some of these chores could be highly unpleasant in severe weather.

A job with the Bank was much prized, in spite of the stringent requirements. Even the clerks had to be possessed of qualities far above those needed for the routine fulfilment of their banking assignments. Although perhaps from across the counter each post seemed limited and clearly defined, the Bank's staff was in reality quite adaptable and its members worked as a team. It is surprising how little evidence there is of conflict or dissatisfaction in those times.

Painting by Stuart Main

in exchange for the Bank-notes paid out to the contractors, which increased the circulation considerably.

A pretty large sum of specie having been gathered together in the Kingston Branch I was ordered to bring it down to Montreal by stage; on one occasion in the month of February, I took down a cargo of specie in boxes and kegs in the ordinary stage, started early in the morning long before daylight, snowing at a great rate, so that in a short time the roads were hardly visible by the river. Between Brockville and Cornwall we had to ascend a very steep hill and in attempting to do so the harness, etc. broke and we were obliged to carry the specie from the bottom of the hill to the top of it, the driver and myself alone were present. At 2 p.m. started off, snow nearly up to my hips, to look out for help and by a light at some distance was directed to a hut and after much talking, I prevailed upon a man to come to our help; he was at the time attending a sick person and it was very doubtful whether we were to have any help, the boxes and kegs were too heavy without further help to carry up that hill.

We got up all right by perseverance and the stage was at last put in order and ascended this steep place, took in all the specie which had been carried up and proceeded on our journey, that is the driver and myself, he swore at a great rate at the hard dollars for giving him so much trouble.

I think we were upwards of two days on the road, it would have been rather hazardous had the driver been a desperate fellow, however, I had not the slightest fear. Near Isle Perrault [Ile Perrot] we rode down again on the small lake. I think its name is St. Francis, and I felt very much relieved at our safe arrival in Montreal.

It has been claimed, in discussing the transactions of the Bank's first period, 1817-22, that premiums as high as twelve to fifteen per cent were realized in specie transactions and that these were the principal source of the Bank's early profits. While the latter part is probably true, no evidence can be found in the records to support the belief that specie at this time commanded a premium of more than five per cent, and rarely that. This, in fact, would account in part for the Bank's immediate success: its ability to handle at lower costs than had existed previously the exchange transactions which were so frequently required in Canadian commercial enterprises.

An interesting by-product of the exchange dealings in New York and Boston was the opportunity they afforded to place the Bank's notes in circulation in the United States. Similar arrangements were made at a very early date with the Burlington Bank at Burlington, Vermont, the Bank of Niagara at Buffalo, and the Niagara Bank, all of which predated any banks in Upper Canada. At one time, also, Prime, Ward & Sands, as the Bank's New York agents, redeemed Montreal Bank notes at a discount of one-half of one per cent, and there was at least one issue of notes of small denomination redeemable in New York, specially endorsed to that effect.

6.

Although the word "branch" did not come into general use in Canada until after the Act of Union became effective in 1841, the evolution of branch banking was no less rapid than that of the Montreal Bank's foreign business. In all probability more has been written about this phase of Canadian banking than any other, a great deal of it based on uninformed assumptions. Until quite recently – and even yet, perhaps – the Canadian system of branch banking was popularly believed to have been borrowed from Scotland. There, agencies had been established late in the seventeenth century, soon after the founding of the Bank of Scotland, but had remained on a poorly organized basis until 1824, when the National Bank of Scotland was founded and the present extensive system of branch banking was introduced. Another assumption was that branch banking in Canada derived directly from the First Bank of the United States, but the branches of that institution appear to have been an afterthought arising from the location of its head office in Philadelphia, which made imperative the establishment of agencies in the large trading cities to serve as repositories for government funds. For like reasons, it seems altogether probable that branch banking in Canada owed as much to the exigencies of geography and politics as to the assimilation of systems existing elsewhere. The geographic and economic position of Montreal and governmental obstruction of the chartering of new banks made expansion inevitable. As late as 1808, it may be recalled, the sponsors of the bill to incorporate the Bank of Lower-Canada included representatives of the mercantile interests of both Montreal and Quebec City. Why, during the ensuing nine-year interval, the latter should have withdrawn or been excluded from participation in the adventure of 1817 remains a mystery, but it is obvious that any bank located in Montreal would have to have an office in Quebec if it expected to do business with the government, the principal source of bills on London. It would be reasonable to conclude, therefore, that the branch banking system that has served Canada so successfully was an indigenous phenomenon.

The first discussions concerning an agency at Quebec took place at the first meeting of the Board following the Bank's unostentatious opening. Ten days later a resolution was passed to offer Daniel Sutherland the post of agent, and the Cashier, Robert Griffin, was directed to write to the gentleman to that effect. At the time, Sutherland occupied the position of Deputy Postmaster General for British North America and his salary of $7,000 made him the most highly paid colonial official next to the Governor General. In 1818, and even up to 1847, the post office was an Imperial Government operation and was regarded as a tax-gathering rather than a servicing organization. As such it was one of the principal sources of Imperial revenue along with Customs and Internal Revenues.

Prior to his post-office appointment, Sutherland had been engaged in the fur trade, but after the union of the XY and North West companies he allowed his interest to expire. At the turn of the century, he and four others, among them John Gray, received a charter to supply Montreal with pure water. However, their system of wooden pipes proved too unreliable and the Montreal Water-Works went up for sale at a heavy loss in 1815, eventually being bought by another Bank of Montreal man, Thomas Porteous.

In spite of his lucrative office, Sutherland accepted the Bank's offer, and the Board made his appointment as agent official on November 28, allowing him one-eighth of one per cent commission on all transactions, the same to cover his expenses. He was required to provide a security of £5,000. The cashier in Montreal was authorized to sell drafts on Quebec at three days sight for one-half of one per cent, bills on the Commissary General being sent to Sutherland to cover any such demands. The president, vice-president and director-of-the-week were also empowered to discount Quebec bills bearing the signatures of two responsible residents of Montreal at three days and ten days sight for commercial and government paper respectively, the differential no doubt resulting from the more deliberate manner of official processing. Within six weeks of its opening in Montreal, the Bank was in business in Quebec and its agent at that point was authorized to furnish himself with "a large Wrought Iron Chest" at the Bank's expense, with the admonition that he would be held responsible, except for accidents and robbery, for any person to whom he might entrust the property committed to his care. The same letter of instructions charged Daniel Sutherland with the need for "Care, Integrity, and Diligence" in the conduct of the Bank's affairs.

It can be assumed that the agent's official connections at the seat of government were held to be somewhat more than promising, so quickly were rules and regulations for the conduct of the Quebec agency drawn up and forwarded. Incorporated in the Minutes of December 5 and transmitted nine days later, the rules were signed by the Vice-President and took the form of "Instructions from the President and Directors of the Montreal Bank to their Agent at Quebec." The eleven clauses dealt with the collection of drafts sent from Montreal, the requirements for Quebec drafts sent to Montreal for discount, the acceptance of Montreal Bank notes offered in payment of all transactions, the submission of frequent reports on the fluctuations of exchange and mercantile credit, and a statement, to be abstracted every Saturday, reporting the amount of specie, bank-notes, bills, and drafts in the chest. Along with these instructions, the agent was sent $4,000 in notes of five-dollar and ten-dollar denominations to put into circulation as opportunity offered.

There is nothing more in the Minutes about the Quebec agency until May 11, 1818, but the Bank's first ledger records transactions with the agency totalling more than £50,000 between the first entry on December 17, 1817, and July 18, 1818. It was because of this, no doubt, that a special meeting of the full board of directors was called at 7 p.m. on May 15, to discuss the expediency of establishing an Office of Discount and Deposit at Quebec, the title used by the Second Bank of the United States on opening its New York agency. Just what was the difference between an "Office of Discount and Deposit" and a branch is not altogether clear; the word "branch" occurs in connection with the discussion of the proposed change of status of the Quebec agency, but does not recur for many years. Both had the power to accept deposits, issue and redeem notes, discount bills and other commercial paper, and deal in exchange. One limitation, apparently, was the export of specie, which was controlled exclusively by the Board of Directors. The proposals concerning the Office of Discount and Deposit having been adopted, Sutherland was invited to inform the Board how far, in his opinion, the installation would serve the mercantile interests at Quebec. The move was undoubtedly made to forestall efforts then being made by those same interests to establish a bank of their own in Quebec City.

Meanwhile the legislature of Upper Canada had passed a bill, in 1817, incorporating a Bank of Upper Canada on the petition of Thomas Markland and divers merchants of Kingston. This was actually the first banking legislation passed in Canada, since the bill incorporating the Montreal Bank was not passed by the Lower Canada legislature until March 1818. The Kingston bill, however, was reserved for royal assent by the Lieutenant-Governor, a rider providing for its natural demise should assent not be granted before January 1, 1819. It was this situation no doubt that prompted discussions around the board-room table of the Montreal Bank, with respect to "the most eligible mode of establishing an agent or agents at York and other places in Upper Canada with a view to putting our bills into general circulation in that quarter." At successive meetings of the Board, two committees were appointed to deal with the Quebec and Upper Canada proposals. On both sat Gates, Ermatinger, and Cuvillier, with the President *ex officio*; in addition James Leslie served on the Quebec committee and George Garden on the other.

Resolutions were adopted on June 16, 1818, appointing William Allan of York and Thomas Markland of Kingston as the Bank's agents at these points in Upper Canada, and advising John Caldwell in Quebec of the Bank's plans to reorganize the Quebec agency. Allan and Markland were up-country merchants and the correspondents of many firms connected with the Montreal Bank, and Caldwell was the Receiver General in Quebec. Later to succeed to the baronetcy of a cousin, Sir John Caldwell is distinguished in Canadian history for defalcations amounting to £96,000, a sum greatly in excess of the average annual provincial revenues. Dismissed from his post in 1823, he made partial restitution.

Beautifully situated at the foot of Lake Ontario, Kingston was then a town of some 2,000 inhabitants and the principal community west of Montreal. Long known as Cataraqui, and famous as the site of Fort Frontenac, which was established there in 1673, it took the name of Kingston when the United Empire Loyalists arrived and made it the base for their occupation of the adjacent Bay of Quinte area. York, renamed Toronto in 1834, but known as "Muddy York," was a small settlement of a few hundred inhabitants situated on a sheltered bay 150 miles west on Lake Ontario. The site was first occupied by a French trading post and was chosen as the location of the provincial capital, in 1793, by the first Lieutenant-Governor, John Graves Simcoe. In 1818 stage-coaches ran twice weekly between Montreal and Kingston, and once a week between Kingston and York.

Rather casually, it would seem, the letters to each of the newly appointed agents in Upper Canada contained enclosures of $10,000 in bank-notes "to be put in circulation," together with instructions similar to those forwarded earlier to the Quebec agency for the conduct of the banking business. This proved sufficiently lucrative from the outset to warrant sending additional quantities of bank-notes to the upper province and rapidly widening the authority of the Bank's agents there with respect to discounts and the transfer of funds between the head office and themselves. Before a year had passed, both Allan and Markland were in reality acting as branch managers and additional agencies had been established at Queenston and Amherstburg. The former was discontinued within two years but another was opened at Perth, a thriving settlement south of the Ottawa River founded a few years before by the officers and men of disbanded Scottish regiments. The four agencies were continued until the Bank of Upper Canada at York was chartered, with the government a twenty-per-cent stockholder. Legislation followed in 1824, outlawing branches of banks with head offices outside the province.

Meanwhile, the expansion of the Quebec business had followed a more complicated course. In conformity with the plan mentioned above and approved by the Receiver General, the Office of Discount and Deposit of the Montreal Bank, though continuing under the same style, had in reality become a duplicate, on a small scale, of the banking house in Montreal, with its own directors, an assured working capital of £50,000, and Daniel Sutherland's title no longer that of agent, but cashier. These changes were brought about by allotting 300 shares of Montreal Bank stock for purchase by Quebec subscribers to ensure support, participation, and virtual management by local interests. As in other Canadian banking ventures of the period, the capital available proved insufficient, and no more than 184 shares could be disposed of. Horatio Gates, however, took up the balance, making possible the election of a board of nine directors, of whom five were to constitute a quorum and conduct the business under a chairman elected by them weekly. Except for the smaller number of directors, the establishments in Quebec and Montreal appear to have been identical, although that in Quebec remained subordinate. The Articles of Association and Rules and Regulations applied alike to both, and in Quebec as in Montreal the local board was empowered to secure suitable premises in which to carry on the banking business and to employ competent persons for that purpose. As stipulated in the Minutes of the Montreal Board, the staff was to comprise a "Manager and Cash-keeper" (cashier) at £300 per annum, a combined Bookkeeper and Discount Clerk at £200, an "Under Clerk" (receiving and paying teller) at from £150 to £200, and a messenger-porter at £100.

Of even greater interest was the establishment, in the course of perfecting the Quebec arrangement in the summer of 1818, of an agency in Boston. Since its inception, the Bank had concluded transactions with Boston business men totalling nearly $350,000, and in the course of these dealings had, at times, built up substantial credits with the Manufacturers and Mechanics Bank. There was also, it will be remembered, a large number of stockholders in the Boston area and it was necessary to make special arrangements for the instalment payments on their shares. For these reasons, the Board resolved, on July 7, "That Messrs. Bellows, Cochran and H. G. Otis jr. with such of the stockholders resident in Boston as they may think necessary, be authorized to manage the Funds belonging to the Montreal Bank now actually deposited in the Manufacturers and Mechanics Bank at Boston in the manner they may think most conducive to the interest of this Institution." Of this group, we have already met Mr. Bellows. Harrison Gray Otis was a leading lawyer of his day and had just completed fifteen years in the Massachusetts legislature; he was at this time ensconced in the U.S. Senate and he would later become Mayor of Boston. William Cochran, a Boston broker, had shown an avid interest in banks and banking. Together with another Montreal Bank shareholder, Nathan Appleton, he devised a plan to "blackmail" Massachusetts country banks into redeeming their notes in specie. The success of this venture forced many of the weaker institutions out of business, and Cochran was later able to found a country bank of his own in Pittsfield, Massachusetts. The Montreal Bank's funds in Boston appear to have been in most capable hands.

SEVEN

BY ROYAL
CONSENT

BY ROYAL CONSENT

I.

In the summer of 1822, almost five years after the Montreal Bank had started in business under Articles of Association, the long-sought royal charter was finally granted. Incorporating the "President, Directors and the Company of the Bank of Montreal," the act changed not only the corporation's official name but also its status, from a private to a public company, imposed legally-enforceable obligations on its directors, and greatly enhanced its prestige as a centre for deposits and the issuing of notes.

It may be recalled that at a shareholders' meeting held in October 1817, before the Bank was fully organized, a decision was reached to apply to the legislature for an act of incorporation; in other words, a charter. As in previous attempts, the task of introducing a bill fell to Austin Cuvillier, a member of the Assembly and also of the Board. A bill to incorporate certain persons under the name of the Montreal Bank was introduced on January 19, 1818, and although the actual bill has been lost, the petition prays that the bank may be incorporated under the terms of the original Articles of Asso-

ciation and it is assumed that the bill was identical with those introduced in
1815 and 1816. The bill was given its first and second readings and debated in
general committee, at which point it was amended to make the shareholders
personally responsible for all transactions of the corporation. To this the
Board was unalterably opposed, and Cuvillier was advised that any charter
containing such a clause would be summarily rejected. Other amendments
were not considered of any consequence, except one limiting the voting rights
of alien stockholders. It was the opinion of the Board that such a proscription
was inadvisable and that foreigners should be allowed to vote by proxy the
same as other shareholders. These matters occupied the attention of the Board
during two consecutive meetings on March 17 and 21, 1818, when a letter was
drafted instructing Cuvillier to exert his influence to have the objectionable
amendment expunged as a departure from the prayer of petition and highly
prejudicial to the Bank. The Bank's solicitor, James Stuart, later to become
Chief Justice of Lower Canada (1838-41) and of United Canada (1841-53),
was given similar instructions on leaving for Quebec the same day.

The controversial question of shareholders' personal liability would continue to command the attention of legislative bodies for several decades but
at this time was apparently dropped. On March 26, 1818, "An Act for the
establishment of a Bank at the City of Montreal in the Province of Lower
Canada" was passed by the legislature and was reserved on April 1 by the
Governor, Sir John Coape Sherbrooke, "for an expression of His Majesty's
pleasure." Confident that the end of the trail was finally in sight, the directors
dispatched letters to Inglis, Ellice & Co., Hon. John Richardson, and Adam
Gordon, the provincial agent, in London, enclosing copies of the Act and
urging that their influence and interest be exerted to hasten passage through
the proper channels. However, the campaign to secure a charter continued
to be attended by misfortune. That the Canadian lobby in London tried long
and hard to procure royal assent is deduced from a Board Minute of July
21, 1820, which provides for the payment of £100 to Adam Gordon "as a
compliment for his services in aiding to obtain an Act for Incorporating the
Bank." From Gordon, apparently, came the information that all efforts had
failed.

With patience and fortitude, a bill was again submitted, January 19, 1821,
to the session of the provincial parliament summoned a month earlier by
Lord Dalhousie, who was then governor. Again an act was passed, incorporating this time the "Bank of Montreal," and again it was reserved for the

royal pleasure. When the new act reached London, Adam Gordon once more intervened on behalf of the Bank. His main opposition on this occasion came from the Chief Justice of Lower Canada, Jonathan Sewell, who expressed doubts as to the legality of the Act, and another year elapsed before royal assent was finally granted. The letter from Earl Bathurst, the Colonial Secretary, to the Earl of Dalhousie giving notice of the action reads as follows:

> Downing Street
> 29 May, 1822.
>
> My Lord,
> Herewith I have the honour to transmit to your Lordship an order of the King in Council bearing date the 18th instant confirming the Act passed by the Legislature of the Province of Lower Canada in the month of March, 1821, entitled:
>> "An Act for incorporating certain persons therein named under the name of President, Directors and Company of the Bank of Montreal."
>
> Your Lordship's
> Most obedient
> Humble servant
> BATHURST.
>
> Earl of Dalhousie.

Appended to the letter is a copy of the Order in Council referred to:

> At the Court at Carlton House
> the 18th May, 1822.
>
> Present:

The King's Most Excellent Majesty	
Lord Chancellor	Earl Cathcart
Lord President	Viscount Melville
Lord Privy Seal	Viscount Sidmouth
Lord Chamberlain	Lord George Beresford
Duke of Dorset	Lord Maryborough
Duke of Wellington	Mr. Robinson
Lord Steward	Mr. Secretary Peel

Marquis of Winchester   Lord Chief Justice Abbott
Marquis of Londonderry   Mr. Wynn
Earl Bathurst
Earl of Liverpool

Whereas by Commission under the Great Seal of Great Britain the Governor, Council and Assembly of His Majesty's Province of Lower Canada, are authorized and empowered to make, constitute and ordain Laws, Statutes and Ordinances for the Public Peace, Welfare and Good Government of the said Province, which Laws, Statutes and Ordinances are to be as near as conveniently may be agreeable to the Laws and Statutes of this Kingdom and are to be transmitted to His Majesty for His Majesty's Approbation or Disallowance. And Whereas in pursuance of the said Powers a Bill has been passed in the said Province and transmitted, entitled as follows, viz:

"An Act for incorporating certain Persons therein named under the name of President, Directors and Company of the Bank of Montreal."

Which Bill having been referred to the Committee of the Lords of His Majesty's Most Honourable Privy Council appointed for the consideration of all matters relating to Trade and Foreign Plantations the said Lords of the Committee have reported as their opinion to His Majesty, that the said Bill is proper, to be confirmed, His Majesty was thereupon this day pleased, by and with the advice of His Privy Council, to Declare His Approbation of the said Bill, and pursuant to His Majesty's Royal Pleasure thereupon expressed, the said Bill is hereby confirmed, finally enacted and ratified accordingly. Whereof the Governor, Lieutenant Governor or Commander-in-Chief of His Majesty's said Province of Lower Canada for the time being, and all other persons whom it may concern, are to take notice, and govern themselves accordingly.

GRENVILLE.

Dated at London, May 18, the confirmation of the Act for incorporating the Bank of Montreal arrived at Quebec on July 19, and was proclaimed by the Governor in Council on July 22, 1822.

2.

The provisions and regulations of the Act were not materially different from those of the Articles of Association under which the unincorporated company had been operating since 1817. In this respect, the petitioners were granted everything they asked for: a parliamentary enactment giving them the statutory right to carry on their business "under the provisions and regulations as nearly corresponding with the terms of their original Association as may be." In other words, the Canadian banking legislation known as I George IV, cap. 25 (L.C.) did nothing to change or even modify the chain of descent that was begun with the short-lived Canada Banking Company in 1792. However, since it forms the statutory basis of a banking system whose essential features are still with us, its further consideration is required.

The contentious clauses limiting stockholders' liability to the amount of their personal stock holdings remained unaltered, as did those clauses limiting the debt to three times the paid-up capital plus deposits of specie. As formerly, the Bank's business was restricted to dealing in bills of exchange, gold and silver coin and bullion, and discounting notes on which the discount was to be collected at the time of the transaction. Also, as before, no more than six per cent could be charged on loans or discounts and the Bank was prohibited from dealing in land or holding any other than that acquired for its own use or hypothecated to it in payment for undischarged debts. Nevertheless, it would be an error to assume that the Act and the Articles of Association were identical. Not only are there differences in the wording and style of the two instruments, but several clauses in the Articles are omitted in the Act and others added. During the course of its two passings the bill had been subjected to amendments of various sorts, which would account for the differences, and it would have been only natural, of course, for the lawmakers to use pre-existing bills rather than take the trouble to draft another. However, since the earlier bills were derived directly from the Act of Congress which chartered the First Bank of the United States, the influence of Alexander Hamilton on Canadian banking became, in the Act of 1821, irrefutably established.

One of the principal differences between the two documents arose from the fact that the Articles provided for the establishment of a banking business while the Act simply incorporated a business that was already in existence. In the Act, therefore, there was no need to provide for the opening of

HIGHWAY 2 — CIRCA 1820

Now one of Canada's main thoroughfares, the highway between Montreal and Toronto in 1820 was little more than a rutted mud track through a primeval forest. The section pictured here between Kingston and York (now Toronto) received most of its use during the winter. In summer, heavy loads would have been transported by sail or steam along Lake Ontario, and travellers, unless prone to seasickness, would have chosen the same route.

According to one traveller of the day, the road "should have been included by Dante as the highway to Pandemonium, for none can be more decidedly infernal."

141

subscription books nor to require that so much capital be paid in before the Bank could begin operations. It had been conducting such operations successfully for several years. Instead of these provisions, we find a list of subscribers appended to the Act. Incidentally, whereas the name "Bank of Montreal" appears for the first time in the Act of Incorporation, in French the Bank was always "Banque de Montréal," before and after its receipt of the royal charter. Other departures from the Articles are seen in changes with respect to foreign stockholders' voting rights and in the penalties for embezzlement, forgery, and counterfeiting. A curious discrepancy occurs in connection with voting rights: Clause IV prohibits any stockholder not a British subject by birth, conquest, or an act of the British parliament from voting either in person or by proxy at any meeting of shareholders for the election of directors, the adoption of by-laws, or "for any purpose or purposes whatsoever." Clause IX, section 2, on the other hand, provides that anyone holding ten shares or more of stock who has been a resident of the province for seven years and of Montreal for three, may be elected a director, irrespective of citizenship.

Any explanation of the inconsistency would be wholly conjectural, but it may be noted that the obvious repugnance to foreign participation shown in Clause IV recurs in Clause XX, which prohibits loans to any foreign state or foreign prince upon pain of immediate dissolution of the corporation. The Act deals also with criminal violations which, of course, were outside the scope of the Articles. Four clauses are devoted to embezzlement, theft, counterfeiting and forgery, of which the first three were adjudged felonies punishable by death without benefit of clergy. Forgery, including counterfeiting the Bank's seal, could bring six years' imprisonment for the first offence, with hard labour, whipping, the pillory, or all three added at the discretion of the court; the penalty for the second offence was death. The severity of these punishments reflected the brutality of contemporary criminal justice but could also have been a reaction to the widespread counterfeiting of Montreal Bank notes a year or two before. Other features may be noted in the Act: one was a clause which continued the life of the charter to June 1, 1831, unless in the meantime the government should decide to establish a Provincial Bank, in which event the charter of the Bank of Montreal would be vacated after seven years; another was a requirement, "for the better security of the public," that a statement of the Bank's affairs be given the Governor or other properly constituted authority who might demand it.

The Articles had required only that statements should be submitted to the shareholders annually.

The act proclaimed in 1822 marks the beginning of a banking system that owed its success not only to the principles on which it had been founded, but also to the personal ability and integrity of those who operated it. In this connection, it is significant that the petitioners named in the Act of Incorporation were 144 in number, as against the original subscription list of 289. As noted in the preceding chapter, most of the American-owned stock had been repatriated, leaving not more than a dozen stockholders in the United States, among whom were such original stalwarts as Abel Bellows, Nathan Appleton and William Cochran in Boston, John Hinsdale in Middletown, and Nathan Prime, Samuel Ward and the Brevoorts, senior and junior, in New York. Between them they probably owned no more than five hundred shares of stock, or around ten per cent. It is evident, therefore, that the chartered Bank of Montreal, in contradistinction to the earlier private institution, the Montreal Bank, was a Canadian-controlled enterprise.

The parliament of Lower Canada which passed the Act of Incorporation of the Bank of Montreal in 1821 also incorporated two other banks in the same session: the Quebec Bank in Quebec City, with a capital of £75,000, and the Bank of Canada in Montreal, with a capital of £200,000. Both had begun business in 1818 under articles of association almost identical with those of the Montreal Bank. The Quebec Bank petitioned for a charter in 1818 and again in 1819; in the latter instance the bill was passed by the Assembly but was lost in the Legislative Council. The Bank of Canada's first petition for incorporation was submitted in December 1820 and was followed by the Quebec Bank's renewed attempt.

Acts for the incorporation of these two banks were finally passed but, along with that incorporating the Bank of Montreal, were reserved for royal approbation. Assent was granted in September 1822 and proclaimed in Quebec on November 30. In both instances the names of the petitioners, that is, the associated stockholders, were included in the preamble of the Act, as they were in that incorporating the Bank of Montreal. It becomes possible, therefore, by combining the three lists, to establish a roster of most of the persons in Lower Canada who, in 1818, had money and were interested in promoting trade and commerce. But such a combination is almost meaningless for the reason that most of the names are now unidentifiable; all that can be surmised is that the capital assets of the province were much larger than the earlier experience of the Montreal Bank would imply, and that there existed considerable antipathy, if not actual animosity, to the founders of the pioneer institution. Whether prompted by personal envy or commercial jealousy, rivalry of the sort was by no means restricted to Lower Canada. As Fritz Redlich points out in *The Molding of American Banking*, this was the experience of all North American communities when banks were first established. In Lower Canada, knowledge of such rivalries makes for a better understanding of the attacks to which the Bank of Montreal was subjected for many years.

At the time of their incorporation, the stockholders of the Quebec Bank numbered 88 and those of the Bank of Canada, 110. The reason for establishing the former are fairly obvious. The merchants of Quebec simply wanted a bank of their own. In 1808, it may be recalled, they had joined in the petition to incorporate a bank in Lower Canada. In 1815 and thereafter they no longer appeared among the petitioners. When the Montreal Bank opened its Office of Discount and Deposit in Quebec City, so great was the resentment there that for several months it seemed doubtful that sufficient business could be obtained to make the venture profitable. As will be seen shortly, the animosity toward the Bank of Montreal was strong enough to bring on a legislative investigation.

The reasons for the establishment of the Bank of Canada remain obscure. This was a rival Montreal undertaking and, in works on Canadian banking, is usually described as having been the creation of a group of American traders interested mainly in dealing in specie and foreign exchange. In that case the name could only have been a calculated euphemism, but in the light of the non-voting limitations placed on foreign stockholders the assumption seems somewhat improbable, although the Bank of Canada charter did not contain the clause in the Bank of Montreal charter which limited the choice of directors to British subjects by birth, conquest or naturalization, or to persons who had resided for seven years in the province. However, the list of subscribers to the stock of the Bank of Canada, as appended to the petition for incorporation published in the *Journals of the Legislative Assembly of the Province of Lower Canada*, contains only four names that are readily identifiable as American – Gates, Bancroft, Nathaniel Jones Jr., and Thayer – and all four were also shareholders of the Bank of Montreal. The list, of course, also contains many important Montreal business names of the day including several, such as Peter McCutcheon (later to be known as Peter McGill), John Torrance,

Charles Brooke, Joseph Masson, and John Try, who had not initially sub-scribed to the Montreal Bank but who would later become closely associated with that institution. About all that can be deduced from these puzzling records is that human drama and conflict were not lacking in the early days of Canadian banking.

Thomas A. Turner was President of the Bank of Canada, and Robert Armour was its Cashier. It had a relatively short and unsuccessful career and was taken over by the Bank of Montreal in 1831. The Quebec Bank, on the other hand, operated as a successful rival to the Bank of Montreal's Office of Discount and Deposit in the provincial capital for many years.

3.

Until royal assent was granted to its incorporation, Canada's first permanent bank had encountered little criticism, the consensus being apparently that as a private business venture it was the personal concern of the shareholders who owned it and those who chose to deal with it as depositors or borrowers. A growing familiarity with the actual practice of banking, however, gave rise to questioning, criticism, and, finally, to political opposition which made concerted attempts to destroy the banks by undermining public confidence in them. At each stage, the Bank of Montreal was the principal object of attack. The reasons for public reaction are not hard to estimate. In the first place, the introduction of bank-notes in a community suffering from a chronic insufficiency of currency would have had profound reverberations; in the second, the formation of three banks in Lower Canada, where none had existed previously, would have raised questions as to the nature, purpose, and need of such institutions; and, third, the efforts of the banks themselves to obtain charters automatically removed them from the domain of private enterprise to that of public concern.

The first definite indication of such concern appeared in 1820 with the publication of a pamphlet entitled *An Inquiry into the Origin and Present System of Colonial Banks and their Dangerous Effects. With a Proposition for a National Bank.* As Shortt points out, the criticism was directed at the banks while they were still in an unchartered condition; nevertheless, the observations made with respect to the lack of elementary safeguards for the protection of the public interest seem to support the view that Canadian banking owed considerably more to the character of the men who developed it than to any virtues inherent in the system itself.

In the United States, whence the system was derived, the same virtues neither protected the public from innumerable bank failures nor provided a satisfactory national banking system; in Great Britain, another quarter century elapsed before Peel's Bank Act of 1844 finally placed English banking on a stable basis. In the light of these facts and the dangers pointed out in the pamphlet on colonial banking, the Canadian achievement in providing at the very outset a safe, secure, and flexible banking system becomes the more extraordinary, explainable only on a human rather than a mechanistic basis. Like the Canadian bush pilots of a much later generation, Canada's pioneer bankers seem to have been guided more by empirical observations than by theoretical considerations. The writer of the pamphlet chose to remain anonymous and explains the reason in a preface, which concludes with this sentence: "Its [the pamphlet's] purpose is so hostile to the interest of many, that concealment will not be wondered at; but those who are disposed to attribute personal fear or opprobrium, as having the smallest share in it, will very much deceive themselves, and misrepresent it to others." Though written with a Johnsonian pomposity which often obscures its meaning, the pamphlet itself represents an informed analysis of the putative dangers in Canadian banking as it existed at the time. It comments, for example, on "the very singular and unprecedented manner in which the Banks of this country issue their bills," and goes on to question the wisdom of allowing "a Commercial Association, formed for the interest of few at the risk of many," to engage in business "as a public body with whom the interest of everyone is assimilated" without subjecting such associations to searching scrutiny and criticism. Commenting on the fact that in England similar associations would be adjudged illegal, the author goes on to say:

> To prevent monopoly, and for the protection of the general interests of society, it has been the wisdom and practice of every government, to enact the severest penalties; and therefore the Parliament of Great Britain prohibits the Association of any number exceeding six, in any Firm, or Stock Company, unless incorporated by its authority. . . . Without this [protection], the public would be ever liable to the fraudulent impositions of adventuring individuals, who with an ostentatious appearance of fictitious capital, might pillage the credulous, and by an invented prospectus of anticipated gains, induce the sanguine to hazard their hard-earned savings.

CANADA'S
FIRST BRANCH BANK

It was only a matter of weeks after its opening in Montreal that the Bank acquired Daniel Sutherland, the Deputy Postmaster General of British North America, as its agent in Quebec. As the port of entry, seat of the governor and base of military operations, Quebec, with a population of 20,000, was an essential link in the Bank's chain of organization.

The Quebec business proved to be of such importance that on July 20, 1818, Sutherland opened an Office of Discount and Deposit which was, in effect, the first branch-banking office in the colonies. The branch bank was situated at 3 St. Peter Street, one of the two principal commercial thoroughfares, in a building owned by Henry Atkinson. Sharing office space with the Bank was William Price, who had been sent out by the British government during the Napoleonic Wars to procure lumber, and whose descendants built up a large business in Canada's wood and paper industries.

The Bank's operations in Quebec were conducted initially by a staff of three under the management of Sutherland, who held the post of cashier until he retired in 1824. Here we see him bidding "au revoir" to several of his directors on a cold winter day after one of their meetings, which, following the pattern in Montreal, were held twice a week. These directors, nine in number, and headed by a president, constituted the Quebec office's own Board. Chosen independently from amongst the stockholders in that city, they were responsible for all transactions except those in foreign exchange. The Quebec office also issued its own notes, which were distinguished from those of the parent institution by a stamp reading "Payable at Quebec."

Painting by Gerald L. Sevier, A.O.C.A., O.S.A.

Discussing the colonial economy before, during, and after the late war, the writer points out that the mere issue of paper currency will not pay for Canada's import surplus, as so many people seemed to imagine, and maintains that an uncontrolled expansion of bank credit by issue of paper currency could lead only to inflation and ultimate disaster. To avoid that peril, he proposes that bank-note issues be backed equally by specie, but believes that the colonies could support at most one bank for domestic purposes. This should not be a private company, but a government-controlled national bank, a proposal which is set forth in these words:

> It therefore only remains for some impartial member of the present Parliament to do his duty. The general interests and safety of the public, demand this sacrifice of private feeling. The House ought to order a Committee of Inspectors, or Auditors of their Accounts; or enjoin beyond future altercation, the responsibility of the Directors and Stockholders to all the engagements of the Banks. . . .
>
> To attempt the reformation of an evil by the substitution of a solid good, ought not to provoke criticism, or awaken censure. Against perils so conspicuous my design is not to create fear, but to propose an antidote.
>
> To remedy every evil, and to ensure lasting benefit, and success to these Provinces, nothing now remains, but for the Government to establish a National Bank – the profits to be only locally applied, in removing obstructed [sic] navigation, forwarding new settlements, internal improvement, and civic polity. Thus this country might be benefitted, and the mother country, in time, be relieved of some of her burthen.

Disclaiming his ability to formulate the details of such a plan, the writer calls on more able heads to do so, before concluding with this panegyric: "The future Historian of this Colony would say, 'The success of it was entirely owing to the zealous endeavours of ————.' Here, my Lord, is a blank! The name of that Governor who shall fill it up, will be more memorable in future times than that of Maecenas. His be the honor; let the Colony reap the benefit! His grave will have a living monument!"

Like Brutus in his misgivings about Caesar, the anonymous pamphleteer feared the banks not so much for what they were as for what they might become. The subsequent management of Canadian banks shows this fear to have been largely groundless; nevertheless, it reflected opinion current at the time, particularly with respect to the issue of paper currency, dealings in exchange and discounting, and the rapid multiplication of bank charters. To have restricted banking to a single institution would, of course, have created a monopoly, as was the case in Upper Canada; on the other hand, the chartering of three banks led to jealousies which erupted in a legislative inquiry in the closing days of 1823. Aimed primarily at the Bank of Montreal, the investigation sought to determine "if any and what inconveniences have resulted from the Establishment of Banks in this Province." On December 30 a Select Committee of the Assembly was appointed to report with all convenient speed.

While the committee was considering ways and means of conducting its inquiry, two of its members, on January 5, 1824, introduced the following resolution in the House:

> That the President, Vice-President and Directors of the Bank of *Montreal*, of the *Quebec* Bank and of the Bank of *Canada* respectively, be required, pursuant to the several Acts of the Legislature incorporating the said Banks, to lay before the House of Assembly, statements of the Amount of the Capital Stock paid into each of the said Banks, of the Debts due to the same, of the Monies deposited, of the Notes in circulation and of the Cash on hand.

The financial statements of the three banks were laid before the House by the Speaker on January 13, 1824. Published, as was the committee of inquiry's subsequent report, in the *Journals* of the Assembly, they provide the first comprehensive statistical data on Canadian banking available.

The most conspicuous feature of the statements is the ratio of cash on hand to circulation and deposits. In the case of the Bank of Montreal, for example, the ratio was fifty-four per cent, while the cash on hand exceeded the total of the notes in circulation, the first being £102,303 and the second £92,727. The unusually liquid position can be accounted for by the inability of the banks to draw rapidly on supplies of specie as was possible in the United States or Europe, and the consequent need to maintain cash balances large enough to meet any probable demand. Although convertibility does not in itself guarantee against currency inflation, it is evident from these figures that the officers of the Bank of Montreal were most conservative in their issuance of paper money, and contemporary fears of "over-issue" were largely groundless. The corresponding ratios maintained by the other banks in Lower

Canada support the observation. The report also reveals the modest limits within which the banking business was conducted at the period – the total paid-up capital for all three banks was £331,702 and debts receivable from loans and discounts came to £529,364, well under the statutory limit of treble the paid-up capital.

The findings of the committee of inquiry, presented to the House of Assembly on February 28, 1824, were largely inconclusive. Twelve witnesses in all were heard, four of them from the Bank of Montreal, which throughout the proceedings found itself on the defensive. Noah Freer, the Cashier of the Quebec Bank and a prominent figure in the world of business in that city, charged that the directors of the Bank of Montreal were without legal power under their charter to conduct a banking business at any place but Montreal; that the establishment of an Office of Discount and Deposit in Quebec had been not only unnecessary but prejudicial to the Quebec Bank and the public interest; and that the president and directors in Quebec City were mere agents of the mother bank, to which all but minor transactions had to be submitted for approval. The witness also claimed that the Bank of Montreal, as the government depository, was able to draw funds from Quebec City which rightfully belonged there and which should have been used to finance local business. Details of the government account were not forthcoming from Bank of Montreal witnesses, but a government inspector testified that deposits of public monies had varied from £3,000 to £15,000. It was disclosed that this had been a practice for several years, although the Directors' Minutes make no special reference to the government's opening an account with the Bank's Quebec branch.

Freer maintained also that by heavy purchases of Commissariat bills, the Bank of Montreal had been responsible for raising the exchange from a discount to a premium of eight per cent. In Freer's opinion there was room in the province for one bank in Quebec and one in Montreal only, and banks should be prohibited from dealing in foreign exchange. Witnesses from the Agricultural Society of Lower Canada testified that on one occasion they had been refused payment at the Bank of Montreal branch of a warrant for £500, except in dollars at a premium of one per cent or "thirteen penny pieces," but had readily obtained dollars at par from its rival – the point apparently being that as a branch in Quebec of the parent bank, the Office of Discount and Deposit was unable or unwilling to render the service that could properly be expected of a publicly chartered corporation. The references to payment by cheque and to thirteen penny pieces are both interesting, the first reflecting the early use of that form of transferring funds in Canada; the second, the unsatisfactory condition of the metallic currency. Other witnesses dealt principally with the knotty problem of foreign exchange, some agreeing with the Cashier of the Quebec Bank that bank dealings in foreign exchange had been disadvantageous to the public and should be abolished, and others pointing out that were banks in the province to desist from dealing in exchange, the vacuum would be quickly filled by private bill dealers or American banks.

Four witnesses appeared on behalf of the Bank of Montreal: John Stewart, Daniel Sutherland, William Lindsay – the President, Cashier and teller respectively of the Office of Discount and Deposit in Quebec – and Horatio Gates, who made the wearisome three-day journey from Montreal to do so. The burden of their testimony, not unnaturally, refuted most of that which others had delivered: the Quebec branch was operated to provide commercial accommodation and not to drain the community of its resources; the Bank's dealings in foreign exchange were principally on its own account for the purpose of establishing credits in New York and London, and such dealings could in no way affect exchange rates since the latter were governed by conditions in the New York money market. As the final witness, Horatio Gates contended that the Bank's exchange operations kept the rate steadier by preventing speculative fluctuations. A further charge that the Bank invariably stopped discounting (*i.e.*, lending) when buying Commissariat bills was categorically denied. Daniel Sutherland's testimony dealt largely with relations between the head office and the Quebec branch.

The committee agreed to present the report to the House without rendering an opinion, but with the recommendation of the Chairman that it be referred to a Committee of the Whole. It was so ordered, but before any conclusion had been reached the House was prorogued on March 9. Officially, the first of many legislative inquiries resulted in a whitewash. Notwithstanding, the charges of discrimination did contain a semblance of truth. When the Bank of Montreal undertook a house-cleaning a few years later, it was revealed that some borrowers had received favoured treatment at the hands of a few members of the Board. The same charge in fact was to hound the Bank for more than twenty years, particularly during the recurrent financial crises which plagued Canada with the regularity of seven-year locusts. However, legislative interest in the Bank of Montreal remained quiescent until 1829.

4.

In Upper Canada a different set of circumstances combined to give the Bank of Montreal a serious setback and to curb the expansion of its branches for almost twenty years. No political animus was involved directly, nor were the Bank's methods of doing business criticized; the trouble arose instead from its remote and alien character and the desire of the commercial interests of Upper Canada to have a bank, or banks, which they would finance and control themselves. With the rapid growth of the upper province following the War of 1812, it was inevitable that this should have been the case both for reasons of local pride and to satisfy the special banking needs of agriculture and of those merchants whose principal trade was with the United States. Since that trade required cash, the metallic currency of Upper Canada was more depleted than even that of the lower province, where the over-rated silver coins of the French regime still circulated as legal tender and where supplies of silver were more readily procurable from American sources. To make good the deficiency of hard money, merchants' *bons*, or promissory notes for change and small transactions, circulated freely; the upper province had also been flooded with American bank-notes, some of dubious value. In Upper Canada, therefore, as elsewhere in North America, the primary reason for a bank was to supplement the depleted supply of specie by the introduction of bank-notes as a circulating medium; the functions of deposit and discount were secondary and ancillary, and served as the means by which notes were put into circulation.

The first discussions about a bank in Upper Canada occurred in Kingston as early as 1808, inspired by the attempts then being made in Montreal to obtain a charter. Conducting local trade was a small number of merchants, some of whom had engaged originally in the fur trade and had later become agents of large mercantile houses in Montreal. Others had come to Upper Canada after the American Revolution from Albany, Sackett's Harbor, Oswego, and other trading places. It was principally this latter group which initially would have been interested in establishing local banking facilities.

The discussions held in 1808 in Kingston were inconclusive and nothing more was heard on the subject until 1817, by which time the Army Bills had come and gone and the upper province was again experiencing the scarcity of money that had prevailed before the war. Although the decision of the founders of the Montreal Bank to do business under articles of association was not made public until May of 1817, a petition signed in Kingston on

TRIALS OF TRANSPORTATION—EARLY 1800'S

Before the Lachine Canal was built, water transport around Montreal Island was a highly formidable enterprise, the crews having to go ashore and haul their bateaux or Durham boats up the rapids.

The Durham boats pictured here were introduced on the St. Lawrence about 1809, and with a freight capacity ten times that of the bateaux, they replaced many of the smaller craft which had had a monopoly of the traffic above Montreal.

The bateau was flat-bottomed and pointed at both ends, while the Durham boat had a centre-board or slip keel and a transom stern, but both were of shallow draft and could be rowed, poled, or sailed. Downstream from Kingston to Montreal, a Durham boat could transport 35 tons of produce in five days. Upstream, however, the load was reduced to eight tons and, travelling in one- to three-mile spurts called *pipes* (between which the crew stopped for a smoke), the boat took twelve days to make the 200-mile trip.

January 20, 1817, by Thomas Markland and others, was presented to the House of Assembly in Upper Canada on March 3, praying for incorporation as "The Bank of Upper Canada." As in other petitions examined earlier in these pages, the preamble refers to "the great utility and advantage of banks to a commercial people," but unlike any of the others, it refers specifically to the establishment of banks in the United States and continues with these words: "feeling the benefit which the latter [the United States] derive from the ready aid afforded by their banks, to carry on their establishments and improvements in their western territory, which, although of a much more recent date, is in a more flourishing state than any part of this Province, [we] are of the opinion that if found so beneficial in those countries [England and the U.S.], they cannot fail of tending to the prosperity of this Province."

It is apparent that, at the beginning at least, Kingston's incipient bankers were influenced rather more by their knowledge of banking across the Great Lakes than by the example of their mercantile confrères down the river. The capital for the proposed Bank of Upper Canada was to be £100,000 divided into 8,000 shares of $50 each. For some reason, the promoters chose to quote the capital in pounds, and the share denominations in dollars.

The Kingston petition was accorded a much more friendly reception at York than were its predecessors at Quebec. Within four weeks of its introduction into the House, a bill was passed without division on March 27, 1817, as "An Act to incorporate sundry persons under the style and title of the President, Directors and Company of the Bank of Upper Canada." Concurrence of the Legislative Council with some amendments followed on April 1, and the Act was sent to the Lieutenant-Governor for royal assent. However, one of the amendments made the Act forfeit if royal assent were not granted by January 1, 1819. This was indeed what happened. The royal assent was not proclaimed in York until after the appointed date, by which time the Act of Incorporation had expired and had to be passed a second time. In the meantime, a number of associated events occurred. The first of these was the appearance of another banking group in York, the seat of government and home base of the Family Compact, the notorious oligarchy of professional U.E. Loyalists, large landowners, and government officials that ruled Upper Canada for several decades. Observing the success met by the Kingston petitioners in the Assembly, the York group promptly presented a similar petition over several signatures of persons in the Family Compact, praying for incorporation as the Upper Canada Banking Company with a share capital of £100,000 in shares of £12. 10s. provincial currency. Although identical in purpose, the two petitions differed somewhat in content, that from Kingston bearing evidence of originality, and that from York being derived directly from the Montreal Bank's earlier submissions to the Assembly of Lower Canada. While no action was taken on the York petition, it served notice that the entrenched oligarchs of the Family Compact were not insensible to the advantages a bank could bring them and only awaited a propitious moment to secure those advantages for themselves.

It will be recalled that on June 16, 1818, the Board of the Montreal Bank offered agencies in Upper Canada to Thomas Markland in Kingston and William Allan in York, both of whom had Montreal connections. Before further action had been taken, however, a meeting was called in Kingston on July 1 to consider the expediency of forming a private banking association in that city, the local merchants having decided apparently that there was no point in waiting longer for royal assent to their act of incorporation. The meeting resulted in the publication a week later of the Articles of Association of the Bank of Upper Canada, similar to those adopted by the Associates of the Montreal Bank a year before, the only significant difference being a capital of £125,000 divided into shares of £25 each.

An interesting provision made the shares payable on call in gold, silver, or Montreal Bank bills, showing what a high degree of acceptability these latter had attained even at this early date. According to Shortt, the shares were subscribed pretty freely, yet on July 27, Thomas Markland, one of the prime movers of the Kingston enterprise, published a notice that he had been appointed the local agent for the Montreal Bank and that any sum could be obtained at his office for good bills on Montreal or Quebec or for specie. Despite this competition and the opening of a Kingston agency of the Bank of Canada, whose head office was also in Montreal, the promoters of the Bank of Upper Canada raised enough capital to engage in business and to hold their own against their rivals from down-river.

The next act in the bizarre drama occurred during the ensuing session of the Upper Canada parliament, in July 1819, after the new Lieutenant-Governor, Sir Peregrine Maitland, announced that he had received authority to give royal assent to the now defunct Act to incorporate the Bank of Upper Canada. Why London should have granted authority to Upper Canada at a time when the three banking acts of Lower Canada had disappeared into limbo remains a mystery. In any case, the Kingston bill was again submitted and again passed, after which it went to the Legislative Council for concurrence or amendment. When returned to the Assembly early in July, the bill had undergone significant alterations. The most extraordinary was the replacement of the Kingston names by those of members of the Family Compact, again petitioners for incorporation as the Upper Canada Banking Company. The location of the bank was also changed from Kingston to "the seat of government," and a third change provided for government participation, as had the Lower Canada petition of 1808. It now appeared that the Compact had not only captured the Kingston charter but had added thereto a most advantageous clause, since in essence the government and the Compact were as one. In a burst of gratitude for the blessings they had received, the victors lent their support to yet a third bill for the incorporation of the Bank of Kingston with provision to open subscription books in York, Niagara, Amherstburg, and other towns. But at this juncture occurred a new complication. On July 12, 1819, Maitland gave assent to the Bank of Kingston act but reserved that of the Bank of Upper Canada for the royal pleasure.

Having lost the shadow and retained the substance, the Kingston people continued a private banking business under the name of the Bank of Upper Canada, with the intention apparently of raising the enlarged capital required by the charter and combining both institutions as the Bank of Kingston. The plan was never realized. The charter provided for an 8,000-share capital of £200,000, of which £50,000 had to be subscribed and £20,000 paid in before the bank could begin business. By the time subscription books were opened in Kingston and other places in the late summer of 1819, the post-war depression, compounded by the imposition of prohibitive British tariffs, had fallen on Upper Canada, and it was found impossible to raise the required £20,000. As agricultural and commercial activity progressively deteriorated during the two following years, the banking needs of the province were served as they had been before: by the agencies of the Montreal Bank and the private Bank of Upper Canada. As we have seen, the Montreal Bank had no difficulty in circulating its notes through its agents in Kingston and York, but since these note issues withdrew specie from the province, the tendency was to deplete the metallic currency, particularly the silver needed for American payments.

So pronounced had this trend become by the summer of 1820 that the currency in circulation consisted mostly of bank-notes, coins of small denomination, and merchants' IOU's, or tokens made out of brass buttons flattened on a blacksmith's anvil and stamped with the issuer's name. In this situation, the Bank of Upper Canada did a flourishing business by extending credit on security which the conservative Montreal banks refused to consider.

In a community where much mystery still surrounded the business of banking, and where the lack of a satisfactory circulating medium was blamed for the depressed state of business conditions, there were bound to be repercussions. These were heard at the session of parliament held at York in 1821, when a petition was submitted calling for the establishment of a provincial government bank which would issue legal-tender notes against the security of land. The petition was regarded as sufficiently serious to call for consideration by a parliamentary committee. The latter's report repudiated the issue of paper money in uncontrollable amounts but showed concern for the unsatisfactory condition of banking in the province. Commenting on "the great embarrassment experienced throughout this province for want of a circulating medium," the committee further declared that "almost all the money transactions of this province are carried on through the means of the paper of a private bank of this province, not established by charter, or by bills of banks in Lower Canada, which it is obviously contrary to good policy to suffer to continue."

In point of critical appraisal of banking practices the committee's findings were more searching than any previous reports in Canada and can be regarded as a portent of later inquiries which would lead in time to effective banking legislation. The immediate result, however, was the introduction of a bill to incorporate yet a third Bank of Upper Canada, based on the charter of the Bank of Kingston. The bill passed the legislature without difficulty and was accorded royal assent on April 14, 1821.

Few dramatists would dare the invention of the next development. Within a day or two after the incorporation of the third Bank of Upper Canada, there arrived from London royal approbation of the second Act, automatically giving it precedence over the third. Under such curious circumstances was the Family Compact possessed of a charter which would prove financially profitable but politically embarrassing. Of the fifteen members who composed the first board of directors, nine were members of either the Legislative or the Executive Council, and most of the others held similar positions some years later.

The Bank of Upper Canada, despite the eminence of its sponsors, got off to a slow start. The capital was set at £200,000, of which £50,000 had to be subscribed and £20,000 paid in before the bank could engage in business. When it became evident after several months that such a sum could not be raised, a law was passed on January 17, 1822, reducing to £10,000 the requirement as to paid-up capital before beginning business. Of this the government promptly took up its 2,000-share allotment and on March 1, 1822, made a first payment of £1. 5s. a share, or ten per cent, amounting to £2,500. A second call of ten per cent dated June 10, 1822, was made, increasing the government subscription to £5,000, or half the required paid-up capital. Nevertheless, the bank opened for business in July. Much speculation has been devoted by Shortt, Breckenridge and others as to how it was able to do so legally until the government's instalments had been matched from other sources. The strong presumption is that it did so illegally.

There were now two banks named the Bank of Upper Canada in business in the province, the one known as the Kingston or "pretended" bank, and the other as the York bank. The conflict was abruptly resolved in the failure, through irresponsible management bordering on dishonesty, of the Kingston bank, late in September 1822. This was the first bank failure in Canada, and while less serious in extent than contemporary American bank failures (liabilities at the time of the failure aggregated £30,212 against theoretical assets totalling £29,111), the bankruptcy led to another debate on banking practices at the next session of the legislature. One result was a law placing the affairs of the defunct bank in the hands of a commission to be wound up for the benefit of the creditors; another was the reduction of the authorized capital of the Bank of Upper Canada to £100,000, a sum considered more in keeping with the requirements of the provincial economy; and a third was the passage, on January 19, 1824, of an act giving the Bank of Upper Canada a monopoly of note issue by prohibiting any banks which did not "return their notes in specie therein" from carrying on business in the province. The Bank of Upper Canada thus became the provincial bank in fact as well as in name.

The immediate effect of the legislation on the Bank of Montreal was to cause it to close its agencies in Upper Canada, though this went unrecorded in the Minutes. Until the Bank of Upper Canada established foreign connections, the Bank of Montreal remained the main source of bills of exchange; its notes stayed in circulation, and it was able, at an unestablished date, to retain as its representative J. H. Dunn, the Receiver General. Nevertheless, loss of business in the upper province may well have contributed to the difficulties in which the Bank found itself two years later.

EIGHT

EXTERNAL
CONFLICTS

EXTERNAL CONFLICTS

I.

John Gray, the first president, relinquished the office in 1820 at his own request. He continued to serve as a director until the fourth annual meeting of
the Montreal Bank in June 1821, when he declined to stand for re-election.
No further reference to this pioneer banker occurs until March 20, 1888,
when the following Minute was recorded: "The Board authorized a grant of
£50 sterling to Mrs. Thwaites, Aukland [sic], granddaughter of Mr. John
Gray the first president of the Bank." The Civil Status lists at the Old Court
House in Montreal show that John Gray was married in 1806 to Mary Pullman, that his age at the time was "about forty years," and that they had two
children, Martin Eccles and Mary. The latter died in Montreal at the age of
twenty-four, but nothing more is recorded about the son.

John Gray's term of office coincided with the dramatic struggle between
the two great organizations, the Canadian North West Company and the
English Hudson's Bay Company, for control of the fur trade of British North
America. Old loyalties and friendships among Montreal's elite were broken

and emotions ran high as the drama unfolded with the inevitability of a Greek tragedy. Both parties to the conflict were represented on the Bank of Montreal directorate, and it was thanks perhaps to John Gray's gentle personality that the business of the Bank was conducted without any outward signs of tension. During his incumbency also the foundations of Canadian banking were firmly laid and its superstructure successfully projected. He was undoubtedly helped in the labours of management by the previous experience of the vice-presidents who served with him, Thomas A. Turner and George Garden, both of whom had engaged in private banking in the course of their mercantile pursuits.

Whatever the assistance given him, John Gray contributed substantially to the Bank's early success, yet little information about him has been preserved and even the place of his birth remains unknown. As already mentioned, he lived in the village of St. Catherines, now Outremont, and had to drive to the city by carriage. Judging from his frequent absences from Board meetings he suffered from poor health, and this appears to have been the cause of his retirement from active business. He was a member of St. Gabriel's Presbyterian Church, whose congregation constituted the English Protestant social register of the day, but apparently he took no part in the numerous civic activities to which other directors gave generously of their time and money. He died September 13, 1829, aged about sixty-three.

Two men more different in temperament and personality than the first president and his successor, Samuel Gerrard, would be difficult to imagine. Gray was retiring almost to the point of self-effacement; Gerrard was hearty in manner, robust, and mentally and physically powerful – he lived to the age of ninety. In addition to serving as president during six turbulent years, he engaged actively in private business and in the many philanthropic and cultural pursuits which had begun to enlist the support of well-to-do Montrealers. The second president's extramural involvements reflect a range of interests typical of the public spirit which actuated most of the Bank's directors. He was a major in the Volunteer Militia, Justice of the Peace, Director of the Montreal Library, Treasurer and Life-Governor of the Montreal General Hospital, Warden of the House of Industry, Very Worshipful Grand Treasurer of the Provincial Grand Lodge for Montreal and the Borough of William Henry, member of the Montreal Centre Auxiliary Society for the promotion of Education and Industry in Canada, President of the British and Canadian School Society, and President of the Auxiliary Bible Society.

Samuel Gerrard was born in Ireland in 1767 and came to Canada about 1787. He was well connected and probably brought capital with him since he shortly became a partner in the firm of Parker, Gerrard & Ogilvy, then still engaged in the Michilimackinac trade in association with Forsyth, Richardson & Co. and other southwest traders. In 1797 Parker, Gerrard & Ogilvy took part in financing the New North West or XY Company and in 1804, when the rival fur companies were reunited, the firm acquired an interest in the expanded North West Company. Apart from a small stock interest in the company, Gerrard never actively engaged in the fur trade. Instead, he was one of the first Montreal merchants to sense the future importance of the grain trade of Upper Canada and in connection therewith to engage in a wide range of mercantile activities, including the establishment of a branch office in London, England. The firm of Parker, Gerrard & Ogilvy was dissolved sometime after 1811 when Gerrard acquired its former North West interests and founded a new partnership with Robert and Alexander Gillespie, both former fur traders. At the time of Samuel Gerrard's election to the presidency of the Montreal Bank the firm had become Gerrard, Gillespie, Moffatt & Co. and included among its several partners George Moffatt, one of the Bank's original directors.

Nothing untoward occurred to mark the succession of the second president. Elected a director at the annual meeting held in June 1820, he became president the day following, took over the duties of management, and conducted the Bank's business in the conservative manner established by his predecessor. Nine new directors had joined the Board since its inception three years before, among them two future officers – Peter McCutcheon and Thomas Thain, chief accountant of the North West Company, who was to succeed George Garden as vice-president in January 1822. Four of the original American directors had been replaced, leaving Horatio Gates as the sole remaining connection with the United States, and their places had been occupied by such representative Montreal business men as Thomas Torrance of the St. Lawrence Steamboat Co., a rival of the Molson shipping interests, and François Larocque, a retired French-Canadian fur trader.

The staff, too, had undergone several changes since the Bank's opening, the most notable of which was the departure of Henry B. Stone for Boston in March, 1818, causing a general reshuffling of the remaining employees. James Jackson acceded to the position of first, or paying, teller, Benjamin Holmes taking his place as second, or receiving, teller, and Allan McDonell being advanced to discount clerk. This left the second bookkeeper's high desk unoccupied and William Radenhurst was brought in to complete the staff. Shortly afterwards, however, McDonell retired, necessitating the promotion of Radenhurst to fill the vacancy, and the hiring of Lawrence Castle as an assistant clerk. Following the general meeting of 1820, all were confirmed in their latest positions with the customary sureties and continued to discharge their several duties as laid down in the Rules and Regulations. The director of the week was named as formerly, on the allotted discount days commercial paper was subjected to the same careful scrutiny, and Benjamin Holmes continued to make frequent trips to New York to take down gold and bills of exchange on London or bring up silver. Despite a depression which began in 1819 and by 1820 had brought activity in the grain and lumber trades almost to a standstill, the Bank's affairs were in good shape.

The small reserve of £1,957 had to be depleted in 1821 to meet dividend payments, but immigration and conservative banking practice enabled the Bank to maintain a slow but steady growth which was accelerated in the spring of 1822 when the English market for Canadian goods picked up again. While specie dealings with New York declined, those with the Receiver General's office increased. In 1821, also, was begun the construction of the Lachine Canal, the first link in the St. Lawrence waterway and the first important internal improvement voted by the Assembly of Lower Canada. It was financed in part by the Bank of Montreal through advances made on the personal security of two of the commissioners, John Richardson and George Garden.

The stimulating effects of the improved economic environment are reflected in the annual statements presented to the legislature and published in the *Journals* of the Assembly. While the capital stood at £187,500 during the four-year period 1821-25, the Rest was built up from £1,501 to £7,695; the deposits increased to £105,518, discounts to an annual total of £1,851,559, and note circulation to £137,580. By 1822 Gerrard's duties as president had become so demanding that the shareholders voted him an honorarium of £500 at their annual meeting.

Such are the impressions conveyed by the Resolve Book. Studiously impersonal, or made deliberately obscure to conform with the banker's rigid code of secrecy, the Minutes present the same picture of stability and steady growth as had been established during the regime of the first president. The picture is supported by the legislative *Journals*. In contrast with the confused

and mountainous seas through which American banking was then steering
an erratic course, those met by the Bank of Montreal seem uniformly placid,
as if affected only by the long ebb and swell of seasonal commercial activity.
But this would be a most erroneous assumption. In point of fact, the weather
encountered during the six-year incumbency of the second president proved
as stormy as any in the Bank's entire history.

2.

The loss of the Upper Canada agencies was but one of the many problems the
Bank of Montreal had to contend with before the end of its first business
decade. The period was marked by growing political dissension in Lower
Canada, domestic and external economic ferment, and increased criticism of
banks and their operations. Other difficulties, such as the legislative inquiry
of 1824, were relatively minor in effect, but the total made the latter half of
Samuel Gerrard's presidency much more arduous than the first. Although
the Bank's returns to the legislature reveal nothing of the travails of the
period, yet these caused serious cleavages within the Board and finally
brought about a change of management and revisions in the by-laws governing the institution.

Foremost among the domestic difficulties was the close of the long struggle
between the North West Company and the Hudson's Bay Company for control of the Canadian fur trade. Begun in 1804, when the North West Company
and the XY Company reunited to challenge the hegemony of the Hudson's
Bay Company, the conflict found the Canadian company at a competitive
disadvantage because of its extended lines of communication and the high
costs of transportation. Yet the Nor'Westers, led by William and Simon
McGillivray, were able to push their domain to the mouth of the Columbia,
establish posts on all the waters flowing into Hudson Bay, and force their
older rival to adopt their system of trading with the Indians. Before then, the
English company had made the Indians bring their furs to Hudson Bay; under
the goad of North West competition it had to duplicate the latter's posts
wherever they appeared – on the Saskatchewan, the Athabasca and the Peace.

The competition soon became ruinous to both parties, but more particularly to the Hudson's Bay Company, whose stock dropped from £250 a share
in 1809 to £50 in 1814. The decline encouraged Thomas Douglas, fifth Earl
of Selkirk, to accelerate the purchases of Hudson's Bay stock which he had
started in 1808, and by about 1810 he had acquired control of the Honourable

YORK—EARLY 1800'S

First established as a French fort to discourage the Indians from trading with the British, Toronto – or York, as it was called from 1793 to 1834 – had only 456 inhabitants when this painting was done in 1803. Most of these were either soldiers or persons connected with the government of Upper Canada which had moved there in 1797.

Surgeon Walsh's painting shows the waterfront road when it was still known as King Street, a name which was replaced in 1821 by Palace Street and again in 1829 by the present Front Street.

Seen from left to right are the residences of Duncan Cameron, one of the Nor'Westers; Dr. W. W. Baldwin, doctor, lawyer and school-teacher; William Allan, merchant, government inspector and future agent of the Montreal Bank; and Hon. Peter Russell.

Mr. Allan's establishment, to be seen immediately beyond the soldier in conversation with the Indians in the foreground, was at the corner of Frederick Street.

Company, in association with Andrew Wedderburn Colvile. A philanthropist and humanitarian, Selkirk had already attempted, with only limited success, to establish colonies of dispossessed Scottish crofters in Prince Edward Island and Upper Canada, and later had obtained from the Hudson's Bay Company a large tract of land for the same purpose in the Red River Valley.

The first group of the Selkirk settlers travelled to the territory via Hudson Bay in 1811 and were joined by other contingents between 1812 and 1815. From the outset, however, every effort to establish a colony was obstructed by the Nor'Westers, who believed agricultural settlement and the fur trade to be incompatible. In 1816 occurred the massacre at Seven Oaks, in which a party of half-breeds, led by Cuthbert Grant of the North West Company, wantonly killed the governor of the Red River colony and nineteen of his men. The news reached Lord Selkirk at Sault Ste. Marie while he was on his way to the Red River with a party of Swiss mercenaries recruited in Canada, ostensibly as settlers. Reprisals quickly followed. On his arrival at the North West Company headquarters at Fort William, Selkirk, a Justice of the Peace of Upper Canada, arrested William McGillivray and fifteen other North West officers on charges of conspiracy, treason and being accessary to murder, and seized the fort, together with furs to the value of £100,000. The North West captives were sent east under guard while Selkirk and his troops took over Fort William to wreak what vengeance they could for the outrage of Seven Oaks.

From this point on, the struggle for commercial supremacy was enacted on several stages simultaneously: in the northwest, where Selkirk, in 1816 and 1817, committed crippling depredations against North West Company posts; in the courts of Canada, where the actions and counter-actions between Selkirk and McGillivray were not finally settled until 1827; in Washington, where John Jacob Astor induced Congress to pass an act restricting trade licences with the Indians to American citizens; in London, where Simon McGillivray and Edward Ellice, now head of the Phyn-Ellice-Inglis complex, tried first to secure control of the Hudson's Bay Company, but failing that were forced to negotiate a merger which lost to Montreal its oldest and once most profitable single enterprise; and, finally, in the Board Room of the Bank of Montreal, where the declining fortunes of the North West Company threatened to bring ruin to some of the Bank's most important customers.

The confused and complicated story may never be known in its entirety. For one thing, the burning of the North West Company's records at Fort

William before Selkirk's actual occupation of the post leaves a gap which never can be bridged; for another, the precise nature of the negotiations between Ellice, representing the North West Company, and Wedderburn Colvile, representing the Hudson's Bay Company, has yet to be determined. As early as 1792, it may be recalled, the old "Marquis," Simon McTavish, had tried to obtain the right to supply his posts in the northwest by way of Hudson Bay. The attempt was unsuccessful. Neither the Honourable Company nor the British government would consider any modification of the 1670 charter which made Hudson Bay a private sea. In the course of the next two decades the Nor'Westers, first under McTavish and then, after his death in 1804, under William McGillivray, had made various efforts to breach the wall of monopolistic privilege, but the petitions of the Canadians always fell on deaf ears. It was not until 1815 that a crack in the wall appeared. This took the form of conciliatory overtures on Selkirk's part, made in Montreal to William McGillivray. Selkirk was then on his way from New York to the Red River Settlement.

At this juncture the fortunes of the Canadian fur barons were probably at their zenith. In a relatively few years they had extended their domain to the Pacific, established posts throughout the Canadian and American northwest, and induced their arch-enemy to become their supplicant. In the proud mood engendered by these accomplishments, McGillivray countered Selkirk's grudging offer of transit rights through Hudson Bay with a proposal that the companies merge on a basis of two to one, the ratio being in favour of the Nor'Westers. In terms of enterprise and managerial ability this was probably a fair offer, but the negotiations collapsed, leaving both contestants determined to fight to the bitter end.

The struggle was now transferred to the Canadian courts and to the forum of public opinion, where Selkirk pamphleteered to establish the legality of his position, and Edward Ellice, under the pseudonym "Mercator," wrote in rebuttal a series of lengthy articles which were published in the Montreal *Herald* and appeared in translation in the *Spectateur*. The Nor'Westers won the polemical duel and the legal actions that had provoked it. Lord Selkirk was assessed £2,000 damages and left Montreal for Scotland in 1818, a sick and defeated man, while his Canadian opponents remained to reckon the costs of victory. Upon William McGillivray's return from the annual meeting with the wintering partners at Fort William in the summer of 1819, these were revealed to be more serious than anyone in Montreal imagined. The internecine warfare had caused a loss to the company of furs, trade goods, and food supplies, and the far-flung transportation system throughout the west had been disrupted. Many of the wintering partners had become dissatisfied with McGillivray's administration. Even more serious were the effects on the company's cash position.

From its inception, the unincorporated alliance of wintering partners and their Montreal suppliers had been held together by the strength of character of two single individuals, first McTavish and then McGillivray, who financed the company's operations through long-term credits obtained against the seasonal sale of furs in London. The profits had been divided among the several partners with no provision ever having been made to put aside reserves or establish a working capital. The loss of sales in 1817 and greatly diminished returns in the ensuing year now made it apparent that the situation could only be saved by recourse to London. It was under these circumstances that William McGillivray, accompanied by his brother Simon, sailed for England in 1819 to confer with Edward Ellice.

Three alternate solutions were possible: one, to obtain payment from the British government for losses suffered and services rendered by the company in the War of 1812; two, to induce the government to grant transit rights through Hudson Bay and Rupert's Land; three, to effect a merger of the two fur-trading companies while the Nor'Westers were still in a position to negotiate from strength. As on all previous occasions, overtures to the government in London received a negative response; but negotiations with the rival fur company opened favourably. These were again conducted by Edward Ellice for the Nor'Westers and by Andrew Wedderburn Colvile, who after the death of his brother-in-law, Lord Selkirk, wielded controlling interest in the Hudson's Bay Company. The debts of the Honourable Company, according to Ellice, were then around £100,000 against an inventory value of Nor'West assets totalling more than £160,000. The actual financial position of the two companies is obscure, but it seems likely that the more spectacular accomplishments of the Canadians gave them an advantage. Had the negotiations been conducted a few years later, after William Huskisson had become President of the British Board of Trade and begun his attacks on the old mercantile system, it is possible that Edward Ellice could have dictated his own terms as an alternative to being granted the long-sought transit rights.

During the winter of 1820-21, however, there arrived in London two disgruntled North West wintering partners, Dr. John McLoughlin and Angus

BANKING COMES TO YORK

York's thousand inhabitants were still bartering with the Indians when the Montreal Bank inaugurated the community's first banking services in July, 1818 – eight months after its own founding in Montreal. This was sixteen years before York was incorporated as the City of Toronto, with a population of 9,000.

Here we see William Allan, newly appointed agent of the Bank at York, leading to his house – where the Bank's business would regularly be conducted – an emissary from the head office in Montreal.

Allan was one of the little community's most respected citizens, and one of its most versatile. Besides being York's first postmaster, he was the collector of customs duties and the inspector of products for export, and he operated a substantial mercantile establishment as well.

Born in Scotland in 1770, William Allan came to Canada at the age of seventeen, settling first in Montreal where he worked as a junior clerk in the great mercantile firm of Forsyth, Richardson & Co. Later he moved to Niagara and finally to York where he established himself about 1800, going into partnership with another young Scot, Alexander Wood. He was instrumental in organizing the Militia, and during the War of 1812 served with distinction as a major under General Brock. At the end of hostilities, he had attained the rank of colonel.

Allan's establishment was situated at the foot of Frederick Street, at the corner of what was then called King Street, now known as Front Street. An important adjunct to this establishment was the jetty at which the *Frontenac*, shown here, has just docked with the Bank's representative as one of her passengers. Known as the Merchants' Wharf, this property of York's first banker is believed to have been the earliest landing-place for larger craft on Lake Ontario.

Painting by Roy Hewetson

Bethune. In Montreal they had already made overtures to the Hudson's Bay
Company to obtain supplies; in London, their presence revealed a serious rift
in the Canadian ranks. On the strength of it, Wedderburn Colvile's attitude
became less cordial and negotiations which had given promise of reaching a
speedy conclusion were temporarily suspended. Few details are known about
the negotiations that continued in London throughout the spring of 1821, but
on March 26, an agreement was finally reached merging the North West and
the Hudson's Bay Company on a hundred-share basis, of which twenty shares
were to go to the Governor and Company, twenty to the Montreal partners of
the North West Company, and forty jointly to the chief factors and traders
of the two companies. Of the remaining twenty shares, two and a half each
went to Edward Ellice and Simon McGillivray in compensation for their
services as negotiators, five went to "Gov. & Co.," five to the "winterers," and
five to the Hudson's Bay Company "subject to an arrangement with the
Representatives of the late Earl of Selkirk." A further agreement, on March
28, divided the proceeds from land sales, three-fifths to the Hudson's Bay
Company and two-fifths to Ellice and the McGillivrays. Later revisions between the Montreal partners on the one hand and the McGillivrays and Ellice
on the other, as well as between the Hudson's Bay Company and the winterers,
did not alter the original distributions very much, and when all such agreements were finally concluded about 1826, it appears that the Canadian faction
had acquired approximately a 49-per-cent interest in the reorganized Hudson's
Bay Company.

In view of the split in their ranks and their weakened financial position, the
Canadians seem to have come off pretty well, but the North West Company
lost its identity, the headquarters of the trade were moved from Montreal to
London, and the status of the wintering partners was reduced to that of
employees of the new company. Control of the rejuvenated Hudson's Bay
Company, and thus of the famous royal charter of 1670, remained lodged in
the hands of the "Gov. & Co." The Governor and Deputy Governor, with two
members of the Hudson's Bay Company and two of the North West Company,
were to constitute a committee to direct the new company's affairs. Edward
Ellice represented the Nor'Westers on the committee along with Simon Mc-
Gillivray, but when the terms of the merger were revised in 1824, Ellice became
the only representative of the Nor'Westers to remain on the directorate.

Who won the substance and who the shadow? Under the direction of the
London committee and the brilliant management of George Simpson as Gov-

ernor in Canada (he was later knighted for his achievements) the Ancient and Honourable Company went forward to greater and more enduring successes and the former North West partners received dividends according to their interests. But a great Canadian adventure had ended. Soon the old stone warehouse on St. Paul Street was known by another name, and the wharves and depots at Lachine were abandoned to decay, leaving none but a few old Nor'Westers such as David Thompson to mourn the glories of the past. Today hardly a trace remains to mark the place of departure of the mighty fur brigades, the military expeditions, the dedicated missionaries, the explorers and discoverers of much of the interior of North America.

In the voluminous literature on the Canadian fur trade the name of the Bank of Montreal is rarely encountered except perhaps in biographical footnotes. Similarly, the name of the North West Company is singularly absent in the records of the Bank of Montreal. Yet the two were intimately connected. One of the factors that inspired the attempt to establish the Canada Banking Company in 1792 was a need to rationalize the haphazard methods by which the Canadian fur trade was being operated; among the founders and shareholders of the Montreal Bank were several firms which acted as the trade's suppliers, and when the last hand was finally dealt, one of the players was heavily indebted to the Bank while another was its most influential shareholder.

In 1821 no less than four directors had an interest in the fur trade as partners in large supply houses: John Forsyth, John McTavish, George Moffatt, and George Garden. As already mentioned, there had also been elected as members of the Board in 1819 and 1820, when the strife between the rival fur-trading companies had reached the boiling point, Thomas Thain and François Larocque. Thain was a cousin of John Richardson and, in addition to the post he held in the North West Company, was a partner in McTavish-McGillivrays. Larocque was a former XY and North West partner who had the distinction of opening the headwaters of the Missouri to Canadian enterprise. Their election could no more have been coincidental than was that of Simon McGillivray in 1825.

That the Bank's direct concern with the fur trade ever extended beyond the acceptance of commercial paper, endorsed and amply secured, is most unlikely. Nevertheless, after the headquarters of the fur trade were transferred to London, making the Montreal district a minor department of the Hudson's Bay Company, the city was estimated to have lost some £40,000 annually in payments for wages and supplies. Insignificant though the sum may seem today, it was sufficiently large then to bring bankruptcy to several of the Bank's customers and to precipitate the crisis in its affairs referred to earlier in this chapter.

3.

The agreement merging the Hudson's Bay and North West Companies was signed at London and Fort William in the spring and early summer of 1821, but it was not until 1823 that its repercussions were felt by the Bank of Montreal and not until 1825 that they assumed critical proportions. The immediate cause was the assignment and undeclared bankruptcy of McTavish, McGillivrays & Co., the doyen of the fur trade, whose liquidation was greatly complicated by financial conditions in England, where speculation in South American stock promotions had reached proportions comparable with those of the earlier Mississippi and South Sea Bubbles. The boom ended in the closing months of 1825 in the worst financial crisis Great Britain had yet experienced.

The final act in the drama of the northwest fur trade took place on two stages simultaneously, remote from one another but intimately connected; the one in Montreal, the other in London, England. The Bank of Montreal was financially concerned with developments in both theatres. Thus was added a third dimension to the range of its operations, the two others being its Canadian and American activities. With the added dimension came the need for far-reaching decisions respecting managerial responsibilities and banking practices. Complicated by personal loyalties, these led first to serious disagreement among the directors, and eventually to the change in control and management already referred to. While the dissensions were mainly of an internal nature and provoked litttle public notice or reaction at the time, they had a salutary effect on Canadian banking. Before proceeding with the history of the stormy years between 1821 and 1826, consideration of the economic forces that made them so will obviate digressive explanations later. Most of these forces emanated from Great Britain and the United States, but to bring them into a common focus an understanding of the Canadian political and economic environment of the period is indispensable.

Viewed as an isolated occurrence, the loss to Canada of the northwest fur trade appears to have been due to economic forces solely; a simple triumph of logistics over such admirable qualities as initiative, enterprise, and indefatigable purpose. This is the consensus of most economic historians, with the rider that the growth of agriculture would have doomed the fur trade anyway. When viewed in the broader context of Canadian relations with Britain, however, the incident takes on a different aspect. Far from being unique, it becomes but one of numerous frustrations, failures and disappointments suffered by Canada's commercial interests, centred largely in the Bank of Montreal, in their efforts to establish a viable provincial economy within the framework of the colonial-mercantile system. Stating the proposition in another way, may not the final outcome of the struggle between the North West and Hudson's Bay companies have been decided as much by the superior political position of the English company as by blind economic forces?

True, the Nor'Westers had gravely weakened themselves by over-extending their operations, building extravagant installations at Fort William and engaging in costly warfare with their venerable competitors. Nevertheless, the Canadian organization was by far the more capable and aggressive, and, had the Nor'Westers been able to secure transit rights through Hudson Bay, they would probably have continued as a Canadian enterprise. They were unable to do so largely because of their political weakness as colonials in competition with one of the most ancient of all English mercantile monopolies. Furs actually counted for an insignificant part of Britain's external commerce and were of importance only to those who traded in them and those who sold them in the luxury market. But so long as the rights granted by Charles II in 1670 were held by members of the social, political, and financial hierarchy in London, and so long as the mercantile system survived, no outsiders, even those as devoted in their British allegiance as the Canadian commercial group, could have breached, much less scaled, the ramparts of monopolistic privilege.

Considered in this light, much that is confusing in the colonial history of Canada becomes understandable. It seems clear, for example, that the country's slow, erratic, and difficult economic growth, particularly in comparison with that of the United States, was attributable as much to her inferior colonial status as to the causes commonly put forward – the smallness of the population, the meagreness of finance capital, and the obstacles imposed by physical geography. From 1817 to 1834, immigration to Canada from the British Isles was actually greater than to the United States (386,531 and 258,751 respectively); Canada's financial capital, while relatively small, was sufficient to found a number of prosperous banks, promote infant industries, and even embark on such a grandiose project as the Welland Canal. The

Nor'Westers themselves showed the way to the conquest of Canadian geography by spanning the elongated east-west axis with no greater technological assistance than was provided by two primitive inventions – the birch-bark canoe and pemmican.

Notwithstanding such evidence of economic potentiality – and of the capability to realize it, given sufficient capital – the Canadian bourgeoisie could neither overcome official British indifference to colonial economic needs nor compete with the burgeoning American states for the private English capital required to improve Canada's greatest single asset – the St. Lawrence River-Great Lakes navigation system. It was not until the 1820's that Canadian land companies first attracted private British investment, and then only to serve as an outlet for surplus population produced by the industrial revolution. Similarly, it was not until the 1840's, after the Act of Union, that the Imperial Government guaranteed a loan of £1,500,000 to complete the St. Lawrence canal system; the first substantial financial assistance, other than that derived from military expenditures, afforded by the government in London to a Canadian province. It was left instead to such institutions as the Bank of Montreal to channel numerous small individual deposits into productive endeavours.

More has been written about the struggle for self-government in Lower Canada than about any other phase of Canadian history, possibly because it is the most contentious whether from an English- or French-Canadian point of view. It was in essence a struggle for self-determination on the part of the two contending groups, the French-Canadian majority and the English-speaking minority, and as such has been interpreted as almost wholly constitutional and political in character. But if one follows the repeated failures of the minority, as represented by the English commercial group, to influence Imperial policy with respect to Canada's economic and commercial needs, a different picture emerges.

Shorn of its racial and religious complications, the struggle for self-government in Lower Canada closely resembles that which occurred in the Thirteen American Colonies half a century earlier. The parallels are seen in the emergence of constitutionally opposed parties, popular and loyalist; in the clashes between royal governors and elected assemblies; in the bitter controversies over the powers of the judiciary; in the frequent prorogations of legislatures; in the suppressions of newspapers and the arrests of editors on charges of seditious libel; and finally, in the prolonged struggles for responsible govern-

SCENE OF FUR-TRADE STRUGGLE—1816

Fort Kaministikwia was renamed Fort William in 1807 in honour of the chief Nor'Wester, William McGillivray. Inside the palisade lay a complete settlement which was reputed to have cost £50,000 and where at times as many as 3,000 people gathered in celebration of a year's business.

The building in the centre was the luxuriously appointed dining hall where each summer the winterers met with their agents from Montreal. The "ranges" surrounding it contained living quarters, and the smaller buildings housed offices, stores, workshops and a jail.

The fort was captured in 1816 by Lord Selkirk in reprisal for the massacre at Seven Oaks, and five years later, Simon McGillivray, at a highly emotional meeting in the great hall, informed the wintering partners that henceforth they were working for the Hudson's Bay Company. Thereafter, the fort decayed because the trade routes were changed, but it was not closed until 1878.

ment (*i.e.*, democratic institutions) through control of the purse. So many effects in common suggest a common origin. It is to be found in the incompatibility of exploitative mercantilism and British parliamentary institutions, however limited their form.

While the struggle against colonialism can be easily followed in all its stages in the Thirteen Colonies, the identical struggle in the Canadian colonies a half century later was confused and inconclusive. In the Thirteen Colonies, heterogeneous groups of Anglo-Saxons with infusions of Dutch, Huguenot-French and Swedes divided along lines of personal loyalties, economic self-interest and political conviction to produce the American Revolution. Inspired by the radical teachings of the French school of political philosophy, the War of Independence was largely ideological in character and split the colonies into two clearly defined parties, loyalist and rebel—it was in fact a civil war. In Canada, on the other hand, no philosophic principles were involved, no important ideological dialogue was inspired, and rebellion produced abortive insurrection and nothing more. The Canadian background engendered three disparate forces divided along political and economic lines: a colonial administration which was predominantly military in character until 1791; a French-Canadian population which grew from 65,000 to 145,000 people during the same period but remained aloof and quiescent; and a commercial group made up of Anglo-American victualling contractors and traders who came to Canada with the British armies and who, augmented in numbers by the arrival of other new settlers, American and Scottish, quickly took over the trade and commerce of the country.

From the outset, the interests of the two language groups, the old and new Canadians, were divergent and conflicting, making the position of the Executive virtually that of referee between them, or failing that, of intermediary between one or the other and the Imperial Government in London. The French were determined to defend their own way of life; the others insisted on their rights as British subjects. Today it would seem that irrespective of differences in race, language, and religion, the French-Canadian and commercial groups, as colonial subjects occupying a common land and dependent on it for their living, shared a community of interest which should have made them allies against the laws and ordinances of a well-intentioned but poorly informed Imperial power. Had such a community of interest become apparent at the time, or had either of the political groups produced the leadership to recognize it, the history of Canada might have been very different. Instead, cleavages developed, particularly after the introduction of British parliamentary government on the limited legislative level, cleavages that both distorted and retarded the growth of Canada for decades and may, indeed, have left their permanent effects.

Incongruously enough, it was the commercial English-speaking group rather than the French-Canadian that first became intransigent, and it is its fortunes, and misfortunes, that principally concern us here. The commercial-political pressure group first appeared on the Canadian scene in 1764, when its small membership began agitating against Governor James Murray's reform of the currency, eventually forcing his recall to London in 1766. Thereafter, the political efforts of the minority group were distinguished more by failure than success. Despised by a succession of aristocratically-minded soldier governors, the group was unable to modify those provisions of the Quebec Act which retained the French seigneurial system of land tenure and made the outmoded and uncodified *Coutume de Paris* the commercial law of the province, rendering business contracts virtually unenforceable. As the commercial interests of the colonies were ignored in 1763 and 1774, so the Imperial Government failed to take account of their position during the next two decades in the negotiation of the border in 1783 and 1794 and the imposition and retraction of the Navigation Acts.

Meanwhile, the demands of yet another Canadian political force, the newly arrived United Empire Loyalists, had brought about the division of old Quebec into two provinces. Each was given a royal government of the type tried unsuccessfully in the Thirteen Colonies forty years earlier, consisting of an executive, legislative council, and judiciary, all responsible to the Crown, and a popular assembly. In this instance, members of the commercial party, among them John Richardson and Adam Lymburner, another leading Canadian merchant, appeared before the House of Commons in London to explain the realities of Canadian geography and demography. They warned particularly against any division of Quebec that would make its English-speaking minority politically helpless while creating an interior province dependent on revenues derived mostly from customs duties imposed and collected in the maritime province. Despite this advice the Canada or Constitutional Act was passed in London and became effective in the closing days of 1791 with the economic and fiscal results foreseen by Richardson, Lymburner, McGill and other Canadians.

The introduction of representative government in Lower Canada resulted in the polarization of two divergent points of view and the emergence of two political parties to press for them. Yet the first few parliaments passed in relative harmony, the French Canadians seemingly content with the *status quo* and eloquently appreciative of the magnanimous treatment accorded them by the British Crown, the English-speaking or commercial party not yet fully sensible of their ineffectuality as a progressive enclave in a static agrarian environment. This position did not become entirely apparent until the legislative session of 1805, when bills introduced for internal improvements foundered on the rocky question of taxation. In the ensuing impasse, the French-Canadian leadership was not so much opposed to economic progress *per se* as to any kind of progress for which the local population would have to pay. If the commercial interests of Montreal and Upper Canada wanted internal improvements let them get the money from the Imperial Government or elsewhere, not by direct land taxes wrung from the hard-earned savings of the farmers on the banks of the St. Lawrence.

It is at this time that the economic motivations of the struggle for political power in Lower Canada are seen more clearly – in the widening breach over the question of taxation and the disposition of provincial revenues; in the identification of the English and French as "have" and "have-not" parties; and in the rising costs of government rife with patronage bestowed on favourites many of whom never set foot in Canada. Known as the Château Clique, from the Château St. Louis in Quebec where the governor resided, the last-named group, because of alleged corruption, precipitated the demand for responsible government that led finally to rebellion. Political attitudes and social connections made most members of the commercial class allies of the Château Clique – the Executive Council and Legislative Council – rather than of their fellow-colonials, the French Canadians.

It is commonly believed that the War of 1812 engendered a new spirit in Canada and marked the dawn of Canadian nationhood. It seems rather to have widened the political chasm dividing the "have" and "have-not" parties in both provinces by bringing unprecedented prosperity to the "haves" while leaving the position of the "have-nots," particularly in the lower province, virtually unaltered. A legislative stalemate next developed in which the French-Canadian popular party adopted the strategy of obstruction, and the commercial English party the tactics of expediency. Blocked in most of their efforts to strengthen the economy, the commercial interests were also frustrated in their attempts to come to agreement with Upper Canada with respect

FIRST
FOREIGN-EXCHANGE
TRANSACTION

Although the notes of the fledgeling Montreal Bank were rapidly accepted at their face value, many transactions, especially those with merchants in other countries, continued to be conducted with gold and silver coins.

The Bank soon saw that through its foreign connections and its dealings with the Commissary General it would be able to satisfy most of its customers' foreign needs with bills of exchange. Consequently, the directors began to seek buyers for specie not needed by the Bank as a reserve against the redemption of notes; it was soon found that merchants in Boston and New York needed silver for their dealings with the East Indies, a trade in which Canada could not partake because of the British navigation laws.

The first of the resulting foreign-exchange transactions took place in the middle of January 1818 when the Bank's vice-president, Thomas Turner, set out for Boston with 130,000 Spanish silver dollars in 65 kegs weighing 100 pounds each. Most of this coin had come to the Bank in payments on account of capital stock, or as deposits.

As noted in the text, such transactions formed a common and rewarding part of the Bank's early business, but this particular instance, as well as being the first, was probably the most ambitious. To transport an unrelenting load of 6,500 pounds along primitive roads through the mountain passes of New England must have been a gruelling task indeed. The convoy is seen here as it prepares to depart from one of the large hostelries which even at this time were to be found snuggled in the valleys of Vermont and New Hampshire.

Painting by James Walker

179

to import tariffs and the division of customs revenues. As was predicted by Richardson, the creation of two separate provinces gave rise to irreconcilable economic interests.

Finding the Executive as powerless against the Assembly as themselves, the leaders of the commercial party now turned to London. With the support of the Governor, Lord Dalhousie, and a strong London lobby, they presented their grievances and recommendations to the British government. The principal grievance concerned French-Canadian domination, which, it was asserted, was negative, racially prejudiced, and under reactionary clerical influence. To correct these allegedly intolerable conditions, the petitioners urged that the provinces of Lower and Upper Canada be united under a single government in which English would become the single official language and English ascendancy would be assured by requiring a property qualification of £500 – far beyond the ability of most French Canadians to meet – and unequal representation. Lower Canada, with around 400,000 people, was to receive fifty seats, while Upper Canada, with a population of less than 130,000, was to have forty. Provision was made for frequent redistribution, Upper Canada then being the faster-growing province.

The proposed bill would have given the petitioners almost everything they wanted. Even without French-Canadian consultation, however, objections raised in the British House of Commons resulted in two separate bills: the Canada Trade Act, 1822, and a revised Union Act, which was held in abeyance to sound out Canadian opinion.

The Trade Act was generally innocuous in that it did no more than set up arbitration machinery for the customs dispute between the provinces; the Union bill, on the other hand, foreshadowing the assimilation of the French-Canadian community, aroused an immediate storm of protest in both Lower and Upper Canada. The bill was dropped in London until its resurrection by Lord Durham almost twenty years later, but the incident left both parties bitter and revengeful: the French-Canadian for the attempted betrayal of their constitutional rights; the English because of the failure, and by so little, of a manoeuvre designed to remedy the weaknesses in their position as an ineffectual political minority in Lower Canada, cut off from their English-speaking compatriots in the upper province.

The Union bill of 1822 was without immediate economic significance; nevertheless, its withdrawal constituted a major set-back to Canada's commercial interests, as did two other events that followed. One was the failure to have Montreal annexed to Upper Canada: this would have removed the commercial metropolis from French-Canadian "domination," and would also have had far-reaching effects from the point of view of the whole Canadian banking system; for then the Bank of Montreal would have been able to establish branches in Upper Canada at an early date, thereby promoting the growth of that province and perhaps averting the stunting influence of the Family Compact and the worst effects of the financial disaster of 1837. The other factor was the outcome of a campaign to induce the British government to build a St. Lawrence canal system at the expense of the British taxpayers. A canal was built, but military defence rather than social or economic needs provided the necessary sanctions. The result was a waterway from Montreal to Kingston, on Lake Ontario, via the Ottawa River and a series of small connecting lakes and rivers. Even before it was well begun, American canals joining the Hudson River with Lake Champlain to the north and Lake Erie to the west were in operation. With the addition of a feeder line from Lake Ontario southward to the Erie Canal, Upper Canada's exports were attracted to the American route by the economics of transportation and later by the advantages of bonding privileges. Thereafter ended the splendid dream of making the commerce of the expanding American middle west tributary to Montreal and the St. Lawrence River.

.

4.

Mercantilism cannot be held solely responsible for the succession of obstacles encountered by every attempt to lay the foundations of a broader Canadian economy. For example, British agricultural, rather than mercantile, interests were responsible for the long delay in securing preferences on Canadian wheat and flour while the beneficial preferences granted colonial timber in 1807 were dictated by naval and mining needs and were actually inimical to the long-established London-Baltic timber trade. However, it can be stated categorically that where British and Canadian economic interests came in conflict those of the colonies were invariably sacrificed.

Not only was this inherent in the mercantilist philosophy, it was enhanced by the smallness of the Canadian population and the few products the provinces had to offer. Limited, as they were, to the southerly range of the coniferous forest, their products were confined to fish, fur, timber, potash, and finally wheat, in contrast with such valuable staples as indigo, cotton, tobacco, and sugar grown in the United States. In fact, it was not until industrialization in Britain had produced large-scale emigration that the Canadian colonies attained pronounced utility, and not until the middle of the century that the growth in population was sufficient to attract British venture capital in appreciable amounts.

Another factor, which may have had a more unfortunate effect on Canadian economic progress than any other, was the preoccupation of Great Britain and of the United States with their own tremendous affairs. In competition with the problems and opportunities present in both countries, Canada's economic or political difficulties had little significance to anyone save the habitants along the banks of the St. Lawrence, the pioneer settlers of Upper Canada, the merchants of the little towns, and the small band of Montreal enterprisers, seized prematurely with the promise of the future.

From 1791, the year that saw the creation of the provinces of Lower and Upper Canada, until 1841, the year of their federation, Great Britain was almost continuously engaged in conflict abroad or convulsive readjustment at home. In the international arena were the wars with France and the diplomatic and military manoeuvrings that followed; in the domestic, the ideological ferment provoked by the American and French revolutions and the economic, social, and political dislocations caused by the industrial revolution.

Such was the magnitude of the twenty-year war with France, and so great were its demands on Britain's resources, that every facet of Imperial policy, whether fiscal, financial, industrial, naval or military, had of elementary necessity to be directed towards the single goal of victory. By the time that was attained, and France temporarily reduced to the position of a secondary European power, the British national debt stood at £846,000,000, the world's largest until World War I. The ability to sustain and win the prolonged contest was based on two main factors: naval supremacy, and industrialization. With command of the seas, Britain was able to increase her world-wide commerce while effectively blockading the European continent; the industrial revolution made her the world's first great industrial power, a position she would maintain throughout the nineteenth century. But she reaped other fruits of her industrial transformation—mass unemployment, financial panic, and the periodic disruption of her monetary and banking systems.

Under such circumstances, is it to be wondered at that the distant and quite unimportant British North American colonies should have been left almost wholly to themselves and to the succession of unimaginative proconsuls appointed to administer their affairs? Yet Britain's preoccupation with her own immense concerns was no greater than that of the United States, the one other country whose policies, actions, and even mere presence, exerted profound influences on life in Canada.

In 1792, the year of the first parliamentary sessions in Lower and Upper Canada, the United States had a population of four million against Canada's 160,000, and was on the threshold of an expansion that by 1850 would multiply its population sixfold and extend its boundaries to the shores of the Gulf of Mexico and the Pacific Ocean. The westward surge to occupy the virgin lands began soon after the Revolution. Such was its volume that by 1803 Kentucky, Tennessee and Ohio had the necessary 60,000 population to acquire statehood. Swelled by immigration after the close of the Napoleonic Wars, the tide rolled westward to Illinois, Indiana and Missouri, the cotton-growing lands of Alabama and Mississippi, and along the trails that led on to the southwest, the Oregon Country, and finally across the Rockies and the Sierras to California. Meanwhile new manufacturing industries had come into being in New England while in the south the cotton gin and slave labour had given rise to one of the richest agricultural empires ever known. Accompanying the explosive growth that registered an increase of one-third in population every decade were political adjustments that kept the Republic in a constant state of intellectual turmoil as the centre of power shifted from federalist New England to agrarian Virginia and eventually to the egalitarian Tennessee of Andrew Jackson.

The question recurs: under the circumstances, how could the United States, involved in the demands and excitements of its own development, have been other than indifferent to the small colonies beyond its northern frontier, the one alien and French, the other Anglo-Saxon and frankly hostile to republican institutions? There are of course many events and circumstances that seem to indicate a desire on the part of the United States, from the time of the Revolution onwards, to annex Canada. The most obvious and frequently cited of these are the War of 1812, the Hunters' Lodges of the 1830's, "Fifty-four forty or fight," the Fenian raids, and the cry of "Manifest destiny" heard throughout the westward expansion. However, their significance can be greatly exaggerated. As stated earlier, the United States turned its back on Canada during the revolution and, except for markets and investments, has maintained much the same attitude to the present day, despite seeming contradictions. During the War of 1812 the refusal of American militia to cross the border was probably a truer indication of American public opinion than the demands of the western War Hawks outraged by the brutal savagery of Indian guerrilla warfare in the Ohio Country – "The Bloody Ground." The war itself, often .called the Second War of Independence, was essentially a maritime conflict, provoked by the French and British blockades with their contemptuous disregard for neutral shipping rights. Had there been any desire to annex Canada, it is inconceivable that the Monroe Doctrine should have been proclaimed within a decade. The other events cited to support the annexation myth require less consideration. The border forays of 1838 and 1866 amounted to little more than armed banditry and were without public support; the Oregon boundary question never did result in fighting, and Manifest Destiny, once the Texas and Oregon questions had been settled, was little more than an electioneering slogan, never seriously debated in the United States Congress. Even had these incidents been more serious, another factor precluded any possibility of annexation, That was the slavery question, which became one of the dominant forces in American politics as early as the Missouri Compromise of 1819. From that date on, the Southern States would not have tolerated the addition of four or more abolitionist states which the annexation of the Canadian provinces would have entailed. Any doubts on this point are dissipated by reference to the American reaction to Canadian annexation overtures in 1849, by which time North-South tensions had already made the proposal a political impossibility. Objective appraisal of American attitudes and reactions toward Canada shows in fact that they were identical with Britain's: like the mother country, the United States used the colonies when it was profitable to do so.

As frustrating to English Canadians as the indifference of both Britain and the United States was the attraction that the erstwhile American colonies continued to exert in the mother country, particularly on her bankers, private investors, and commercial interests. Before the Revolution, the Thirteen Colonies had been Britain's best customer, and vice versa; no sooner was peace declared than the old trading relations between London on the one hand and Philadelphia, New York, and Boston on the other, were renewed. As early as 1783 John and Francis Baring & Co., later the House of Baring, opened negotiations with Robert Morris to represent them in the United States. To this connection were shortly added those of other English correspondents of equal stature in New York, Charleston, Baltimore, and Boston. With the stability given to American finances by Hamilton's fiscal policies and his establishment of the First Bank of the United States, British and Dutch capital flowed to the

United States to profit by mercantile ventures, land speculation, and the financial needs of both federal and state governments. Through these overseas correspondents were arranged the negotiations with the Barbary pirates, the liquidation of the government's stock in the First Bank of the United States, and the funds required to conclude the Louisiana Purchase. So great was London's faith in the American future that by 1809, when application was made to Congress by Secretary of the Treasury Gallatin to renew the twenty-year charter of the First Bank of the United States, it was found that a majority of the stock was owned in England, although no alien could serve as a director.

Interrupted for seven years by the continental blockades of France and England, Anglo-American commercial relations were resumed as soon as news of the Treaty of Ghent could cross the Atlantic. Peace found the United States almost bankrupt, its currency depreciated, and dependent on an inadequate private and state banking system, but with the beginnings of industry established in New England and a merchant marine grown capable by years of blockade and privateering. Once again Britain stepped into the breach; her government by revising the Navigation Laws to place American shipping in a competitive position; her bankers by supplying the capital to tide the federal government over its financial crisis. With the establishment of the Second Bank of the United States and a return to Hamilton's fiscal policies, dynamic growth resumed—in the shipyards and on the seas, in the shops and factories of New England, in the cotton fields of the south and along the wagon roads leading to the west. Indiana gained statehood in 1816, Illinois in 1818 and Missouri in 1821. In 1807, there were but fifteen mills with 8,000 spindles in operation in the United States; by 1815 the number of spindles had risen to 500,000, tended by 76,000 workers.

Accompanying and supporting the explosive energies of the people, bold plans for roads, canals and internal improvements of all kinds were undertaken in New York, in Pennsylvania and in each new state as it was formed, with seeming disregard for the difficulties or the costs involved. Most of those costs were met, of course, by the dynamic growth of the economy itself, although in many instances public indebtedness was repudiated, usually because of financial crises in Great Britain, which spread to the United States and Canada. To a very large extent, however, the enormous sums of capital required to finance state governments, construct great public works, and start new industries was supplied by British and European investors through the agency of English, Dutch, and French banking houses, notably the House of Baring. In contrast with the British capital that flowed freely to the "rebel" United States, that received by the loyal Canadian provinces was almost negligible. To quote J. B. Brebner: "Caught up in this interplay of overpowering forces, the colonies [Canadian provinces] had to puzzle out their individual courses as best they could in terms of their local interests and ambitions, and of the best accommodation to them that they could extract from each other, from Great Britain, and from the United States. Mere survival was an achievement in itself. Anything beyond that evidenced abilities of a high order in the colonial leaders."

5.

In terms of survival and leadership, it is interesting to compare the experience of the Bank of Montreal during the protracted period of political unrest with that of its great contemporary, the Second Bank of the United States. Despite the difference in magnitude and the fact that the government was a stockholder of the U.S. bank, the two institutions were similar in many respects. They were based on identical principles of specie convertibility; both were government depositories, and their note issues were accepted for the payment of public and private debt. The Second Bank of the United States, however, at the end of its twenty-year charter, was destroyed by its political enemies, while during the same period the Bank of Montreal continued its growth without serious challenge to its position as Canada's leading financial institution.

The explanation is to be found in part, of course, in the dissimilar functions and environments of the two banks, the one national in scope and the other provincial. In the United States, the collection and management of the public debt put the Second Bank of the United States in a position where it could indirectly affect the fortunes of people everywhere, particularly those in new states and territories where capital was needed for expansion and little better security could be offered than the promise of the future. In such circumstances political pressures developed in favour of local and state banking facilities, becoming in time so strong that they were able to destroy the federally controlled monopoly. Public debt in the Canadian provinces, on the other hand, was negligible, the finances being largely the concern of the Imperial Government in London. With neither the problems nor the opportunities deriving from the management of such a debt, the Bank of Montreal, while serving as the government depository, was able to continue as it was begun: a commercial bank making carefully selected short-term loans, buying and selling foreign exchange, and circulating its notes to an extent determined by its specie reserves and the changing economic requirements of the country.

It may appear from the foregoing that the uninterrupted growth of the Bank of Montreal, and of banking in Canada generally, was due less to management than to the colonial environment. In part this is true. While the political structure of the United States, coupled with its explosive expansion, fostered divisive experiments that kept American banking in a fractured condition for almost a hundred years, that of Canada, together with a much less rapid rate of growth, fostered both the survival of conservative banking practice and, by the proliferation of branches, its eventual extension to all parts of the national domain.

Except for its later national expansion, the Bank of Montreal was not unique, of course. Commercial banks of great stability and strength were established in many individual states of the Union. Nevertheless, there were factors present in the Canadian scene that were lacking in the American, and these contributed importantly to the growth of the Bank of Montreal along lines of cautious conservatism. One of those factors was the limited nature of the colonial economy and its dependence on a single overseas market characterized by erratic and unforeseeable fluctuations in price and demand. There resulted problems with respect to domestic financing which could be met satisfactorily only by the exercise of constant vigilance and the willingness to adapt to new situations without jeopardizing the basic tenets of commercial banking. To deviate from them was to court disaster, as will be seen in the succeeding chapter. Unlike the expansive economic climate across the border, that of Canada rarely inspired, much less encouraged, gambling on the future.

Another factor in the moulding of Canadian banking as exemplified by the Bank of Montreal was the manner in which the corporation, unlike the Second Bank of the United States, succeeded in remaining politically aloof in the midst of confused and even chaotic political tensions. Although subjected to two legislative investigations, one of which has already been dealt with, the Bank did not become a focus for the kind of political attack that bedevilled its American contemporary throughout its twenty-year existence – this despite the fact that, to Papineau and other leaders of the popular party, the Montreal institution was an instrument of sinister financial power controlled by a ruling oligarchy of which the Château Clique was the detested symbol.

As a corporate entity the Bank of Montreal was never in its early days a participant in political controversy. Until 1827, the only legislative councillor connected with the Bank was the Honourable John Richardson; in that year his partner, John Forsyth, became a member of the Council as did other officers subsequently. Four directors – John Molson Sr., George Garden, Austin Cuvillier, and James Leslie – were elected to the Assembly between 1817 and 1827 but while Molson was an ardent partisan of the English connection, Garden was a moderate, and Cuvillier and Leslie were both adherents of the popular party until 1834, when the incendiary "Ninety-two Resolutions" paved the way to rebellion and lost Louis-Joseph Papineau most of his moderate followers. It goes without saying that many, and perhaps most, of the Bank's shareholders, and hence directors and officers, were supporters of the English party. It is true, also, that John Richardson and others closely associated with the Bank received their full measure of government patronage. Nevertheless, when all the evidence has been appraised, an impressive fact emerges: the men who managed the Bank during its formative years were able to maintain a political detachment as bankers and at the same time subjugate their own personal points of view, rivalries, and interests to the needs of the shareholders and customers and the commercial community at large.

The ability to do these things came not only from strength of character and hard-headed commercial instinct but also, as already shown, from the fact that the members of the Board were representative of the three principal commercial groups in Montreal: the older mercantile houses trading in British exports and imports; the former American nationals with U.S. banking connections engaged in the Vermont and New England trade, and firms and individuals whose business dealings were confined largely to domestic trade or other enterprise. From its very inception, therefore, the Bank of Montreal reflected, as did no other institution of the time, the three-way character of Canada's economic situation as a trading country. Serving both the needs of government and the commercial community, the Bank thus became the principal intermediary for payments and collections arising from the commercial and financial relationships between Canada, Great Britain and the United States. While hardly the "linchpin" of Churchillian oratory, the Bank was an indispensable link in the complex apparatus of Canadian trade and commerce.

NINE

INTERNAL

CRISIS

INTERNAL CRISIS

I.

Addressing the eighth annual meeting of the Bank of Montreal on June 6, 1825, the President, Samuel Gerrard, was able to report the most satisfactory twelve months' business the corporation had yet experienced. The dividend of six per cent had been maintained, and the rest fund had grown to £7,695. In a period when the practice of building a reserve from undivided profits had yet to become widely established, a rest fund amounting to approximately four per cent of the paid-up capital was a matter to be viewed with satisfaction. As for the other indices of activity and growth – deposits, note circulation, and discounts – each showed a satisfactory gain over the preceding year: so satisfactory, in fact, that the stockholders unanimously resolved that the President "be requested to accept the sum of one thousand pounds cy as a remuneration for his valuable services" and "in acknowledgement of the benefits and advantages which the Bank has derived from his superintendence of its transactions." Meeting the next day, a new Board of Directors re-elected Samuel Gerrard president and Thomas Thain vice-president for the ensuing year and raised the salary of the Cashier, Robert Griffin, to £600 with the customary perquisites. Both the remuneration to the President and the increased salary granted the Cashier were generous for the day and indicated a strong endorsement of the manner in which the Bank's business had been conducted. Yet, before three months had passed, Samuel Gerrard was charged with irregular conduct, and four months later was declared a defaulter to the Bank. As such he could neither transfer any Bank shares standing in his name nor have access to his own account.

At the time Samuel Gerrard was one of the pillars of Montreal society, a leader of its financial and commercial world, and the recipient of the most distinguished tributes the city had to offer. His personal honesty and integrity were never questioned; he was, in fact, specifically absolved from having any personal interest in or receiving any personal gain from the transactions brought under scrutiny. In this light, it is difficult to understand why he should have been placed in such an invidious position. At worst he was guilty of a technical and by no means unprecedented violation of the by-laws. Was he the object of some personal animosity, or were larger issues and principles involved?

The first impression is that Gerrard was indeed the victim of persecution at the hands of a former business partner. But as the story unfolds in the studiously obscure pages of the Resolve Book, it becomes manifest that larger issues were in question, among them problems arising from economic developments in Great Britain and the inability of the Gerrard management to cope with them. Actually at stake was not only the solvency of the banking business but the ability of the institution to meet the future in a changing Canadian environment. Viewed in this light, the impeachment of Samuel Gerrard is seen to have been the first encounter in a prolonged struggle between two historically opposed groups for control of the Bank's management and policies. Enacted against a background of economic collapse in Great Britain and failure, foreclosure and bankruptcy in Canada, the conflict marks a significant turning in the history of the Bank of Montreal.

Largely responsible for both the conflict and the changes it brought about was George Moffatt, one of the Bank's founders and a director from 1817 to 1819 and again from 1822 to 1835. Described in 1833 by Governor Simpson of the Hudson's Bay Company as "without exception the most influential man in Canada," Moffatt was born in Durham County, England, in 1787, and came to Canada in 1801 when thirteen years of age. While still in his teens young

Moffatt entered the service of Parker, Gerrard & Ogilvy, transferred to McTavish, McGillivrays & Co., and saw service as a brigade clerk with both the XY and North West companies until 1810, when he formed a brief partnership with Alexander Dowie, a nephew of Sir Alexander Mackenzie. Soon afterward he rejoined the Gerrard-Ogilvy house, becoming a partner in Gerrard, Gillespie, Moffatt & Co., and subsequently in Gillespie, Moffatt & Co., which he eventually controlled. With branches in Quebec, Upper Canada, and London, the Moffatt company shared the commercial leadership of Montreal for a decade or more with the still powerful house of Forsyth, Richardson & Co. and with the several partnerships of the former Vermonter, Horatio Gates. In association with Gates, Moffatt organized a commercial intelligence service to keep dealers in Upper Canada informed as to British prices and marketing prospects for such colonial products as wheat, flour, timber, and potash. He also took a leading part in the agitation for Union and the granting of wider colonial preferences on Canadian export commodities. He served in 1824 as a member of the committee for the improvement of Montreal's harbour.

Despite his earlier allegiance, George Moffatt became one of the most fervent partisans of Lord Selkirk and the Hudson's Bay Company in their feud with the McGillivrays and the North West Company. In September 1819, he became the connecting link between Wedderburn Colvile of the Hudson's Bay Company in London and the two Nor'West partners, Angus Bethune and Dr. John McLoughlin, later "the father of Oregon," whose disaffection prolonged the negotiations several months and undoubtedly weakened the Nor'West position. While Moffatt had no part in the negotiations leading to the merger, he seems to have been disappointed in the outcome, believing that his partisanship in the Hudson's Bay cause, together with his standing in the Canadian business community, should have entitled him, rather than Simon McGillivray, to a place in the councils of the reorganized company.

It is against this background that Moffatt's persistent and at times single-handed campaign to produce changes in the Bank of Montreal must be considered. He was one of the giants of his day, a man of formidable personality and ability and without doubt one of the most interesting and forceful characters that appeared on the Canadian scene during the first half of the last century. He was also a man of indomitable purpose in pursuit of any objective he believed in, whether it had to do with the preservation of colonial relationships, the development of Canadian commerce, the improvement of internal communications, or banking reform. As a result of the last endeavour, Moffatt was charged by Simon McGillivray with engaging in a personal vendetta to bring about his ruin. As will be seen, McGillivray's charges were closely reasoned and bear considerable conviction; yet as one studies the Minutes recorded in the directors' Resolve Book during 1825 and 1826, it is seen that every action taken by Moffatt, whatever his personal motivation, was based on sound banking practice.

In any case, Moffatt's contentions were upheld and, in August, Gerrard was adjudged guilty of defalcation, by a five-to-four vote among nine directors. The charge was that he had been guilty of illegal action on two counts: one, that he had granted discounts on his individual responsibility; two, that in granting discounts he had augmented the debt of a borrower beyond the permissible limit of £10,000. Moffatt based his case on that clause in the Act of Incorporation which held directors jointly and severally liable for the debts of the corporation in excess of three times the paid-up capital, with the proviso that any individual director could exonerate himself by publishing, within eight days of an illegal action, his non-concurrence.

At issue was a series of complicated actions totalling more than £10,000 and involving a number of notes and bills discounted for two mercantile houses – Maitland, Garden & Auldjo, and Spragg & Hutchinson – and signed by four private individuals as promisors and/or endorsers. Maitland, Garden & Auldjo was one of the leading commercial houses in Montreal at the time. The Montreal *Gazette* for April 23, 1825, reported the launching of "the beautiful ship *Lady Rowena*, 328 tons measurement" for the firm, and it may be recalled that when the new banking house for the Bank of Montreal was planned in 1818, the specifications referred to the handsome building then being erected on St. Paul Street for Maitland, Garden & Auldjo. One of the partners, George Garden, was twice a director of the Bank, from 1817 to 1822 and from 1823 to 1826; during his first tenure he also served as vice-president for four years. Another partner, George Auldjo, alternated with Garden as a director during the latter's absence in the old country in 1822. Little is known about the senior member of the firm, Maitland, but it is presumed that he was one of the many Montreal merchants of the early nineteenth century who withdrew themselves and their capital to England or Scotland after they had secured a competence. Little more is known about Spragg and Hutchinson except that they advertised ship's auctions frequently in the *Gazette* and apparently were dealers in the unconsigned ship's cargoes which played an important role in the wholesale trade of Montreal after the Napoleonic Wars. Among the four individual promisors or endorsers, Messrs. Porteous, Nesbitt, Bernard, and Thompson, only the first has been identified. Thomas Porteous was a director of the Bank from 1818 to 1823 and again for a year in 1826-27.

Except for the foregoing data, taken from the Directors' Minutes, no references to the Gerrard embroilment have been brought to light. Without commercial documents or correspondence bearing directly on the matter, it is impossible of course to know precisely why two such well-established houses should have found themselves delinquent in the relatively small sum of £3,546, or why that delinquency should have been seized upon to precipitate a struggle for control within the Bank of Montreal. It is possible, however, to find an explanation in the economic and political conditions in Canada, Great Britain, and the United States at the time. Thus, the euphoria that marked the annual meeting held in June, 1825, can be attributed to the uninterrupted strengthening of Canadian business conditions over a three-year period; the dissident note sounded by George Moffatt less than two months later can be traced to an awakened concern over financial conditions in England, then in the final stages of a speculative boom of unprecedented dimensions.

2.

The feeling of confidence and satisfaction that permeated the annual meeting of Canada's first bank in June, 1825, reflected the commercial climate of the day. In four years the population of the two Canadian provinces had increased from 526,000 to 637,000, a gain of more than twenty per cent; and business generally, although not as wildly profitable as during the war years of the preceding decade, was in a healthier condition than ever before. Although the full effects of the Hudson's Bay - North West merger were still to be felt in Montreal, the transfer of the trade to London and the Hudson Bay route had fortunately coincided with the post-war recovery that had begun in Britain during 1821. With recovery had come increasing demands for a wide range of Canadian forest products such as timber, staves, and ashes, and also for wheat and flour. Next to the timber and ashes derived from the land-clearing process, wheat ordinarily provided the pioneer settler with his first cash crop, but all cereals were virtually excluded from the British market under the Corn Laws enacted in 1815 in the interests of British landowners and agricultural producers.

COLONIZATION—LOWER CANADA

By 1835 two companies, the Canada Company and the British American Land Company, were actively promoting colonization, the first in Upper Canada and the second in Lower Canada. The proprietors bought large tracts of crown land from the government on long-term arrangements, whereby as much as half the debt could be paid off in the form of capital improvements, such as roads, mills and schools, on the company lands.

Here we see an area around Stanstead near the Quebec-Vermont border which was settled largely under the auspices of the British American Land Company.

The country derived great benefit from the work of the companies in stimulating immigration and facilitating settlement. This latter service had the important effect of shortening the period between an immigrant's arrival and the time when he became a productive citizen.

From 1821 onward, the problem of colonial preferences had been a major concern of Canadian commercial and agricultural interests and as such had been the subject of numerous resolutions and petitions to the Colonial Office through the Governor-in-Chief and by direct representations in London by Canadians, either as emissaries or as resident partners of the several Montreal branch houses located there. At the outset, however, these efforts were wholly unsuccessful. In 1821, for example, a committee of the House of Commons recommended a discontinuance of the duty of £3. 5s. per load (approximately 600 board feet or 50 cubic feet) which had been imposed on Baltic timber since 1809 and which had led to the establishment of the Canadian timber trade. The grounds for the recommendation were that the bounty granted the North American colonies was unnecessarily large for the reason that the Canadian products, particularly oak, were held to be inferior to those of northern Europe and because a large percentage of Canadian timber exports originated in the United States.

This was indeed the case. Until the 1830's, Vermont and northern New York were the principal suppliers. The timber trade, however, was almost wholly a British enterprise financed by British capital and operated by agents of British companies sent over to Quebec. These interests proved sufficiently powerful to avert the threat of free trade by accepting a reduction in the Baltic tariff of only one pound per load. Thanks to sustained demand, the reduced preferences had little effect on the Canadian timber trade, which continued to dominate the British market until mid century. However, the incident is indicative of the attitude of British governments to Canadian economic problems. Had the Canadian timber trade not involved important British vested interests, it is unlikely that any preference would have been extended in 1821.

The next year again found the British government concerned with Canadian affairs, this time in connection with the bill to unite the provinces of Lower and Upper Canada. While the failure to secure passage of the measure was a defeat for the Canadian commercial lobby, the debate on the political situation in British North America undoubtedly focused attention on the Canadian provinces and their problems. Of much greater significance to the future of colonial relations, however, was the change in the complexion of the British government that took place the same year. Following the death of Castlereagh, a reorganization of the cabinet resulted in the inclusion of liberal-reform elements in the persons of George Canning as Foreign Minister, Sir

Robert Peel as Home Secretary, and William Huskisson as President of the Board of Trade. Canning, a champion of self-determination, is principally known for having "called the New World into existence to redress the balance of the Old"; Peel was the son of a self-made factory owner and had won recognition as a fiscal and financial authority through his work on the House of Commons committee of 1819 which finally reinstated cash payments by the Bank of England after two decades of inconvertibility; and William Huskisson was a successful Liverpool financier and disciple of Adam Smith who had already established himself as a liberal parliamentarian of great ability.

In office from 1822 to 1830, the trio represented the rise of industrial laissez-faire liberalism and was responsible for initiating many domestic reforms and paving the way for free trade two decades later. From a colonial point of view, its most important activities were the assaults made by Huskisson on the old mercantile system of protective tariffs and restrictive trade and navigation regulations. The first of such assaults was made in 1822 by the liberalization of the shipping laws in the interests of freer trade with the United States and between Britain's colonial possessions, and was followed in 1825 by a proposal of Huskisson's for a drastic modification of the Corn Laws. These had provided for a sliding scale of duties on Canadian wheat which virtually prohibited import until the price in Britain rose above 67s. a quarter, about $1.68 a bushel. Huskisson now proposed, in the interests of Britain's growing industrial masses rather than with any concern for the Canadian farmer, that Canadian wheat be admitted at a fixed duty of 5s. a quarter, that is, 12.5 cents a bushel, irrespective of the price in Britain. This was less favourable than the free entry Canadian merchants had been asking for since 1821 but nevertheless it represented a boon to a farming community slowly emerging from subsistence agriculture, and the progress of the proposal was followed eagerly in Montreal and Upper Canada. Before its introduction in the House of Commons the proposed measure met severe opposition from the supporters of the old system of protective tariffs and from agricultural interests. As with the timber question earlier, it was held that the lower duty would lead to a flooding of the British market by American wheat, smuggled across the border and shipped down the St. Lawrence as Canadian produce. Nevertheless, the bill passed in the House of Commons, and in its issue of June 18, 1825, the Montreal *Gazette* printed the following dispatch:

Quebec, Monday, 12th June, 1825:– By the attention of a mercantile friend, we have been favored with a copy of the Liverpool *Courier* of the 11th May, brought by the Canadian *Udney*, arrived on Saturday in thirty days passage.

The resolutions subjoined were proposed by Mr. Huskisson in the House of Commons, on the 2nd May, and agreed to without opposition. They propose the admission of Canadian wheat at 5s the quarter, which is about 8d. currency on each of our minots. There appears little doubt that an act to effect this change will be passed during the Session of the Imperial Parliament. It will have the effect of raising the price of our wheat immediately, from one to two shillings per minot, and prove very advantageous to our farmers and to the holders of large quantities of the article. The price of provisions and labor will also rise. About 50,000 bushels of wheat have already been shipped for Great Britain at this port, and a very great quantity more will immediately be shipped.

Comparing the dates–London, May 2; Quebec, June 12, and Montreal, June 18–it is likely that the intelligence had already reached Montreal through private channels via a Black Ball packet from Liverpool to New York and the New York-Montreal mail, which was running three times a week in 1825. While the news could hardly have reached Montreal as early as June 6, its nature had already been anticipated and doubtless contributed to the expansive mood of the annual meeting of the Bank of Montreal shareholders. Other benefits stemmed from Huskisson's liberalization of the Navigation Laws, an important result of which was the establishment of direct trade between the Far East and Canada. On April 16, 1825, for example, Forsyth, Richardson & Co. announced their appointment as agents for the East India Company and on July 16 the *Gazette* hailed the arrival of the *Moffatt* and *Juliana* direct from Canton, with tea, as providing the means "effectively to check the system of smuggling [East Indian goods from the U.S.], which has so long prevailed in these provinces to the detriment of morals and the public revenue."

The pages of the *Gazette* for the first six months of 1825 are replete with other indications of economic well-being. On May 19, for example, the shareholders of the Welland Canal met in Montreal with Simon McGillivray in the chair and John Fleming acting as secretary; and on June 14 a largely attended meeting was held to organize the Lower Canada Land Company. Modelled on

FIRST GREAT CANAL
PROJECT

Although attempts had been made to build a canal around the Lachine Rapids as early as 1700, it was not until 1819 that a charter to build such a canal was granted to a group of Montreal merchants – men who were no doubt concerned with the threat which the Erie Canal, when completed, would pose to Montreal's importance as a trade centre. Little progress was made, and two years later the charter was revoked by the Lower Canada legislature, the provincial government itself taking on the responsibility of building this important artery.

The first sod was turned by Hon. John Richardson, chairman of the Lachine Canal Commission which was appointed by the government in 1821. Mr. Richardson is seen here, leaning on his cane and surveying the completion of the first lock of the Lachine Canal at Windmill Point, near the foot of McGill Street. With him are his colleagues of the Commission, to which the Bank of Montreal had advanced quite a sizable sum so that the work on the waterway could proceed as planned.

Completed in 1825, the canal was 28 feet wide at the bottom and generally 48 feet wide at water level. It contained seven locks, each a hundred feet long and twenty feet wide, with five-foot water depth on the sills. The total fall of these locks, over the 8½ mile length, was forty feet. The cost of this first great project in the field of Canadian water transportation was $440,000.

Painting by Jack Tremblay

the Canada Company, which had lately been formed in England to promote colonization in Upper Canada, the Montreal company was capitalized at £1,000,000 sterling to acquire lands in the Eastern Townships of Lower Canada (counties adjacent to Vermont and New Hampshire) for the purpose of development and sale to selected immigrants. Forty-nine persons resident in Montreal and Quebec attended the meeting and subscribed a total of £182,000 for 1,820 shares of stock. Most of the subscribers were shareholders of the Bank of Montreal and several were past or present directors. On May 14, Francis Rasco announced the opening of the Masonic Hall, yet another of the famous innkeeper's hostelries, one of which, built in 1836, is still standing near Bonsecours Market in Montreal. The same issue of the *Gazette* noted the launching of seven ships from three separate shipyards below the Current and the edition of June 25 describes the launching at the Ile d'Orléans of the *Baron Renfrew*, a 5,280-ton timber carrier whose unprecedented dimensions and seaworthiness aroused great interest in both Canada and the United States.

Other shipping items report arrivals at Quebec and Montreal averaging more than seventy vessels weekly, most of them in ballast, suggesting a thriving export business, while advertisements reveal the expansion of steamboat navigation since the launching of John Molson's *Accommodation* in 1809. An interesting notice, dated June 1, announces the purchase of the apparatus of St. Mary's Foundry, established by the Molsons to machine the engine parts for the *Accommodation*, and its removal to a new site at St. Catherines (Outremont). Other foundries and machine shops made their appearance in Montreal at this time or shortly after, the first to supply the potash kettles and the gear for the lumber industry, the second to build steamboat engines. Montreal was one of the foremost pioneers of river steamboat navigation and for a time led the world in towing, both in tonnage and in distance. The run from Quebec to Montreal was 186 miles and most sailing vessels reached Montreal by tow-boats. One of these, the *Hercules*, at the time of its launching in 1822, carried the world's most powerful engine, 100 hp., constructed by John D. Ward at his recently established Eagle Foundry. It should be pointed out, too, that manifestations of optimism were not confined to items of material progress only. The Molsons were currently engaged in promoting the construction of the Theatre Royal, which was to open in the autumn of 1825; although not Montreal's first theatre, it would soon become its most famous, playing host to such celebrities as Edmund Kean and Charles Dickens. The Montreal *Gazette* was also in the throes of expansion; this most venerable of all Canadian newspapers, founded in 1778 by Benjamin Franklin's printer, Fleury Mesplet, was purchased in 1822 by Thomas A. Turner, the former vice-president of the Bank of Montreal, who soon changed it from a bilingual weekly to a semi-weekly English publication.

Despite all signs of flourishing business conditions, with improved prospects for the future, at least one director of the Bank of Montreal, George Moffatt, seems to have sensed the approach of disaster in the summer of 1825.

3.

At the close of the Napoleonic Wars, Britain was the world's richest country. Although the prolonged struggle had cost hundreds of millions of pounds, her export trade had doubled and her revenues had trebled. Despite severe war-time shipping losses, her merchant marine had increased in tonnage from one million to two and a half million, and, with the protection of the British Navy, had penetrated to every trade mart in the world. Under the stimulus of war, the methods of both agricultural and industrial production had been revolutionized, and in the closing years of the war her farmers, drovers, factory workers, miners, navvies, and tradespeople were fully employed at higher wages than they had ever received. Never before in Europe had all classes of any nation ever attained such heights of prosperity and well-being.

With no previous experience to go on, it was confidently expected that the war-time prosperity would not only continue after Waterloo, but would rapidly increase with the reopening of European markets and those of the United States, once the abortive American War could be concluded. Instead of anticipated prosperity, peace brought with it depression and distress and finally spread misery as the war-supported economy fell rapidly into stagnation. A sick and devastated Europe had neither the means nor the organization to absorb surplus British manufactures; the government's demands for war supplies ceased; prices of manufactures fell precipitously, and thousands were thrown out of work at the same time that more than 400,000 demobilized men of the armed forces joined the ranks of the unemployed. The conclusion of the American War six months later did not help matters. The United States stood in need of British products and vice versa, but the States, like Europe, was virtually bankrupt; the still-sacrosanct British trade and navigation laws also remained on the statute books to delay the resumption of the profitable North Atlantic trade.

Primarily responsible for Britain's victory were the Royal Navy and the historical conjunction of her agricultural and industrial revolutions; the economic collapse that followed was brought about by the sudden removal of governmental support and financing of the war-time economy. The latter had been accomplished by the levying of increased taxes of all kinds, including an unprecedented ten-per-cent income tax, the creation of a huge funded debt, and the issuance of fiat money by the Bank of England. Under the provisions of the Bank Restriction Act, passed in 1797, its bank-notes ceased to be redeemable in specie and, although not made full legal tender, were accorded legal sanctions for the payment of public and private debt. In the opinion of leading financial experts of the day, the use of fiat money was held to be as much responsible for Britain's 1815 victory as her navy, the industrial revolution, or even the playing fields of Eton.

In 1815 Adam Smith had been dead twenty-five years but the study of economics was still in its infancy. It is not surprising, therefore, that the steps taken to cope with the first of the great nineteenth-century depressions should have been faltering and unsuccessful. Under a Tory government controlled by the landed aristocracy they proved, in fact, to be largely contradictory. Thus the Corn Laws of 1815, passed in the interests of British landowners and food producers, raised the price of bread to the workers and the unemployed, while the abolition of the ten-per-cent income tax in 1816, lifting the now onerous burden of taxation from those with incomes, was accompanied by the imposition of new taxes on articles consumed principally by those whose earnings were next to non-existent. As unemployment spread in the rural districts, the Poor Rates of Elizabeth's reign were revived in an effort to aid the needy without having recourse to more radical measures for the purpose. The effect was to depress wages and lower mass purchasing-power still further. In the cities, factory towns, and ports, social unrest was expressed in riots and political agitation to which a reactionary government could reply only with repressive measures: the Coercion Acts of 1817 which, breaking with constitutional tradition, abolished the cherished right of habeas corpus; and, after the Peterloo massacre, the Six Acts of 1819, which restricted the right of assemblage and the freedom of the press.

Largely unaffected by the poverty and distress around them, the landowning class that controlled the government were content with the *status quo* in the belief that the situation would right itself in time; for their part, the unemployed sought relief in demands for parliamentary reform and the abolition of the hated Corn Laws, which they held responsible for the rising price of food. Yet another body of opinion, made up of financiers, bankers and economic theorists in and out of Parliament, blamed the over-issue of the temporarily inconvertible bank-note currency, and its consequent fall in value in terms of bullion, for the rise in general prices. As Andréadès has pointed out in his *History of the Bank of England*, a debate ensued in both Houses of Parliament which ran the gamut of economic theory as it was known at the time. One school maintained that without the Restriction Act of 1797 the war never could have been won and that the Act should therefore be regarded as inviolable; another that convertibility should be resumed if Britain was to be spared the experience of Continental countries resulting from the uncontrolled issue of paper currency.

These questions had been thoroughly explored by the Bullion Committee of 1810. Among the members were William Huskisson and Sir Francis Baring, but their recommendations to amend the Restriction Act were ignored until 1819, when an act was passed providing for a graduated return to a free gold standard. Historians and economists remain in disagreement as to the true effects of the resumption of cash payments. With Keynesian aftersight perhaps, Arthur Bryant puts it this way in his disillusioned study of the period, *The Age of Elegance*:

> With agricultural and industrial production lagging behind both capacity and demand, an expansive financial policy might have changed the whole course of the nineteenth century. By using direct taxation to check inflation in boom periods and judiciously expanding the currency to facilitate reduction of taxation in a depression, a far-seeing Government might have raised the workers' standards of living step by step with the rising wealth of the capitalists. Britain might then have emerged from the Industrial Revolution one nation instead of two.

On the other hand, David Ricardo, whose pamphleteering at the period made him the most popular economic theorist in Britain, argued in favour of Adam Smith's faith in the inexorable law of the market place, and confidently predicted that conditions would automatically improve when that point had been reached where they could no longer worsen.

Ricardo's predictions were realized. After industrial unemployment, agrarian contraction, and governmental indifference had driven Britain to the brink of revolution, the economy began to stir again; but to what extent the resumption of specie payments was responsible remains an open question.

Andréadès notes that the ease with which the Bank of England conformed to the terms of the Bullion Law "quickly restored public confidence." But other factors appear to have been involved. Bryant makes this observation: "The prices of manufactures having fallen to rock-bottom, foreign customers began to buy again, and, employment improving as a result, internal purchasing-power became more plentiful." But other potent restorative influences were present: the restoration of European purchasing-power resulting from massive British loans to the Continental states; the betterment of commercial relations with the United States; the opening of great new markets in South America as its colonies declared their independence from Spain and Portugal, and the addition of liberal elements to the cabinet in the persons of Canning, Peel and Huskisson.

The quickening of the economy that began in 1821 reached boom proportions by 1824, and by 1825 had produced an orgy of speculation comparable to the stock-market boom in the United States a century later. To quote Andréadès: "Companies were formed with the most absurd objects, and as the first subscriptions paid up did not often exceed 5 per cent of the nominal value of the shares, persons of very modest fortunes were able to take part in the transactions. The number of companies formed rose to 624, involving a nominal capital of £372,173,100. This enormous sum represented £150 per head for the 13 million persons who then constituted the population of England, and was equivalent to a third of the total wealth of the country."

Despite storm warnings toward the end of 1824, prices continued rising through the first quarter of 1825, but after a period of market indecision the inevitable contraction set in. The summer witnessed an increasing number of country bank failures, but such was the momentum of the boom that it was not until the autumn that disaster finally struck like a hurricane, bringing panic with it and leaving commercial devastation and economic chaos in its wake. Generally held responsible was the failure of the English banking system to cope with the credit and exchange problems of the industrialized peace-time economy, although it had functioned with remarkable success and flexibility in meeting the financial demands of war in the two preceding decades.

Country banking had made its appearance in England early in the eighteenth century and during the Napoleonic Wars embraced more than 750 institutions; by 1825 the number had been reduced to 544 through failures and amalgamations. After 1826, when joint-stock banking was permitted beyond a radius of sixty-five miles of London for the first time, country banking rapidly declined as it was supplanted by the more responsible joint-stock type of organization. Whatever its weaknesses, English country banking was an essential link in the chain of circumstances which produced the phenomenal increase in England's wealth during the second half of the eighteenth century. As L. S. Pressnell has established in his *Country Banking in the Industrial Revolution*, the country banks were the agencies which mobilized the credit by which England's mercantile adventures, colonial plantations, world-wide trade, and agrarian and industrial revolutions were mostly financed. They seem to have appeared spontaneously in the west country to finance commercial ventures: in the farming counties to extend the enclosure system and promote the introduction of scientific livestock breeding, and in the midlands to open mines, improve roads, construct canals, build factories, and supply machinery – all this in addition to performing the customary services rendered by banks of issue, discount, and deposit, while providing the exchange apparatus that linked the provinces with London and vice versa. Despite a record of economic utility, the system broke down during crises in 1793 and 1797, when country bank suspensions, though not necessarily bankruptcies, reached serious proportions. The same situation developed again in 1825, when it became apparent that the entire English system, grown up like Topsy, would have to be placed under legislative controls.

Many theories have been offered to explain the breakdown of a system that benefited England so greatly during one of the most dynamic periods in the history of her economy. The theories include matters such as the inherent instability of a system based on the largely uncontrolled issuance of bank-note currency; the drain of bullion to meet the reconstruction needs of France and other European countries; the resumption of cash payments in 1821, and the expansionist policies of the Bank of England during a period of spiralling speculative frenzy. Cited to support the last assumption was the drop in the Bank of England's gold reserves during 1824 and 1825. In January 1824, the reserves stood at £13,500,000; a year later they had decreased to £9,400,000, and by the end of 1825 had sunk to £1,200,000. In more general terms it can now be seen that the rather pragmatic system that had largely marshalled the capital required for economic growth was no longer capable of dealing with the complexities of the mature economy it had helped to create.

As pointed out above, the post-Napoleonic War boom had its beginnings in 1821, when the ease with which the Bank of England was able to anticipate the resumption of cash payments, scheduled for 1823, restored public confidence and resulted in a rise in prices. A year later an act empowering the Bank of England and the country banks to increase their issues resulted in a further rise in prices and enabled the government to refund £215 million of the public debt at 3½ and 4 per cent instead of 4 and 5 per cent. The effect of the reduction in interest was to induce holders of government securities to move their funds to more lucrative investments – particularly in the issues of Latin American republics and companies, and speculations in overseas commodities, especially cotton. The first signs of warning came toward the end of 1824 with the failure of several large dealers in the American staple. The warning went unheeded. Prices continued to rise in the first quarter of 1825, new companies were formed, and the Bank of England, which had already been loaning on mortgages and on its own stock, ignored the policy of contraction pursued in 1797 and increased its issues freely, resulting in the drain on its reserves already noted.

It was not until the last day of 1824 that the Bank of England increased its discount rate to five per cent, indicating a return to a policy of contraction, but the immediate impact was softened by increased discounts. As soon as the effects became noticeable in the London money market, country banks, many of which, particularly in the west of England, had extended long-term transatlantic credits, began to call in their loans. By May, the London money market was "in a very feverish state" as stock-market holdings were liquidated to transfer money to safer and more secure English funds, and in midsummer the policy of retrenchment of the country banks, already well advanced, was intensified by parliamentary discussions which concluded with the opinion that all banks, in common with the Bank of England, must redeem their notes in gold when a note-holder so demanded. While no banking legislation was passed for several months, the opinion was accepted as a mandate to the unchartered banks to pay specie on demand. Since many such banks had no reserves of metal, the inevitable happened as note-holders and other creditors demanded specie which could not be produced, either because it was non-existent or because it could not be transported quickly enough from London.

The first failure was that of a small agricultural bank at the end of August. The crack widened in September, with more serious disasters, and runs on country banks became more common; in October the stoppage of payment on £517,000 of acceptances by S. Williams & Co., a leading house in the American trade, produced grave anxiety, particularly in those cities and ports where most of the trade with Canada originated – Bristol, Liverpool, Manchester, and Birmingham. The nadir was reached in December when thirty-three banks throughout England closed their doors, precipitating the worst economic depression yet experienced and with it an eighteen-month stagnation of British overseas commerce. To quote Pressnell: "Britain had been importing goods and exporting capital and sending goods overseas on credit and in hope." It is only in relation to this background and its disastrous results that contemporary developments in Canada can be fully understood.

4.

The effects of the tightening of English money appear to have been felt in Canada in July, 1825, when the firm of Maitland, Garden & Auldjo began extensive purchases of bills of exchange on London to meet the demands of its English creditors. This conclusion is based on the sequence of events in England; the firm's sudden need for money, and its subsequent turning to the President of the Bank of Montreal for advances beyond the £10,000 limit permitted an individual borrower. Unfortunately, little is known about the particular agencies through which the Canada Trade was supplied or the agencies through which it was financed, but the general pattern has been well established. All the leading Montreal houses at the time had representatives in England, usually in the persons of partners who had returned home after making their fortune in the colony, and who arranged for the shipment of goods to the ports of the St. Lawrence and for the disposal of the staple commodities received in return. Since most of the export trade with Canada was in articles manufactured in Birmingham and Manchester, financing was arranged through private banks which had both manufacturing and shipping connections in the area.

The condition of the Maitland account was first brought formally to the attention of the Board on June 28, when the firm was specifically named in a resolution authorizing the acceptance by the President of its ninety-day draft on Quebec in payment of overdue paper. Since similar transactions were ordinarily noted in the Resolve Book simply as "discounts accepted," the identification was unusual. Three days later the firm negotiated £5,000 in bills of exchange on London and a week later gave its demand bond for

£15,700 to cover protested notes for which it had become liable as endorser. When the President passed further notes totalling £10,000, or £25,700 in all, George Moffatt challenged the complacency of his fellow directors, first, by serving notice of his non-concurrence in the President's actions, and second, by charging him with serious violations of the by-laws governing the activities of the institution. It appears from the Minutes that the Bank had ample cause to be concerned but that the Board was satisfied to deal with the situation leniently, and rather than make the position of old friends more difficult, the discounts were reaffirmed.

Gerrard was already in a difficult position in regard to the notes he had discounted the previous April for Spragg & Hutchinson, who also appear to have been doing considerable business with Maitland, Garden & Auldjo. Moffatt had charged Gerrard with favouritism, implying that he had an outside interest in these discounts, some of which had come under protest. A committee of three which had been appointed to report on this matter absolved the President from any sinister motive in the transactions or receiving any personal gain therefrom, but, on another motion introduced by Moffatt, the Board declared him liable for the unpaid balance of the protested notes he had accepted on his own responsibility. The alignment of interests and personalities among the directors is now seen for the first time. Voting to exonerate Gerrard were Forsyth, Garden, Larocque and McGill, all formerly connected with the fur trade and now constituting an old-guard phalanx: to hold him liable, Moffatt, Leslie, Gates, Millar, and Torrance, a tentative grouping of intransigent elements. George Moffatt's position as the reforming crusader has already been established; James Leslie occupied a distinctive place in English commercial circles through his support of the French-Canadian party in the Assembly, where he was one of the members for the District of Montreal; Horatio Gates, with his connections in the United States, was essentially interested in the Bank's exchange operations; James Millar was a transatlantic ship-owner and commission agent, heading the firm of Millar, Parlane & Co. which later as the Montreal Ocean Steamship Company, under Sir Hugh Allan, would acquire world renown for its Allan Line; and Thomas Torrance was a general trader who had successfully entered the forwarding business on the St. Lawrence, a purely Canadian enterprise.

Having voted to hold the President liable for the unpaid balance of £4,046. 14s. 9d., the directors took no other steps at the time to enforce payment. The Moffatt faction had gained only a token victory in its first two forays,

LUMBER CAPITAL OF CANADA

Although timber rafts had been descending the Ottawa River for many years, there were few settlers at the present site of Ottawa until Colonel By arrived to start the Rideau Canal in 1826.

By's chief contractor was Thomas McKay, a stone-mason with previous experience on the Lachine Canal and other military and public works. His profits went into land at the junction of the Rideau and Ottawa rivers, where he built the mill complex depicted here, using power from the Rideau Falls to run grist and saw mills, a cloth factory and a brewery.

In 1838 McKay built a splendid home for himself and called it Rideau Hall. It has long since become the residence of Canada's governors general.

During its early years, Bytown, as Ottawa was called until 1855, was a wild and lawless place, but it grew rapidly and soon became the lumber capital of Canada, its annual timber trade approximating $4,000,000 by 1850.

and there the matter rested until the first board meeting in November, called to consider the semi-annual dividend and to elect a director in the place of James Millar, who had recently resigned. The customary three-per-cent dividend was declared with only Moffatt and Leslie dissenting, no doubt because they had heard by this time of the beginning of the collapse in England and would have preferred to fortify the Bank's reserve rather than pay a dividend of £5,625 on the paid-up capital of £187,500. The names of the directors voting to declare a dividend were not recorded, but it is evident that the Moffatt-Leslie faction had yet to consolidate its strength. This became possible through the election of Simon McGillivray to the vacant seat on the Board. The strength of the crusader faction was not reinforced by any support McGillivray gave it—he remained inactive during his five and a half months' tenure as a director—but the extraordinary misfortunes that overtook him in winding up the affairs of the North West Company set the stage for the final defeat of the old regime.

Curiously enough, the Minutes of the Board contain only two references to McGillivray—his election in November and that of his successor the following April—until July 1826, when legal action was instituted to collect his debt of some £22,000 then owing to the Bank. The debt itself, however, originated in October and November of 1825, when Simon McGillivray sold drafts on his London house of McTavish, Fraser & Co. to the extent of £28,500.

As set forth in the preceding chapter, the agreement amalgamating the Hudson's Bay Company and the North West Company was signed in London on March 26, 1821. Shortly afterwards Simon McGillivray made the long journey to Fort William, the Nor'West headquarters on Lake Superior, to secure the approval of the other North West partners. He arrived there on July 1, and after lengthy and acrimonious discussions returned to Montreal, arriving some time in September. For the next two months he and his brother William attempted to settle the affairs of McTavish, McGillivrays & Co. but departed for London in November, leaving to Thomas Thain the onerous task of assembling in Montreal records and accounts scattered across half the continent. A provisional balance was reached on November 30, 1821, and the books were then closed, the partnership agreement having another year to run. Precisely on November 30, 1822, a new firm, McGillivrays, Thain & Co., came into being without formal articles of partnership to wind up the affairs of McTavish, McGillivrays & Co. and to manage "the trade and concerns" of the Hudson's Bay Company, for whom McGillivrays, Thain & Co. had been appointed agents for the Montreal department, now a relatively small segment of the once mighty Canadian fur-trading empire. Thomas Thain became the "managing Agent and Financier and Book-keeper of the North West Company, and of Sir Alexander Mackenzie & Co. [a heritage of the XY-N.W. Co. feud] and the managing Partner and Financier of the firm of McGillivrays, Thain & Co."

In failing health after nearly forty years of unceasing activity in the fur trade, William McGillivray, on his return to England late in 1821, left to Simon, eighteen years his junior, and to Edward Ellice the laborious negotiations with the Hudson's Bay Company to determine the value to be placed on the North West Company's properties and inventories in Canada. To this effect an agreement was signed between the brothers in May, 1822, to pool their fur-trade interests and to make the survivor the residuary legatee. Finally, on March 26, 1823, after months of continuing negotiation, the value of the Nor'West assets was fixed at "£164,000 [currency] or a sum of £123,000 sterling," and this amount was to be the North West Company's share in the capital of the new organization. The McGillivrays themselves agreed to supply half this sum, and to surrender their "shares and interest in the trade, *present, reversionary*, and *contingent*," in return for "a certain sum of *Hudson's Bay Stock*."

Having completed these arrangments in London in 1824, Simon McGillivray sailed for New York in January 1825 with the intention of winding up his Canadian affairs as speedily as possible. By this time, his partner, Thomas Thain, had been engaged for more than three years in Herculean accounting labours for which he seems to have been quite indifferently fitted. When Simon reached Montreal in March or thereabouts he found the books and accounts of McGillivrays, Thain & Co. in a state of hopeless confusion and Thain himself on the verge of mental collapse. The inference is drawn from a letter written by Thain in England in February 1826, in which he stated that he had left Montreal in August "to obtain medical advice in the country and visit relatives . . ." Before leaving he persuaded Simon McGillivray that no one but himself could untangle the mess of material he had brought together in the company's offices, now known as Hudson's Bay House, for which reason he locked the door behind him and took the key. He continued as a director and Vice-President of the Bank of Montreal until June 1826, his colleagues on the Board postponing the naming of a successor in expectation of his return.

Upon Thain's departure from Montreal, Simon McGillivray appointed

Pierre de Rocheblave, a former Nor'Wester with a long and able career, to take over the management of the Hudson's Bay interests in Montreal while he attempted to bring order to four years of accumulated records. In this he had the understanding and support of old confrères such as John Richardson, John Forsyth, and Samuel Gerrard, along with the confidence of the Bank of Montreal. In spite of Simon's feeling that he had little or no moral responsibility for the debts of the Canadian house, most of which had been contracted by the partners in his absence, he was nevertheless anxious and willing to discharge these obligations. Although he was uncertain of the amount of the debts, he calculated that the recently concluded agreement of 1824 had made available immediate resources exceeding £100,000, which was the value he placed on the Hudson's Bay stock received by his brother and himself. He also estimated his separate personal estate to be worth another £100,000, which he was ready to sacrifice if need be. Thus, on his arrival in Canada, little question could have existed, either in his mind or in that of the public, as to his ability to satisfy his creditors. It was on this assumption, no doubt, that he was elected a director of the Bank of Montreal and was able, during October and November, to cash drafts on McTavish, Fraser & Co. totalling £28,500. The transactions with the Bank were intended to permit the orderly reduction of his Canadian indebtedness, as were loans of £23,600 obtained separately: £12,600 from Hon. J. H. Dunn, the Receiver General of Upper Canada, of public monies belonging to the province, and £11,000 privately from Samuel Gerrard. As security for these loans, McGillivray pledged £9,000 of Hudson's Bay stock owned by him and valued at £24,300, an action that led to bitter and prolonged controversy afterwards. He raised a further sum of £3,450 in December by selling sixty shares of Bank of Montreal stock standing in his name and thirty-two shares in that of McGillivrays, Thain & Co. Interestingly enough, the sales were made to Henry Brevoort of New York, Charles Carroll of Carrollton, Md., and John McTavish of Baltimore, and also to Samuel Gerrard in his private capacity. By mid December, 1825, the total sum raised by Simon, without tapping his brother's resources, amounted to £55,550 currency.

At this juncture McGillivray received a letter that completely dislocated his plans. Written by Edward Ellice and posted in London on October 26, it contained the distressing news of William McGillivray's death at St. John's Wood ten days before. A will signed on the tenth named the younger brother as principal heir and executor, William's dying concern, according to Ellice, being the interests of his creditors. Ellice's letter also conveyed the alarming news of financial panic, the suspension of all commercial credit, and the depreciation of all property. The great speculative orgy of 1825 had reached its final phase of crisis.

Faced with the wholly unexpected deterioration of his resources, and after anxious talks with his friends, Simon McGillivray came to the conclusion that he "could not meet all the engagements of the House" and quickly decided that "it was useless to put off the evil day." Convinced that no possible alternative existed, he immediately notified his creditors and called a preliminary meeting for December 27, 1825, when he offered to make a voluntary assignment of the whole of his own and his brother's estate "for the payment of the House's debts." Little did he realize how much the value of this estate had deteriorated as a result of the sudden depression and the activities of his London associates in the speculative markets.

In a series of epistles written later, Simon blamed the final debacle on the costly feud with the Hudson's Bay Company, on the time and money consumed in collecting records, and on the social indulgences of former Nor'-West partners, who "launched into all sorts of expenses; – got married, – set up establishment, – and gave entertainments, – without considering whether or not they could afford the means." Probably a full explanation will never be discovered, the records left by Thain having been disposed of at auction after the bankruptcy. Although some documents have since come to light in Canada, Scotland, and elsewhere, the contradictions contained in Simon McGillivray's lengthy letters to his creditors have yet to be reconciled.

The news of the bankruptcy must have shocked the relatively small commercial community of Montreal as nothing had done since the loss of the fur trade four years before. Not only was the sum involved more than a million dollars, unprecedented in Canadian commercial experience, but the event itself reflected gravely on the business acumen of some of Montreal's most exalted personages. So infallible, however, was the discretion of the Montreal press that no notice of the failure was taken by any of the three journals published locally. In fact, the only reference that has been uncovered is in the Quebec *Gazette* for January 22, 1826, which printed an excerpt from a letter in a New York paper of January 7, quoting in its turn parts of a letter "from a Gentleman, now in Montreal, dated Montreal, December 28, 1825," as follows:

Gentlemen:—Saturday the mercantile community of this place was thrown into confusion in consequence of the reported failure of a heavy house. This morning, on enquiry, I find it to be the North West Hudson Bay Company, under control of McGillivrays, Thain and Co.—they have stopped payment for about Eight Hundred and Fifty Thousand Dollars. The principal loss, if any, will fall on individuals who have retired from business and loaned this company their money. Not a mercantile house, as I can learn, will be the losers.

After noting the confusion as to names, the *Gazette* article contains these further comments: "The failure, we are well informed, is not for 'eight hundred and fifty thousands dollars,' but the claims . . . amount to about £150,000 and property to about £180,000 is exhibited. . . . The premature demand for specie on the Montreal Bank, in consequence of this failure, has ceased, and we understand that not much more than £7,000 was paid out."

The reticence exhibited by the local press was no greater than that prevailing in the inner councils of the Bank of Montreal. Although the Board met on December 23 and 30, before and after McGillivray's meeting with his creditors, no reference to that event is contained in the Directors' Minutes, nor was the Bank officially represented at the meeting. While the coffee houses around the Hay Market and along St. Paul Street echoed with gossip about the assignment, the Bank remained resolutely aloof. One explanation is to be found in the fact that the Bank was not yet sure of its actual position, nor would it be until it received advice from its London agents, Thomas Wilson & Co., with respect to the acceptance or non-acceptance of McGillivray's drafts on London. Another, and perhaps better, explanation is to be seen in his relation to the Board, in his long-standing friendship with many of the Bank's most influential shareholders, and in the pledge of secrecy of the banking profession generally, as binding as that observed in law or medicine.

Whatever the reasons, a veil of silence was drawn about the McGillivray embroglio for the next six months and the chief character in the drama relegated to the wings. Nevertheless, McGillivray's off-stage presence can be felt in the resumption of George Moffatt's attack on the existing management: in fact, the McGillivray affair, though never mentioned, provided Moffatt with his most effective ammunition in his campaign to bring an end to the laxity with which the Bank's business was being conducted. On December 23, for

example, soon after McGillivray's notice to his creditors, Moffatt reintro-
duced a resolution to replace any directors who had been absent for three
months, and a second for the election of a vice-president pro tem. in the place
of Thomas Thain, who had been away in Scotland since August. The following Tuesday, John Forsyth was named vice-president.

On December 30, three days after McGillivray's meeting with his creditors,
Leslie introduced a series of resolutions which was tantamount to proposing
a vote of want of confidence in the Bank's management. The first called for a
statement of the losses incurred by the Bank since its formation in 1817, with
particulars as to all persons and circumstances, together with all due and
protested paper in the hands of the cashier; the second provided that no stock
could be transferred by the president, vice-president or cashier in future
without the concurrence of the Board; the third, that no bills of exchange
could be taken without observing the same procedure, and the fourth called
for a statement of all bills of exchange purchased during the preceding six-
month period with the names of the endorsers. A fifth resolution provided
for the appointment of a committee to draft a new code of by-laws and regulations for the future conduct of the banking business. The five resolutions
carried unanimously but were effectively pigeon-holed by the failure to
implement them.

Resuming his attack on January 6, 1826, Moffatt moved that the Cashier be
directed to write to the President demanding payment of the indebtedness for
which he had been found liable back in August. Gerrard's answer, tabled on
the 10th, was a statement that "he owed the bank nothing," whereupon
Moffatt moved that the President be declared a defaulter without power to
transfer his stock or have access to his account (that is, cash cheques or drafts
or serve as endorser) as long as he remained in default. The motion was
carried after the defeat of an amendment by Garden to strike out the prohibition with respect to cheques and drafts. As recorded, the final vote read: for
the affirmative, Moffatt, Leslie, Gates, Ermatinger, and John Molson Jr. (who
had replaced David David as a director in 1824); for the negative, Forsyth,
Garden, and McGill. Flushed with victory, Moffatt and Leslie now tried to
persuade their colleagues to call a special shareholders' meeting on the first
Monday in March, but lost by a vote of six to two.

That the Bank's own position was more serious than yet shown by the
Minutes is seen in three resolutions tabled at a meeting of the Board on
January 17, the day following McGillivray's preliminary explanation of his

accounts to his creditors. Introduced by F. W. Ermatinger, the resolutions provided (1) that no loans above £10,000 were to be granted without the unanimous consent of the Board; (2) that no bills of exchange, except government bills, were to be taken from any firm or house without a responsible endorser approved of by the Board; and (3) that notices be posted conspicuously in the banking chamber advising customers that after the lapse of a fortnight full payment of notes would be required on maturity, thus putting an end to the practice of granting renewals upon a fractional reduction of the principal.

The resolutions, sponsored by one of the old guard, represented a significant defection and constituted an even more severe criticism of management than those introduced by Leslie some two weeks earlier. However, so evenly were the opposing factions now divided that the Ermatinger motions were laid over for one week and were again postponed until January 27, two days after McGillivray's second meeting with his creditors. With George Moffatt in the chair as director of the week, the Board approved the Ermatinger resolutions without a recorded vote and then proceeded to appoint a committee of three, Moffatt, McGill, and Fleming, a new director, to draft new by-laws in accordance with Leslie's motion of December 30.

With an aura of uncertainty enveloping the presidency and vice-presidency, responsibility for the day-by-day management of the Bank devolved upon the Board and the director of the week. This situation was to extend over a four-month period. During the interregnum, George Moffatt marshalled his forces, inside and outside the Bank.

TEN

A NEW
APPROACH

A NEW APPROACH

I.

On April 28, 1826, the directors of the Bank of Montreal unanimously resolved "that no dividend be declared for the 6 months from 1st December last
to 1st June ensuing." This was the first time that the semi-annual dividend
was passed. Three and a half years intervened before the declaration of another. The four-year interval has been interpreted by Breckenridge and Shortt
as an indication of the severe losses suffered by the Bank as a consequence of
the financial panic in England in 1825 and the commercial depression that
followed in Canada. Corroboration for the interpretation is contained in the
letter written some forty years later by Henry Dupuy, the first accountant,
after his retirement. It contains the statement: "About the year 1824 the
Bank of Montreal met with some severe losses, chiefly in Quebec, by lumber
merchants, others in Montreal, and about £80,000 was lost and carried to the
debit of profit and loss. Dividends were stopped for one year and a half or
perhaps two years. I think the stock was offered at 40 and 50 [per cent] discount and the public became very uneasy." Shortt also refers to a loss of

£80,000, and to a drop of 40 to 50 per cent in the value of the Bank's stock, but without giving the source of his information.

Despite his retentive memory, the aging first accountant seems to have been somewhat confused on financial matters. It was virtually impossible for the Bank to have lost £80,000 in 1824, for this would have represented nearly one-fifth of its total assets, and yet, after payment of the regular six-per-cent dividend, the rest account was increased in June of that year by £1,794, which was with one exception the largest sum so allocated out of undivided profits up to that time. The next year, it is true, saw a pitiful addition of only £38, but the six-per-cent dividend was maintained, and the £11,250 was paid without touching the reserves. In point of fact, the only net loss took place in 1826, when £4,679 had to be transferred from the rest account, leaving a balance of around £3,000. At this time, the Moffatt faction had grown sufficiently in strength to secure the adoption of more cautious policies with regard to dividend payments. As a result, the rest account was built up to more than £25,000 before a dividend was again declared, although the undivided profits transferred to the rest account in 1827 and 1828 were sufficient to pay annual dividends of six per cent had the Board so determined.

Other evidence bearing on the Bank's operations during the critical years of the 1820's is contained in the annual returns submitted to the provincial legislature and published in the *Journals* of the Assembly. These show that the volume of loans and discounts, the Bank's principal source of earnings, dropped, in round figures, from £1,850,000 in 1825 to £1,175,000 in 1827. Following the opening of navigation in the spring of 1826 the first ships up the St. Lawrence carried news of the widening depression in the British Isles. Thereafter, business in Montreal ground almost to a standstill. During the two years or more of commercial stagnation that followed, the Bank of Montreal's overdue advances at one point reached £86,800, more than half of which, however, resulted from the failure of the two largest customers, the Maitland house and Simon McGillivray, both of whose accounts, along with many of the others, were eventually recovered without serious loss to the Bank.

In contrast with the spate of bank failures in Great Britain and the United States, the Bank of Montreal maintained a record of financial stability and competent direction. Responsible was the *ad hoc* management brought into being after the President had been declared a defaulter and little hope remained for the Vice-President's return from Scotland. After acting decisively to place severe curbs on loans and improve collections, George Moffatt continued as its dominant figure until the annual meeting held in June 1826. Throughout the intervening months the Minutes of the Board refer mainly to routine banking matters, which were generally dealt with by unanimous action in conformity with sound banking practice. Even in the mute pages of the Resolve Book, however, a human drama of continuing conflict can be sensed. Despite the recent tensions, and the more stringent banking procedures that had been adopted, a resolution was passed on February 24, with only Moffatt dissenting, to reinstate Samuel Gerrard as a promisor and endorser. The incident marked a victory for the old guard. Much more significant was the success of its principal adherents – Forsyth, Garden, and McGill – in blocking the repeated efforts of Moffatt or Leslie to call a special meeting of the shareholders as provided by the charter.

The clash of principles and personalities continued against a background of worsening economic conditions in Canada and England. In Canada, April brought the final capitulation of the Maitland house after months of effort to avoid bankruptcy, together with a marked increase in the number of delinquent accounts. And from England, early in the same month, came information that serious apprehensions existed about the solvency of the Bank's London agents, Thomas Wilson & Co., who had over-extended their South American investments. Noting that "great inconvenience might result to the Bank from the suspension of the London Agency," the Board authorized, "in the event of the failure of the said Firm, the opening of an account with another House in that City." Letters to this effect went forward to Edward Ellice, Hart Logan and Robert Gillespie in London with instructions to proceed "at their discretion." The seriousness of the situation is indicated by a resolution, passed at the same special meeting of the Board, to request a loan of £25,000 for four months "on the security of the notes of the institution" from Prime, Ward, King & Co., successors to Prime, Ward & Sands, the Bank's New York agents.

While the Board recorded its deliberations with the utmost circumspection and the press was even more discreet, the public could not have been wholly unaware of the tensions existing within Montreal's foremost financial institution. Confirmation is to be read in a resolution passed at a July meeting of the Board:

> The Board, having had under its consideration the evil tendency of
> disagreement among the officers of the Bank, deem it necessary to de-

clare that it is their bounden duty individually and collectively to uphold the character and respectability of the Institution by the performance of their daily avocations with temper and forbearance – thereby conciliating the confidence of the public and the respect and esteem of each other – And the Directors are fully determined to mark any instance of neglect of such duty or breach of decorum in the Bank with the severest displeasure of the Board.

Apparently, gossip about the Bank had reached an unwholesome pitch much earlier. The conclusion is reinforced by the sentence in Dupuy's letter, "The public became very uneasy." Its uneasiness was to acquire gale force resulting in legislative inquiries in 1829 and 1830. In 1826, however, it was inspired by a general feeling of insecurity concerning the trend of events in England, by rumours of the Bank's losses following the failure of two of its principal customers, and by the introduction of a tight money policy at the very moment when the commercial community stood urgently in need of accommodation. Cancellation of the customary dividend in April did not help. It was also felt that the Bank, as the largest exchange dealer in the community, was responsible for the high rate on English exchange. All these circumstances combined to give George Moffatt the opportunity he needed.

2.

As we have seen, the commercial community of Montreal was not the monolithic hegemony it has often been pictured. Instead it was made up of diverse interests among which were persons who had capital to invest but who did not choose to accept the financial leadership of the Bank of Montreal alliance between the old fur-trading hierarchy and Yankee middlemen from across the border. Unlike many of the business men, whether English, Scottish, Irish, or American, who looked forward to returning "home" when fortune had favoured them sufficiently, these others looked on Canada as home and intended to remain there. While some were merchants – importing dry goods, hardware and liquor; exporting ashes, staves and wheat – their interests were not mercantile in the classic exploitative sense but were rooted in the domestic economic activities of the country. It was this group, as genuinely Canadian as *les Canadiens* who lumped together all English-speaking business men as exploitative interlopers, that was instrumental in founding the Bank of Canada as a separate financial institution, dissociated from the reigning financial oligarchy, for the same reasons that had prompted similarly situated groups in New England, New York, and other states to found their own separate banks. The Canadians were less successful than most of their American compeers. Although Montreal had become the commercial capital of Canada by the 1820's, the city could not yet support two banks; the Bank of Canada enjoyed only a few years' activity and upon the automatic termination of its ten-year charter was absorbed by the Bank of Montreal. Nevertheless, from the ranks of its subscribers came the added strength needed by George Moffatt to bring about the transformation within the Bank of Montreal he had begun at the onset of the 1826 depression.

Two factors combined to make the transformation virtually inevitable: the disappearance of one commercial generation and the appearance of another, younger and more aggressive. Helpful also no doubt was the swift onslaught of the depression, a circumstance always inimical to the older business generation. This is not to suggest that the giants of an earlier day had lost their power or were suffering a decline in fortune. Forsyth, Richardson & Co., as the agents for the East India Company and the financial agents of Upper Canada, still exerted a potent influence in Canadian affairs, as did others whose earlier successes won them posts on the Legislative Council or enviable positions on the boards of the many official and civic organizations with which the city now abounded – the Lachine Canal commission and Montreal harbour commission, the General Hospital, the Masonic Order, the Agricultural Society, and the numerous institutions for the promotion of education and learning. It is simply that one business generation was coming to its end. As John Irwin Cooper points out in *Montreal, the Story of Three Hundred Years*, by 1826 Montreal had become a city of 25,000 inhabitants and its wealth was no longer founded on the fur pack. Instead, a growth in the Canadian provinces proportionately greater than that occurring in the United States had brought about an expansion of the domestic economy and was laying the foundation of new fortunes and a shift in the locus of financial power.

Representative of this trend was John Molson, who had arrived in Montreal in 1782 at the age of eighteen years to engage successfully in brewing, lumber milling, real-estate speculation, and river transportation, and to become, by the 1820's, a leading figure in the city's life. One of the most remarkable men Canada has produced, he introduced steam navigation to the

TORONTO FISH MARKET—1840

Visiting Toronto in 1842, Charles Dickens wrote: "The country around this town being very flat is bare of scenic interest, but the town itself is full of life and motion, bustle, business and improvement." Much of this improvement dated from 1834 when the town of York was incorporated as the City of Toronto.

Fresh meat was often difficult to procure in those days, but Lake Ontario provided a good diet of salmon, bass, whitefish and perch, which was supplemented by imports of fresh oysters, lobsters and herring. The fish market was just south of today's St. Lawrence Market. Near the junction of Wellington and Front streets, at right, can be seen William Weller's stage depot and the City Hotel.

By 1840, Toronto had a population approaching 15,000 and landed property values in excess of £1,000,000. Up to fifteen steamboats plying Lake Ontario called at its wharves, and no less than ten newspapers reported the events of the day.

St. Lawrence River in 1809 with the successful voyage of the *Accommodation* from Montreal to Quebec, only two years after Robert Fulton's *Clermont* appeared on the Hudson River. Molson's second steamboat, the *Swiftsure*, a larger and more sophisticated river steamer, powered by twin engines built at the famous Soho works of Boulton & Watt, served as a troop carrier during the War of 1812 – the first use of steam navigation in military history – and afterwards enabled the brewing family to carry on a highly successful business in exchange, buying bills in Montreal at a discount and selling them twenty-four to thirty-six hours later in Quebec at an appreciable advance in price. This may explain why John Molson Sr. was not listed among the early subscribers to either the Montreal Bank or the Bank of Canada. More than four years passed before he became one. The Montreal Bank's transfer register for January 8, 1822, records the purchase of thirty shares each by John Molson Sr., John Molson Jr., and Thomas Molson, and ten shares by the youngest son, William. The Molson family has been closely associated with the Bank of Montreal ever since.

When John Molson Jr. was elected a director of the Bank in 1824, he was thirty-seven years of age, the youngest member of the Board, and, with the exception of Austin Cuvillier, the first director born in Canada. Understandably self-effacing during his first years of service as a director, he later became an active supporter of the Moffatt faction in the schism that developed over the President's alleged irregularities. The Moffatt ranks received their second reinforcement with the election of John Fleming to fill the place on the Board left vacant by the resignation of François Larocque, the former Nor'Wester, at the height of the McGillivray crisis. Born in Aberdeenshire in 1786, Fleming had come to Canada in 1803 to serve as a clerk with Hart, Logan & Co., and had quickly carved out a niche for himself in Montreal society, being a man of considerable taste and literary aspiration. Not only did he collect a library of some 11,000 volumes, but he was also adept at the writing of poetry and prose, his most ambitious work being *The Political Annals of Lower Canada*, which, however, provoked criticism as "a work as full of information as it is of prejudice against the French Canadians." In addition to literary and business pursuits, he was a member of many civic bodies and trade committees, and served as a Justice of the Peace. Although born in Scotland, John Fleming embraced the nascent Canadianism already noted and from the outset of his association with the Bank of Montreal was a staunch supporter of the forces working for its rejuvenation.

3.

Despite the growing strength of the Moffatt faction, a stalemate persisted between the old guard and the new during the early spring of 1826, with the independents on the Board occupying a neutral position. So intense was the struggle that despite the retirement of the unfortunate Simon McGillivray, the death of Thomas Torrance and the absence of Vice-President Thain, now confined in an asylum in Scotland, the election of further substitute directors was put off until the annual meeting in June. In the interval, the remaining ten directors were divided, four, three and three. In the old guard were Forsyth, Garden, staunchly loyal to old comrades of another day, the much younger McGill and the partially deposed President Gerrard. In the ranks of the insurgents were Moffatt, Leslie, and the newcomer, Fleming, while on the sidelines, standing seemingly aloof from what might have been regarded as a family quarrel within the empire, were Gates, Ermatinger and John Molson Jr. The forces being distributed as they were, the three independents obviously held the balance of power; it was through their support, in fact, that the dissident Moffatt had attained a very real measure of success before he was able to acquire voting strength. With the independents, he nullified the power of the Bank's chief officer, secured the adoption of more rigid banking practices, and to all practical intents and purposes, took over the management of the institution from mid January to early June. With only three votes, however, the rebels had insufficient strength to attain their third and most important objective – to bring matters out into the open by calling a special meeting of shareholders which would consider the charges laid against the President and approve or disapprove amendments to the existing code of by-laws and regulations. Notwithstanding the legitimate, and quite likely necessary, nature of this objective from a corporate point of view, all efforts to induce the Board to call a shareholders' meeting proved unavailing.

During the spring of 1826, confidence in both the Bank's financial strength and the character of the management was seriously weakened by the increasing number of failures and foreclosures among commercial houses doing business with the Bank, by the growing sense of doubt and insecurity as each new ship arriving from abroad brought more alarming news of the British depression, and by the rumours, rampant in the city – of divided management, of financial losses, of stock depreciation – recalled so vividly by Henry Dupuy nearly half a century after. Some of these rumours were undoubtedly justified. We know that a serious cleavage existed within the councils of the institution and that news of the dissension had not been kept within the confines of the board room. The injured tone of the Board's manifesto to the staff clearly indicated that every counting room, coffee house, and tavern in the city must have reeked with gossip about the Bank's affairs and the personalities involved in them. Compounding the undesirable situation still further was the Bank's enigmatic behaviour with respect to the McGillivray bankruptcy, now become a *cause célèbre* surrounded in mystery to all but the trustees.

Under such circumstances it was inevitable that loss of public confidence would develop. The acid test of any bank's solvency at the time, of course, was the ability to make good the promise to redeem its notes in specie on demand. This the Bank of Montreal could have had no difficulty in doing, for during the past year it had imported over £223,000 in specie from New York to cover a note issue which fluctuated between £133,000 and £138,000. With its new tight-money policy, the Bank's financial position was thus actually better than was suspected, and there is no real evidence that the shares suffered any marked depreciation. It is informative to note that only nine transfers of Bank of Montreal stock occurred between January 1 and June 1, 1826, and of these, only two were for more than ten shares each. The lack of undue trading activity reveals an interesting fact: no attempt was made by either faction in the power struggle to secure voting control by stock purchases. Whatever George Moffatt's innermost motivation may have been, his campaign to bring an end to favouritism in banking was fought on the grounds of principle alone.

Weighing the various aspects of the situation, it seems that the question that split the Board was not the validity of Moffatt's demands, for this had already been confirmed, but what in modern terminology would be called a question of public relations policy. We have no way of knowing, of course, what conversations were held, what arguments were presented, what pressures were brought to bear, or what realignments were effected within the Board or among the shareholders, but we can be certain, from what is known of George Moffatt's subsequent political career, that the debate was vigorous and comprehensive. The question was whether to proceed immediately with the agreed-upon housecleaning or let matters rest as long as possible. The first alternative involved a gamble with public opinion. Had immediate action been taken, and a frank disclosure made of the facts, there was the possibility that public confidence would have been greatly strengthened; yet any

IMMIGRANTS ON
THE MONTREAL DOCKS

The trip from Europe to America for immigrants in the nineteenth century was often a dreadful experience. Steerage passengers were confined to holds universally condemned for their filth, stench and overcrowding. On a rough passage, the hatches would rarely be opened and the dank quarters where the poor slept five to a berth would turn into hotbeds of fever and dysentery, often killing as many as a quarter of the passengers before they could reach their new homeland. Even on calmer voyages there was great hardship, for both food and water were scarce and, as often as not, unfit for human consumption toward the end of the two-month voyage.

To while away the endless hours, the people would read their bibles or play cards, although lighting was limited because of the terrible threat of fire. For the men, there were tasks imposed by the Captain, but all too much time remained in which to listen to the complaints of the sick. Entertainments in the form of dances were sometimes held on the rolling decks, and for those who could afford it there was rum to be purchased from the ship's stores; but this often led to drunkenness and fighting, which made life even worse.

Landfall brought anguish as well as joy, for it meant medical inspections and the transfer of the sick to quarantine stations. Sometimes the ailing members of a family would be sent to hospital at Grosse Isle, twenty-five miles below Quebec, never to be heard of again despite pitiful advertisements placed in the newspapers by their relatives. Those who survived were landed on the docks as we see them here, in a weakened condition and seldom with any specific place to go. It is little wonder that they look fatigued and forlorn, but their courage and strength are to be marvelled at; of such people was Canada made.

Painting by Fred Oakley

precipitate action might have caused alarm by creating the impression that things were much worse than was actually the case. To let sleeping dogs lie, on the other hand, involved no risks whatever, except that of enduring for a few more weeks the gossip that eventually infuriated the Board. It may be noted too, that the Bank of Montreal was a chartered institution, responsible to the public through the government, and no question of illegality of any kind was involved. Under these circumstances it is not surprising that cooler heads among the directors—suspicion points to Gates, Ermatinger and Molson—effected a compromise which gave both factions what they wanted: on April 20 an advertisement appeared in the Montreal newspapers signed by thirty of the Bank's stockholders, serving notice of a special meeting to take place after the close of the statutory annual meeting, to consider amendments to the by-laws.

4.

Under date of June 5, 1826, the following Minute was recorded in the Resolve Book:

> At a General Meeting of Stockholders held this day for the purpose of electing by Ballot, directors for the ensuing year, when by a majority of Votes, Messrs. Jamieson, Logan and William Molson, appointed to act as scrutineers, declared the following persons to be duly elected, viz: Samuel Gerrard, John Fleming, George Moffatt, John Torrance, John Forsyth, Horatio Gates, Joseph Masson, Wm. Blackwood, Peter McGill, Thomas Porteous, F. W. Ermatinger, John Molson Jr., James Leslie.

George Garden is believed to have retired permanently from business about this time, and it had become known that Thomas Thain would never return to Canada. After a trip to Scotland to attend to some personal matters, Garden returned to Montreal where he died in 1828; Thain died in Scotland four years later. The two vacancies on the Board were filled by William Blackwood and Thomas Porteous. Blackwood was the senior partner in Blackwood & Larocque, general merchants; Porteous had already served as a director. Both were supporters of Moffatt, as were Joseph Masson and John Torrance, the former elected to succeed Simon McGillivray, retired, and John Torrance his deceased older brother Thomas, a director of the Bank since 1818. Born in St. Eustache, Quebec Province, in 1791, of well-to-do parents, Joseph Masson was the third Canadian-born director of the Bank and at the time of his election was already a successful business man with a reputation for great shrewdness and ability. Coming to Montreal in 1814, he first secured a partnership in a Canadian branch of a Glasgow house, W. & H. Robertson, which was succeeded later by Joseph Masson, Sons & Co. with branches in Quebec and Glasgow. Joseph Masson is said to have been Canada's first millionaire. John Torrance was one of three brothers who came to Canada from Britain by way of New York before the War of 1812; Thomas and John set up as general merchants in Montreal, dealing principally in wines and liquors, and James at Kingston in Upper Canada. The three brothers were pioneers of the forwarding business on the upper St. Lawrence, became prosperous during the War of 1812, and with the purchase of the *Hercules* in 1826 successfully challenged the Molson transportation monopoly between Montreal and Quebec City. Not long thereafter the Torrance firm also challenged the East Indian monopoly of Forsyth, Richardson & Co. by becoming the first Canadian firm to deal directly with the Orient. With all four of the new directors on its side, the Moffatt group was thus now in a clear majority.

In view of the highly formal character of modern annual bank meetings, the somewhat irregular procedure followed at this annual meeting held in 1826 invites comment. No financial statement was tabled, to show profit and loss, notes in circulation, or bad and doubtful debts. As the statement was submitted to the legislature, it must be supposed that the figures had been made available to the stockholders but were omitted from the Resolve Book as redundant or irrelevant.

Following the record of the annual meeting, the next Minute reads:

At a General Meeting of Stockholders held this day pursuant to an advertisement duly published in the newspapers of this city bearing date the 20th April were present:

The Hon. John Richardson		The Hon. Matthew Bell	
Samuel Gerrard	George Moffatt	James Leslie	John Fleming
Robert Froste	Daniel Sutherland	John Forsyth	Thomas Porteous
William Blackwood	Peter McGill	H. G. Brevoort Jr.	Samuel Hall
Charles L. Ogden	John Try	James Eccles	John Molson Sr.
William Molson	Daniel Grant	Horatio Gates	F. W. Ermatinger
Cornelius Peck	Thomas Busby	Charles Stewart	Charles Brooke
John Bouthillier	John Ashworth	James Logan	John Jamieson
Frederick Griffin			

At this special meeting, the stockholders (evidently including the younger John Molson also, though he is not listed) proceeded to deal with the controversy that had agitated the Board for several months. The patriarchal Hon. John Richardson was unanimously elected Chairman, with Frederick Griffin, the Bank's lawyer, as Secretary. The meeting was called to order. The entry continues: "Mr. Gerrard presented a code of Bye Laws or Rules & Regulations for the Management of the Affairs of the Bank, and for prescribing the respective Duties of the President, Cashier and subordinate officers thereof for the approval of the Stockholders."

This code, representing the first revision of the rules set down in 1817, had been drafted by a committee made up of Moffatt, Fleming and McGill, appointed on January 27 "to draw up by-laws for the regulation of this institution according to the Act of Incorporation." Reporting back on February 7, the committee noted that irregularities had been found in the bonding requirements of subordinate officers but recommended that the existing code, adopted in 1817, remain in force until such time as a revised and amended code could be submitted to a general meeting of the stockholders for their approval. The recommendation was adopted but a motion to call a meeting for the purpose was defeated. On the date of its submission to the stockholders, June 5, the revised code had therefore been under consideration for almost four months. Thirty-six clauses were read and debated separately before acceptance or rejection by a *viva voce* vote. Significantly, perhaps, the only individuals taking part in the debate were Moffatt, Leslie, John Molson Jr., Gates, Gerrard and one Samuel Hall, who, after this brief appearance on the stage of history, is heard of no more. He was a supporter of Samuel Gerrard, and with the latter provided the only opposition to the revised code, and then only to those clauses governing the executive duties of the president. At the conclusion of the reading (but not the meeting, as will be seen), an amended and approved code of thirty-five articles was ordered printed for distribution among the stockholders, only one of the suggested provisions having been rejected.

The occasion represented a pronounced victory for George Moffatt and the group he had brought into being and had led for several months. In addition to holding a comfortable majority of the thirteen seats on the newly-elected Board of Directors, the group had also won the valuable support of the senior directors, Gates and Ermatinger, and of John Molson, junior, and had received approval, without important alterations, of the code that had been drafted under its direction. Considering the length of time that instrument had been in preparation and the consequent suspense engendered, the revised by-laws seem on first impression to represent a Pyrrhic victory for what had now become the second banking generation; a more detailed study shows, however, that such was not the case. Although twenty-six of the forty-two original clauses were incorporated without changes of any kind and six others were dropped in their entirety, the new code of thirty-five by-laws so strengthened the rules of governance of the Bank as to make the Board of Directors as a whole more truly responsible for the conduct of the banking business. This was accomplished by incorporating in the revised code the resolution that had already been adopted by the Board to restrict the discretionary powers of the senior officers of the institution. Thus Clause Seven of the 1817 code (Clause Six, 1826), governing the management of the Bank during recesses of the Board, was amended by the addition of these words: "no notes shall be discounted or Bills of Exchange purchased during the recess under any circumstances whatsoever." Similar proscriptions were placed on discounting practices and dealings in exchange. Clauses Eight and Nine of the 1817 code provided that discounts would be determined by a majority of votes but that two negative votes would be sufficient to check the passing of a note. The comparable 1826 by-law, Clause Nine, reads as follows:

> No individual or firm shall be promisor or 1st endorser for a sum exceeding in either case Ten Thousand pounds without the unanimous consent of the Board. Nor shall any Bills of Exchange, except Government Bills, be taken from any individual or firm, when Bills are depending on account of the Bank for a sum exceeding Five Thousand pounds sterling; nor in any case shall Bills of Exchange, except Government Bills, be taken without a responsible endorser, unless by the unanimous consent of the Board, of which seven Directors, at least, shall be present.

The discretionary powers of the weekly management committee were further restricted by an amendment to the clause relating to delinquent paper. Clause Eighteen of the 1817 code required that the cashier turn over to the solicitor all overdue notes "to be put in suit unless otherwise ordered by the President or Vice-President and Directors of the Week." In the 1826 code the modifying direction reads: "unless otherwise ordered by the Board."

As the 1817 code has already been discussed in some detail in Chapter Five, it will suffice here to note only other significant changes. One of these occurs in Clause One, establishing days and hours during which the Bank would remain open for business. Omitted from the 1826 code are the Catholic holy days—Epiphany, Annunciation, Corpus Christi or Fête Dieu, St. Peter and St. Paul, All Saints, and Conception—a reflection no doubt of the growing schism in Lower Canada. The holidays retained were New Year's Day, Good Friday, His Majesty's Birthday and Christmas Day. The Bank continued to remain open on Saturdays as theretofore, and banking hours were from ten to three o'clock during the winter and from nine to three during the summer. From several points of view, however, the most interesting amendment to the old code is that contained in Clause Thirty-two of the new by the addition of these words: "So soon as a permanent provision for the services of the President shall be made, he shall not, directly or indirectly, use Trade or Business of any kind on his private account, but devote himself entirely to the Superintendence of the affairs of the Bank." Not only was the now-familiar "conflict of interests" principle involved but the time had arrived when bank management would require full-time professional attention. As had been the experience in chartered banking across the border, the day of friendly accommodations among a small circle of mercantile associates was drawing to a close.

One other change may be noted: the omission of Clause Four of the 1817 code, pledging Bank stock held by any borrower to the institution as security so long as his debt remained undischarged. Otherwise all additional amendments or omissions were of minor importance.

The reading of the thirty-five clauses concluded, Captain James Eccles, one of the largest stockholders present, requested "some information respecting certain transactions said to have taken place some time since between Mr. Gerrard and Messrs. Spragg and Hutchinson." A motion that the Journals of the Bank be produced was carried by a voice vote of 19 to 8, a few stockholders abstaining, and the proceedings of the Board of Directors on August 27, 1825, and January 6 and 10, 1826, were read, whereupon "Mr. Moffatt moved to Resolve, seconded by Mr. Leslie, that the decision of the Board of Directors of the 27 August last, as to Mr. Gerrard's liability to the Bank be confirmed. It was Resolved that the sense of the meeting on this motion be taken, according to the number of votes." The votes were as follows:

Yeas	Votes	Nays	Votes
Mr. T. Porteous	5	Mr. Forsyth	32
Ermatinger	31	Richardson	130
Eccles	25	Hall	40
C. Stewart	5	McGill	11
Gates	5	Try	20
Moffatt	96	M. Bell	5
Molson Sr.	20		
Molson Jr.	20		
Peck	11		
Fleming	5		
(for Torrance)			
Leslie	37		
Froste	5		
Jamieson	5		
Wm. Molson	10		
Logan	11		
	———		———
	291		238

The voting on a share basis is of particular interest for the reason that it had never been resorted to before and for the information it reveals as to the alignment of the contending forces. Unfortunately, the restriction on voting, by which the holder of 100 shares or more was limited to 20 votes, makes it impossible to determine where stock control rested or how many of the 5,000 shares were actually voted, either in person or by proxy. Such questions, however, were mainly of academic interest: the important thing about the June meeting of 1826 was that George Moffatt and his staunch board-room ally James Leslie – strongly opposed to each other politically, by the way – had won their well-fought battle of principle: henceforth the corporation would be run under the provisions of the charter in the interests of the share-holders, not as a benevolent partnership. Having won the victory, the substance as it were, they now pressed to collect the shadow – the money owed by the ex-president. With this end in view, Leslie moved, and Moffatt seconded, a resolution to instruct the Directors "to proceed immediately to the recovery of the money decided by this meeting to be owing by Samuel

Gerrard, Esq., to the Bank of Montreal." However, an amendment was offered by John Molson Jr., who "moved to Resolve, seconded by Mr. Bell, that the Stockholders do relinquish their claim on Mr. Gerrard." The recorded vote follows:

Yeas	Votes	Nays	Votes
Mr. Hall	40	Mr. Peck	11
W. Molson	10	Fleming	5
J. Molson Sr.	20	Porteous	5
J. Molson Jr.	20	Stewart	5
McGill	11	Leslie	37
Bell	5	Moffatt	96
Forsyth	32	Froste	5
Try	20	Jamieson	5
Richardson	130	Logan	11
Gates	5		
	293		180

A final resolution, proposed again by Leslie and Moffatt, "that a Committee of Five Stockholders, not being of the number of the late Directors, be appointed to examine into the concerns of the Bank and report thereon at a meeting of the Stockholders to be called for that purpose on the first day of August next," was defeated, 170 votes being cast in favour and 303 against. So ended the momentous sequel to the ninth annual meeting of the Bank of Montreal.

5.

The events of June 5, 1826, marked an important milestone in the history of the Bank of Montreal. The day also marked a personal triumph for the indomitable crusader, George Moffatt. It brought not only a sweeping vindication of his principles, decently tempered by mercy, but the election of a Board of Directors whom he could rely on for support. When the stockholders dispersed on the Monday afternoon, the Honourable John Richardson was still the doyen of financial Montreal, but he was no longer its unchallenged leader; a younger man, more attuned to the changing Canadian environment, had occupied his place. Yet the final act in the drama of transition had still to

QUEENSTON, 1820 — EARLY BANKING POINT

Located below the falls on the Niagara River, Queenston formed the lower terminus of the old Niagara portage. The town was founded toward the end of the eighteenth century by Robert Hamilton, a Scottish trader who decided to move west from Kingston.

As one of the main stopping-places on the east-west transportation axis, Queenston became the site of warehouses and trading activity. Consequently, the Montreal Bank, a year after its opening, decided to appoint an agent there, and early in 1819 the services of Messrs. Grant and Kirby were engaged.

As the fur trade on the Great Lakes was replaced by agriculture and lumbering, the Bank withdrew its agency to concentrate on the developing areas farther east. Years later, in 1839, the first railway in Upper Canada, a portage road around Niagara Falls called the Erie and Ontario, was built between Queenston and Chippawa.

be concluded. Despite the demands of Monday's two meetings, the newly elected directors returned to the banking house on St. James Street early the next morning to perform their first statutory duty: the election of officers for the ensuing year. Any politicking that may have taken place was not noted in the Minutes, but when a vote was taken, Horatio Gates was awarded the presidency and John Fleming was named vice-president.

Still the dramatic interlude continued. The chief officers having been elected, the Board adjourned until Friday, June 9, when F. W. Ermatinger tendered his resignation as a director and John Molson Sr. was elected in his place. Horatio Gates then resigned the post of president and George Moffatt nominated Molson to succeed him. The election was unanimous, John Fleming, Vice-President, in the chair. So John Molson, brewer, steamboat proprietor, sometime member of the Legislative Assembly, took on the new challenge of the Bank's presidency at a most difficult time.

It is obvious that the elder Molson had been tendered the post earlier but had refused to accept it until he was satisfied that his services were needed in the interests of the Bank and hence of the financial and commercial community. But why did George Moffatt not assume the position himself? He was eminently qualified, enjoyed the confidence of the public, and commanded a majority of the votes of the directors; he appears, in fact, to have been the more logical choice. And failing Moffatt, why did Horatio Gates not continue as president? From the standpoint of banking experience, particularly with reference to the exchange operations that bulked so largely in the business of the Bank, he was probably the best qualified of any of the directors. Yet his acceptance of the post was on the understanding apparently that it would be on a stop-gap basis only.

Several explanations suggest themselves. Moffatt may simply have preferred to remain the power behind the throne as John Richardson had been before him. As head of a large and successful business then being expanded in Upper Canada, he may not have been willing to risk the sacrifice which he would have to make if the new "conflict of interests" clause were to be implemented during his tenure. About this time, too, as a close friend of the Governor, Lord Dalhousie, he had begun to interest himself more in politics. Horatio Gates's interests, as always, pointed southward, and at this time the conditions arising from the depression must have required his close attention. These factors, coupled with the increasing responsibilities devolving on the bank president, may have persuaded both gentlemen to forgo the honour. There is, however, another and perhaps more satisfactory explanation: the fact that the elder Molson had taken no part, openly at least, in the dissensions that had stirred the Board for months. He would thus have been more acceptable to the several interests among the shareholders and directors than any committed partisan. His wide variety of enterprises also made him rather more representative of the new Canadian commercial community than any other available candidate for the post.

As for the delay in his accepting the presidency, a knowledge of the history of the Molson family suggests that it was probably based on personal considerations. The second son, Thomas, after disagreements with his father and two brothers over the conduct of the family business, had moved to Kingston, Upper Canada, where he had set himself up as an independent brewer and distiller. John the elder, then contemplating retirement, had been forced to return to harness again, and had taken over the direction of business interests which included not only brewing and steamboat operations but farming and the management of Montreal's first foundry. Under the circumstances, his hesitancy in assuming added duties becomes understandable. The impasse was resolved when his sons John and William agreed to take over the management of the family business, leaving their father free to accept the post of president; and on June 20, F. W. Ermatinger was persuaded to rejoin the Board of Directors in place of John Molson Jr.

John Molson, the founder of the noted Canadian family of the name, was born in Lincolnshire three days after Christmas in 1763 and was therefore sixty-two years of age at the time of his accession as President of the Bank of Montreal. With a reputation for unswerving honesty, creative imagination, and bold achievement, he made his influence immediately felt in the conduct of the Bank's affairs. The presence of a new captain on the bridge is at once reflected in the pages of the Resolve Book – in the greater frequency with which meetings of the Board were held; in the increased attendance of directors at the meetings; in the greater number of items brought under consideration, and in the more conscientious manner these were dealt with and recorded.

The items of business fall into two general categories: those having to do with customer relations – the granting of discounts, collections and so forth – and those having to do with exchange operations, in Quebec with the Receiver-General's department, in New York with the Bank's agents, Prime, Ward, King & Co., and between Lower and Upper Canada, involving principally the relations of the Bank of Montreal with the now flourishing Bank of Upper Canada. One of the early steps taken to emphasize the new impartiality was the declaration "that this Board does not deem it expedient to retain the account of His Majesty's Receiver General on any other terms than those which are applicable to other depositors."

There was, however, another separate and more special problem, the delinquent account of Simon McGillivray. This had been permitted, so far as any direct action on the part of the Bank of Montreal was concerned, to lie dormant since the preceding January. As the story embraces the valedictory of the great Nor'Westers in Canada, it will be dealt with next, leaving the more general aspects of the Bank's activities for discussion in a later context.

At the first regular meeting after the election of the new president on June 9, 1826, the twelve directors in attendance lost no time in grappling with the McGillivray matter. Following the routine appointment of George Moffatt as the Bank's representative on the Maitland company estate, the first item of business on the agenda was a resolution, tendered by Moffatt and passed by a vote of ten to two, to appoint a committee consisting of John Fleming the Vice-President, James Leslie, and Thomas Porteous, "to wait on the Trustees of Messrs. McGillivray & Co. to see the statement of the affairs of that House and to report what instructions should be sent to Messrs. Wilson & Co. in regard to the transactions between them and Simon McGillivray, Esq."

As early as April 1826, Thomas Wilson & Co. had taken independent action to protest bills in the amount of £18,000 drawn by Simon McGillivray against his London house, McTavish, Fraser & Co., and sold to the Bank of Montreal. It was to come to grips finally with this situation that the committee had been appointed. By pure coincidence, two days later, a letter was received from Wilson & Co. enclosing a report from their legal counsellors, dated London, April 28, setting forth developments in London together with the legal costs to date, and enclosing the recommendations of counsel that the debt be prosecuted vigorously. It had now mounted to £22,000 with interest and legal fees.

The report of the committee appointed to wait on the Honourable John Richardson and Samuel Gerrard, the McGillivray trustees, was submitted on June 16 and considered in conjunction with the letter received from the London agents the preceding day. The committee's conclusions follow:

> . . . the conditions of the Assignment appeared so favourable to the Bankrupts and the Accounts so incomplete and unsatisfactory, that your

Committee could under no probable circumstances advise the accession of the Bank to said Assignment before having exhausted every other means of obtaining payment of the claim in question. On this head your Committee beg leave to remark that one half of the Creditors either in Number or Amount have not acceded to the Assignment, and it is probable that the want of regular Accounts and clear Statements will induce many to withhold their signatures, more particularly as the Memorandums and Accounts referred to, prove that after the Bankruptcy, large payments were made by the said Firm to some Creditors, to the prejudice of others equally entitled.

*   *   *   *   *

The probability of obtaining proof on these points from a disclosure in a Court of Justice, of the facts respecting the appropriation to be found in correspondence between Mr. W. McGillivray, Messrs. McTavish, Fraser & Co., and Mr. Ellice is a principal motive for approving the measures adopted by Messrs. Thomas Wilson & Co., and their Solicitors. Your Committee, while recommending to serious consideration the inconveniences, expenses and delay that may attend the suits in London, are humbly of the opinion that the character and respectability of the Bank, require that some sacrifices should be submitted to, with the view of prosecuting a claim which appears deserving of Investigation in an English Court of Justice, and the enforcement of which might be the most effectual means of preventing the occurrence of important breaches of engagement prejudicial to the Interests of the Stockholders and to the Public at large. – All which is nevertheless humbly submitted.

Montreal, 16 June, 1826.
John Fleming, T. Porteous, J. Leslie.

The payments and appropriations under question refer to £9,000 of Hudson's Bay Company stock set aside in his assignment by Simon McGillivray to secure his "private" debts to Samuel Gerrard for the latter's endorsement of a note for £11,000 discounted by McGillivray at the Bank of Montreal, and to the Honourable J. H. Dunn for the advance of £12,600 of the public monies of Upper Canada. It was these stock transfers, worth two to two and a half times their par value, together with usurpation of other McGillivray funds in London, that the Bank's directors were principally concerned about.

The committee report was concurred in by a vote of ten to two, J. Forsyth and P. McGill alone dissenting. There the matter rested for a week, when a letter of acknowledgement was dispatched to Wilson & Co., together with payment of the legal account and approval of the action previously taken: further instructions were to be "transmitted by the packet on the 8th proximo" (July 8), presumably via New York City. The McGillivray committee was instructed to wait again upon the trustees to ask that they assemble the creditors "to consider compromising on this side of the Water the claim of the Bank for the amount of returned Bills, as a means of stopping further legal proceedings in London by Thos. Wilson & Co." The meeting was held July 5, when the Bank's committee, with George Moffatt as an added member, presented an offer to settle the Bank's claim for £10,000 currency with interest and the transfer of Bank of Montreal stock standing in the names of the various individuals or firms party to the bankruptcy – McGillivrays, Thain & Co., Simon and William McGillivray, and Thomas Thain. In the event of the refusal of the offered compromise the Board of Directors would consider it their duty to instruct Wilson & Co. to proceed with the suit already instituted. While the reaction of the McGillivray creditors is omitted in the Minutes of the next meeting of the Board, it is evident that the Bank's proposal was favourably received. A similar proposal was then transmitted to Thomas Wilson & Co. for submission to Simon McGillivray and Edward Ellice in England.

That Simon McGillivray was kept fully cognizant of these proceedings by some person or persons who had detailed knowledge of them and, in addition, had access to the books of the Bank of Montreal, is clearly revealed by a letter to his Canadian creditors written in London, February 26, 1827, by McGillivray, and published for private circulation by B. MacMillan, Bow Street, Covent Garden, printer in ordinary to His Majesty.

The letter with its several appendices is nearly 25,000 words in length and contains McGillivray's detailed explanation of the causes of his bankruptcy and a discussion of subsequent events, especially the depreciation and mismanagement of his estate while he was in Canada. The document is a most able literary production and is at one and the same time a polemic, an apologia, a personal vindication, and an attack on the Bank of Montreal for instituting litigation designed to throw the entire estate into chancery and the author into debtors' prison. Since most of the ground covered by the letter has already been dealt with in these pages it will suffice now to remark upon the latter accusation. The charges against the Bank of Montreal are also contained in a letter to the Board dated July 25, 1826. These are summarized in the publication of February 1827:

> It appears to me perfectly demonstrated by the facts herein stated, that the interests of the Proprietors [the stockholders of the Bank] *have been* trifled with and sacrificed, by *a party* who had obtained a temporary ascendancy in the management of the Bank, but who had scarcely any interest in its prosperity; and whether their conduct is to be imputed to ignorance, or prejudice, or obstinacy, or party spirit, I care not, but I think it quite impossible to imagine, that it could have proceeded merely from a due regard for the interests of those constituents whose benefit they professed to have principally in view.

To elucidate, it was McGillivray's contention that the Bank's efforts to collect from him were not "actuated by a stern sense of public duty" but by a personal and venomous desire on the part of three directors, Messrs. Moffatt, Leslie and Porteous, to bring about his complete and final ruination. In the furtherance of this goal, it was maintained by McGillivray, these men, supported by a bare majority of the directors, had been willing to sacrifice the interests of both the stockholders and the creditors, by forcing him to become a legal bankrupt in England.

McGillivray argued his case brilliantly and in great detail, citing at length the deliberations of the Bank's directors, the votes and resolutions regarding the continuation of litigation, and the individual interests of the three pernicious directors with special reference to their ownership of Bank stock. Since their shareholdings were shown by McGillivray to have been only enough to qualify them as directors, the inference was that they had, indeed, been motivated by base personal enmity. The points involved in McGillivray's voluntary assignment, or acknowledgement of bankruptcy in Canada, were of a highly legal nature, and were never adjudicated in a court of law. It is thus a matter of personal opinion whether or not McGillivray's protestations as to his *bona fides* were genuine.

It is unquestionable that he had been placed in an abominable situation for which he was at most only indirectly responsible, but he compounded his difficulties by a desire to acquit himself honourably of the extravagant debts inherited from his partners. Nevertheless, the several letters to the creditors leave a good deal to be explained and give the impression that their author protests too much.

It seems unlikely that the directors, charged with gross malevolence, would have chosen to engage in open controversy, but no information on this point is available. Of the forty-two volumes of Directors' Minutes of the Bank of Montreal, only one is missing: Resolve Book No. 2, covering the years 1827-34. Existing Minutes of 1826, however, suggest that McGillivray's letter of July 25, 1826, reached Montreal shortly before September 9, when its contents were communicated to the Board at a special meeting. It was then decided to instruct Wilson & Co. to stay litigation in the prospect that McGillivray could return to Canada.

During the ensuing six weeks, the Board was kept busy tidying up the numerous other accounts and suits that had resulted from the depression. By October 24, however, the directors were becoming nervous about their second largest delinquent account and on that date they submitted several procedural problems for the consideration of their lawyers. Their basic dilemma was whether to sue McGillivray separately, subscribe to his deed of assignment, or carry the debt until he could disentangle his finances, gainfully employ his resources, and thereby tender repayment; the old guard was still reluctant to embarrass a friend and associate of long standing. The specific points of interest to the Bank in the case were the status of the McGillivray estate in Scotland, and the legality both of Simon's transfer of Hudson's Bay stock to Gerrard and Dunn after his bankruptcy and of his sale of Bank of Montreal stock just prior to his declaration of insolvency. The majority of the Board favoured accepting the deed of assignment, but before committing themselves they wanted to be sure that the Scottish property and the Hudson's Bay stock would be included in the assigned estate and that the Bank of Montreal stock, to which they felt they had prior claim, would not.

On receipt of their solicitors' opinion, the directors, after several prolonged meetings in early November, 1826, agreed to subscribe to the deed of assignment, providing, however, that all other rights of recourse to the aforementioned stock and property were reserved. The trustees of the McGillivray estate, needless to say, politely rejected the Bank's highly conditional offer. In so far as the Bank's records are concerned, the final denouement was reached on December 12, when the ten directors in attendance debated a resolution to transmit all documents and opinions to Messrs. Thomas Wilson and Company for submission to barristers of eminence in the Court of Chancery and to take such steps as they might advise to cancel the transfer of Hudson's Bay stock and return it to the estate to be divided among the creditors thereof.

This was the ninth in a series of related resolutions introduced by George Moffatt and seconded by James Leslie or John Fleming. Seven, setting out the facts of the case, passed unanimously, but the eighth, calling for immediate legal action by the Bank, was lost by a vote of six to five through the exercise of the presidential prerogative by John Molson Sr. The ninth was then amended by Peter McGill, who had remained McGillivray's unswerving supporter from the beginning of the controversy, as follows:

> Resolve – that any steps taken by this Board similar to the raising of the proposed question tending to make Mr. Simon McGillivray a Bankrupt, thereby throwing his Estate into the Court of Chancery, and depriving the Trustees of the Benefit of his Services in winding up and settling many complicated Accounts, will be ruinous to the Estate generally, and most injurious to the Interests of this Institution:

> YEAS: Messrs. Molson, Blackwood, Forsyth, Fleming, McGill.
> NAYS: Messrs. Porteous, Leslie, Masson, Torrance, Moffatt.

The amendment was carried by the casting vote of the President, whereupon Moffatt offered a tenth resolution to clarify the Bank's position, and possibly his own:

> Resolved that this corporation neither desires nor seeks to establish any exclusive right or claim in the distribution of the Assets of the said House of Messrs. McGillivrays, Thain & Co. except as related to the Stock of the Bank held by the Partners of the said House – and that it has offered to relinquish and is still willing to relinquish all claim and demand against the said Simon McGillivray, in respect of the Debt due by his House to the Bank, upon the single condition of a full participation in the Assets thereof, as to right and justice may appertain.

The record closes with the words, "Which resolve was carried unanimously."

On this inconclusive note ends the extraordinary story of the Nor'Westers, in so far as it is pictured from the existing records of the Bank of Montreal. Little more information has been discovered elsewhere. A submission by the Bank during a legislative inquiry in 1829 reveals that as of November 6, 1828, the Bank was carrying the McGillivray account at five shillings on the pound plus the Bank stock at 95 per cent, making an estimated £11,336. 3s. 4d. recoverable out of a debt which by then had grown to £22,117. 17s. The stock transfer register confirms that on October 1, 1829, the trustees of the McGillivray estate transferred to the President of the Bank of Montreal in trust the 163 shares of Bank stock standing in the name of McGillivrays, Thain & Co., Thomas Thain, Hon. William McGillivray and Simon McGillivray. At their previous evaluation, this would have represented the recovery by the Bank of £5,806. 17s. 6d., but it remains unknown if, when, and in what amount the balance of the debt was settled.

ELEVEN

PUBLIC CRITICISM
AND LEGISLATIVE
VINDICATION

PUBLIC CRITICISM AND
LEGISLATIVE VINDICATION

I.

Of the great economic depressions of modern times, that of 1825-26 was one of the shortest in duration but one of the most revolutionary in its social and political effects. Starting with the failure of country banks in the west and south of England, it moved to the crisis stage in December 1825, and throughout 1826 was attended by the now familiar phenomena of financial failure, commercial contraction, falling land values and commodity prices, large-scale unemployment, and great social unrest. Yet so resilient were the forces of industrial recovery that the trough of the depression had been reached by the summer of 1827 and a new cycle of rising prices, investment, industrial expansion, and world-wide commercial activity was begun, to reach its peak midway through the 1830's.

As the depression that began in 1929 brought the New Deal to the United States, so in 1825-26 a similar crisis became the catalyst of profound economic, social and political change. The depression of 1825 gave rise to the great exodus of people from the British Isles to seek new opportunities beyond the seas and was responsible for the first drastic changes in more than a century of the laws governing English banking and currency. The effects of the depression were not confined to the British Isles, but were felt with equal force in Europe and the United States.

Although still relatively unimportant members of the North Atlantic commercial community, the Canadian provinces were also affected by the winds of change that swept across their boundaries. The most important effect of course was the tide of immigration that began in 1826, as a result of a combination of British unemployment and the cheap passages available on timber vessels returning to Quebec. The twin forces of British repulsion and Canadian attraction tripled the population of Upper Canada in fifteen years, resulting in the development of an agricultural economy, providing labour for public works, and adding to the political discontent that led to armed rebellion before the next decade was ended. Other effects can be noted in the resumption of the trade war between Britain and the United States and in the Imperial decision to strengthen Canada's defences against the United States. The trade war was largely a maritime concern precipitated by Britain's final effort to monopolize the carrying trade between herself and North America; the building of the Rideau-Ottawa canals and construction of fortifications on the Richelieu River were military undertakings to provide for a war which had already been fought and which – in the light of the Missouri Compromise and the declaration of the Monroe Doctrine – would never, in all likelihood, be fought again.

Recommended to the Duke of Wellington by engineers who had served in Canada during the War of 1812, the Rideau system was designed ostensibly to provide a network of interior military communications secure from American attack along the frontier of the upper St. Lawrence. Despite the efforts of the Montreal commercial group and of people in Upper Canada to win Imperial aid for the improvement of the St. Lawrence River itself, the military recommendations were accepted and work was begun in 1826, less than a year after the opening of the Erie Canal. Built under the supervision of Colonel John By of the Royal Engineers, the Rideau Canal was completed in 1832 at a cost of approximately £800,000 sterling. It had considerable importance as a "make-work" project in view of the steady increase in immigration, and it helped, when finished, to open up the country between Lake Ontario and the Ottawa River for the new settlers, but its small, shallow-draft locks and the absence of a tow-path greatly limited its value for general transportation purposes. The bulk of its traffic, in fact, soon consisted of floating timber and, later, barges piled with milled lumber.

The years between 1826 and 1841 were to prove the most trying in the history of the Canadian provinces. In both Lower and Upper Canada the struggle for popular government through control of the purse culminated in short-lived rebellion, while the economy suffered from the intractable nature of the geography and the division of a single economic area into separate provinces with different cultural backgrounds and commercial attitudes. As hitherto, military expenditures continued as one of the principal supports of the economy in both provinces, as did the square-timber trade even under the reduced colonial preferences of 1821. However, the latter merely exploited the country's natural resources, as the fur trade had done before it. Operated from Quebec until mid century and controlled from England, it required small capital investments and, apart from subsistence wages, left little money in the country.

As we have seen, the changes within the Bank were wrought by the introduction of more stringent lending and collection policies and by the adoption of a more effective code of rules and regulations to conform with the principles of commercial banking. Within a month of its election in June 1826, the new Board of Directors also took steps to provide greater management efficiency and to effect economies.

Since it was not yet possible to make the president a full-time salaried officer, standing committees on finance and correspondence were named to assist him in his labours; Horatio Gates, James Leslie and George Moffatt serving on the first, and Peter McGill, F. W. Ermatinger and William Blackwood on the second. With the same end in view, the responsibilities of the cashier, already increased during the period of board management, were extended to relieve the president of merely routine duties. The staff of nine was reduced to eight, but a further attempt at a general salary cut was defeated by a vote of seven to five. Instead, each salary was individually debated during the course of a spirited session of the Board held on June 30, 1826. Two, those of the discount clerk and second bookkeeper, were reduced by £50, while the messenger received a £25 raise. The staff retained at that time comprised Robert Griffin, Cashier, £600 per annum; Benjamin Holmes, first teller, £350; Henry Dupuy, bookkeeper, £300; James Finlay, discount clerk, £200; William Radenhurst, second teller, £300; Lawrence Castle, second bookkeeper, £150; A. Jackson, messenger, £100; and a porter, unidentified, at £75. James Jackson, who had replaced H. B. Stone as first teller in 1818, was retired with six months' leave of absence, and the resignation of Robert Griffin was accepted, to take effect at the end of the year. He subsequently financed Montreal's first speculative real-estate development, the area still known as Griffintown being named for him.

A more significant reaction to the depression, however, was the decision made some months before to withhold dividend payments until a reserve equal to ten per cent of the authorized capital of $250,000 had been accumulated out of earnings. The Directors' Minutes show that this was made possible by increased dealings in foreign exchange. A Minute of June 20, 1826, for example, contains a resolution "that gold and British Silver Coins be prepared in parcels of £500 and £1000 to be forwarded to Prime & Co. as good opportunities recommended by Mr. Gates may offer." A fortnight later the Board resolved to purchase "Government Bills of Exchange at the rate of 10% premium for 30 days and also to pay for British Silver of the New Coinage at the rate of 6½% premium." Again, in August, the Bank tendered through its Quebec office for "all the Government Exchange advertised for sale, namely £20,000 at 10%," and in September, exchange to the value of $222,000 was purchased at the same rate. Most of these purchases were transmitted to the New York agent for sale on the Bank of Montreal account, and again we find the indefatigable Holmes engaging in his itineraries down Lake Champlain and the Hudson River, returning on one occasion with £30,000 in silver coin. Concurrently, William Radenhurst was ordered to York with Bank of Upper Canada notes and instructions "to receive payment for the same by a cheque on this Bank at par, a draft on New York @ 3% at 116 premium or in specie as best may suit the convenience of the Bank of Upper Canada."

2.

These highly profitable exchange activities depended on several factors: the temporary stoppage of the flow of British investment capital to the United States; the imbalance of trade between the two countries in favour of Great Britain; the continued flow of British funds into Canada to support the military and civil establishments; and the concurrent attempt on the part of the British government to establish a uniform currency throughout the Empire, an unsuccessful experiment that increased the shipment of silver into Canada.

Following the British occupation, it will be recalled, no steps were taken to provide a provincial currency, although continuous efforts were made to establish the ratings of the heterogeneous gold and silver coins then in circulation. Among the French Canadians in Lower Canada, the old French coinage with the livre as the unit of value became the principal medium of exchange and in Upper Canada the Spanish or Mexican dollar. In both provinces, however, the dollar was the monetary standard but with different values, Lower Canada adopting the Halifax standard of five shillings to the dollar, and Upper Canada, in spite of legislation to the contrary, the York standard of eight shillings to the dollar.

An effort to improve this extraordinary situation was made by the British government in March 1825, when an Order in Council was passed for the purpose of securing the circulation of British silver and copper money: "In all those colonies where the Spanish dollar is now, either by law, fact, or practice, considered as a legal tender for the discharge of debts, or where the duties to the Government are rated or collected, or the individuals have a right to pay, in that description of coin, that a tender and payment of British silver money to the amount of 4s. 4d. should be considered as equivalent to the tender or payment of one Spanish dollar, and so in proportion for any greater or less amount of debt."

Based on recommendations of the Treasury Board, the Order in Council was a direct outcome of the introduction of a new silver coinage following Britain's return to the gold standard a few years earlier. With a view to preventing silver currency from going abroad, the Treasury at that time had made silver a token money by raising its face or minted value above its bullion value and limiting its use as legal tender to forty shillings. With a higher purchasing value in Britain than elsewhere, the new coinage remained in the country as a permanent medium of exchange, relieving the currency famine that had occurred after the Napoleonic Wars. Not only did the seemingly simple operation accomplish its primary purpose; it was also profitable to the government through the seigniorage involved. Under such circumstances, it was desirable that means should be sought to extend the silver circulation. With this end in view, the Treasury, for the first time, turned its attention to the state of the currencies in British colonies and possessions abroad as they affected the expenditures for public services, both military and civil.

In most of the colonies, the Spanish dollar was the prevailing coin but it was in short supply and over-rated in terms of its intrinsic worth by local ordinances. The first condition was caused by the recent South American revolutions, which had strangled the normal silver supply, and the second by the

BELATED DEFENCE PROJECT

Following the War of 1812, consideration was given to a canal system from the mouth of the Rideau River to Kingston at the foot of Lake Ontario. The British army was anxious to have an east-west supply line that would be less vulnerable in war time than the St. Lawrence route, which was favoured by the merchants.

Britain finally decided to build the Rideau Canal alone, and in 1826 Colonel John By of the Royal Engineers arrived to supervise construction of the 47 locks needed to serve the 133-mile project. Completed in 1832 at a cost of £803,774, it was wide enough to admit steamboats, but since it was just five feet deep, only the smaller craft could use it. W. H. Bartlett's drawing shows the entrance to the canal at Bytown.

One of the contractors associated with Thomas McKay on the canal was John Redpath, a director of the Bank of Montreal. The Bank sent an agent to Bytown soon after construction began but was barred by law from opening a branch there until after 1841.

practice of over-rating in the hope of keeping specie in the colonies. The Lords of the Treasury, in fact, discovered that whereas the government was paying 4s. 8d. for a Spanish dollar, "As compared with British standard silver, the dollar is slightly less than 4s. 4d., while at the prevailing market price for silver it is scarcely above 4s." Add to this the fact that in Lower Canada the dollar traded for 4s. 6d., and one gets an idea of the current commercial quandary. The nominal value of the new British silver coinage was higher than its intrinsic value and it was hoped that this, together with special arrangements for its convertibility into bills on London, would keep it circulating in the colonies and at the same value as in England. It was decided, however, to sell these bills at a three-per-cent premium in the colonies. While the Spanish dollar remained in circulation it was to be rated at 4s. 4d., and provision was made for the fulfilment of existing contracts under the conditions prevailing at the time of engagement. In all future contracts, however, the Commissariat would reserve to itself the option of paying the contractor either in British silver or in bills on the Treasury, at the rate of £100 for every £103 of the contract. It was planned to introduce the new coins into the colonies by way of the government payrolls.

Quoting Adam Shortt, this scheme, it was confidently hoped, "would unite the whole British Empire in the use of one uniform medium of exchange. All parts of the Empire should henceforth hold commercial intercourse in one currency language, to the great benefit of trade within the Empire and its extension beyond it. Wherever the British flag waved the British shilling would circulate, each an emblem of British rule.

"To the eye of pure reason the scheme was faultless. Even official minds trembled on the verge of sentiment in contemplation of its vast imperial possibilities. But, unfortunately, the shield had another side, the colonial, from which it excited little enthusiasm."

The crux of the matter lay in the arbitrary devaluation of the silver dollar from 4s. 6d. to 4s. 4d., which constituted an uncompensated loss of four per cent on silver coins in Canada. In the opinion of James Stephen, the legal adviser to the Colonial Office, the currency Order in Council was *ultra vires*: His Majesty's Government was not privileged to dictate changes in those rates which had been established by the legislatures of the various colonies with respect to the Spanish dollar or any other coin. Despite Stephen's opinion the order was forwarded to all colonial governors with instructions for its proclamation. Received in Lower Canada in the fall of 1825, this high-handed

procedure immediately encountered opposition on the grounds already anticipated by Stephen. Reporting to Bathurst, the Lord Treasurer in England,
Lord Dalhousie, the Commander of the Forces in North America and Governor
of Lower Canada, could see no alternative but to wait for the next meeting
of the legislature in January, when he would recommend the measure but
with little hope of its adoption.

His lordship's forebodings were fulfilled. When the matter was laid before
the Assembly on January 21, 1826, it lay tabled for a month, when a committee of five was appointed to inquire and report on the expediency of changes
in the currency. The matter died in committee. Meanwhile by means of a
special message from the Governor the order was transmitted to the Legislative Council. For once the Council and Assembly found themselves in accord
in a financial-monetary matter, but ironically the usually sycophantic Council
was much the more forthright in its opposition. While no objection was voiced
against British coinage *per se*, the Council pointed out that it could not be
introduced at an altered valuation without alteration of the existing laws. It
was further held that any depreciation in the value of the dollar would
injuriously affect the collection of feudal *rentes* and dues in a province where
most accounts were kept in livres and sols.

The monetary folk-ways of the French Canadians also posed a nice dilemma. In the rural districts of Quebec, the family nest-egg and the bride's modest
dot were still represented by little hoards of specie accumulated by the slow
and difficult process of treasuring silver coins that came into the habitant's
possession. Some of these were French silver of the Ancien Régime and
some of the minting of 1793, a French currency that had found its way to
Canada by way of the West Indies and the American States. Although such
coinage had become worn and mutilated, it still circulated legally at an over-
rated value and, except in Montreal and to a less extent in Quebec City, was
greatly preferred to the bank-notes that often turned up on rural market days.
As a result, the province had become a place of refuge for all the despised and
deteriorated French coin of North America and this in turn had become the
medium of exchange in which most French-Canadian business was reckoned
and conducted. Under such circumstances, any attempt to alter the value of
the common medium, without imaginative preparation and generous compensation, must have led to serious repercussions. After all, there were men
not yet in their seventies who sometimes wondered what might have been
Canada's allegiance after 1775 had the American invaders brought with them

hard currency instead of the worthless paper promises of the Continental Congress.

The situation in the sister province differed considerably. In Upper Canada, the principal medium of exchange was the bank-note—Canadian or American—and there was little or no tendency to hoard specie, for the simple reason that there was so little of it in circulation. Shortt notes that the only gold coin ever seen was that brought in by immigrants or on its way back out of the colony to pay for imports, while silver was also in notoriously short supply. The dearth of copper had already led to a mongrel penny coinage made up of brass buttons and merchants' tokens of various kinds and sizes. Above the rapids of the St. Lawrence, therefore, there was no question of disrupting existing monetary values; instead, the population welcomed the prospect of large infusions of British silver through government expenditures, and no serious objection to devaluation developed. What wrecked the scheme in Upper Canada was the unwillingness to abandon the already assimilated and more convenient North American dollar for British sterling with its pounds, shillings and pence.

The business men of both communities were satisfied with the bank-note circulation that made it possible for them to engage in transactions simply and expeditiously without having to spend time and effort in weighing every small coin that came into their possession. What would have been favoured, and was to be, eventually, was the introduction of a provincial decimal currency. Meanwhile, in a patronizing fashion, the Upper Canada legislature drew up and passed an act which paid lip-service to the Treasury Order: this act simply revalued the few British coins then circulating in Upper Canada without changing the dollar-oriented currency system, thereby effectively ignoring the real intent of the British Treasury Board. This piece of legislative adroitness, however, only made the legal ratings between the two provinces even more disparate.

Despite the unfavourable Canadian reaction, the government in London believed that it held in its own hands the instrument for carrying out its purpose, as it entirely controlled military expenditures in the North American colonies. The building of the Rideau Canal and the projected strengthening of Canadian defences at Quebec, at Kingston and on the Richelieu would give it increased leverage. In other words, if the Canadian provinces could not be persuaded to embrace the British currency by legislation it could be forced on them by sheer weight of metal. The assumption was to prove mistaken,

"THE GIBRALTAR OF AMERICA"

Quebec was long the centre of military strength in Canada, both French and British, and fortifications existed there from the earliest times to augment the natural obstacles to attack. Construction of the present Citadel, however, was not begun until 1820.

As a result of Canadian experience in the War of 1812, Colonel Elias Durnford, commander of the Royal Engineers in North America, submitted plans and an estimate of £70,000 to the British government. These were willingly approved, and the next task became the acquisition of material and its transportation to the top of the 300-foot Cape Diamond. Although much of the needed stone was available locally, one Aberdeen skipper got the idea of using granite as ballast on the westward passage; instead of dumping his ballast in the river as was the custom, he put ashore Scotch granite blocks, some of which weighed over five tons, and was paid for them.

To raise such objects to the site of the Citadel, Durnford designed the inclined plane pictured here, up which cable cars were hauled by a windlass. The latter was worked by a team of horses until about 1830, when a steam engine was installed in a commissariat building at the foot of the tracked incline. This is the first known instance of the use of steam for land transportation in Canada.

Although some modifications have since been made, the Citadel was essentially finished in 1831. Together with the Rideau Canal and other minor feats of military construction during this period, the Citadel was responsible for a very heavy inflow of money which provided an essential boost to the fledgeling Canadian economy.

Painting by Don Anderson

255

but on the strength of it £30,000 of the new silver coinage was shipped to Canada in August 1825 and formal notice was given in the Canadian press that, dating from the preceding May 25, the pay of His Majesty's forces throughout the North American Command would be issued at the par of 4s. 4d. to the Spanish milled dollar. Notice was also served that in future all tenders for supplies must be made in British money, as must all payments to the Military Chest on His Majesty's account. The significance of the last provision relates to the anomalous fact that Canadian customs duties were levied under different statutes, Imperial and Canadian. The effect of the edict was to raise the duty on commodities imported under the Imperial schedules and formerly paid for in dollars or related coins or in bank-notes. Deeming the arbitrary action of the Treasury illegal, Canadian merchants refused to pay the duty, but ensuing litigation ended in a judgement in favour of the Treasury.

In theory, massive infusions of British currency should have led to its eventual adoption. They failed to do so for a number of technical and human reasons. One of these was that the specie sent to Canada never exceeded the requirements of its international exchanges. Indeed, the more the British government spent, the greater the quantity of goods purchased from abroad for which payment could be made only in British silver under the new currency dispensation. So the metal was always in demand and was quickly bought up by those who had to pay customs duties or purchase sterling bills of exchange. In the normal processes of trade, no sooner was the silver put into circulation than it began its journey back through the merchants and the banks to the Treasury or the military chest.

The entire operation was like trying to fill a barrel from which the bung had been removed. The attempt proved that the assumption that the new coinage would be retained in Canada was gravely in error. The over-rated silver was retained in Britain for the reason that it had no place else to go, while in Canada, there was another country, namely Britain itself, that would not only accept the coins at their face value but virtually demanded that they be rendered for any debts due itself or its exporters. In Shortt's opinion, "Their intrinsic deficiency counted only with reference to the American exchanges, and that was one chief reason why they [the new British shillings] were confined to the function of procuring British exchanges. For all purposes of internal trade, the bank-notes and greatly over-rated Spanish pistareens and French coins were still used." Nor did the special arrangements for the convertibility of the new coinage help the situation, as Shortt points out elsewhere: "Owing to the constant demand for British bills of exchange and the declaration of the government that bills of exchange would be issued for British silver at three per cent premium, the British silver was constantly withdrawn from circulation to purchase bills of exchange. Thus the very machinery which was to ensure the circulation in Canada of British coinage resulted in virtually banishing it from circulation, leaving the currency field to the paper issues of Canadian and American banks, supplemented by French silver in Lower Canada and American and Spanish silver in Upper Canada. In course of time it was found that the premium of three per cent on British bills was too high, it being cheaper to export the British silver directly. Before long, therefore, the military chest itself was forced to receive and pay little else than Spanish and American dollars and their fractions."

The records of the Bank of Montreal, together with returns made to the government and the evidence given to legislative committees, suggest other incongruities. Despite the difference in the rated and the intrinsic value of the British coinage, so great was the New York demand for specie that the discount at the rated value was more than compensated by the higher premium it commanded beyond the border. In effect, every effort to place the Imperial currency in circulation, and keep it there, was frustrated by its rapid return to the military chest or its export to New York, where at one point it commanded a recorded premium of sixteen per cent.

The Bank of Montreal must acknowledge a share of responsibility for the failure to implant an Imperial currency on the Canadian provinces. This resulted not so much from direct opposition or obstruction on the Bank's part as from the fact that its notes had become the established circulating medium against which less convenient media of exchange could not compete. While the same held true of the other banks, the unique position of the Bank of Montreal, as the depository of the Receiver General in Quebec and with its network of correspondents abroad, made it the principal dealer in exchange. The Receiver General deposited with the Bank bills on London, against which payments were made by cheque or draft in dollars on the Treasury account. By this arrangement, London bills were transferred to the Bank at a small premium and paid for in the Bank's own notes. Although payable in specie on demand, these notes were seldom presented for redemption because of their reliability and convenience. So the Bank was able to acquire bills of exchange in return for its own promises to pay, and dispose of the former at a profitable premium to Canadian merchants, or its New York agents for specie. In fact, the Treasury's introductory shipment of £30,000 in shillings in 1825 was dwarfed by Bank of Montreal specie imports from the United States which in that same year exceeded in value £198,000.

The commanding position of the Bank with respect to hard currency is attested to by a letter in the Kingston *Chronicle* in 1824, which stated that specie sent to Kingston to pay the troops was not put into circulation but was turned over directly to the agent of the Bank of Montreal who issued bank-notes in return and sent the specie back down the river in the same kegs and boxes in which it had arrived. The statement, or accusation, as it was probably intended to be, is confirmed in the previously quoted memoir of Henry Dupuy where it is noted that a similar situation prevailed during the construction of the Rideau Canal.

3.

The name of Thomas Hart Benton is rarely encountered in Canadian histories; nevertheless, the senator from Missouri exerted a marked influence on Canadian thinking during the 1830's. His fulminations in support of agrarian democracy were echoed in the speeches of Louis-Joseph Papineau and William Lyon Mackenzie, and his tirades against banks, bankers and the "money power" as represented by the Second Bank of the United States provoked legislative inquiries in both provinces and a spate of banking experiments in Upper Canada. At no time in Canadian history was there more discussion of the nature of banking, nor was there a time when the banking system stood in greater jeopardy.

Some of the forces, economic, social, and political, which led to the American bank war of the 1830's and to the destruction of the nationally chartered banks in the United States have received attention in these pages, as have the principal reasons for the survival in Canada of a banking system founded on the same classic principles. Here, we are concerned in a more detailed way with the struggle for free banking south of the international boundary and its quite extensive repercussions in the British colonies to the north. Free banking involved the application of the laissez-faire principle to the incorporation of banks; it was felt that anyone who desired to engage in the business of banking should merely be required to conform to some general statute. Each state would adopt its own laws, under which interference and restrictive regulations were to be held to a minimum, government participation being rejected because it was incompatible with the ideal of free competition.

The American bank war had its origins in the depression of 1825-26, which for some years made capital for further expansion and development almost unattainable, especially in the newly established communities of the Middle West. Actually responsible was the industrial and financial collapse in England brought on by over-expansion and speculation. In the eyes of Andrew Jackson and the leaders of the new agrarian democracy, however, the blame was placed squarely on the Second Bank of the United States, with its command of the government revenues, its manipulation of international exchange, its discount or lending policies, and its access to the London money market, whence came most of the capital for American expansion and development.

In the presidential election campaign of 1828 the banking question became an important issue, and after Jackson was elected the seventh president he conducted a severe attack on the Second Bank of the United States and its guiding genius, Nicholas Biddle, describing the institution as "a hydra of corruption" that had "demoralizing effects upon our citizens" and was "dangerous to our liberties." Its destruction became an *idée fixe*, and while Jackson acted as the chief engineer, its downfall was made possible by a strange alliance between western radicals, who sought a banking system not dissimilar to that comprising the English country banks but without England's immense capital resources, and New York banking interests, who were determined to make that city the financial centre of America in place of Philadelphia, the head office the Second Bank of the United States. In the course of the long battle between political philosophies and financial rivalries, Thomas Benton became one of the most bitter enemies of the centralized control of banking credit vested in the Second Bank of the United States and a most trenchant assailant of the fiscal, financial, and monetary systems of the times. Known as "Old Bullion" for his advocacy of a metallic currency, he disputed the legality of bank-note issues on constitutional grounds and at the same time questioned the right of the government to regulate credit and the currency. He avidly supported Jackson in the series of steps that finally wrecked the Second Bank of the United States. This was accomplished, first, by Jackson's refusal to renew its charter and, second, by his withdrawal of federal deposits and their distribution among favoured state or "pet" banks. The result was an American banking system controlled entirely by the whim or wisdom of the several state legislatures. Benton's attitude throughout the banking crisis is epitomized in a statement from one of his famous speeches: "All the flourishing cities of the West are mortgaged to this money power. They may be devoured by it at any moment. A lump of butter in the mouth of a dog! One gulp, one swallow, and all is gone!"

Any similarity with conditions in Canada seems remote. Not only was there no "money power" in the two provinces; there was very little money. Instead of one nationally chartered bank in control of credit and exchanges, there were two principal banks, the Bank of Montreal and the Bank of Upper Canada, both with sufficient capital to serve the limited commercial needs of their respective provinces and to provide such foreign bills of exchange as were needed. Nevertheless, much of the criticism of banks and banking voiced by Benton and others in the United States awakened responsive echoes in Canada. This was particularly true in Lower Canada, where the Bank of Montreal had come to be regarded by the French-Canadian political leaders as both the symbol and the instrument of the power wielded by the English-speaking minority in the Executive and Legislative Councils. The attitude of Papineau toward the Bank in fact paralleled Benton's toward the Second Bank of the United States. In addition to becoming an object of political attack, the Bank of Montreal also suffered the frequently vague and generalized criticisms levelled against banks and banking in both countries since the introduction of such institutions. These included charges of unfair lending practices that favoured directors and other insiders against the ordinary customer, of contracting loans in times of crisis and augmenting inflation in times of prosperity, and of controlling foreign exchange to the prejudice of the public interest. Further prejudicing the Bank of Montreal's image was the suspicious gossip that had attended its internal reorganization and the implementation of more cautious policies under the presidency of John Molson the elder.

Though festering for some time, dissatisfaction in Lower Canada was not brought out into the open until after the close of Jackson's successful election campaign of 1828. The campaign was followed closely in Canada and without doubt helped inspire the attacks made on the two leading banks in Lower and Upper Canada. That directed at the Bank of Montreal took the form of a petition to the legislature of Lower Canada on January 16, 1829, by several persons who styled themselves merchants and traders of Quebec. Later reduced to its essentials by a committee appointed to investigate, the charges were summarized as follows:

1ST. That the public have suffered much inconvenience and loss from the manner in which said Bank have conducted its affairs.

2ND. That the Bank had no legal right to establish an Office of Discount and Deposit at Quebec.

3RD. That the Office of Discount and Deposit at Quebec refuse to redeem the notes issued by the Mother Bank.

4TH. That the Office of Discount and Deposit at Quebec have issued notes bearing the words "payable at Quebec," and that they refuse to redeem any other.

5TH. That the Montreal Bank traffics in its own notes by buying them up at a Discount.

6TH. That the Bank had traded largely in deteriorated coins.

7TH. That the Bank had not used proper precautions to prevent its paper from being counterfeited.

The petition was signed by obscure persons who seem to have been disgruntled with the Bank of Montreal for purely personal reasons; nevertheless the inquiry developed political overtones. No action was taken to deal with the matter immediately, but the Bank regarded it seriously and on February 2 submitted a counter-petition requesting that a full investigation of the charges be made, the Bank offering to facilitate such an inquiry by presenting details of its business beyond those required by its charter. A committee consisting of Messrs. Vallières, Cuvillier, Lee, Neilson and Young (with the later addition of Messrs. De Rouville and Heney) was appointed, and sat from February 6 to 21, 1829, to hear evidence. None of the committee was associated with the Bank. Although Cuvillier had at an earlier date been a director and the Bank's principal legislative spokesman, his relations with it at this time were far from cordial as a result of certain altercations on financial matters following the depression of 1825-26.

In their interrogations, the committee gave their most serious attention to the matter of redemption. This concerned the refusal of the Quebec office to redeem the notes of the parent bank issued in Montreal, confining payment in specie to notes issued by itself and stamped "Payable at Quebec." Likewise, notes issued at Quebec were not redeemed at the head office in Montreal. The question had particular cogency in Quebec, where all import duties were payable in specie but where there were only two banks, the Quebec Bank and the Bank of Montreal's Office of Discount and Deposit. The matter of convertibility was also one that had agitated critics of the Second Bank of the United States ever since it established branches in 1817. For a while thereafter, the American bank redeemed its notes wherever issued or presented. It was shortly discovered, however, that the seasonal flow of trade between the interior and seaboard involved a difficult choice: to maintain large supplies of specie at every branch, or to engage in the hazardous and expensive transportation of specie or bullion from one place to another. The problem was finally resolved by the universal use of the cheque or personal draft, but in the early nineteenth century, with its fetish of convertibility, it could be taken care of only at considerable cost, risk, and effort because of the poor roads and slow communications. Not long after its establishment, therefore, the Second Bank of the United States decided to redeem its notes only at the place of issue, selling internal exchange in the form of drafts at a small discount to pay for the costs of transmission.

Questioned by the committee, Benjamin Holmes, who had been Cashier of the Bank of Montreal since 1827, cited the experience of the larger American establishment as identical with that of his own. Like the Second Bank of the United States, the Bank of Montreal had begun by redeeming its notes at the Quebec office, but had been forced to discontinue the practice for the same reasons: the cost of transporting shipments of metal. As the Bank was a money-making business, it had to recover such costs by means of a small discount on its notes; hence the charge that it was deliberately trafficking in its own paper, by issuing promises to pay at one point and buying them back at a discount at another. Like its American prototype, the Bank had then discontinued redemption except at the office of issue, selling drafts for internal exchanges.

The Cashier also cited statistics to show the circular movement of specie in Canada: from the government coffers at Quebec to points of disbursement in the lower and upper provinces, and thence into the channels of trade, from which it was collected by the Bank of Montreal, to be returned eventually to Quebec in payment of taxes or used for buying English or American exchange. The cost of this endless flow of gold and silver was borne mainly by the Bank of Montreal and paid for by charges that barely covered the costs of transportation. To meet the Canadian demand for specie by the government and by private firms and individuals, the Bank, as we have seen, also imported considerable amounts of specie from New York and Boston.

QUEBEC'S NERVE CENTRE—1830

This early-winter scene at the foot of Côte de la Montagne shows Quebec's famous Neptune Inn. At one time, Côte de la Montagne was the main highway between the Upper and Lower Town, and up its steep pebbled slope rode the governors on their arrival at the capital of Lower Canada.

The Neptune Inn was opened in 1809 and its location in the Lower Town made it a favourite both with seafarers and with leading business men. Stages for Montreal departed from its front door, and in 1816 its lower floor became the headquarters of the Quebec Exchange. Here, at the nerve and rumour centre of Quebec's commerce, auctions of merchandise were held and advertisements could be posted for a fee.

However, the popularity of the Inn was limited by the fact that, to the less sophisticated, the figure of Neptune with his trident looked too much like the Devil.

Imports from and exports to the United States for the period under review, 1818-1828, were reported to be £665,582 and £150,951 respectively. Most of the imports had taken place between 1822 and 1828, when the Bank's established name enabled it to purchase government bills drawn on London and sell them for specie. Thus the cumbersome transfer of specie down Lake Champlain and the Hudson River was largely circumvented. Private Canadian bills drawn on London against export credits were also purchased by the Bank and were sent to its agents, Thomas Wilson & Co., to provide funds against which bank exchange could be drawn. The Bank's contribution of introducing into the Canadian market more than £500,000 of hard currency, double the amount of its own paid-up capital, is a vital indication of its service to the commerce and trade of the colonies.

Benjamin Holmes appeared before the committee several times, and was questioned at length on the general subject of exchange practices in England, Scotland, and the United States. The extent to which American influence on Canadian banking still prevailed is revealed by his answers. Although an officer of the Bank of Montreal from its commencement, and probably more conversant with the exchange business than any other person, he testified that he had no knowledge of English or Scottish banks. He was entirely conversant, on the other hand, with all phases of banking across the border, and described the operations of leading American banks as being very like those of the Bank of Montreal. Although one of the directives of the committee had been to obtain information on English and Scottish banking practices in this respect, it found itself unable to do so.

From the public point of view, another serious charge was that the Bank had traded largely in deteriorated coin. It is true that at the time a variety of depreciated silver coins was in circulation. The rated values of the smaller French coins, in particular, were considerably in excess of the intrinsic value of their silver content. The Bank, however, was compelled to accept such coins in payment of debts, since they had been declared legal tender, and it had therefore no option but to return them to circulation in exchange for its notes. Furthermore, it would of necessity divest itself of such metallic currency whenever possible since its own larger exchange dealings had to conform to the bullion standard.

The final charge, that the Bank had not taken proper precautions to prevent its notes from being counterfeited, was denied. Not only had care been taken to secure the services of the best American technicians to engrave Bank of

Montreal notes, but whenever counterfeits had been discovered the entire issue had been withdrawn from circulation as rapidly as possible. It might be pointed out that counterfeiting of bank-notes had become a minor industry along the borders of Vermont and northern New York, where Canadian and American paper currency circulated freely. Notes of wholly imaginary banks found their way into circulation, usually in areas far removed from the reputed point of issue, to be discovered worthless only when they had made their slow return through the channels of internal exchange to a non-existing promisor.

Several petitioners were examined by the committee but none made significant contributions to the investigation. Incongruously enough, the two most articulate witnesses, one Ritter, described as a tobacconist, and Sarony, a general merchant, were discovered to be non-naturalized alien residents and as such unable to carry on business legally in the province of Lower Canada. Whether or not any action was taken against them is unknown. Of the other witnesses heard, none could give direct evidence showing that the Bank had been guilty of favouritism or that the public had suffered inconvenience from the way in which it conducted its business.

Dated February 21, 1829, the report of the Legislative Committee determined that there was nothing in its charter to prevent the Bank of Montreal operating an agency or office at Quebec, and furthermore found that the business of the Office of Discount and Deposit had been conducted on fair and honourable principles to the great benefit of the commercial and agricultural interests of the country. The committee's attitude toward the remaining charges is reflected in the report's concluding statement: "Your Committee are of the opinion that the Petition is frivolous."

4.

At first glance the Bank of Montreal appears to have emerged from its second legislative investigation even more strongly than it did from the first, held several years earlier, when substantially similar criticisms and charges were made and similarly dismissed. In the light of the Bank's depression activities and the preponderantly unfavourable attitude toward it in the Legislative Assembly, the second endorsation was even more emphatic than the first. Yet the report of the committee was just as unsatisfactory to the Bank's management as it was to the merchants of Quebec who had been its instigators. Instead of giving the directors a feeling of confidence it brought forebodings of trouble, particularly with respect to the renewal of the charter, which was due to expire June 1, 1831. The management was also concerned about the future for two complementary reasons: the worsening political climate in Lower Canada, and the failure of the legislative investigation to accomplish what the Bank had hoped for. It will be recalled that the original petition was confined to the alleged malpractices of the Office of Discount and Deposit at Quebec, and that it was the Bank itself that later demanded a full-dress investigation. The reasons for doing so were based on a desire to allay the criticism of the institution that had been growing since the depression of 1826 and had been aggravated by inflammatory attacks on banks and bankers in the United States. By using the Assembly as a forum for a presentation of the Bank's affairs and its methods of doing business, it was hoped, naively perhaps, that public opinion would be favourably affected. With the same aim in view, a non-political and as yet uncontroversial figure in the person of Benjamin Holmes was chosen to present the Bank's case rather than the President or Vice-President, the elder Molson and John Fleming having both by this time become closely identified with the English commercial party in the province.

Notwithstanding the able presentation made by Holmes, the results were unsatisfactory, largely because of the superficial nature of the inquiry. Instead of improving the Bank's public image, as was planned, the blanket vindication had rather the opposite effect by giving the general public the impression that immense political power must be wielded by its leading financial institution.

In the sister province, where the governing clique, the Family Compact, owned and controlled the Bank of Upper Canada, political patronage in banking affairs was readily discernible. As shown earlier, however, the corporate activities of the Bank of Montreal had remained largely non-political, once royal assent had been given to the Act of Incorporation and a charter granted. Relatively few of its directors and officers engaged directly in politics, although some prominent shareholders, including two presidents of the Bank, Horatio Gates and John Molson Sr., were appointed to the Legislative Council. However, since the interests of the Bank were essentially those of the commercial community that had brought it into being, it was logical for the two to be looked upon as having the same political allegiance. This identification became stronger after 1822, when the Union bill, supported by many persons prominently associated with the Bank, would have been passed by the House of Commons had it not been for the intervention of Louis-Joseph Papineau and other French-Canadian leaders who eloquently expressed their opinions in London. Thereafter, the cleavage first noted in 1808 over the question of taxation widened to include such other contentious questions as those of land tenure, the powers of the judiciary, internal improvements, and the perennial voting of supplies. At the core of the situation, of course, was the incompatibility of the two ethnic groups, neither of which would admit any virtue in the culture or aspirations of the other, and each of which had the power to block the other in the important business of governing the province.

Even before 1829, matters had been approaching an impasse strongly influenced by outside events—the growing dissatisfaction with the conservative government in England which led to its defeat in 1830, the victory of Jacksonian democracy in the United States, and the political and social unrest boiling up in many parts of Europe. In its extremity the French-Canadian radical party developed more and more obstructive tactics, while the commercial party, now become more colonially-minded than the Colonial Office, pressed the newly formed Canada Committee of the British House of Commons to have the cause of union resurrected, or failing that to bring about the annexation of Montreal to Upper Canada.

The recognized leaders of most of these endeavours were persons known to be closely connected with the Bank of Montreal, either as officers, directors, or shareholders. A rarely quoted petition to the Assembly of Lower Canada at the session of 1830 sheds more direct light on this question of public opinion versus the Bank of Montreal. Filed by one William Price as agent for three London merchants, it sought relief from a peculiar situation in which the petitioners found themselves as respondents in a suit with the Bank. The testimony shows their case had been presented to the Court of Appeals on July 15, 1828, but had not yet been heard for the reason that the Chief Justice of the Court of King's Bench for the District of Montreal, James Reid, and the Honourable John Richardson, and the Honourable John Stewart, had all debarred themselves as members of the court from sitting on the case because they had personal interests in the Bank of Montreal.

Considering the mounting political tension in the province, it is not surprising that the directors of the Bank of Montreal felt somewhat uneasy about the future. Should the intransigence of the popular party in the Assembly continue to increase, might not that body refuse to renew the charter, or perhaps modify it beyond acceptability? The variety of banking experiments passed in state legislatures across the border and the banking developments in Upper Canada suggested that either contingency might happen. Also, in Upper Canada, the provincial government, as the largest shareholder of the Bank of Upper Canada, had earned eight per cent on its investment almost from the inception of the institution. With these considerations in mind, the directors of the Bank of Montreal decided, after the inquiry of 1829 had been concluded, to establish the strength or weakness of the Bank's position as soon as possible rather than wait until 1831, the year the charter would expire. With the approval of the shareholders, a petition praying for the renewal of the charter was prepared for presentation to the legislature at the next session.

Signed by officers and shareholders of the Bank, the petition reached the House on February 3, 1830, was ordered printed, and was debated by the House in committee on March 9 and several times thereafter, the legislative *Journals* of 1830 containing no less than twenty-three separate references to the subject.

It is interesting to note that the Bank now had 176 shareholders, of whom only a handful were resident outside Lower Canada, and only eleven of whom, including three Americans, owned 100 or more shares of stock. Samuel Hall held 254; William Yule, 190; Peter Smith, 183; the Montreal Savings Bank, 120; John Try, 108; Charles Oakes Ermatinger, 102 and Thomas Dickson and Sir Gabriel Wood 100 shares each. The largest American shareholders were now Charles Carroll, 195, Henry Brevoort, 165, and Laura E. Brevoort, 100. Abel Bellows, the original American shareholder who had done so much for the Bank in Boston, still held forty shares.

In praying for renewal of the charter, the petitioners claimed that the Bank had been operated in the best interests of commerce, industry and agriculture, that it had contributed extensively to their growth, and that its continuance had now become indispensable to the prosperity of the country and the development of its resources. James Leslie, a director of the Bank and member of the Assembly for Montreal East, presented the petition; he was supported by Austin Cuvillier, who "spoke for the public good" for "no man was more disinterested than himself in the Bank." The principal speakers in opposition were Papineau and Neilson, leaders of the popular majority in the House, and Thomas Young, a Quebec merchant who was unusually well informed on the general subject of banking.

As the Bank anticipated, the petition provoked more damaging criticism

capital, and send out large quantities of paper, which might in the end turn out to be blank paper in point of value." Referring to the special committee of 1829, the Speaker claimed that that body had desired more to screen the Bank from blame than to conduct a searching, impartial investigation.

Papineau concluded with the statement that banks were not private but public and political institutions and should answer for their conduct to the constituted authority that created them. This, he charged, they had failed to do, and until they did so, and their statements had been carefully examined, the Assembly could not prolong the Bank's corporate existence. Papineau was particularly concerned about the immunity of directors beyond their liability as shareholders and insisted that banking offered a dangerous opportunity to the unscrupulous to amass fortunes at the expense of the innocent, ignorant, and unfortunate. "Private interests invariably more or less sway men in their public capacities; and it is necessary that establishments of this kind be jealously looked at."

Defending the Bank, James Leslie reminded Mr. Neilson that the matter had been before the Assembly for over a month and that, although the charter was not in immediate jeopardy, a decision should be made; otherwise great difficulty would accrue to the Bank and great inconvenience to the public. He was, however, "ready to lay the fullest information before the House." There was in the bill for renewal a clause providing for fuller statements to be rendered to the government which he hoped would prove satisfactory. With respect to the prudence of the Bank's operations, he said that the charter allowed for the issue of paper to the value of three times the amount of the capital, but that it had never gone beyond £200,000. As to the charge concerning small notes: at first the Bank had not issued any notes under five dollars, but there was so much application for small money that they had done so with a view to preventing an inundation of heterogeneous small American bank-notes, which would have been inconvenient to redeem and susceptible to counterfeiting. Currently only about £45,000 of such paper was outstanding.

Neilson agreed that the calling in of the Bank's loans of £600,000 would cause great embarrassment and confusion to the mercantile community "and bring on a break up, such as we had never yet seen." Since the evil would be brought about by the legislature's refusal to renew the charter, the legislature was bound "to make it fall as lightly as possible." This, he said, was the reason for taking time to consider how to act. Papineau then suggested that Leslie produce the documents he had been brandishing and show specifically what the Bank had lost through bad debts.

At this point a sharp clash developed between the Bank's critics and its supporters. The opposition, led by Papineau, Neilson, and Young, was quite evidently on a fishing expedition, inspired by rumours long current regarding various aspects of the Bank's affairs. Leslie replied that he would answer any specific questions that might be asked but refused to divulge other information until the question before the House had been resolved: was the charter to be renewed or wasn't it?

Leslie's inconsistent attitude could only have aggravated the opposition, which was further aroused when Cuvillier joined the debate to remind those present that the whole subject had been investigated by a committee of the House the year before, when charges against the Bank had been found frivolous and groundless and the petition for an inquiry wicked and corrupt. In his opinion, the Speaker had fancied an evil that did not exist and had conjured up a phantom only to combat it. Furthermore, he defied anyone present to understand the financial statements of the Bank when even bankers themselves had difficulty in interpreting them. Duval, an unidentified French-Canadian member, wryly observed that a strange doctrine had been set up: particular measures were to be dealt with by particular classes exclusively – law matters by lawyers, banking business by bankers, and so on; but all members of the Assembly were expected to be competent to take a part on every question. He did not wish to throw any obstacles in the way of the measure, but when he found that the gentlemen themselves said that they did not understand their own accounts, and he verily believed them, he would object to further proceedings until further elucidation was given. He could not but believe, however, that there was something mysterious hidden under all this, for after all, it was but a matter of figures, of common arithmetic. The only way, if it was not understood, was to study it until it was. On this note the debate was adjourned until three days later.

At the resumed session, Young moved that the directors of the Bank of Montreal be ordered to lay before the House detailed statements of their operations. Leslie objected that the statements demanded could not be produced in less than eight to ten days, and that the delay might postpone consideration of the measure to another session of the House. Young replied that he had no intention of causing unnecessary delay. He had been clearly of the opinion that the charter ought to be renewed; but when one member said that he had the information wanted in his pocket but would not produce it until he was sure of a renewal, and another member said that nobody would understand the statements anyway, it was high time to pause.

As the Bank's defenders, both Leslie and Cuvillier appear to have been remarkably inept, and they certainly did not improve its public image. Leslie's evasive tactics in refusing to produce the documents he alternately waved in his hand and returned to his pocket could only have fortified any suspicions concerning the Bank's operations. Cuvillier's fatuous attempt to come to Leslie's rescue simply added fuel to the fire, and when Cuvillier went so far as to admit that Young seemed to know more about the Bank than he did, the whole debate was brought abruptly to a somewhat inconclusive termination, and the matter was referred to a committee.

Meanwhile, the Bank was under fire from other quarters: Quebec merchants again petitioned that care should be taken, in the event of a renewal, "to protect the interest of the public by restricting the said Bank from dealing in bills of exchange and from issuing bills for small sums." Commissary-General Routh, intent on introducing the new Imperial silver currency into Canada, objected also to the Bank's conduct of its exchange business and its issue of small notes, and the author of a series of letters, *Conclusions des Observations d'Anti-Banque sur les Banques du Canada*, claimed that the issuance of small bank-notes had driven metallic currency out of the country. The opposition of the Quebec merchants was doubtless inspired by two conditions: the monopoly of government exchange the Bank commanded with its superior resources, and the continuing prejudice of most French Canadians against paper money. Gold and silver, they knew, retained its value; paper, they also knew from bitter experience, could not be trusted.

The Commissary General's strong objection arose from his inability to keep specie in circulation alongside bank-notes, but his arguments against the Bank were identical, oddly enough, to those being used by bank critics in the United States. "Anti-Banque" was similarly concerned about the powers bestowed on banks through the issuing of paper money; although he based his arguments on leading economic writings of the day, in restating them to fit the Canadian case he invariably upset their logic. In all this discussion, no attempt was made to view the other side of the coin – the very real benefits brought to the country through its chartered banks – nor was any attempt made to explain why the Canadian experience with banking should have been much more fortunate, from the point of view of shareholder and depositor at least, than that of the United States. For its part, the Bank of Montreal refrained where possible from entering into public controversy; it attempted neither to disclose its activities nor satisfy the public curiosity by explaining the relatively simple nature of its business.

The committee of the Assembly eventually reported in favour of a renewal of the charter but recommended that more detailed information be required. It was also recommended that the Bank be allowed to increase its capital, but no prohibitions were included as to dealing in exchange or issuing small notes. The necessary act was passed renewing the charter, but only for six years, to June 1, 1837, with the proviso that in the event that the charter of the Quebec Bank were not renewed, and no other bank chartered, the act continuing the Bank of Montreal was to lapse in ten months after the expiry of the existing charter of the junior bank. The charter of the latter, however, was extended in 1831 to May 1, 1836.

The most important amendment to the original charter was drawn from a recent act of the State of Massachusetts. This required a new and much more comprehensive form of financial statement to be furnished to the governor, or either branch of the legislature, on request. In deference to the generally groundless but nonetheless widespread objections to the circulation of small notes, issues below one dollar (five shillings) were prohibited, and the issue of notes below five dollars was limited to one-fifth the amount of paid-up capital.

Except for the above-mentioned restrictions on the issue of small notes, this act did nothing to change the day-to-day business of the Bank. The new statements still exposed little but the skeleton of this business, and the information divulged therein exceeded only in minor details that which the Bank had voluntarily provided during the investigation of 1829. It is, however, interesting to note that one of the required tabulations was "deposits bearing interest." At this time, the practice of paying interest on deposits was gaining popularity in the United States, but in England it did not become widespread until the late 1830's; the first commercial bank to adopt the custom in Canada was the Agricultural Bank of Toronto in 1834, but several years elapsed before the principle was accorded general acceptance.

TWELVE

ON A WAVE
OF PROSPERITY

ON A WAVE OF PROSPERITY

I.

The debate on the Bank of Montreal in Lower Canada was but one of many on the subject of banking in Canada and the United States during the 1820's and 1830's. For more than two decades state legislatures argued over monetary, financial, and banking theory in their efforts to enact the laws best suited to various constituencies—some with capital resources and a mature commercial economy, others in the first stages of settlement and development.

As we have seen, the land or country banking system served England nobly during the Napoleonic Wars, a period when the economy was continually expanding, but failed when economic retrenchment forced demands for note redemption that bankers were unable to meet. In many respects the English and American experiences were identical, in others markedly divergent. In England the weaknesses of the banking system as it existed at the close of the Napoleonic Wars led gradually to centralized banking with the Bank of England becoming the keystone of the arch: in the United States the system of centralized banking was sacrificed to financial and regional jealousies.

A comparison of the great American debate on banking, as discussed by Redlich in *The Molding of American Banking* and by Hammond in *Banks and Politics in America*, with that which took place in the Assembly of Lower Canada in 1830 throws light on the backward condition of the Canadian economy after seventy years of British rule, the elementary knowledge of banking as exemplified in the Assembly debates, and the strong position occupied by the Bank of Montreal, even at this early stage of its development. As set forth in the petition for renewal, the Bank had actually become "indispensable" to the financial and commercial life of the province.

All students of Canadian history are, of course, familiar with the discrepancies in wealth and growth between the United States and its less fortunate northern neighbour – the one endowed with all the physical advantages the temperate zone could bestow, the other denied all but a fraction of the richness enjoyed by the Republic from the Great Lakes to the Gulf of Mexico. In fact, some forgotten European observer once sardonically described Canada as "the fringe on the Paisley shawl." But this is the essence of the Canadian story – the disadvantages, natural and unnatural, under which a divided people had to labour to ensure survival, subjugate the wilderness, expand their domain peacefully from coast to coast, and finally establish themselves as one of the world's most enviable nations. If the facts of the long struggle were more widely understood – the forbidding character of the environment, the formidable obstacles to communication and transportation, the exploitative nature of colonial mercantilism, and the crippling effects of American protective tariffs – if there were a deeper appreciation of this historic background, there could be no Canadian inferiority complex; Canadians instead would view themselves proudly in the light of their incredible accomplishments.

In 1830, the population of the United States was approximately thirteen million, while that of the Canadian colonies had yet to pass 800,000. In the United States, twenty-four states had already been admitted to the Union, settlement had extended to the foothills of the Rockies, and 1,277 miles of canals had been constructed; in Canada, the people had yet to achieve responsible government, Upper Canada, bedevilled by its Clergy Reserves, remained virtually unsettled except for the accessible concessions fronting on Lake Ontario and Lake Erie, and only a few miles of sorely needed canals had been completed. Meanwhile mills and factories had been established throughout New England; Ohio and Indiana were already herding droves of sheep and cattle to eastern markets across the Alleghenies, and cotton had made New Orleans one of the most prosperous cities on the continent.

A decade and a half earlier the Second Bank of the United States, together with the established commercial banks of the eastern seaboard, had sufficed to fulfil the financial needs of a commercial economy. Now, industrial and agricultural expansion had brought into being new banks better suited to the particular need of the several sectors of the economy, financial, agricultural, and industrial. Lacking specie capital, the west had no recourse but to turn to the system of private country banking which had proven so useful earlier in England. Thus, free banking found great favour in the west as immigration and settlement made the need for credit, any kind of credit that would provide negotiable paper for goods and services, imperative. Along the eastern seaboard, on the other hand, banking retained a more conservative complexion. In New England, the Suffolk Bank, under the presidency of H. B. Stone, was developing the first clearing-house system in the United States, and in 1829 the State of New York, under the governorship of Martin Van Buren, Jackson's ablest adviser and his successor in the presidency, passed the Safety Fund Act. The Suffolk system was designed to organize internal exchange throughout New England and establish a measure of control over the proliferation of private country banks; the New York Safety Fund was a precursor of the Federal Deposit Insurance Corporation of Franklin D. Roosevelt's first administration.

The debate in the United States continued for more than seven years and in the course of it every phase of fiscal, financial, monetary, and banking theory was aired and examined: the management of the public debt and its relation to the credit needs of the country; the ever-present dilemma of foreign exchange; the security of bank-note credit supported by bullion as against that supported by state bonds, corporate securities, and land values which often proved ephemeral. Whether or not the American public actually supported Jackson in his determination to do away with centralized banking, they had every opportunity to become informed on the issue.

In contrast to the fury and tumult of American banking history was the unruffled state at this time of Canadian opinion on the subject of banking. In the debate in the Assembly of Lower Canada, for example, the members were concerned only with the alleged shortcomings of a single institution. No effort was made to explore the questions of banking theory or even to examine the existing bank charters. Instead, the debate was confined to an inquiry into the

Despite the inconclusive character of the Bank of Montreal debate, it would be a mistake to conclude that Canadian opinion was wholly indifferent to the question of banking. On the contrary, in both Upper and Lower Canada, but more particularly in the upper province because of its more rapid growth, the established banking system came under fire for a variety of reasons. In company with Lord Aylmer, most conservative Canadians, impressed by the frequent failure of banks in the United States, regarded all American banking institutions as "little better than gambling speculations"; nevertheless, reform opinion in the upper province clearly followed that prevalent in the adjacent midwestern states. In both communities banks were regarded as quasi-public institutions whose function was to provide in the form of credit the capital needed by trade and commerce and for internal improvements. At a somewhat later date this point of view was to lead to banking experiments in Upper Canada along the lines of American free banking and the English country system.

Several schemes were suggested to stimulate the Canadian economy and correct the deplorable currency situation. The first of these was submitted to the Permanent Under-Secretary for the Colonies, Wilmot Horton, by a Mr. Forbes as early as 1826, at the depth of the depression. Forbes's plan was designed to ensure the loyalty of the colonies by making them even more financially dependent on the mother country than they already were, and by such means strengthen the bonds of empire. Shorn of extraneous details, the plan called for the formation of a banking company in England with a capital of £500,000 or larger, to which the government would grant permission to issue a provincial currency in the form of restamped Spanish dollars. These were to have a value of five shillings and to be exchangeable for London bills at par. The banking company was also to be permitted to issue a limited paper currency, the sum to be redeemable only on the continued good behaviour and loyalty of the colonies.

Another detail of the Forbes plan called for the absorption of the existing Canadian banks in a single comprehensive institution which would become banker to both the Imperial and provincial governments, regulate a uniform currency, and maintain the exchanges at par. The flaw in the scheme, as the British government was soon to discover from its own attempt to introduce an Imperial silver currency, lay in the Canadian economy itself with its chronic excess of imports over exports. Under such circumstances a metallic currency, whatever its nature or designation, would inevitably be used to buy exchange. Quite apart from whatever reactions the Canadian bankers might have had, nothing came of Forbes's scheme for the same reason that quashed Biddle's more practical proposal.

Another scheme, proposed in 1827 by John Galt, the first manager of the Canada Company, was also designed to stabilize the fluctuating Canadian exchange. This was to be done by the government's paying its Canadian accounts in Bank of England notes, thus introducing a paper currency which would soon supersede that already in use and by the very fact of its superiority retain a constant value with respect to foreign payments. Galt not only over-rated the ability of the Bank of England to regulate its own internal exchanges, but lost sight of the fact that a medium of payment redeemable at par in London would command a premium in Canada so long as exchange was in demand.

Two years later, Thomas Dalton, erstwhile banker turned brewer, journalist and radical politician, called on the Bank of England to solve Canada's financial problems. Before the Upper Canada Assembly he maintained that Canada's condition, stagnant and backward in comparison with that of its neighbour, was due to the lack of finance capital. Arguing that the Canadian banks lacked sufficient strength to fill the void, Dalton believed the Bank of England could redress the situation by opening a branch or branches in Canada. Reflecting western American opinion, he spoke eloquently of the undeveloped natural resources of the country and suggested that this latent wealth be made the basis for credit to be supplied through the medium of Bank of England sterling notes issued by local branches of that institution.

The reaction of the British Treasury to the proposal is shown in its refusal to accept notes of the Bank of Montreal in payment of the Canada Company's obligations. If the company had the money it could pay it directly: if it held Bank of Montreal notes it could obtain specie for them; but if it held an accommodation loan from the Bank to meet its indebtedness, as may or may not have been the case, then the Bank must be holding the company's hypothecation of its lands as security. Having but recently corrected some of the worst evils of land-secured English country banking, the Treasury regarded such security as the worst a bank could hold, for the reason that it could not be converted into money at the very time of stress when money was needed to satisfy note-holders and depositors. Even had this feature of Dalton's scheme not made it unacceptable in the British Treasury, there was yet too little interest in colonial affairs to inspire interference in the existing banking system.

It will be noted that most of the proposals for change originated in Upper Canada, where the need for capital had grown more pressing than in the older province and where the control of the Bank of Upper Canada by the Family Compact had provoked mounting denunciations of that institution. In Lower Canada the business and commercial community was reasonably content with the banking system that existed, although more and more was heard about the iniquities of the "money oligarchy" and its alleged political alliance with the executive arm of the provincial government. It was in this unsettled political climate that the Bank of Montreal entered upon one of the more remunerative periods of its career.

2.

Except for immigration and the increased demand for foodstuffs to feed a new British urban population, Canada received little direct benefit from the early decades of the industrial revolution. As Britain and the United States prospered, so in some measure did Canada, but lacking cotton and associated commodities, the northern colonies were denied one of the principal dynamics of the British and American economies. As has so frequently occurred throughout Canadian history, the geographically handicapped and sparsely occupied colonies had to await political change and technological progress elsewhere before they could undertake the development of their own intractable resources.

Curiously enough, one of the most significant of all such advances, from a Canadian point of view, coincided with the commercial, financial, and banking crisis of the middle 1820's. This was the successful opening of Britain's first public steam-operated railway, the Stockton and Darlington, in 1825. The commercial feasibility of the venture was demonstrated in 1830 with the inauguration of a main-line railroad, the Liverpool and Manchester, some thirty miles in length, and the impressive savings in transportation costs led to a railroad construction boom that brought England out of its economic doldrums and revived Canadian prosperity.

The effects of the revival on the Bank can be readily conveyed. From 1830 to 1837 inclusive, it paid dividends totalling 102 per cent on a paid-up capital of £250,000, while increasing the rest fund from £7,840 to

£49,457. Because of the changes in reporting procedure required by the Act of 1830 extending the charter to 1837, it is impossible to determine the exact growth pattern with respect to deposits, loans and discounts, note circulation, or assets and liabilities. Before 1830, for instance, the volume of loans and discounts was shown for the whole year, while the new regulations required the banks to tabulate the amount outstanding on the date of reporting. As a result, loans and discounts, which were tabulated in 1829 as amounting to £1,559,683, were reported for the year following as £478,820. With the resumption of dividend payments in 1829 after a three-year lapse, the Bank has continued to pay dividends every year without interruption from that time to this.

Another factor that helped the Canadian economy in the early 1830's was the expansion of credit in England induced by the Bank Act of 1833, which extended the charter of the Bank of England to 1855, made its notes legal tender for the payment of public debt, and exempted it from the usury laws which had restricted its interest rate on loans to five per cent. The Act of 1833 also affirmed the legality of cheques issued by joint-stock banks in the London area. The first of such banks, the London and Westminster, was established soon after, and by 1836 no less than seventy-two were doing business in the capital.

Easier credit stimulated investment, provided financing for railroad expansion, and accelerated the business upswing that had begun in 1828. Attending the recovery was also a rapid expansion of textile manufacturing as wages put more purchasing power in the hands of factory workers. The United States was the principal beneficiary because of the demand for cotton and because of the ease with which English credit could be obtained for almost any kind of American investment. But Canada was also favourably affected.

Massive stands of hardwoods three hundred to five hundred years old still covered the southern reaches of Upper Canada. To clear this land required time and Herculean labour whose only salable products were the ashes left from burning. Had it not been for the continuing demand of the textile industry for pot and pearl ashes as bleaching agents, agricultural development in Upper Canada must have been delayed a generation. Railroad construction also had important repercussions. Theretofore, Canadian timber had been floated to Quebec for export by British naval contractors in the form of square timber or three-inch deals; the boom created a new demand for railroad ties, pit props for mines, and clear white pine for pattern stock. As a direct consequence, a new group of softwood buyers made their appearance in the coffee houses of Quebec's Lower Town and the Canadian lumber trade entered upon a new phase of its development, in which bank financing assumed a more important role.

Even more significant to the Canadian economy was the phenomenon already referred to—the great transatlantic migration. Begun in the sixteenth century with the introduction of the plantation system, the exodus from Europe to America had been fostered in turn by religious persecution and mercantilist enterprise, but it was not until after the Napoleonic Wars that the tide set in earnest, and not until 1830 that it began to assume economically significant proportions.

The unprecedented increase in Canadian immigration from 13,307 in 1829 to 30,574 in 1830 and 56,067 in 1831 can be attributed to several causes. One of these was distress in Ireland and rising unemployment in the British Isles, another the increase in shipping engaged in the Canadian timber trade, enabling tens of thousands of emigrants to cross the Atlantic for the small sum they could afford. Most of the newcomers were displaced farm labourers who arrived with little or no money but were able to find employment in Upper Canada until they could join the ranks of the pioneer settlers. A considerable number, however, were carpenters, masons, millwrights and mechanics with some means, who readily secured work in city or town. Swelling the flow also, though in smaller numbers, were half-pay army officers, lawyers, doctors, journalists, and tradesmen with some capital to invest and the ability to employ others.

The surge in Canadian immigration during the early 1830's is reflected in many ways. Despite increasing political tensions, French and English Canadians joined forces long enough to approve sorely needed public works. In 1829, for example, the legislature of Lower Canada voted money to build a revetment wall on the Montreal waterfront and install lighthouses along the St. Lawrence. An additional sum was voted in 1830 to improve Montreal's harbour, and in 1832 the City of Montreal was incorporated and made a port of entry. Meanwhile, construction of the Chambly Canal had begun, and plans were being laid for the building of Canada's first railroad, the Champlain and St. Lawrence, which was to run from St. Johns at the foot of Lake Champlain steam navigation to the small village of La Prairie on the south shore of the St. Lawrence River, eight miles upstream from Montreal.

Although the French-Canadian majority in the Quebec House joined the

English-speaking minority to vote money for navigation and canals, it was implacably opposed to immigrant settlement. As a result the great bulk of the 400,000 new Canadians who arrived between 1826 and 1841 passed up the St. Lawrence to find work or take up land in Upper Canada. As settlement spread inland from the lake fronts, pressure for the improvement of communications and transportation became greater with each succeeding year. Trunk and feeder roads were the primary need, but without canals the bulky pioneer staples – potash, flour, oak – had still to be rafted down the St. Lawrence and all imports had to be portaged up-river at prodigious cost and effort.

By 1829 the Welland Canal Company, formed by William Hamilton Merritt and financed initially with New York State lottery money, had succeeded in building a four-foot-deep waterway joining Lake Erie and Lake Ontario. A yet greater problem was that of the St. Lawrence system, a project far beyond the capacities of private enterprise. Failing to secure either Imperial support or the co-operation of Lower Canada, the provincial authorities of Upper Canada determined on a bold and even desperate course of action. In 1834, they authorized the issue of £200,000 sterling of Upper Canada government debentures, which were sold through Thomas Wilson & Co. in London. However, this issue enabled the government only to cancel part of the existing public debt which had been accumulating for a decade. Something still had to be done about the public works; so, the next year, Hon. J. H. Dunn, the Receiver General of Upper Canada, went over to London and there wrote to about a dozen bankers asking them to provide £400,000 against debentures secured by the revenues of the province, to be derived from Upper Canada's share of the customs duties collected at Quebec. Some of the bankers did not trouble to answer, but two – Messrs. Thomas Wilson & Co. and Baring Brothers – each offered to provide the whole amount. The Receiver General divided his favours and each was given £200,000 of the debentures. Still the need was not satisfied, and in 1837-38 the upper province was forced to borrow a further £269,650 in London, against which it issued a like amount of bonds.

These loans, totalling £869,650 sterling, represented the first Canadian public financing of any magnitude and the first time either province had sold government debentures in London. There is no evidence that the Bank of Montreal was directly connected with the sale of the debentures. However, Thomas Wilson & Co. had been the Bank's London agents since 1818, and the Bank's New York correspondent was Prime, Ward, King & Co., the Baring

GATEWAY TO THE UNITED STATES

Situated on the Richelieu River, twenty miles southeast of Montreal, St. Johns served as an outpost first against the Iroquois and later against the Americans. Its site on this vital southern artery made it also a commercial entrepôt, and until about 1800 it was the only port of entry into either of the Canadas from the United States.

The toll bridge across the Richelieu was built in 1826 by Robert Jones for "Travellers, Cattle, and Carriages," the charges being sixpence, twopence, and one shilling each, respectively.

Bank of Montreal interests were in the area early. John Richardson owned a general store there in 1802, and by the time of this picture, in 1839, the Bank had a full-time agent at St. Johns who carried on an extensive business in connection with the customs and the military.

Brothers' representative in the United States, who were given £20,000 of the second series; and although the Bank of Upper Canada secured the patronage of the British Treasury in 1833, the relations between the Receiver General and the Bank of Montreal remained most cordial. The separate links of the several parties with the Bank of Montreal suggest that that institution may have played the role of intermediary in placing the debentures. Once the provincial bonds were accepted by Thomas Wilson & Co., the government could draw bills of exchange on the London house which were then sold in Canada. Bank of Montreal interest in the transaction is confirmed when we see Benjamin Holmes buying substantial blocks of these bills for the Bank, and also Forsyth, Richardson & Co., nominally as financial agents for the government of Upper Canada, taking as much as £90,000 of one issue to negotiate on commission.

The Bank's important role in the economic expansion of the 1830's can be attributed to its London and New York connections, its resources, and the able direction of four successive presidents: John Molson, 1826-30; John Fleming, 1830-32; Horatio Gates, 1832-34; and Peter McGill, who occupied the post from 1834 to 1860, a longer period than any other president to date. All four presidents were experienced bankers, since each had served an apprenticeship as vice-president or director. Molson's steamboat operations had accustomed him to dealing in foreign exchange, as had Fleming's connection with Hart, Logan & Co., one of the largest Scottish import houses in Canada. During the second year of the latter's administration the Bank for the first time declared a bonus on its stock in addition to a seven-per-cent dividend, making a total distribution for the year of £30,000.

John Molson resigned in 1830 after four years in office but remained a director until his death in 1836. His decision seems to have been prompted by his own business interests, which included the building of new river steamboats and barges every year to accommodate the flood of immigrant traffic from Quebec to Montreal and the promotion of the Champlain and St. Lawrence Railroad along with George Moffatt, Peter McGill, John Molson Jr., and others connected with the Bank of Montreal. Some years earlier the elder Molson had proposed retiring to his farm at Boucherville, a few miles down the St. Lawrence from Montreal, and had arranged his affairs accordingly, turning over his business interests to his sons, but within two years he was prevailed upon to head the Bank of Montreal. Having done so successfully during the critical four years that followed, he no doubt felt that the time had come for others to take over the burden of his responsibilities.

When he died, on January 7, 1836, Molson was a leading member of the English-speaking commercial group and as such had often opposed French-Canadian reforms. Yet expressions of regret were universal throughout Lower Canada on his death. Though opposed politically to everything the Montreal bourgeois stood for, *Le Canadien* of Quebec City wrote on the occasion: "We hasten to associate ourselves with the regrets which have been expressed by our Montreal contemporaries, on the loss experienced by Canadian industry through the death of the Hon. John Molson, to whom Lower Canada owes the introduction of steam in inland navigation, and who at all times was a zealous supporter of every important commercial and industrial enterprise. Few men have rendered better service to their country in connection with its material development." As a mark of respect to his memory and to evince their high opinion of John Molson's public spirit, integrity, and social qualities as a citizen, the Board of Directors voted to wear mourning for thirty days.

During John Fleming's brief regime, "net profits on hand," a new reporting category, rose from £15,066 to £31,482, and it is probable that it was about this time that the practice originated of keeping a considerable portion of the reserve in New York to be loaned on call. Fleming was, first, a successful merchant, and secondly, a man with a wide variety of interests. Elected a director of the Bank of Montreal in 1826, he occupied the posts of vice-president and president and was also the wheel-horse on a variety of important business and civic committees.

John Fleming died late in July, 1832, at the height of the cholera epidemic which crossed the Atlantic in the lumber droghers, spread from the immigration reception centre at Grosse Isle to Montreal and thence up the St. Lawrence and along the Lakes to spend itself finally in the remote frontier settlements of the American middle west. The plague caused some seven thousand deaths in Montreal and Quebec City alone and placed almost insupportable burdens on the medical and charitable resources of the province. The fact that Fleming was one of its victims prompted the Board of Health to inquire into "the state of the 'Little Creek' on Craig Street, and its effects upon the public health." Frequently mentioned by Stephen Leacock in his study of Montreal, the small waterway drained the eastern slopes of Mount

Royal and each spring overflowed its banks to flood the stable yard of the Bank premises on St. James Street.

Horatio Gates, the third president of the 1830's, died in Montreal on April 11, 1834, at the age of fifty-six. A heavy load of public and private responsibility undoubtedly contributed to his final illness. His death was followed eight days later by that of his nephew-in-law and partner, Charles Bancroft, of grief and shock. Gates's sons being too young to carry on his extensive enterprises, the firm of Gates & Co. was shortly forced into liquidation.

Of all the founders of the Bank of Montreal, Horatio Gates had in many ways the most interesting, most varied and most influential career. Although Richardson's New York connections through Phyn, Ellice & Co. were far from negligible, those of Gates in financial, banking, and social circles in Boston and New York were unquestionably responsible for giving the Bank's operations the international character they have retained to the present day. As a director, he helped establish the Bank's New York and London connections, guided its early development, and throughout his life was probably its sagest counsellor. In addition to his Bank of Montreal interests, Gates was one of the founders of the ill-starred Bank of Canada, and, together with John Fleming, he arranged for its absorption by the Bank of Montreal upon the expiration of its charter in 1831. As early as 1820, the Montreal Bank had refused to accept the cheques or notes of the Bank of Canada because the latter would redeem its obligations only in half-crowns which, because of their official overvaluation, could not be exported and had become debased coin. This practice of the Bank of Canada had other serious repercussions as its deposits fell drastically in the mid twenties and by 1830 its capital was reduced to £3,555 out of an authorized £200,000. Although the details of Canada's first bank merger are lacking, the affairs of the bank appear to have been wound up without loss to note-holders or depositors, although its shareholders must have suffered quite severely.

3.

Gates's successor to the presidency was Peter McGill, a relatively young man of forty-five who had served temporarily as a director in 1819 and again from 1825 to 1830, when he was elected vice-president. Born Peter McCutcheon in Scotland in 1789, he had come at the age of twenty to Canada where his maternal uncle, the Honourable John McGill, an Executive Councillor and Inspector General of Upper Canada, was one of the foremost personages in

Shown leaving Montreal after having her engines installed is the famous Canadian paddle steamer, *Royal William*. She was built at Quebec for two prominent Quebec City merchants, George Black and John Campbell, and was launched on April 27, 1831. The engines were made at St. Mary's Foundry, formerly owned by John and William Molson.

Purchased by the Quebec and Halifax Steam Navigation Company, with which the Cunards were associated, the *Royal William* first plied the Quebec-Halifax route. In 1833 she was sold again and was sent to Boston, thereupon becoming the first British steamer to enter a port of the United States. On her return to Quebec it was decided to sell the ship in London, and the *Royal William* thus became the first Canadian steamship to cross the Atlantic. She left Pictou, Nova Scotia, on August 18, 1833 under the command of John McDougall, and reached Gravesend on September 12 – a journey of 25 days.

In September of 1834 she was bought by Spain. Converted into a warship, she was the first steamer in the Spanish Navy. Six years later, when repairs were attempted, it was discovered that her timbers were rotten, and this gallant ship spent the rest of her days as a hulk. Her engines were installed in another ship, however, and continued to function until 1860, when that vessel was wrecked.

Painting by Tom McNeely

the colonies. It was the uncle's influence, no doubt, that secured Peter McCutcheon a position with Parker, Gerrard & Ogilvy, but his qualities of character and initiative soon enabled him to master the fundamentals of the Canadian trade situation and he left the firm to found a successful business in partnership with three other young Montrealers. Very likely it was the same qualities and capacities that persuaded the childless John McGill to make McCutcheon his heir, provided that he adopt the name McGill. This was accomplished by royal licence in 1821 and is so registered in the College of Arms.

According to the records, Peter McGill was also blessed with a handsome physique and an attractive personality, both of which must have contributed to his success and enabled him to become a leader of many social, civic, and philanthropic organizations; among the posts he held were Governor of McGill University, Governor of the Montreal General Hospital, President of the Canadian School Society, President of the Montreal Bible Society, and founding president of the St. Andrew's Society. McGill's commercial leadership often took him to London, where he was not unknown at the Colonial Office and the Treasury. On one of these trips, in 1831-32, he married Sarah Elizabeth Wilkins. His appointment to the Legislative Council in 1832 was the start of a long political career, and in addition to his work for the Champlain and St. Lawrence Railroad he was busy at this time providing for the colonization of the Eastern Townships through the British American Land Company, of which he was a Canadian commissioner.

With such a pilot at the helm, it is understandable that the shareholders of the Bank of Montreal (now numbering scarcely more than 100, as compared to the original 289) maintained their confidence despite growing political conflict throughout 1834-35. Nor were they disappointed, for, reviewing the year's business at the eighteenth annual meeting held on June 1, 1835, the new president was able to report the most successful year the Bank had yet experienced. The dividend rate had been maintained, and although the rest fund had been depleted slightly, net profits on hand had increased to the substantial level of £41,167. Reflecting the satisfaction of the shareholders, the meeting awarded the President "the usual allowance of £500 for his services" and voted "donations for the prevention of fires and for preventing the spread of pestilential diseases." In conformity with the charter a new Board of Directors was elected, consisting of Charles Brooke, Thomas Cringan, Hon. Louis Gugy, William Lunn, Hon. Peter McGill, Hon. Joseph Masson, Hon.

George Moffatt, Hon. John Molson, John Redpath, H. L. Routh, Joseph Shuter, John Torrance and William Walker. As usual, the Board represented the leading commercial houses of Montreal.

Meeting on June 2, the new Board continued Peter McGill as president and Joseph Masson as vice-president, and confirmed the appointment of the several officers and clerks. The salary of the paying teller was raised to £350 because of "the hazard attending [his] situation," and the Cashier was directed to examine the existing sureties and satisfy himself that all were in order. At a special meeting held a week afterwards, William Walker resigned as a director and was succeeded by T. B. Anderson, later to become vice-president and president of the Bank. A special interest attaches to this meeting for the appreciation tendered Benjamin Holmes for "the zeal and ability" with which he had discharged his duties as cashier. It was then voted unanimously on a joint motion by Hon. George Moffatt and Hon. John Molson that the cashier's salary for the current year be £900 currency, in addition to the several perquisites which pertained to the office – family living quarters in the banking house, firewood, and free stabling if, indeed, a suitable equipage was not provided at the Bank's expense.

While comparisons are difficult, a salary equal to $3,600 in 1835, with living quarters and transportation found, would have had a purchasing value equivalent to five or six times that sum today. The salary compared more than favourably with those paid by leading banks in the United States at that time. A consideration of these facts leads to the conclusion that Benjamin Holmes, following his appointment in 1827, rapidly became, in fact if not in name, the general manager of the institution. This conclusion is further substantiated by the Directors' Minutes after January 1, 1835, which contain ample evidence of Holmes's growing responsibilities and increased authority. In the trying period that ensued we find him supervising the operations of the Quebec office, dealing directly with the Bank's New York and London agents, negotiating with the banks of Upper Canada, and managing the exchanges on his own responsibility. Apart from the semi-weekly discount activities of the Board, the employment of staff and the wages paid them, Holmes appears to have been in complete charge of the day-by-day conduct of the banking business.

The by-laws adopted in 1826 had given the cashier more responsibility than had those of 1817. But the 1826 by-laws also made a provision for the payment of a salary to the president as the Bank's principal executive officer.

This did not prove feasible for many years—it was not until 1846 that the president's honorarium, voted annually by the shareholders, equalled the salary of the cashier. Although generally overlooked in works on Canadian banking, the point is important and interesting. It marks the appearance in banking of professional management and a significant step in the evolution of the Bank of Montreal.

Benjamin Holmes can properly be said to be the first of a long line of extremely able and influential Canadian bankers. A copy of his portrait hangs in the Bank's Main Office, but his biography remains to be written. The portrait suggests a man of assurance who never suffered fools gladly. As manager, or cashier, he often conducted the Bank's affairs in an arbitrary manner and was frequently in hot water with customers because of his inflexibility in the handling of their accounts. Called on the carpet on several occasions, he defended his actions with such force and vigour that he was invariably exonerated and the customer asked to retract his charges or take himself and his account elsewhere. In addition to his professional career he was a political reformer who drew upon himself the vituperative attacks of newspapers opposed to his ideas. He was also one of the founders of the first Unitarian Church in Montreal. As a political, religious and philosophical nonconformist, he appears to have been an anomaly among the conservative bank directors who had to endure his extramural activities for twenty years. Benjamin Holmes must have been an extraordinarily proficient banker to win such sufferance.

Certain facts about the conduct of the banking business can be deduced from the statements submitted to the legislature under the Act of 1830. These show that the Bank was managed on scrupulously "sound" principles. The charter permitted a note circulation equal to the sum of specie deposits plus three times the paid-up capital—however, it rarely exceeded the paid-up capital itself; more than adequate quantities of specie were kept in the vaults, notwithstanding constant movements of metal, and ample reserves were maintained in the rest and undivided profits accounts against any conceivable contingency. We know that decisions with respect to discounts, exchange rates, sales and purchases, and general policy were governed by the Board. It is apparent, too, that directorships were no sinecure. Meetings were held twice weekly, and in addition there were standing committees on finance, foreign exchanges, branch operation, and other matters, which made severe demands on the time of those concerned.

These general observations have been made by Breckenridge and Shortt and, indeed, by all writers on Canadian banking. Nevertheless, detailed information as to banking practices is almost totally lacking. As far as can be determined, loans were made on personal security only in the form of "two-name paper" – a promissory note bearing the names of a promisor and endorser. Even in those cases where the Bank advanced money to such public bodies as the Lachine Canal Commission, or to private companies like the Welland Canal and the Champlain and St. Lawrence R.R., it was always on the personal security of individuals connected with the undertaking. This practice was of course in line with the broad principles of commercial banking: to lend short-term money for the exchange or production of readily salable commodities, not to provide long-term loans for capital improvements, no matter what their value or necessity. Victor Ross, however, contends in his monumental history of the Canadian Bank of Commerce that the "handling of agricultural produce, alone, could not support a bank. In the undeveloped state of the country, landed property was the principal asset of most of the inhabitants, even of those reputed wealthy. Advances were usually made on the personal security of the endorser, and . . . it came about under these conditions that ultimately the security held for all slow and doubtful transactions was land."

To what extent the foregoing observation holds good with respect to the Bank of Montreal is impossible to determine. In the 1840's, it is true, the Bank began to find itself the owner of large land holdings in Chicago, acquired through real-estate hypothecations, but there is no evidence to show that, prior to its involvement in the west, this situation was as common as Ross suggests. The records show rather that during the prosperous years between 1831 and 1837, bad or doubtful debts were a negligible item. Most of the profits of the period appear to have derived from discounts made to not more than a score of Montreal mercantile houses, from dealings in internal and external exchanges, and from the Bank's position as the depository for government funds. How all these activities were pursued in the day-by-day routine of banking can only be conjectured. However, considering Montreal's geographic situation and the smallness of its commercial group, it is probable that the members of the Board of the Bank of Montreal were collectively conversant with every phase of trade and commercial activity in the provinces. For many years, in fact, Horatio Gates, through his regular letters to the Montreal *Gazette* (a front page feature) reporting on current business trends and commercial prospects, was recognized as the commercial expert of Canada. Under such circumstances it seems likely that the banking business was shrewdly conducted on the basis of both intimate personal knowledge and theoretical considerations, the recognized solvency of borrowers being no less desirable than the liquidity of pledged assets.

4.

On the opening of business in November 1817, the paid-up capital stood at £37,500 and by 1820 the sum had been increased to £187,500. This proved sufficient until 1828, when economic recovery in Britain led to calling in the outstanding balance of £62,500 in four instalments, the last payable in August 1830. In February of the same year, when the Bank petitioned to renew its charter, the Banking Committee of the Assembly recommended that it also be allowed to increase its capital, but for some reason the authorization was omitted from the act of 1830 extending the charter to June 1, 1837. Oddly enough, the Quebec Bank, on being given an extension of its charter in 1831, received authority to increase its capital from £75,000 to £225,000 but was refused permission to open a branch in Montreal as prayed for in its petition.

One can only conjecture as to what lay behind these inconsistencies. Commercial jealousies may have played a part, as may also the animosity toward the Bank of Montreal on the part of the more radical French-Canadian element in the Assembly. It is more likely, however, that the worsening political climate in Lower Canada, coupled with the controversies over banking then current in the United States and Great Britain, was mainly responsible. In other words, the Assembly now chose to await developments elsewhere before tampering with a banking apparatus that had functioned reasonably well and without the slightest taint of scandal. The intention, no doubt, was to review the whole subject at a later date in the light of British and American experience.

By 1831, however, unparalleled prosperity in Lower Canada, coupled with the demise of the Bank of Canada and the failure of the Bank of Montreal to augment its capital, led to a credit stringency and to agitation for increased banking facilities. The latter found expression in February, 1831, in a petition to the legislature to charter the City Bank (Montreal) with a capital of £200,000 divided into 8,000 shares of £25 each to conduct a general banking business in the province. An act of incorporation was passed by the Assembly but shelved by the Legislative Council. Shortt has suggested that this was probably due to the machinations of the Bank of Montreal but there is no evidence to support the imputation: many promoters of the City Bank were also shareholders of the senior institution.

Resubmitted at the next session of the provincial parliament, the City Bank petition passed both the Assembly and Council but was reserved by the Governor, Lord Aylmer, for submission to London. There it was found that the charter contained the clause providing the death penalty "without benefit of clergy" for any servant of the bank "who should secrete, embezzle, or run away with any of the securities of the bank." The British criminal code having recently been tempered, the bill was disallowed on the grounds that it would establish a special criminal code for a specific corporation. Shorn of its objectionable features, the City Bank bill was enacted by both branches of the Lower Canada legislature at its 1832-33 session, was given the Governor's assent, and became law April 3, 1833. The subscription books were opened on May 13 and 1,000 shares were immediately subscribed. The charter required that £40,000 be paid up before the issuance of notes and £36,000 additional within three months thereafter. Apparently the first of these conditions was met by October 14 when the bank opened its doors for business. Shortt comments that paper to the extent of £50,000 was offered for discount on the opening day, £9,600 of which was accepted.

Comparing the relative ease of the new bank's establishment with the twenty-five-year travail that preceded that of the Bank of Montreal, it can be seen that the Canadian economy had made appreciable strides since 1817. Like the Bank of Montreal charter, that of the City Bank was to run to June 1, 1837, with the same provisions for earlier cancellation should the legislature be so minded. Except for the elimination of the death penalty for embezzlement, the City Bank charter was a replica of that of the Bank of Montreal, making it a commercial bank of issue and deposit engaged in the business of discounting sixty and ninety day commercial paper. Most of its exchange dealings were made through the senior institution, thus introducing the latter to its role of a "banker's bank," a function that was to be extended and consolidated as Canadian banking facilities were expanded during the ensuing decade.

The next bank to appear in Lower Canada differed in many respects from the three chartered banks then existing. This was the private banking firm of Viger, Dewitt & Co., which operated under the name of La Banque du Peuple and which opened its doors for business in July 1835, after two years of promotional effort. The first newspaper notice of the new venture appeared in August 1833, and the articles of association, signed by nine leading French-Canadian merchants, were published in January 1836. These provided for an initial capital of £100,000, divided into 8,000 shares of £12. 10s. each, and an eventual capital of £250,000. In general the articles embraced the banking principles and proscriptions contained in the Articles of Association of the Montreal Bank, but the new partnership took the form of a French joint-stock company *en commandite*. Under this system the twelve original partners assumed unlimited liability, jointly and collectively, for all debts of the partnership while the ordinary shareholders were liable only for the amount of their share holdings. The structure contained features of both English country and English joint-stock banking and in theory provided greater security for depositors than did the chartered banks. As in the latter, the directors were chosen by vote of the whole body of the shareholders. The articles of association envisaged the establishment of branches inside and outside the province.

The Banque du Peuple marked an invasion of the Canadian banking scene by French-Canadian financial and commercial interests. As such the venture was hailed in some quarters as a welcome awakening of French-Canadian enterprise; in others as a conspiratorial manoeuvre to weaken the position of the existing English-Canadian banks. While its inspiration has been generally recognized as political rather than commercial, its immediate success suggests that a need existed for banking facilities to serve the French-Canadian community. The Banque du Peuple appears to have filled a vacuum, although for some years it occupied a position of dubious legality with respect to its note issue.

Having failed to apply for a charter, presumably on the grounds that any petition would have been killed by the predominantly English Legislative Council, the Viger, Dewitt enterprise was prohibited from issuing certain notes under the Currency Act of 1830, restricting such issues to chartered banks. To get around the obstacle an ingenious device was resorted to: the notes of the bank were given the appearance of conventional bank-notes, but were actually drafts drawn by Viger, Dewitt & Co. on the teller of the Banque du Peuple, G. Peltier. Accepted by Peltier, these drafts passed into circulation as paper currency and received public acceptance despite initial efforts on the part of the chartered banks to boycott them. The Quebec

BROCKVILLE—1841

The first settler to build his log cabin at Brockville arrived in 1784 and was soon followed by other United Empire Loyalists. The inhabitants had various names for the town in the early years and did not reach a compromise until after the War of 1812, when it was named in honour of General Brock. Meanwhile, adjacent homesteaders had been referring to it as Snarlington.

This drawing, done in 1841, shows the town from the south side of the St. Lawrence. The brick court house on the hill, centre, is flanked on the left by the Presbyterian church and on the right by the Methodist church, while the old blockhouse stands guard on the waterfront. Slightly to the right in the background is St. Peter's Anglican church.

In 1843 the Bank of Montreal opened an office in Brockville, by then a thriving community of 3,000 engaged mainly in farming, lumbering and shipbuilding.

Gazette, in an editorial on August 7, 1835, attacked the new bank, pointing out the devious character of its note issue and drawing attention to the highly irresponsible character of the enterprise. Neither were its affairs to be made public nor was it subject to the statutory controls imposed by the charters of the existing banks. So far as the public had any knowledge, the bank's officers were free without restraint to engage in abuses of any and every kind. As has happened frequently in banking history, however, the public faith in the probity and integrity of Messrs. Viger and Dewitt was such that no action was ever instituted against their enterprise nor was the legality of their note issue ever tested. By May 1837, when the specie crisis struck Canada, the Banque du Peuple had become an accepted member of the Lower Canada banking family.

The success of the Viger, Dewitt excursion into banking inspired the promotion of joint-stock banks on the *en commandite* principle in Chambly, St. Hyacinthe, Boucherville, and Montreal itself. Later, during the acute currency stringency that developed in 1837 and 1838, a number of mercantile houses, among them that of Thomas and William Molson, borrowed from the Viger, Dewitt example to issue their own paper currency in the form of simulated bank-notes. Since these first forays into private banking in Lower Canada either died in infancy or were quashed by government edict they were without lasting significance. Instead, the scene now shifts to Upper Canada where immigration and more rapid economic growth had produced demands for increased credit facilities which led in turn to the multiplication of chartered banks, a great enlargement of bank capital, and the appearance of a number of more successful private banking experiments modelled partly on British and partly on American practice.

5.

Notwithstanding parliamentary investigations and the limited time for which charters were renewed, banking in Lower Canada pursued a relatively even course during the first twenty years of its development. French-Canadian political leaders, it is true, acquired an almost paranoiac hatred of the Bank of Montreal as the seat of English-Canadian commercial power, but no serious efforts were made to challenge the Bank's financial dominance nor to supplant it with some other kind of institution. In marked contrast is the story of banking in Upper Canada where the rapid growth of population in an Anglo-

American frontier environment made banking one of the most bitterly fought political issues of the turbulent 1830's.

The battle lines were first drawn, it will be recalled, by the bizarre manoeuvres and political skullduggery that brought into being simultaneously the two banks of Upper Canada, the one in York, the provincial capital, the other in Kingston, then the leading commercial centre in the upper province. Following the example of the Banks of the United States as to government participation, the York bank had as its principal shareholder the provincial government; consequently it enjoyed the provincial patronage and was controlled by the governing clique. The Kingston bank was promoted by local merchants to finance shipping on Lake Ontario, the growing trade with Watertown, Oswego, and other American communities, and forwarding on the St. Lawrence River.

The so-called "pretended" Bank of Upper Canada at Kingston began business during the prosperity of the early twenties but, in spite of its initial success, it was soon brought to disaster by poor management and irresponsible discounting practices. A government commission was appointed to wind up its affairs, leaving the York bank in a monopolistic position except for the agencies of the Bank of Montreal at Kingston and York. This situation was promptly rectified by the passage in 1824 of the act excluding banks that did not redeem their notes in the province from doing business there. The Bank of Montreal closed its agencies but named the Hon. J. H. Dunn, the Receiver General, as its representative in York. This arrangement ran smoothly until 1826, when Dunn was requested to return all Bank of Montreal notes in his possession; the Cashier, however, assured him of "the high sense which the Board entertained of the very friendly and satisfactory manner in which his agency had invariably been conducted."

The circumstances surrounding this manoeuvre remain obscure, but in 1829, at the behest of army paymasters and Rideau Canal contractors, the Bank re-established an agency under Henry Dupuy, the latter also being charged with the organization and supervision of strategic sub-agencies in the upper province. This defiance of their branch-exclusion act prompted the Family Compact to strike back. Soon, the Bank of Montreal and the Compact's Bank of Upper Canada were engaged in a note war wherein each collected the other's notes and presented them for redemption in specie at hopefully inopportune moments. The specie raids were finally resolved by the Bank of Montreal becoming the correspondent of the Bank of Upper Canada in Lower

Canada and vice versa, although the controversial agency at Kingston remained in operation. Each bank maintained a balance with the other and, despite altercations between the redoubtable Benjamin Holmes and Thomas Ridout, the Bank of Upper Canada's Cashier, they succeeded in lubricating the wheels of trade and commerce between the two provinces. However, the partnership was not a happy one, and in 1833, when the Bank of Upper Canada was made the depository for Imperial funds in the upper province, the Bank of Montreal withdrew from the agreement, closed its Kingston agency, and appointed the newly established Commercial Bank of the Midland District as its Upper Canada correspondent.

The monopoly enjoyed by the Bank of Upper Canada and its affiliation with the reigning political oligarchy enabled its management to practise rank favouritism, discrimination against political opponents, and an investment policy which channelled funds into exchange transactions at the expense of discounts, to the detriment of commercial development. There is, however, no evidence that its directors or officers ever strayed from the letter of the law in the daily conduct of their banking. In that they were eminently successful. Beginning in 1822 with a paid-up capital of no more than £8,500 – most of it furnished by the provincial government – the bank increased this by 1831 to £100,000, with a note circulation of £187,039 and discounts of £260,577. In Lower Canada at this time, the total banking capital amounted to £324,312 with a note circulation of £271,538 and corresponding discounts of £612,345. A comparison of these statistics throws light on the financial famine that prevailed in Upper Canada during the heyday of provincial banking. While well within the statutory limitation, the relation between note circulation and paid-up capital goes far to explain the highly profitable nature of the enterprise. Within nine years, that is by the end of 1831, the Bank of Upper Canada returned £51,000 to its shareholders in annual dividends of eight per cent and two bonus payments of six per cent each. The reports of the bank to the provincial legislature indicate the manner in which this was accomplished.

Discounts and note circulation both show steady increases, clearly pointing to the prosperous condition of the province and to the demand that existed for capital, or credit, for commercial and investment purposes. The public were able to find ready opportunities to employ their savings, and consequently deposits remained relatively small. The bank met the situation by extending its discounts, and its note circulation rose proportionately, at one point exceeding six times its specie reserves. It was therefore ill-prepared to meet a crisis, since its own solvency was dependent on the liquidity of its discounted paper, much of which was secured by inflated land values. For the time being, however, its profits were large and its reputation high because of government participation and, presumably, government backing.

Under the circumstances, it is not altogether surprising that the bank's officers and their legislative confrères, many of them directors of the bank, should have sought to preserve their profitable monopoly against all comers, British, American, and native. In point of fact, the depression of the middle twenties, and the unsavoury failure of the pretended Bank of Upper Canada at Kingston, did preserve the bank's monopoly until returning prosperity in 1829 gave rise to agitation in Kingston, Brockville, Niagara, and other centres for increased banking facilities, either in the form of locally controlled branches of the York bank or newly chartered local institutions. With these aims in view the merchants of Kingston, then the most thriving community in either of the provinces thanks to the Rideau Canal construction, resolved in 1830 to establish a new bank to be known as the Commercial Bank of Upper Canada with its head office in Kingston and branches in other suitable locations throughout the province. The Compact defeated the resultant bill in the Council and the Bank of Upper Canada then countered by establishing an office of deposit and discount at Kingston similar to that operated by the Bank of Montreal at Quebec and like it governed by a local board of directors.

Despite the withdrawal of some Commercial Bank supporters to sit on the Kingston board of the Bank of Upper Canada, a petition for incorporation was again presented to the 1831 session of the legislature. The bill passed the Assembly but was again defeated by the Council. Under the continued attacks of the reformers, the Compact yielded during the next session and permitted a bill incorporating the Commercial Bank of the Midland District to become law, but secured as a *quid pro quo* an increase in the capital of the Bank of Upper Canada from £100,000 to £200,000. The Commercial Bank was incorporated with a capital of £100,000 in shares of £25 each. Its charter followed substantially those of the chartered banks of Lower Canada and included the Massachusetts requirements with respect to reporting assets and liabilities adopted by the legislature of Lower Canada in 1830. The life of the charter extended to June 1, 1856.

The tripling of the banking capital of the province, from £100,000 to £300,000, unleashed an astonishing backlog of funds available for investment in bank stock. The Commercial Bank received pledges of £24,000 while still in the planning stage and experienced no difficulty in disposing of the balance of its shares on the opening of its subscription books in 1832. Six months had been allowed the Kingston venture before the Bank of Upper Canada could enter the investment market, but when it did so the subscription books for the new offering of 8,000 shares were closed in a single day. No person was allowed to subscribe initially for more than eighty shares, yet when the returns were finally in from other parts of the province and elsewhere 25,679 shares to the value of £320,987 had been subscribed. In 1832 the Bank of Upper Canada paid a bonus of eighteen per cent on its original shares and in addition maintained its regular dividend of eight per cent.

The break in the log jam of banking monopoly, coupled with galloping prosperity and a mounting flood of immigration, produced a speculative climate not unlike that which had accompanied the American banking mania a decade and a half earlier. Money, it appeared, could beget money if only a charter and a printing press could be legally wedded. With this romantic end in view, financial and commercial groups in Brockville, Cobourg, Hamilton, London and Niagara circulated bank petitions for submission to the legislature. At this juncture, however, an ironical obstruction was encountered. During the heated and consistently acrimonious debates on the Commercial Bank charter and the Bank of Upper Canada capital expansion, William Lyon Mackenzie, the fiery leader of the Reform party, vowed that should the measures be enacted he would proceed to London to secure their disallowance. He was implacably opposed to any system of banking which enabled the monopolization of the country's currency for either political or personal ends, and for this reason he had at first supported the Commercial Bank as a rival to the Bank of Upper Canada. His apparent about-face took place when it became evident that the charter of the new bank would not contain ample safeguards against the evils he feared. His threat was not an idle one and by representations to the Colonial Office, the Lords of the Treasury and the Board of Trade, he managed to carry it out. A transcript of his submissions has been preserved in the Public Archives of Canada and presents an alarming picture of banking in Upper Canada. Shortt, in his "History of Canadian Currency, Banking and Exchange," succinctly describes the reaction: "The Home Government, in its usual spirit of cheerful ignorance and blind benevolence, attempted untimely interferences. . . ."

When rumours of disallowance reached Canada early in 1833, both banks immediately curtailed discounting, the Commercial in the prospect of having

QUEBEC UPPER TOWN—1820'S

Until an epidemic of Asiatic cholera decimated the population of the city in 1832,
most of Quebec's inhabitants lived in the Lower Town. Thereafter, many moved to
the more spacious Upper Town, although most business continued to be carried on
along the narrow streets near the waterfront.

Pictured here is the Rue des Jardins in the Upper Town with the old Jesuit
College on the right and the bell tower of the English Cathedral in the background.
The college was completed in 1651, but after 1760 most of its pupils and teachers
returned to France and it was taken over by the army for use as barracks.

Rue des Jardins was also the site of the principal market in the Upper Town. Its
stalls and butchers' "shambles" were a hive of activity on market days, and it is
said that cattle were driven all the way from Rimouski, 180 miles down-river, for
sale in Quebec.

to wind up its charter, the York bank facing a fifty-per-cent capital reduction. According to Shortt: "The effect on business was very severe, and several failures resulted. The consequences would have been more serious had not the Bank of Montreal come to the rescue of the merchants and others deprived of their discounts." The unfortunate gap in the Montreal bank's records at this point makes it impossible to cast more light on the nature of the transactions; nevertheless they seem to represent a growing homogeneity among Canadian bankers in the face of what was regarded as the unwarranted interference of a poorly informed Imperial Government then engaged in the reform of its own none-too-satisfactory banking system.

As matters turned out, the threat of disallowance failed to materialize. When the official dispatches relating to the banking controversy reached Canada, they were found to contain nothing more serious than suggestions by the Committee of the Privy Council for Trade and Foreign Plantations for the regulation of banking, with the recommendation that all new charters embody eight conditions. Since five of the clauses were already incorporated in existing Canadian charters, only two provoked serious objections – the second, that banks maintain specie reserves and redeem their note issues at all offices, and the seventh, providing for double liability. The sixth clause, requiring the preparation of weekly balances, was simply regarded as a nuisance. Fearing the loss of its charter, the Commercial Bank was willing to agree to double liability, but such was the temper of both branches of the legislature that Tories and Reformers in unison refused to consider the proposals and instead addressed to the King what was tantamount to a sharp rebuke·to the Home Government. In the formal verbiage of prayer and petition, London was told to mind its own business. The reply, presented to the 1835 session of the legislature, was conciliatory. While expressing surprise at the heat and vehemence of the legislature's rejection of their tentative suggestions and maintaining the right of the Crown to veto any and all colonial enactments, the Lords of the Treasury advised that the King in Council, sensible of the confusion and distress that would follow disallowance, abjured any interference with existing provincial banking statutes. This interesting interchange has been overlooked by most historians despite its obvious relation to the struggle for responsible government then approaching the crisis stage.

Under pressure from all sides to expand existing banking facilities, and emboldened by its successful defiance of Imperial authority, the Assembly of

Upper Canada now introduced bills to charter commercial banks in Cobourg and Hamilton. The Legislative Council countered by offering bills to enlarge the capital of the existing banks. Involved were the two basic theories of banking: the one favoured the existence of a few strong banks; the other, the introduction of a free banking system, then proving so successful in the neighbouring states. So great had become the opposition to further enlarging the Bank of Upper Canada that the proposition was shelved, but when the Commercial Bank applied in 1835 to have its capital increased to £200,000, equal to that of the bank at York (Toronto since 1834), the petition was granted. Led by Mackenzie, the Reform party fought to have the British recommendations embodied in the amended charter but this was unsuccessful, as was an attempt to impose a trifling annual tax of a penny a pound on banking capital.

Encouraged by its successful acquisition of new capital, the Commercial Bank opened its first branch, at Brockville, in March 1835. Meanwhile, the Bank of Upper Canada had branches operating in Brockville, Kingston, Cobourg, Hamilton and Niagara. Despite the rapid expansion of facilities, efforts persisted to charter other independent local banks in Cobourg, Hamilton, St. Catharines and London. Only one was successful. In 1835 the Gore Bank of Hamilton was chartered with an authorized capital of £100,000, only £10,000 of which had to be paid in before opening for business.

Responsible for the Gore Bank was the political adroitness of Allan MacNab, whose baronial establishment, Dundurn Castle, still overlooks Hamilton harbour as an historic shrine. The previous year the Assembly had granted a charter for the bank, only to have it blocked by Bank of Upper Canada directors on the Council. A long-time associate of the Compact himself, the Laird then proceeded to expose the motives and methods of the junta, "much to the delight," says Shortt, "of the enemies of the Compact and the edification of the public in general." A year later the Act of Incorporation was duly promulgated and in November, 1835, the subscription books were opened at the head office and the branches of the Bank of Upper Canada. Although it was the first bank in Upper Canada to carry double liability, its stock was heavily oversubscribed, as had been the issues of the other chartered banks before it. The Gore Bank opened for business in May 1836 and enjoyed its share of the inflated prosperity that terminated abruptly with the American specie crisis of May 1837.

6.

At the close of the 1835 session of the Upper Canada legislature, the population of the province was 400,000 and its chartered banking capital £500,000. During the next session, 1836-37, nine new banks were chartered, with an aggregate capital of £4,000,000. All the enactments were reserved by the Lieutenant-Governor, Sir Francis Bond Head, and sent to England, where, to quote Breckenridge, "they met the scathing criticism they deserved." Neither the Treasury nor the Board of Trade, however, formally allowed or disallowed the bills; instead they were returned to the Upper Canada legislature for a more objective reconsideration along the lines noted earlier. Before this proposal could be acted upon, the calamitous events of 1837 reduced to embers the fiery enthusiasm for crossroads banking that had enlivened a brief interlude of halcyon prosperity.

The banking craze that swept Upper Canada in the 1830's was a North American phenomenon. With their economic development retarded by the staggering transportation costs imposed by the obstacles of the St. Lawrence – to say nothing of the caprices of British and American tariff policies – the farmers, millers, merchants, lumbermen and forwarders of the interior province had only to look southward to learn the apparent ease with which an abundance of money, or what passed for money, could be obtained to finance any and every kind of enterprise – public works, settlement, agriculture, commerce, industry. While much of this financial capital came from England in exchange for commodities or as investments in American enterprises, even more seemed to be a product of spontaneous generation, propagated and proliferated in the manner of lichen growing from wind-blown spores.

Economic historians are still debating the significance of this free banking in the dynamic growth of the United States, but to many Upper Canadians of the 1830's, starved for some form of financial capital, it seemed to be the only key that would open the Pandora's box of illimitably rich natural resources. Herein lies the explanation of the passion for banks and more banks which possessed the reform elements of Upper Canada, both radical and moderate, but which had no parallel in Lower Canada; the first having a borrower's environment, the latter, established commercial interests restricted to Quebec and Montreal.

The subject had other ramifications, of course. The successful establishment of the Banque du Peuple and City Bank in Lower Canada indicated a legitimate need for increased banking facilities. In Upper Canada, on the other hand, the scramble for bank charters encountered the opposition of the established chartered banks as well as that provided by viceregal and Imperial resistance to any kind of change. The existing banks argued on entirely logical grounds that a few strong, well-managed banks were preferable to a plethora of weak and poorly financed note-issuing ventures such as existed across the American border. All factions, however, conservative, moderate, and radical, were opposed to interference on the part of the Home Government and urged that the governor no longer be permitted to dissent from future enactments of a purely local nature. In the debate on the constitutional issue, a number of solutions to the provincial banking dilemma were proposed.

The most interesting of these was the plan put forward in 1835 by W. H. Merritt of Welland Canal fame for the establishment of a Provincial Bank patterned on the dying Second Bank of the United States and the Bank of Upper Canada. It was to contain the best features of both, and for good measure the injection of Scottish open credits and interest payments on deposits. The Provincial Bank was to be capitalized at £500,000, £350,000 to be raised abroad by the sale of provincial securities; £25,000 directly by the province; and £125,000 by the sale of stock to the local investing public. Branches were to be established in each of the districts of the province with a capital of £100,000 each, £75,000 furnished by bank debentures bearing six per cent interest, and £25,000 by local subscription. Merritt's proposals were embodied in a bill which produced one of the most interesting discussions on banking yet reported in Canada, and which contained economic theories in some respects not dissimilar from those expounded in support of Social Credit a century later.

Merritt's scheme for a Provincial Bank was defeated by a narrow majority only after extended debate and then mainly on the grounds that any institution combining public credit and private interest could only exaggerate the evils already exposed by the operations of the Second Bank of the United States and those of the Bank of Upper Canada. Shortt observed: "The scheme was vigorously supported in the Assembly, yet the pessimistic element prevailed, and the friends of free paper were left to marvel at the blindness and selfishness of their fellow men."

Much praise has been bestowed on the Home Government for restraining the Upper Canadian banking enthusiasm in the 1830's, but a skeptical footnote may be added. After the passage of the English Bank Act of 1833, extending the powers of the joint-stock banks established by the Act of 1826, there appeared in Toronto two English gentlemen, Captain George Truscott of the Royal Navy and John C. Green, a retired commissary general, who began business under the firm name of Truscott, Green & Co., and proceeded to organize the Agricultural Bank of the City of Toronto in 1834. The men had a little capital and some experience in English joint-stock banking. They established their Toronto bank on the same principles, the partners being liable for all the debts of the institution. The bank drew upon itself the ire of other Canadian financial institutions by being the first to introduce the Scottish practice of paying interest on deposits. It also adopted the Scottish open credit system and proved moderately successful, surviving both the attacks of the Bank of Upper Canada and other chartered banks on its note issue and those of William Lyon Mackenzie on the politics of its directors.

The success of the Agricultural Bank inspired the establishment of a second joint-stock enterprise, the Farmers' Bank, with which Truscott was briefly connected because of his experience, and of which Henry Dupuy, the former Bank of Montreal agent at Kingston, became the Manager, a term not hitherto used in Canadian banking. Mackenzie now turned from criticism to action by petitioning for a charter for the Bank of the People, to be run on joint-stock principles. Still a fourth joint-stock bank, the Niagara Suspension Bridge Bank, a hybrid invention having offices in Niagara Falls (Upper Canada) and Lockport (New York), next appeared upon the scene, and there is reason to believe that several obscure improvisations circulated notes as reputed joint-stock undertakings before the legislature, with growing concern for the mounting circulation of heterogeneous paper currency, finally acted to prohibit the issue of notes or other paper intended to pass as currency except by express legislative authority. Exempted from the provisions of the act were the chartered banks and the private or joint-stock banks already doing business.

Private banking ventures in Upper Canada functioned satisfactorily until the crisis of 1837. Even then, the Bank of the People, which had secured as its cashier Francis Hincks, an Irishman of wide financial and banking experience, was the only Canadian bank which continued to make specie payments during the crises of 1837-39. Both Hincks and the Bank of the People will return to the limelight at a later date, the first as a leading member of various parliamentary committees on banking, and the second in connection with its absorption by the Bank of Montreal. Meanwhile other events impinged on the Canadian economy and its banking system.

THIRTEEN

UNCHALLENGED

LEADERSHIP

UNCHALLENGED LEADERSHIP

I.

As related, the first sizable infusions of British capital in the Canadian economy for other than administrative, military, or mercantile purposes occurred between 1834 and 1838 when Upper Canada was able to sell £869,650 sterling of provincial debentures in London. A number of considerations prompted English financiers, such as Baring Brothers and Thomas Wilson & Co., to invest their funds in Canada rather than in the United States as had hitherto been their habit: the re-election of Andrew Jackson in 1832 with a virtual mandate to exterminate the Second Bank of the United States; Jackson's transfer of federal funds from the branches of the doomed bank to politically favoured "pet banks" soon after his inauguration in 1833; and the devaluation of silver coinage by the United States government the following year. According to Ralph W. Hidy, Baring Brothers' historian and chronicler, the British government's large indemnity loan to West Indies planters for freeing their slaves "also deflected attention and funds from America." This situation throws a new light on J. H. Dunn's placement of the £400,000 of Upper Canada debentures in London in 1835.

However, there were other signs of a growing interest in Canada about that time. Early in 1836, two financial groups in London undertook the formation of new colonial banks to do business in North America. One of these was connected with the recently formed Provincial Bank of Ireland, the other, headed by W. Medley, "a Lombard Street banking genius," with British North American mercantile houses in London. Separate charters were sought under the provisions of the Bank Act of 1833, but neither petition was immediately successful. Nevertheless, the two banks began operations as private companies, one in the West Indies, the other in the British North American provinces.

Much confusion has surrounded the origins and early operations of the Bank of British North America. Absorbed by the Bank of Montreal in 1918, it was one of Canada's most enterprising financial institutions throughout the nineteenth century, pioneering the way through the prairies to British Columbia, the Yukon, and California. Yet Adam Shortt, writing his monographs on the history of Canadian currency and banking in the 1890's, had to rely on a publication of the 1870's, *History, Statistics and Geography of Upper and Lower Canada*, for information about the B.B.N.A. Written by R. M. Martin, a former London journalist, the book was one of a number by the same author dealing with the Canadian provinces before Confederation. In that on Lower Canada, Martin claimed to have originated the idea of forming a colonial bank in London, and to have passed it along to his friend, W. Medley, who then carried it forward to a successful conclusion. This indeed may have been the case. The first Minute Book of the Court Committee in London, the governing body of the Bank of British North America, shows that the institution had its genesis in a meeting called by W. Medley, 10 Lombard Street, London, on March 4, 1836. Eight gentlemen from "the City" attended, and adopted the following proposal:

> That in consequence of the increasing importance, especially in their Commercial relations with Great Britain, of the North American Colonies, the high rate of interest there, the great difference of Exchange with England, the rapid progress of emigration, and the increasing facility of communication between Europe and North America, now averaging only 20 days on the homeward passage, a Banking Company should be established in London, for the formation of Banks of issue and deposit at Quebec, Montreal, Toronto, Halifax, Sydney (Cape Breton), St. John's (Newfoundland).

The proposal goes on to mention the newly formed Bank of Australia, the shares of which were selling at a premium of eighty per cent, and the Provincial Bank of Ireland, which had shown the facility with which control over colonial branches could be exercised through a "London Board of Management." The first Minute closes with the statement: "In fact next to Ireland the Canadas are the nearest points for extending the Banking System of England with the improved advantage of a local direction to act with the Managers."

Following the first meeting of the "Committee of Investigation," Medley and his friends forged ahead to place their banking venture on a working basis. In eight days a second meeting was held, at which representatives of Canadian mercantile interests included Robert Gillespie of R. Gillespie & Co., the English branch of Gillespie, Moffatt & Co., and James Dowie of Gould, Dowie & Co. of Quebec, Halifax and New York. In attendance also were representatives of the Provincial Bank of Ireland and British mercantile houses with important interests in continental Europe. Resolutions were adopted to apply forthwith for a charter and to invite the participation of such banking houses as Baring Brothers; N. M. Rothschild; Reid, Irving & Co.; Ellice, Kinnear & Co., and also R. N. Hunt of Newman, Hunt & Co., St. John's, Newfoundland. At a succeeding meeting, the presence of George Forsyth and Russell Ellice added other well-known Canadian commercial names to those already mentioned. Oddly enough, there was no reference to Thomas Wilson & Co. nor to the Bank of Montreal, although Robert Gillespie submitted a lengthy report on Canadian banks and banking.

In less than two weeks from the first meeting, conversations with Sir George Grey, Under-Secretary for the Colonies, disclosed that "*at present* there are insuperable obstacles to obtaining a Charter from the government." Nothing daunted, the promoters decided to proceed without benefit of charter and later modified their petition to pray for an act enabling them to sue and be sued as a corporate body.

Given public advertisement on May 2, the prospectus of the Bank of British North America announced the formation of a joint-stock banking company with a capital of £600,000 divided into 12,000 shares of £50 each of which one-quarter were to be reserved for colonial subscription. Thirteen directors were listed and Glyn, Hallifax, Mills & Co. and I. &. S. Pearce, Phillips & Bolger named as the bankers and solicitors respectively. The preamble was unlike any of those heretofore examined. Whereas the promotional material of the early American and Canadian banks strongly emphasized the public benefits

COBOURG WHEN THE BANK ARRIVED

Founded in 1798, Cobourg, on Lake Ontario, claimed a population of one hundred in 1824 and grew to 1,653 in 1837. First named Amherst, then Hamilton—and nicknamed Hardscrabble because of the quality of its soil—the settlement became known as Cobourg in 1819. This water-colour by Lieutenant Bainbrigge is dated 1840.

The East Pier storehouse, at the entrance to the wharf, served as both a custom house and a warehouse, the passageway through its centre facilitating the inspection and storage of merchandise. Behind this building can be seen Victoria College which had opened as the Upper Canada Academy in 1836, while at the far right is St. Peter's Anglican church dating back to 1820.

The Bank of Montreal came to Cobourg in 1840, attracted possibly by the resourcefulness of its inhabitants who had received several patents during the 1830's for inventions in the fields of transportation, carpentry and agriculture. In 1833 they had proudly launched their own steamboat, pictured here at the wharf.

to be gained from banking institutions, that of the Bank of British North America confined itself to prospective profits:

> The rapidity with which the Colonies have advanced in prosperity and commercial importance, the vast increase of their population, the high rate of interest, the fluctuations of Exchange, the inadequacy of the Capital already employed for banking operations, and the increasing facility of intercourse with the Mother Country point out the different settlements of British North America as affording a secure field for the profitable employment of Capital.

Provision for management was vested in a London Court of Directors and those of branches in boards of directors chosen locally but approved by the Court in London. To secure to the shareholders "the advantages of limited responsibility" a clause was inserted in the deed of settlement to compel the directors to call an extraordinary general meeting of the shareholders should the books ever show a loss of one-third the capital, when the expediency of dissolving or continuing the company would be determined. Shares were to be allotted on an initial payment of £10, preferably on the recommendation of a director, and voted on the ratio of one to five shares – one vote; five to ten shares – two votes; ten to twenty-five shares – three votes; etc.

So great was the public response that within a week the Court decided to increase the capital to £1,000,000 divided into 20,000 shares of £50 each, of which 5,000 were allocated to the Colonies. Meeting on May 7, the Court further resolved: "That it is absolutely indispensable to send out to the Colonies, for the purpose of getting information, and making preliminary arrangements, a gentleman of the first talent and respectability, and in some degree acquainted and connected with the Colonies." The choice fell on Robert C. Carter of Leadenhall Street. After brief negotiations, he agreed to proceed to the Colonies on June 1, 1836, and to remain there, if need be, until March 1, 1837, for a monthly stipend of £200 sterling and an allocation of 175 shares. He was appointed a director and, after a farewell dinner at the Albion Tavern on the evening of May 30, tendered by the members of the Court at a cost of £15. 18s., sailed for America on the next westbound packet. Following Carter on later June packets went dispatches "suggesting to him, not to lose time in attempting to overcome any extraordinary difficulties that might occur in establishing Banks in Lower Canada, but to turn his attention to the Upper Province, and to the Lower Parts, with as little delay as possible."

Robert Carter resumed his seat at the London Court of the Bank on March 9, 1837. During his nine months' absence overseas he had travelled by steamboat, stage-coach, sleigh or other conveyances more than five thousand miles in the British colonies and the United States, and had visited all the principal cities in the Canadian provinces. Arriving in New York in July 1836, he proceeded to Quebec, Montreal, Halifax, Fredericton, Saint John, Toronto, and Kingston, returning to New York via Montreal early in 1837.

The extent of the accomplishments of the colonial commissioner was reported to the proprietors of the B.B.N.A. at their first annual meeting held at the Bank's premises, 7 St. Helen's place, on June 27, 1837. They included the placement of 3,427 shares of the 5,000 allotted to the Colonies, the collection of £34,270 sterling for deposits thereon, the establishment of branches with local boards of directors at Montreal, Quebec, Toronto and St. John's, Newfoundland, and the completion of arrangements for the establishment of branches and agencies or sub-branches in Saint John, N.B., Halifax, Kingston, Fredericton, Miramichi, Pictou, and Charlottetown, as soon as statutory difficulties could be overcome. An act of the Imperial Parliament passed July 5, 1836, enabled the Bank to sue and be sued in the United Kingdom. Similar acts passed by the legislatures of Upper Canada and Prince Edward Island also gave the bank legal status in those provinces. Enabling legislation had been delayed in Lower Canada by an enforced recess of the Assembly, and in the Atlantic provinces by local banking interests with strong political connections. The accession of Samuel Cunard to the Halifax board was rightly expected to overcome this obstacle.

The Maritime Provinces excepted, Robert Carter encountered no "extraordinary difficulties" on his transatlantic mission. In New York he had studied American banking and had completed arrangements for Prime, Ward, King & Co. to become the New York agents of the B.B.N.A. In Quebec he had been welcomed by the mercantile houses already represented on the London Court and had been able to announce in the Quebec *Gazette* of August 19, 1836, that a provisional committee had been formed to conduct the bank's business and that the shares allotted to the district (1,300) had been taken up and a deposit of £10 paid on each. Compared with the paid-up capital of £8,512 with which the Bank of Upper Canada had started business, £13,000 sterling was an impressive sum for a branch bank to have at its disposal. The actual opening awaited only the arrival of a manager and an accountant appointed by the London Court, and of iron doors for the strong-room, a set of books, and a supply of printed documents and bank-notes to be sent from England.

Despite some misgivings about the reaction of Montreal's financial interests, mainly the Bank of Montreal, the Commissioner's reception there had been as cordial as in Quebec. Dispatches dated August 31, 1836, give the names of the provisional directors – Messrs. William Cunningham, Austin Cuvillier, Robert Gillespie Jr., Albert Furniss, and James Millar – and recommend that a manager and accountant be sent out as soon as possible. No references to Robert Carter's Montreal visits appear in the records of the Bank of Montreal, but those of the London Court of the B.B.N.A. indicate that a merger of the institutions was seriously contemplated when Carter returned to Montreal in the spring of 1837.

Swinging eastward, Carter reached the Maritimes in November 1836, setting up provisional committees at Halifax, Saint John, N.B., Fredericton and Miramichi; the St. John's, Newfoundland, branch had already been arranged directly by the Court in London. Moving west via Albany and Rochester, Carter arrived at Toronto in time for Christmas, and the legislature obligingly passed an act enabling the London bank to sue and be sued in Upper Canada, imposing the same restrictions with respect to returns and note issues as those already governing the existing banks. In Kingston, a committee headed by William Strange, the Vice-President of the Commercial Bank, was waiting to solicit the establishment of a branch in that city.

Considering all the circumstances, there appears to have been no reason why the emissary of the Bank of British North America should have been greeted otherwise than with open arms. At the time, the crying need in the British American colonies was for capital, and this, according to its prospectus, the bank would furnish to the extent of £1,000,000 sterling, almost as much as that of all the banks in Canada combined. Had there been any objection to the transfusion it must have come from the chartered banks, but they were easily persuaded that they would profit from the introduction of new supplies of sorely needed specie since it was a foregone conclusion that some of the money would end up as deposits in their vaults. Furthermore, the cachet of English banking carried tremendous weight in the business and political circles of Upper Canada, although the banking system established by the Bank of Montreal had attained in the course of its brief evolution a greater flexibility and stability than had yet been achieved in England.

MOMENTOUS MEETING
DURING 1837 DEPRESSION

In the autumn of 1836, economic depression started in England. It was soon felt across the Atlantic, and in May 1837 the New York banks were forced to suspend specie payments.

Closed off by the ice until spring, Montreal was feeling only the first symptoms of the impending malady when the news from New York shocked the city's financial leaders into abrupt action. At the instigation of the Bank of Montreal, hurried consultations took place between the heads of business and the banks. Drafts of petitions to the government were composed, but it was obvious that, with no gold available in the United States, runs would soon start on the Canadian banks. Business and banking could not wait for Lower Canada's crippled parliament to take the lead.

The situation called for an immediate response. Thus, on May 16, the public was summoned to the meeting hall in St. Ann's Market. They arrived, as can be seen, to find the details of the proposed tactics not yet worked out, but they unanimously approved a set of resolutions to suspend specie payments, dramatically presented by the chairman, Hon. George Moffatt, who was one of the commercial fathers of Montreal and a former director of the Bank. By this independent manoeuvre, the people of Lower Canada saved themselves from the worst of the ensuing chaos; they had to look only as far as their sister province to see the greater evils that could have befallen them.

Painting by Lewis Parker

The rosy expectations awakened by the opening of B.B.N.A. branches went unrealized. For one thing, their establishment took place during a period of great political unrest which affected operations for several years, particularly with respect to note circulation. For another, the bank's early dealings consisted largely of loans to firms engaged in commerce: and as such credits were readily available from the established chartered banks, the B.B.N.A. introduced relatively small amounts of specie into the country. What Canada needed was financial capital for internal improvements and the development of the country's natural resources. However, the B.B.N.A. simply conformed to the practices of the existing banks, guarding its specie carefully, dealing in profitable exchange, and discounting warily only the best commercial paper. According to the Minutes of the London Court, not much more than £100,000 sterling, including £34,270 received from local subscriptions, was used by the bank during the first years of its operations in Lower and Upper Canada.

One of the more interesting features of these operations was the bank's role as a financial agent for immigrants. The B.B.N.A. early developed close relations with the Provincial Bank of Ireland and the National Bank of Scotland, into whose branches prospective emigrants were encouraged to deposit their funds. Upon arriving in America, the settlers could then draw cheques on any of the widespread branches of the B.B.N.A. and receive its notes in return. While this system greatly facilitated immigration and settlement and was a source of substantial exchange profits to the bank, it also impeded an important flow of specie to the colonies, as many immigrants no longer brought with them their pouches of gold and silver coins.

Notwithstanding the failure of the Bank of British North America to realize fully its early promise, the institution had far-reaching effects on the evolution of Canadian banking. It is probable, in fact, that the persistent legend of Scottish banking as the dominant influence on Canadian banking stems from practices introduced by the London bank. Prior to 1837, for example, the Canadian banks had recruited their personnel locally among trained bookkeepers or accountants who carried on the system introduced by H. B. Stone, Horatio Gates and Charles Bancroft in the Bank of Montreal. In contrast, the London Court of the B.B.N.A. recruited its managers (cashiers), accountants and tellers, with few exceptions, in Great Britain. At the outset, candidates with experience in the Provincial Bank of Ireland were favoured, but owing to the strong representation of Greenock-Newfoundland mercantile houses on the London Court of Directors, the field of recruitment soon shifted to Scotland, where the services of managers and accountants could be secured for salaries of £400 per annum for the one category and £200 for the other. At the time when the cashier of the Bank of Montreal received an annual salary of £900 with perquisites, that of the secretary of the London Court and those of managers sent to the colonies were £400 without other emoluments. The saving in wages to be effected by recruiting staff in Scotland was not overlooked by Canadian bankers.

Other Scottish practices introduced by the Bank of British North America were the system of cash credits, long a feature of Scots banking, and the payment of interest on inactive deposit accounts. Although this last practice had already been introduced into Upper Canada by the Agricultural Bank, its endorsement by the London colonial bank led to its general acceptance first in Upper Canada and later in the other provinces. The change is significant as it marks a major deviation in Canadian banking from those principles of American commercial banking which had hitherto prevailed.

The influence actually exerted on Canadian banking legislation by the London-governed institution is now obscure. The dispatches of Robert Carter and later of the several managers of branches would no doubt throw light upon the matter. Unfortunately they are no longer in existence. Stored under Holborn Viaduct in London, all the letter books and other voluminous records of the London Court of the Bank of British North America including some of the minute books were destroyed in 1940 by the same German air raid that wiped out a large area of the city near St. Paul's Cathedral.

These facts are known, however: Baring Brothers and Thomas Wilson & Co. acquired a lively interest in the financial affairs of Upper Canada by their assumption of the role of provincial investment bankers. To this interest were added those of the London directors and shareholders of the Bank of British North America with such powerful connections in the City as Glyn, Hallifax, Mills & Co. and, in Downing Street and Westminster, as Lord Glenelg, Sir George Grey and Poulett Thomson, later to become Governor General of Canada as Baron Sydenham. This potent combination suggests a new explanation for the unprecedented concern shown by the Colonial Office during the closing years of the 1830's in the banking legislation of Upper Canada. Imperial interference found expression in persistent acts of reservation, disallowance and instruction, none of which was received gladly by the provincial legislature. Nevertheless, the effect was to modify the strong American influence on Canadian banking and give it a more distinctive native character.

2.

While the British Treasury and Colonial Office evinced a growing tendency after 1835 to question all banking legislation enacted in Upper Canada, bank bills passed in the sister province enjoyed virtual immunity. This contradiction bore paradoxical results. Although Imperial paternalism in Upper Canada may have saved the Canadian banking system from the worst American excesses, as so often stated, the absence of Imperial interest in Lower Canada undoubtedly preserved the principles of commercial banking introduced by the Bank of Montreal in 1817. Concurrently, the triangular apparatus of exchange, also introduced by the Bank of Montreal, was greatly strengthened, and with it the Bank's position in the financial world of Canada. In a satisfactory position at the beginning of the 1830's, the Bank emerged, at the end of a decade of temporary prosperity, economic disaster, political conflict and constitutional change, as the country's unchallenged financial leader. Each transition left the institution in a stronger position than it had enjoyed before.

Many factors, British, American, and Canadian, contributed to its rise to undisputed eminence. One of the most important was the Bank's position as the principal government banker in the Canadian provinces and its access to foreign exchange through its New York connections. Equally important was the strategic location of Montreal, the trans-shipment point of most of the imports and all of the economically significant exports of Upper Canada. These advantages alone placed the Bank in much the same relationship to the Bank of Upper Canada as that of the larger eastern American banks to their western correspondents.

Another factor in the Bank's progress at this time has been indicated above – the apparent lack of interest of the Treasury and the Colonial Office in Lower Canadian banking when that of Upper Canada was subjected to alarmed scrutiny. A possible explanation lies in the fact that the one was deemed satisfactory and the other in danger of corruption from American influences. But present also in the upper province was the newly established British investment interest, attracted by phenomenal population growth and economic expansion, while the largely subsistence economy of Lower Canada remained relatively static.

Yet another influence is seen in the ethnic backgrounds of the two provinces. In both, agitation for political reform was rampant and later reached a point of crisis. In Upper Canada, however, the homogeneity of the Anglo-American population enabled parliamentary government to continue without interruption. In Lower Canada, on the other hand, the conflict between two alien peoples, opposed in every facet of tradition and endeavour, culminated in armed rebellion, the suspension of the elective process, and government by administrative council.

The schism between agrarian Catholicism and commercial Protestantism in Lower Canada actually occurred some years before. As early as 1832, the Assembly and Executive had reached a virtual impasse, after which legislative action became less and less effective as successive sessions were prorogued or stalemated. Previously, the Assembly had refused to extend the existing bank charters beyond June 1, 1837, no doubt with the intention of making drastic changes in the laws governing banking before that time. Legislative incapacity made this impossible, even had the collapse of prosperity in England and a banking crisis in the United States not had severe repercussions in the Canadian provinces. In consequence no new banking legislation reached London from Lower Canada for several years and the existing banks, unlike those of Upper Canada, continued to function without interference. The situation persisted until a new constitution for the Canadian provinces could be adopted and the first parliament of the Province of Canada could enact new banking legislation.

It is idle to speculate as to the changes that might have taken place had environmental influences been different. The fact remains, however, that the legislative hiatus in Lower Canada enabled commercial banking to become firmly established in Canada during a period when the banking systems of both England and the United States were undergoing searching reappraisal. Contributory, no doubt, was the absence of those incentives in the economy of Lower Canada that inspired other areas in North America to turn to land or state banking as a means of providing credit for development. But although it is apparent that a combination of such circumstances enabled the Bank of Montreal to exert an influence that is without a parallel in the history of banking in other countries, there was of course one other essential factor – exceptionally able management.

The Bank's progress under the presidencies of John Molson Sr., John Fleming, and Horatio Gates has already been reviewed. Their tenures of office encompassed a period of economic expansion that was felt in all parts of North America. Immigrants flowed into Canada and the United States, and for several years the British colonies received more from the British Isles than did their republican neighbour. Investment capital soon accompanied the exodus; land companies were formed to engage in the organized development of frontier areas in Upper and Lower Canada; public works were undertaken, and new enterprises established. The flood of immigration brought with it serious epidemics of Asiatic cholera in 1832 and 1834, but the tide continued until the collapse of British prosperity in 1836. Meanwhile, the Bank paid dividends of fourteen per cent for three consecutive years. While high dividend payments may reflect nothing more than general prosperity, the steady increase in reserves bears evidence of conservative, long-sighted management.

Such achievements were not attained without arousing suspicion and animosity. As the agitation for reform intensified, the Bank became more closely associated in the minds of Papineau and his followers with the governing clique of the province; it was therefore a target for political hatred and invective. While platform oratory seems to have had little actual effect on circulation or deposits, it did lead on one occasion to violence. During the bitterly fought of elections of 1832 a mob converged on the Place d'Armes, and during the course of the rioting the facade of the Bank of Montreal was stoned and most of the windows broken. Troops from the garrison at St. Helen's Island arrived to put down the riot and in the ensuing fracas three men lost their lives by gunfire. Two officers were arrested, but the indictment was later thrown out by a grand jury. The incident brought Papineau one step nearer to rebellion and the English commercial group to a renewal of its agitation for Montreal's annexation to Upper Canada.

Politically, an uneasy calm endured throughout 1833; financially, however, the year posed new problems. In Upper Canada the Bank of Montreal agencies were withdrawn following the transfer of government patronage to the Bank of Upper Canada, beginning a period of higher charges for exchange between the provinces, and the removal of federal deposits from the Second Bank of the United States had repercussions that affected all of North America. Under the much-hated management of Nicholas Biddle, the Second Bank of the United States, as the government depository, had in a large measure been able to control an inflationary trend through its command of specie and conservative discounting practices. With the transfer of federal funds to state-regulated banks, controls vanished, lending practices were relaxed, and both money and credit became easier. Under the added stimulus of seemingly inexhaustible supplies of British capital and manufactured products obtained on long-term credits, an orgy of speculation in railroads, canals, banks, industry, real estate, in fact, enterprises of every kind, ensued.

The effects in Canada of the Jacksonian easy-money era have yet to be fully assessed. Some were relatively minor, as for instance the increased circulation of American bank-notes in Canada, and the invitation they gave counterfeiting gangs along the border to produce worthless paper currency without discrimination as to the country of origin. Other American influences had wider significance. The example of spectacular growth and prosperity across the border added to the political discontent in both provinces and invited the banking experiments launched in Upper Canada. While not patterned directly on American models they were largely inspired and made acceptable by the initial spectacular success of the U.S. ventures. A parallel development occurred in Lower Canada with the establishment of the Banque du Peuple and other private banks. The Jacksonian influence had another expression in the growing enmity of Louis-Joseph Papineau toward the oligarchy represented by the executive and the financial interests of Lower Canada, notably those connected with the Bank of Montreal. Denied the creation of an elective legislative council by Lord Aylmer, Papineau introduced in the 1834 session of parliament his inflammatory "Ninety-two Resolutions" in which the "money power" was referred to in terms reminiscent of Thomas Hart Benton's excoriations of the banking Moloch in the United States Senate. In November, Papineau's radical followers made an effort to undermine confidence in the banks by posting notices in French on the doors of parish churches and other public places. The translation reads:

NOTICE TO CANADIANS

From the public press you will have learned that the confidence of the public of Quebec in the Banks, and above all those of Montreal, has ceased, that within a few days £12,000 has been withdrawn from them, and that the principal Bank at Montreal has been forced on two occasions to send hard coin to its branch in Quebec. Those of you who have Bills of this Bank in your possession, and who do not wish to be exposed to the risk of losing their value, wholly or in part, would do well to exchange them as soon as possible, for hard coin at the Bank of Montreal, St. James Street. Let the example of the United States be a warning to Canadians. Several hundred banks have failed, and those who had confidence in these institutions, which are enemies of the liberty of the people, have sustained considerable losses on their rags of paper, which they pretend to be equivalent to hard coin. Be on your guard, Canadians! Take no more bills, rid yourself as soon as possible of those you now have!

November 8, 1834.

A copy of the notice is preserved in the Bank's museum. Along the margin is written: "Posted at the County Church door, and read, too, by order of Papineau & Co., December, 1834, and produced very little effect."

That the notice had some effect is apparent from the mere fact of notation but no estimate of its extent is possible. The Bank's returns to the government for 1834 show a drop in discounts of approximately seventeen per cent from 1833, indicating that commercial lending had been curtailed to profit from the exchange market in New York, but dividends totalling fourteen per cent show that the banking business in Lower Canada was not adversely affected by the worsening political climate.

By the close of 1834, the Crown had refused to grant any constitutional reforms, echoing events that had transpired in the British Province of New York eighty years before, and an infuriated Assembly had traditionally responded by voting to impeach the Governor and by refusing to vote supplies. Another ghost of a forgotten past was seen in the formation of Committees of Correspondence and of the opposed Constitutional Association. Yet despite the gathering storm clouds on the political horizon, the year 1834 was one of continuing prosperity. Notwithstanding the second visitation of cholera, immigration was the third largest on record to that time, and the British American Land Company was chartered with George Moffatt and Peter McGill as its Canadian commissioners to develop "the waste lands" of Quebec's southernmost tier of counties.

As always, however, the dynamics of Canadian prosperity had their origin elsewhere, in a fiscal phenomenon that had been taking place in the United States during the early 1830's. Almost miraculously, it seemed, after the frantic financial conditions produced by the redistribution of federal funds, the national debt was finally reduced to zero in 1835, thanks to the excess of government receipts over expenditures (the former from customs and from sales of public land) during the seven years of Jackson's administration. In theory, the retirement of the public debt was "the result of public thrift, honesty and grit," and the faith of British bankers and investors, shaken in 1833, was renewed, to produce the frenzied speculation that would climax the business cycle. As Hammond comments:

Since the government's income was derived mainly from customs, since the customs were derived from the importation of goods, and since the importations put the economy in debt to Britain, the seeming prosperity of the American government was in fact incidental to prodigal purchases abroad; and liquidation of the federal debt was concomitant with an extravagant expansion of the debt owed to Europe by private business and by individual states . . . The eagerness of the New World to borrow was matched by the eagerness of the Old to lend. There was not only American speculation proper but also speculation in America by Europeans.

Though on a more modest scale, the Canadian economy responded to the same influences. Despite a sharp drop in immigration following the cholera epidemic of the previous year, 1835 witnessed the strengthening of the British investment interest in Canada already noted, pioneer industries made their appearance in many towns of Upper Canada, and the demands for expanded banking capital and facilities, discussed in the previous chapter, were translated into action. Construction was begun on the Champlain and St. Lawrence Railroad; William Weller's Royal Mail Line of four-horse coaches was inaugurated between Toronto and Montreal; the provincial government of Upper Canada increased its debt to embark on an ambitious program of public works, and the Bank of Montreal, now under the presidency of Hon. Peter McGill, for the third consecutive year paid its shareholders two dividends of four per cent and a bonus of six per cent. But on the political front, a year of British obstruction and inertia had heightened political tensions in both provinces, and on the economic front unfavourable portents had appeared. Presaging the adoption of free trade in Britain, ominous rumblings were heard in the British House of Commons against the existing colonial timber preferences and an abundant British harvest drove the price of wheat in Toronto down to thirty-two cents a bushel during the winter of 1834-35. In 1835, also, the costly British defence works at Quebec and Kingston were nearing completion, and in the United States crop failures throughout the Middle West placed a severe strain on a flimsy and disjointed banking system. The system was able to function so long as the flow of British capital and goods continued, but before another year was out these twin founts of North American prosperity suddenly dried up at their source.

3.

In the spring of 1837 Canadian prosperity suddenly collapsed, bringing to an end a period of exceptional economic expansion and precipitating a financial crisis of unprecedented severity. The causes were so remote that only a few Canadians were aware of their existence until commercial stagnation was upon them and armed rebellion threatened. As in 1825, the business cycle had reached its climax and, as in 1825, so in the early autumn of 1836, the first weakness in the airy superstructure of international credit appeared in the failure of a small and relatively obscure Irish provincial bank on the periphery of the English banking system. Other Irish banks, expecting a run on their own gold reserves, appealed to the Bank of England and secured a loan of £2,000,000, but while the Irish situation was relieved, another of more ominous dimensions appeared less than two months later when the Northern and Central Bank of Manchester also found itself in difficulties. An appeal to the Bank of England was at first refused, but the failure of an institution with thirty-nine branches in the industrial districts would have been so disastrous that the bank was forced to make advances, first of £500,000 and finally of £1,370,000.

Storm signals had actually been flying since early in the year. At the beginning of 1836 the gold reserves of the Bank of England were £8,000,000, but in March a decline set in and by the end of November they stood at only £3,600,000. In an attempt to halt the drain, the bank had raised its discount rate, first to $4\frac{1}{2}$ per cent and then to 5 per cent. In the speculative climate then prevailing the gestures had little meaning, and in the middle of August the bank announced that it would no longer rediscount paper that had already been discounted by a joint-stock bank. The effect was to render virtually worthless a vast quantity of American commercial paper and government securities then circulating in Britain, forcing demands for specie payments on the United States which could not be met. There followed the threat of bank failures in Ireland and the Midlands, the two trading areas most heavily involved in American credits. Retrenchment, liquidation, and deflation ensued with attendant bankruptcies, bank failures, commercial stagnation, and unemployment.

Up to this point the crisis of 1837 followed the pattern set in 1825, but complicating the current situation were the capricious fiscal, banking, and monetary policies pursued by the United States: Jackson's attacks on the Second Bank of the United States, his redistribution of Treasury funds among "pet banks," and the astonishing Specie Circular of July 1836, requiring specie payments for the purchase of public lands. Designed to protect the poor individual homesteader, this last measure actually benefited the speculator who had a command of specie, creating unusual and often insupportable strains on the over-extended laissez-faire banking system. Aggravating the complex financial situation was Jackson's decision to distribute the federal surplus, amounting by 1837 to more than $37,000,000, among the several states. To meet the demand for specie, the "pet banks" were forced to call loans made against Treasury deposits, thus adding to the financial chaos caused by the retrenchment begun in Britain.

Most of the above developments have been discussed in an earlier context; here it will suffice to note that their cumulative effect, taken in conjunction with the financial situation in Britain, subjected the apparatus of international payments to insupportable strains. Outraged Canadians, unaware of its source, considered themselves the innocent victims of the ensuing crisis. Much of the anti-American sentiment in the years that followed sprang not from United Empire Loyalists' grievances or War of 1812 memories but from the crippling financial, commercial, and political effects of the collapse of 1837.

Although financial chaos had been heralded by events in England during the previous year, it was not until the suspension of specie payments by New York banks on May 10, 1837, that the Canadian public knew of the disaster that had overtaken them. Even the directors of the Bank of Montreal, more sensitive to the financial climate than any group in the country, do not appear to have become alerted until a month before the crash.

While the dividend rate was dropped to twelve per cent in 1836, the reduction was not made for economic reasons but because of the uneasiness which the Board felt as a result of the difficulty that they were encountering in renewing the charter, which would expire in June 1837. Discounts, however, were maintained at a high level, and the rest fund was increased by thirty-five per cent, thus placing the Bank in an unusually secure position compared with many across the border. Discussions were also under way for a new branch building at Quebec, and in November the stockholders approved a resolution to increase the Bank's capital because the current sum of £250,000 had "been found inadequate to the exigencies of the growing and extensive Trade of the Province."

Curiously enough, the Bank's sound and confident position gives no inkling of the widespread suffering in Lower Canada caused by the poor harvest of the previous autumn. During the winter many areas in the province were dependent for food on government support.

The first mention in the Directors' Minutes of the financial weather outside Canada is contained in a reference on March 21, 1837, to the receipt of a letter from Thomas Wilson & Co. disclosing the state of the London market and offering to raise a loan in London should the Bank find itself in need. The Board declined the offer but directed the President to keep the negotiations open. Reading between the lines, it can be surmised that the trade between Britain and Canada, financed directly by a few strong mercantile houses, had not yet been severely affected by the rapid deterioration of financial and commercial affairs in London and New York. Letters presented to the Board on April 4, however, revealed that markets in both cities "were depressed to a most unprecedented degree," and that doubts had arisen as to the solvency of Thomas Wilson & Co. The President, Hon. Peter McGill, addressing the Board, stated that "however alarming the position in which the Institution was placed in consequence of the difficulties to which its agents were liable, it would be prudent, by pursuing a liberal line of Discount, to ward off any pressure and consequent want of confidence in this city." The Minutes note that the Board then passed most of the discounts offered.

Even at this advanced date, little was known in Canada about the alarming condition of financial affairs elsewhere. Nevertheless, the finance committee, comprising the President, Vice-President Joseph Masson, T. B. Anderson, and John Jamieson, a director since the resignation of Hon. George Moffatt in 1835, was empowered "to adopt such proceedings as upon the instant might in their judgment be required as respects the purchasing and selling of Exchange, importing of Specie, or the making of such other general arrangements or disposition of the funds of the Bank as the urgency of the case might require." A letter was dispatched to Robert Gillespie and Nathaniel Gould giving them power of attorney "to open an account or make such other arrangements in London as might be in their opinion requisite should any disaster have overtaken the present agents of the Bank."

Three days later, on April 7, the finance committee reported the measures taken to bring in £30,000 in specie, the arrival of £12,500 in gold, the purchase of bills of exchange in the amount of £30,172, and the transmission to Gillespie and Gould in London, for collection by Thomas Wilson & Co., of a bill for £10,000 drawn by the Receiver General of Upper Canada. A week later the finance committee submitted a proposal to transmit to Gillespie and

TIMBER—CHIEF COLONIAL EXPORT

In the 1830's the timber trade was of prime importance to the Canadian provinces. At Quebec City, buyers from Britain met the weary raftsmen after their two-month journey from Upper Canada, and when the timber had been inspected by government agents, the product of the previous winter's cutting was finally sold.

The rafts were broken up and the logs left floating in the calm backwaters of coves such as this one near Cape Diamond. When the British agent had filled his contract, a lumber drogher, like those dotting the river here, anchored alongside the boom.

The logs were loaded by "snaffling" them to a chain and then winching them into the hold through ports in the bow, a series of which were used in succession as the ship settled with its load. On their trip over to Canada, these ships filled up with whatever cargo they could get; this often meant immigrants, for whom the trip was far from pleasant.

Gould a guarantee for £60,000 sterling, signed by "the members of the Board and others acquainted with and having confidence in the Institution," to protect bills of the Bank of Montreal in London.

Having strengthened the Bank's defences to the best of their ability, the members of the Board could only sit back to await developments. These took the form of a marked increase in the number of the Bank's notes presented for redemption, mostly by persons who, the Cashier reported, "again and again appeared at the counter." It was evident that speculators were acquiring specie to be exported to the States. Early in May the necessity of importing a further supply of metal became pressing. Samuel Gerrard, the former president, consented to proceed to New York to procure specie to the extent of £16,000 and to obtain information which would enable the Board to decide on the further continuance of the Bank's connection with Thomas Wilson & Co. Gerrard left for New York on May 12 accompanied by a messenger and taking with him exchange drawn on Thomas Wilson & Co., together with bills on the Bank of British North America which were to be negotiated according to circumstances. The train that took Samuel Gerrard to St. Johns brought back to Montreal the news of the suspension of specie payments by the New York banks two days earlier. There followed the most dramatic interval in the early history of Canadian banking.

In response to urgent notices, the directors of the Bank of Montreal assembled on Saturday morning, May 13, in the banking house, with Hon. George Moffatt, John Frothingham, President of the City Bank, William Price of Quebec, and the Bank's solicitor, present by request. The fact that a premium of five per cent was being "freely offered for Canada funds in New York rendered it evident that every bill would be purchased up, and sent for specie, and under the existing suspension of specie payments in New York it was equally evident that no supplies of coin could be obtained." After reviewing the situation, the meeting was adjourned until eight o'clock so that representatives of all the financial institutions of the city could be brought together for consultation. Present at the evening meeting were the officers and directors of the Bank of Montreal, representatives of the Banque du Peuple and the City Bank, Hon. George Moffatt, Allan Good, Manager of the Montreal branch of the Bank of British North America, and Robert Gillespie Jr., a local director of that institution. Mr. Price of Quebec was also in attendance. It was agreed that suspension was necessary if general bankruptcy was to be avoided, and on Monday more concrete resolutions were passed, but immediate action was postponed to arrange a public meeting and to enable Hon. Peter McGill to obtain the opinion of the heads of the departments most directly involved in government payments and collections: the Commissary General, the Receiver General, and the Collector of His Majesty's Customs.

With the support of the Montreal Committee of Trade, the banks presented a series of resolutions in both French and English to a large gathering of "merchants, tradesmen and citizens generally" of the City of Montreal assembled at St. Ann's Market on the evening of May 16, 1837. With Hon. George Moffatt in the chair, the suspension of specie payments was unanimously approved and a copy of the proceedings sent to the Governor at Quebec. Although somewhat jingoistic in expression, the resolutions so clearly convey the feeling of the day as to warrant inclusion in their entirety:

Resolved 1.—That the Commercial community of Montreal and of the Canadas generally, experience at the present moment great alarm at the posture of financial matters in the United States, that the suspension of Specie payments by the Banks of New York is an event threatening the most deplorable consequences to these Provinces unless measures to avert them be promptly adopted.

Resolved 2.—That the circumstances which have led to the suspension of specie payments in the adjoining States are deeply to be regretted, and that although these Provinces are happily free from the apprehension of similar circumstances as arising out of the business of the Country, yet there can be no doubt from our proximity to, and general intimate relation with, the United States that our interests will be injuriously affected and that immediately, unless we resolve to protect ourselves.

Resolved 3.—That certain information has been received that individuals have been employed in New York and elsewhere to proceed to these Provinces for the purpose of withdrawing the Specie from the Vaults of our Banks and that consequently no time should be lost in frustrating their designs thus preserving ourselves from the effect of calamities produced by no fault of our own, and that the only measure which can meet the present emergency and prevent the evil so much dreaded is a suspension of Specie payments by the Banks.

Resolved 4.–That we have the utmost confidence not merely in the solvency and stability of our Banks, but in their management and likewise their ability to meet with coin all their bills in circulation, yet we feel assured that if not protected against foreign abstraction of Specie, they will only be able to sustain themselves, at the expense of the mercantile body, thereby producing results that cannot be contemplated without dismay.

Resolved 5.–Whereas every consideration of prudence and policy and of self defence demands that this calamitous result should be averted, that this meeting recommends to the Banking institutions of the Provinces, but more particularly to those of our own City, that is, the Chartered Banks of this city, and the People's Bank [Banque du Peuple], a suspension of specie payments for the present.

Resolved 6.–That this meeting recommends to the several Banking institutions of the City a mutual forbearance to and confidence in each other and to the Citizens generally that any and every attempt to disturb the public confidence in those institutions be discountenanced.

At the close of the meeting, representatives of the several banks again met in the board room of the Bank of Montreal, this time to agree on immediate action, and at 12.30 a.m. the several cashiers proceeded to draft a public notice. It was decided, however, that each bank would advertise separately in all the newspapers, possibly to avoid criticism of the guiding role taken by the Bank of Montreal. The notice of that institution follows:

In accordance with the expressed opinion of their fellow Citizens, conveyed to them in certain resolutions unanimously adopted at a General Meeting held yesterday by the Inhabitants of this City, for the purpose of taking into consideration the existing difficulties in the Money market, the Directors although confident in the capacity of this Institution, come forward with much reluctance to announce the assent of the Board to accede to the request therein expressed of suspending, for the present, specie payments, and in so doing, they claim from the public that confidence and support which the urgency demands.

The Bills of the People's Bank and of the City Bank will be taken in payment and Deposits as heretofore.

By Order of the Board
(Signed) Benjamin Holmes, Cashier
Montreal, 17th May, 1837

Meanwhile the Quebec Bank and the Bank of Montreal's Office of Discount and Deposit in Quebec had passed similar resolutions at a meeting on May 16.

The public response to the Bank of Montreal's notice was gratifying; the drain on specie reserves ended and business resumed its normal course, though cautiously and at a slackened tempo. As yet, there was little awareness among the commercial community of the true nature of the disaster that had overtaken it. In the isolated position of Montreal this was natural enough. The great pine timber rafts with their cargoes of flour, ashes, oak, and other export staples had yet to come down the Ottawa and the St. Lawrence, and the spring fleet had yet to start coming up the river, bringing with it first-hand intelligence of the state of affairs in Britain. Not until these events occurred could any just estimate be made of the season's prospects. As for the Bank of Montreal, information received from Samuel Gerrard in New York brought assurance that, while the firm of Thomas Wilson & Co. was in precarious straits and would doubtless go under, the Bank's position would be protected. Gerrard also reported that the New York crisis was fundamentally a matter of specie payments rather than a general collapse of the American economy. Concerted efforts to control the unfortunate American banking situation were being made, and Biddle and other eastern bankers were negotiating for a credit with the Bank of England. It was a foregone conclusion that there would be a drastic business contraction and much enforced liquidation but it was believed that conditions would right themselves once the requisite arrangements between New York and London had been completed.

From every point of view the Bank of Montreal's position was unassailably secure. By assuming the initiative in winning public confidence and securing suspension, it had gained virtual control of the financial situation in Lower Canada. With these and other factors in mind, including the prosperous state of the Bank's affairs, the directors on May 19 voted the usual half-yearly dividend of four per cent to be paid on June 1. The notice was duly advertised with a rider postponing the allocation of further undistributed profits until such time as final adjustments with the London agents had been concluded. Having been in almost continuous session for more than a week, the Board then recessed until May 23.

Meanwhile events in Upper Canada followed a strangely divergent course. In Toronto, as in Montreal, the first reaction of the banks on learning of the financial crisis in New York had been to suspend specie payments since they, like those of Montreal, were dependent on the New York money market. In Upper Canada, however, a provision in the banking statutes called for the loss of the charter if redemption in specie was interrupted for more than sixty days without the express approval of the government. This the two larger banks, the Bank of Upper Canada and the Commercial Bank of the Midland District at Kingston, tried immediately to obtain, only to encounter a firm refusal from Sir Francis Bond Head, Knight Commander of the Royal Hano-verian Guelphic Order, Knight of the Prussian Military Order of Merit, and Lieutenant-Governor of Upper Canada. Waving imminent financial disaster aside as an unworthy consideration in the face of national honour and moral commitment, the quixotic knight took the stand that the banks having prom-ised to redeem their notes in specie, redeem in specie they must so long as a single coin remained in their vaults. No bank chartered by His Britannic Majesty, and particularly the Bank of Upper Canada, of which the Sovereign was the largest shareholder through his provincial government, could do otherwise. The immediate effects were runs on the banks, both chartered and private; the calling in of loans, and cessation of all commercial accommoda-tion. In the course of a few days, business ground to a standstill, real estate tumbled in value, and belts were tightened with a vengeance as the banks, no longer able to sustain speculation, reduced their discounts to the vanishing-point.

The first intimation of these dire developments was brought to the atten-tion of the Bank of Montreal on May 23 when Thomas Ridout, the Cashier of the Bank of Upper Canada, appeared before the Board to apply for a loan of £20,000 in specie to enable his institution to survive the viceroy's pronun-ciamento. Although relations between the banks were cordial at the time, the application was refused. Having suspended specie payments with a view to preventing the exportation of coin from Lower Canada, the directors refused to entertain any proposal "having for its object abstraction of specie from the vaults of the Bank." Thomas Ridout then continued his journey to Quebec with a view to enlisting the help of the Commissary General. Four days later, however, there arrived another emissary of the Bank of Upper Canada in the person of Samuel Jarvis, this time to request an advance of £40,000 in Bank of Montreal notes against sixty-day interest-bearing bills of the Bank of Upper Canada payable in Montreal. This, the Toronto bank believed, was the only means by which it would be able to afford even a modicum of accommodation to its customers.

The proposal was taken into consideration over the week-end and, when Thomas Ridout returned from Quebec on Tuesday to report the failure of his mission, the Board agreed to advance its distressed confrère not £40,000 in notes as originally requested, but £50,000, on condition that Bank of Montreal notes be received in payment by the Bank of Upper Canada and all its agencies for all debts due, including bills sent up for collection. On the last day of the month, an advance of £20,000 in the inconvertible notes of the Montreal bank was also made to the Commercial Bank on the same conditions. Since £70,000 was equivalent to about fourteen per cent of the total bank-note circulation in Upper Canada at the time, these transactions relieved some of the financial pressure produced by Head's romantic policy and, temporarily at least, ameliorated the more disastrous effects of enforced liquidation due to the sudden contraction of commercial credit.

Concurrently with these negotiations with the Upper Canada banks were others conducted by Alexander Simpson, the Cashier of the Office of Discount and Deposit at Quebec, with the Receiver General, regarding a moratorium on specie payments for debts due to the government. This the executive would grant only to September 20 and then only by payment being tendered in bank drafts against which the issuing bank would hold in its vaults, until called for, a like amount of specie. Normally, the specie moved into the economic stream via military payrolls, whence it reached the public through the market place and, unless hoarded, finally found its way back into the coffers of the banks. There it remained until the circular movement was resumed through its purchase by the Commissary General in exchange for Treasury bills or by merchants having debts to the government to meet, or having balances to settle in Britain or the United States.

At the time of suspension the Bank of Montreal held a supply of specie amounting to around £80,000, most of which had been imported originally by the Bank on government account to finance the military establishment. On the other hand, the total customs duties collected by the Province of

Lower Canada in 1835 (its last year of reporting) exceeded £170,000, most of which would have been assessed during the summer months of open navigation. If the Bank had agreed to the government's plan, it can be easily seen that, with the circular flow of specie frozen by suspension, the Bank's coffers would have been drained on September 20 when it had to redeem its drafts in specie.

In consequence, the Bank of Montreal rejected the government's offer, on the grounds that "however much it was the desire of the Board to facilitate any measure connected with the trade of the country or the public service, it was, under the peculiar circumstances, . . . impossible for the Board of Directors to undertake what it might not be in their power to perform, and consequently they could not assent to a measure which must necessarily entail no inconsiderable direct loss to the Bank if carried into effect, and the practicability of which must at present be doubtful." While the action compelled importers to obtain specie for customs duties by paying the market premium, which rose to 16 per cent in June and to $22\frac{1}{2}$ per cent in July and August, it also insured the flexibility of the Bank's position by securing for it the control of its own specie. Although the position adopted by the Bank was to prove beneficial to the economy of Lower Canada, it represented a defiance of constituted authority at a time when the future legal status of the Bank had become precarious.

FOURTEEN

THROUGH
DEPRESSION
AND REBELLION

THROUGH DEPRESSION
AND REBELLION

I.

Addressing the twentieth annual general meeting of the Bank of Montreal shareholders on June 1, 1837, the Honourable Peter McGill reported on "the prosperous condition of the business, congratulated the stockholders on their continued participation, and justified the suspension of specie payments to the satisfaction of all concerned." The officers and staff were tendered the traditional vote of thanks for their zeal and diligence, the President was voted the customary honorarium of £500, and thirteen members of the out-going Board of Directors were reinstated for another term. As in 1826, when the Bank stood on another threshold of depression, the tone of the meeting was buoyant and assured. In the five years 1833-1837, dividends totalling 77 per cent had been paid; the rest fund had been increased to almost £50,000, and the growth of the business had warranted a capital expansion from £250,000 to £500,000. Even more significant for the future was the unchallenged financial leadership so ably acquired during the recent specie crisis. Notwithstanding manifold reasons for confidence and mutual congratulations, the officers of the Bank of Montreal must have entertained some misgivings about the future of the institution on June 1, 1837.

It may be recalled that no banking legislation was passed in Lower Canada after the parliamentary session of 1835-36. At the time all three banks petitioned for extensions of their charters but were blocked in the Assembly, largely through the impassioned opposition of Louis-Joseph Papineau. Repeating the arguments he had used in 1830, the popular leader denounced the entire banking system and promised to introduce a bill at the next session which would embody fundamental changes. What those changes would have been remains a matter for conjecture since the 1836 session marked the virtual demise of parliamentary government in Lower Canada. However, as a result of Papineau's opposition the only banking legislation was an act extending the charter of the Quebec Bank to June 1, 1837, in conformity with those of the Bank of Montreal and City Bank.

There the matter had rested until the annual general meeting of the Bank of Montreal in June 1836, when a resolution to petition the legislature was again adopted with the proviso that failing a favourable outcome a general meeting of the shareholders would be held to determine "the most eligible and safe mode of continuing the business." The petition was duly prepared and approved by the Board on September 20. Its principal interest lies not in its contents, which were repetitive, but in the fact that Louis-Hippolyte Lafontaine, later to become a joint premier of United Canada, but then the member for Terrebonne and a Papineau supporter, agreed to translate the document and present it in French when the legislature reassembled. The belated public-relations gesture never materialized, the Governor General, Lord Gosford, failing to call the expected session, and on November 21, 1836, a general shareholders' meeting was held "to take into consideration the best means of continuing the business . . . in case the Charter shall expire before the Provincial Parliament is again called together for the dispatch of business, or in the event of any unexpected contingency preventing its renewal before the first of June next."

Three decisions were unanimously approved; one, to continue the business after June 1, 1837, under articles of association and deed of settlement; two, to increase the capital, and three, to open subscription books of a successor institution on April 1, 1837, should no charter have been received before that date. Further to protect the stockholders' interests, the members of the Board, on February 14, 1837, addressed petitions to the Lieutenant-Governor, the

Legislative Council and Legislative Assembly of Upper Canada praying for the enactment of a law which would empower the Bank to collect its debts in the upper province after the expiration of its charter. Reference was made to the large sums the Bank had advanced to merchants and others in Upper Canada on promissory notes, bills and other securities, and to the liability of loss if legal means were lacking for their collection.

Considerable mystery attaches to the next act of the drama which concerns the granting of a royal charter. Having lost hope of legislative action early in 1837, the Bank of Montreal, in association with the Quebec Bank and the City Bank, appealed directly to the Sovereign. No reference to any such petition is contained in the Bank of Montreal Minutes at the time, but other sources show that all three petitions set forth the intolerable situation under which the banks of Lower Canada laboured, the injury to themselves and Canadian commercial interests should they be forced out of business, and the need for royal charters to enable them to ride out this difficult period. The Bank of Montreal petition also prayed for authorization to increase its capital to £500,000, which was £250,000 less than the amount proposed in November of the previous year.

Little hope apparently was held for the success of the appeal as, on March 14, 1837, the Bank's directors resolved to advertise in the Montreal and Quebec newspapers that books would be opened in both cities to receive subscriptions for shares in a new company to take over the assets of the Bank of Montreal and carry on the banking business. These books were to remain open until April 10; the next day a second set would be opened to receive subscriptions for £250,000 new stock divided into 5,000 shares of £50 each. Subscriptions were limited to 50 shares for any single firm or individual, with a down payment of £5 with each subscription and a further payment of fifteen per cent, or £7. 5s., by May 15. The advertisement also made reference to the undistributed profits of the expiring establishment as "safely estimated to be 20 per cent or one-fifth of the capital stock." Such was the public confidence in the Bank that the new stock was oversubscribed, and the records show that by June 1, over thirty-five per cent had been paid up.

Meanwhile the petition for a royal charter reached London where, with limiting modifications, it finally received royal assent. Instead of the £500,000 asked for, the capital was limited to £250,000 and the life of the charter to twelve months from the conclusion of the next session of the provincial legislature. The charter was signed at Westminster on May 31, 1837, but by

the time it reached Canada the Bank of Montreal had become a private banking company with a capital of £500,000. Since the royal charter limited the
capital to £250,000, compliance with its terms would have required the dissolution of the newly formed company and the return of the payments made
on the increased capital. Furthermore, the added limitation as to duration
made the charter no more than a temporary stop-gap. Under such circumstances it can be seen that the officers would prefer to abide by the new arrangements, discreetly ignoring London's dispensation which, incidentally,
cost £564. 18s. 8d. including stamp duties of £110; in consequence no reference to the receipt of a royal charter is included in the Minutes.

Under the articles of association the Bank of Montreal became a private
banking company similar to the English banks established under the Joint-
Stock Bank Act of 1826 and the Act of 1833. Nevertheless, it was operating
without any specific legal sanction, a situation which exposed it to the
attacks of unfriendly newspapers in Montreal and Quebec on both political
and financial grounds. Its position was made secure, however, by the unchallenged presence of the Banque du Peuple, operating *en commandite*, and by
the nature of the functions it was ordinarily able to perform through the
strength of its American connections. There was in fact no other machinery
by which the government could satisfy its needs for specie unless, of course,
it chose to accept the costs and hazards of importing coin from London or
establishing its own agency in New York as Nicholas Biddle had once
suggested.

Why, then, should the officers and others connected with the institution
have had any misgivings about the future? Because there was, firstly, uncertainty as to the Executive's possible reaction to the banks' independent
suspension of specie payments without prior referral to the government;
secondly, the possibility of some reprisal for the Bank's summary rejection of
the proffered four months' moratorium, and thirdly, the possibility that the
damaging banking legislation threatened by Papineau might be enacted at
the forthcoming session of the legislature, scheduled for August 1837. There
were other anxieties of a broader nature: the alarming condition of affairs in
Upper Canada; the worsening political climate in both provinces, and the
collapse of the British market for all Canadian products save timber. The men
who guided the destinies of the Bank of Montreal greatly underestimated the
strength of their position.

2.

Historians are generally agreed that the depression of 1837-39 bore more heavily on Upper Canada than on any other part of North America: in contrast, the records of the Bank of Montreal suggest that Lower Canada may have suffered least. During the first year of the depression, for example, the Bank's returns contain little evidence that a financial crisis had occurred: discounts show only minor fluctuations from preceding years and the carefully nurtured rest fund was augmented by £22,207 to bring the total up to £49,457, an increase of nearly fifty per cent from the year before. Concurrently, the business of the Quebec branch, still known as the Office of Discount and Deposit, was in such a flourishing condition in the spring of 1837 that the local board of directors was increased from nine to thirteen members, the capital from £95,000 to £125,000, and in the fall a site was purchased in the Lower Town at Quebec at a cost of £2,000 for a new banking house to replace the rented quarters occupied since 1818. The price hardly reflects a falling-off of land values in Quebec.

Further confirmation of business activity is provided by the Board Minutes of the Bank of Montreal for June 2, 1837, the day after the reconstituted company began operation, when salary increases were granted to four members of the staff and three new employees were added. It should be noted on the other hand that one of the semi-annual dividend payments was reduced from four to three per cent in 1837, but since this payment was made on a paid-up capital of £388,251, as against £250,000, the actual amount paid out was greater. The Board was also able to make a sixteen-per-cent distribution from the surplus funds of the antecedent institution. Significantly, there were no further calls on the shareholders from June 15 to December 1839, when a balance of only £47,500 was outstanding, most subscribers having paid up in full before that date.

Compromising this clear-cut picture of continued stability is a letter from President McGill to W. H. Merritt, now in the Public Archives at Ottawa and written in the late summer of 1837 in response to Merritt's urgent request for a loan to keep the work going on the Welland Canal. McGill replied in part, "We all here feel the importance of affording facilities to the purchase of wheat in Up: Can: but the Banks of L: Can: cannot give them, and but few Individual Houses will be able to supply their Correspondents with the needful from hence, because their Capital is already in Up: Canada Credits, and nothing coming down. In my day such times have never been experienced."

Other sources support the gloomy outlook. One Montreal journalist reported that "An excessive languor pervades nearly every branch of commerce and our streets have, so far as relates to business, the appearance they are wont to exhibit on a close holiday or a Sunday."

How can the discrepancies between banking facts and the consensus of recorded observation be reconciled? One procedure is to examine the anatomy of the depression in Upper and Lower Canada separately rather than to treat them as a single economic unit; in this way the factors that made it possible for the Bank of Montreal to maintain a satisfactory profit ratio during a period of commercial stagnation and political upheaval become apparent.

That the people of Upper Canada should have been hit so severely by the financial crisis is readily understandable: belonging geographically to the Great Lakes region, they were denied their logical economic associations by the political barrier that divided them from the United States; belonging politically to the British Empire, they were denied whatever benefits the mercantile-colonial system could bestow on them by the physical barrier of the St. Lawrence rapids and the high transportation costs involved. To these fundamental handicaps were added others: Pitt's legacies of the Clergy Reserves and inequitably allotted customs revenues; Simcoe's semi-feudalistic invention of the Family Compact, and the crowning misfortune of Sir Francis Bond Head. Despite such formidable obstacles to nineteenth-century progress, Upper Canada during the 1830's became one of the fastest-growing areas on the continent. Immigration from the States and overseas nearly doubled the population; ambitious public works were undertaken, and the people, seized by the promise of the future, quite humanly proceeded to borrow to the limit of their abilities. The banks lent money on almost any security, new banks were formed, and speculation became as fevered as across the southern border: for a time, in fact, Upper Canada exhibited more the spirit and behaviour of an American state than of a Canadian province, and republicanism became a force in political discussion.

The financial crisis of May 1837 struck without prior warning, producing devastating effects on the banks, the business community and the public at large, and finally the government. Thanks to the Lieutenant-Governor's insistence on note redemption, the circulation of the chartered banks fell by 23 per cent and the specie reserves by 22 per cent between May 15 and June 15. So crippling were the effects of contraction and liquidation that an extraordinary session of the legislature was called on June 19 to consider the financial and commercial difficulties that beset the province, but the Golden Knight remained unshakable. Not only was British honour at stake, the Lieutenant-Governor proclaimed, but also the confidence of British investors in Upper Canada.

The Assembly then passed a bill providing for suspension without loss of charter, but this was promptly amended by the Council on the advice, no doubt, of the Bank of Upper Canada. In consequence a compromise was effected whereby a bank would be allowed to suspend without prejudice to its charter on appeal to the Governor in Council when its specie reserve neared exhaustion. Under the influence of the Bank of Upper Canada, in effect the provincial treasury, no further appeal was made until the Commercial Bank had to suspend on September 29. The Agricultural Bank went bankrupt in November. One of the partners was arrested in Buffalo; Truscott, the founder, decamped for Europe leaving unsatisfied claims of £30,000 behind him. The Farmers' Bank suspended for two weeks in December, but the Bank of the People, under the management of Francis Hincks, continued to redeem its notes throughout the depression.

The Bank of Upper Canada did not suspend until March 1838. Meanwhile, commercial paralysis had become endemic; goods, chattels, lands and houses would not bring half their value at forced sale; thousands of settlers had cashed in on their possessions to trek on to Michigan and farther west; the provincial government had become bankrupt, and the public works were halted. Thomas Wilson & Co., who were responsible for paying the interest and cashing drafts on half the provincial debentures issued in 1835, closed their doors on June 2, but while Glyn, Hallifax, Mills & Co. came nobly to the rescue on June 12 by voluntarily assuming the burden of the Canadian debt, £83,000 of provincial funds were trapped in the collapse. The sum was afterwards recovered with interest but the scare thrown into Upper Canada's creditors, already made jittery by the rebellions, caused the credit standing of the province on the London market to be compromised for several years.

The economic debacle that prostrated the interior province at this period failed to materialize in Lower Canada for many reasons; with an outlet to the sea the province suffered none of the geographic disadvantages of the neighbour colony and as entrepôt and forwarder continued to levy tribute on its far-flung hinterland. The great timber rafts, contracted for at the height of the preceding boom, continued to come down the Ottawa and the St. Lawrence, and up the river from Quebec came the luxurious steamers of the

GOVERNMENT BANKER
WORKS WITH THE
BRITISH ARMY

From the earliest days, the Bank of Montreal was intimately associated with the military life which was so important to the colonies.

In its first year of operation, the Bank was "given the right of supplying the Government in this country with such moneys as may be wanted by the different departments in Upper and Lower Canada."

In line with this understanding, the Bank later opened an agency at Ile-aux-Noix, site of the great Fort Lennox on the Richelieu River. The island, a dozen miles down the river from Lake Champlain, had been the site of fortifications for many years under the French regime. Fort Ile-aux-Noix was, indeed, one of the last strongholds of that regime.

The strategic value of the site was recognized by the British when they occupied the island in 1760, but it was not until 1782 that the Imperial Government decided to undertake a reconstruction of the fortifications.

During the War of 1812, it was found that the fortress was still insufficient for defence purposes, and further work was carried out. On completion, the fort was called Lennox, presumably from the family name of the Duke of Richmond, Governor-in-Chief of Canada in 1818-19.

British troops were regularly stationed at Fort Lennox until 1870. This painting depicts a regular pay-parade some thirty years earlier, when the 70th Foot Regiment was on duty at the fort. The funds being paid the troops have just been handed over to the paymaster by the Bank's agent at Ile-aux-Noix, George Gunn, who is seen here standing with the officer commanding the regiment.

Painting by Huntley Brown

Molson-Torrance Line towing behind them the same immigrant-packed vessels as in former years. Most of the newcomers passed on up the river to swell the ranks of the unemployed in Upper Canada but, in passing, left behind an appreciable quantity of shillings and pence, and even a few sovereigns. A measure of the value of the combined traffic outward and inward can be seen in the prosperous condition of business at the Quebec office of the Bank of Montreal.

Other factors helped to moderate the full impact of the commercial crisis that prostrated the sister province. The speculative fever had never attained the heights in Lower Canada that it reached in other parts of the continent and in consequence the process of deflation was less convulsive. Also into consideration must be taken the prompt and independent action of the Bank of Montreal in suspending specie payments: had the banks done otherwise, or had they met the obstacles encountered in Upper Canada, there is little doubt that commercial activity would have been similarly affected. Ironically enough, it was Papineau and his more belligerent followers who rendered an unwitting service to the Lower Canadian economy by engaging in open rebellion, resulting in the reinforcement of the British garrison in Montreal and Quebec and the calling into service of volunteer militia units which had remained inactive since 1815.

In Upper Canada the romantic monetary convictions of the viceroy, combined with the short-sighted profit-making policies of the government bank which drastically curtailed discounts and kept as large a spread as possible between its buying and selling price of specie, produced economic chaos: in Lower Canada the contrasting quiescence of the Executive, combined with the sense of public responsibility shown by the officers and directors of the Bank of Montreal and the three other banks, kept the economy on a fairly even keel. The story could have been different. The profit-making opportunities of the Bank of Montreal were actually much greater than those of its Toronto confrère, had it chosen to pursue the same policies; instead, the immediate gain of the shareholders was made subservient to the long-term public interest. A conservative policy was instituted, following suspension, but discounts for the remainder of the year fell only $9\frac{1}{2}$ per cent below those for the same period of 1836, which had witnessed the height of the boom. The result was that failures were much less common than in Upper Canada or in the United States, and the accumulation of bad debts was negligible. Between 1837 and 1839, for example, there was only one bankruptcy of sufficient magnitude to engage more than the passing attention of the Board. The firm involved was a large trader in grain and other staples, and in the process of liquidation it hypothecated to the Bank some real-estate holdings in Upper and Lower Canada and also in New York and the American middle west. These became the property of the Bank and a management problem for many years. To their acquisition and that of other American properties at a later date can be traced the Bank's decision in the 1860's to establish its own Chicago branch.

There is of course another side to the picture. While the Bank of Montreal managed its own affairs with prudent perspicacity, it could hardly have remained immune to a depression that affected the economic climate of Europe and North America alike. As the summer of 1837 wore on, fewer staples came down from the upper country, while sterling exchange in July and August rose to a high point of 22½ per cent premium, imposing a further burden on merchants who required exchange to pay for goods ordered in the buoyant mood of the preceding autumn, or to pay customs duties.

Directly connected also with the suspension of specie payments were two other interesting phenomena: one, the famine in fractional metallic currency that rapidly developed as silver coin commanded a premium; and two, the appearance in Montreal and the surrounding area of a number of bogus banks designed to cash in on the good repute of Lower Canadian bank-note currency by circulating simulated paper currency in the American middle west. Involved were half a dozen or more spurious institutions bearing such plausible names as the Merchants' Bank of Montreal, the Mechanics' Bank of St. Johns, L.C., and the Canadian Bank of St. Hyacinthe, which circulated excellently engraved and printed notes in Buffalo and other border cities for several months after suspension. The success of the operation was based on the initial redemption of a small amount of notes by an agent in Montreal, after which the notes were counted on to remain in circulation, a circumstance which the heterogeneous bank-note currency of the period strongly favoured. While the pretended banks caused few losses in Lower Canada, their circulation reached considerable proportions across the border.

The rapid disappearance from circulation of small coins under the value of one dollar had wider and more serious repercussions. The phenomenon was due in part to a law which prohibited the banks from issuing notes under the denomination of a dollar. Some light is thrown on the state of the currency even in normal times by a diary kept by Thomas Molson on a journey to England in 1836. This shows that on leaving Montreal for New York he carried with him £177. 2s. 10d. made up as follows: 67 U.S. dollars, 521 half dollars, 1,200 quarter dollars, and the rest in Spanish dollars, English gold and silver, and notes of the Bank of Montreal. In the summer of 1837 he would have experienced much difficulty in putting together the same collection of coin. In consequence of the shortage, firms having day-by-day business in the market place and general merchants in both provinces revived the old system of issuing I O U's or *bons* to take the place of the vanished silver, and some firms, including Thomas and William Molson, issued their own notes in denominations of one, two and five dollars after the manner introduced by the Banque du Peuple. The first issue of Molson notes took place in August, 1837, but the Bank of Montreal refused to accept them even though John Molson had replaced his deceased father as one of its directors in 1836.

The merchants' *bons* were redeemable by the issuing firm or individual in even amounts of one dollar, and from a practical standpoint were as satisfactory for restricted local circulation as were the inconvertible notes of the chartered banks for provincial circulation. However, the system was exposed to fraudulent or insolvent issues and steps were taken to control it; finally an ordinance was passed by the Special Council which prohibited the issue of notes, bills, or any other undertaking to pay money intended for circulation under £5 currency except by licence as a private banker. No notes were to be issued under five shillings and no licences were to extend beyond one year. This was the first general law passed in Lower Canada, except those dealing with currency valuation, which was designed to exert some direct control over banking. Meanwhile the Bank of Montreal, separately and in association with the other chartered banks, brought in copper to the extent of almost £5,000 which was coined into "bank tokens" in an effort to relieve the situation. However, this, too, quickly vanished from circulation with the result that in many parts of the country, particularly in the rural districts of Upper Canada, business intercourse could only be conducted by the primitive method of barter.

Added to the financial, commercial, and monetary crises that occurred in Canada after May 17, 1837, was another that is generally regarded as having greater historical importance: the political crisis that developed during the summer and autumn to reach its climax in the rebellious outbreaks of November and December. To what extent the economic crisis influenced the political situation or vice versa is a moot question. The tight money situation in Lower Canada was probably somewhat relieved by the military expenditures required to put down the rebellion: on the other hand the abortive uprising so influenced public opinion outside Canada as to retard economic recovery for two or three years. Apart from these general observations, the rebellion and the political clashes that led up to it seem to have remained curiously detached from the concurrent economic disruption.

The actual point of political crisis was reached in Lower Canada on August 26, 1837, when Lord Gosford again prorogued the Parliament of Lower Canada after a two-day session during which the Assembly once more refused to vote supplies, and during which still another Bank of Montreal petition came to nothing. Political tensions steadily mounted during September, and on October 23 the first great rally of Patriotes was held at the village of St. Charles. while a similar gathering of loyalists took place in Place d'Armes with Peter McGill in the chair. The porter or night watchman of the Bank was found in such a state of nervous excitement when the Cashier arrived to open the bank the next morning that his proffered resignation was accepted. However, there seems to have been no violence at either gathering, and the first open clash between the opposing Patriotes and loyalists did not occur until November 6. During this riot in Montreal between the Fils de la Liberté and the loyalist Doric Club, the Patriotes were routed, and on November 16 warrants were issued for the arrest of Papineau and the other French leaders. Meanwhile, the Commissary General had called on the Bank of Montreal to furnish him with $50,000 in United States' coin, and as a precaution the Bank shipped £21,699. 9s. 10d. in specie by steamboat to Quebec to be stored in the Citadel for safe keeping.

Begun with an ambush of troops on the Richelieu River plain on November 16, the pitiful uprising was completely crushed on December 14 at the battle of St. Eustache, where one hundred and fifty Patriotes were incinerated in the parish church by a force of two thousand regulars and a horde of volunteers from across the Upper Canada border. Meanwhile, martial law had been declared on December 5, and most of the rebel leaders had sought refuge in Vermont. The revolutionary fever having gradually subsided, February 26, 1838 was declared a day of public thanksgiving in Lower Canada. By this time Lord Gosford had returned to England and the House of Commons in London had passed an act to establish a provisional government for Lower Canada. The act was proclaimed in Canada by Gosford's successor, the interim administrator, Sir John Colborne, who then proceeded to name twenty-two persons to a Special Council. Three of these, Peter McGill, Samuel Gerrard, and John Molson, were closely connected with the Bank of Montreal. The first session of the Special Council lasted from April 18 to May 5, 1838, and at its last sitting the provisional government finally caught up with the times by passing an ordinance legalizing the suspension of specie payments which had taken place almost a year before, and continuing it until June 1, 1839.

The Council also passed an act incorporating the President, Directors and Company of the Bank of Montreal with a capital of £500,000.

The preamble to the latter stated that four-fifths of the subscribed stock had already been paid in, but it contained no mention of the royal charter granted on May 31, 1837, to extend for "one year from the end of the next session of the provincial legislature." Since that session had ended in August 1837, the royal charter had only three months to run. Discussing this event, Shortt regarded the omission of any mention of the royal charter as remarkable; however, the explanation has already been given. To have accepted the royal charter, on its belated arrival in Montreal, would have required the dissolution of the private company and the cancellation of the increased capitalization. The 1838 act of incorporation extended to November 1, 1842, and was identical in all essential respects to the original charter and preceding articles of association, even to the inclusion of the death penalty for embezzlement and forgery. Since an act in favour of the Bank of British North America passed at the same session of the Special Council was disallowed in London because of this penal clause, it may be assumed that the Bank of Montreal ordinance was examined rather casually by the Lords of the Treasury.

When Thomas Wilson & Co. were finally "obliged to yield to the pressures of the times" in June 1837, the Bank of Montreal agency in London was taken over by Smith, Payne & Smiths, a long-established private banking firm which also had overseas interests in Australia, New Zealand, and the East Indies. Although this connection was destined to last for several years, the Bank also procured a second English agency in February, 1838, by a reciprocal agreement with the Bank of Liverpool, an institution founded in 1831 to service the trade of the Midlands. Under the agreement the Liverpool bank extended to the Bank of Montreal an uncovered credit of £25,000 to be drawn against at five per cent, in support of which remittances were to be made at three-month intervals and balances to be struck once a year. The connection proved both profitable and convenient and has continued to this day, the Bank of

Montreal being one of the oldest correspondents of the Bank of Liverpool, or Martin's Bank as it is now called.

Although Canada remained in the economic doldrums for another year, the financial skies showed signs of brightening elsewhere. In Britain the trough of the commercial cycle had been passed by 1838; in the United States, gold imports from England had alleviated the money stringency that had seized the country in 1837. Reacting to these influences the rate of sterling exchange in Canada gradually receded from the high point reached in August; at the turn of the year it was as low as 12½ per cent and by May, 1838, it had dipped to 7 per cent. By this time conditions were so much improved that New York banks resumed specie payments on May 10, and as a result the Special Council invoked a clause in the suspension ordinance which gave it the power to demand redemption by the banks on two months' notice. The Bank of Montreal, after carefully considering its own situation and that in New York, decided not to wait for the July 17 deadline but voluntarily to resume paying specie on May 23, 1838. The other Montreal banks concurred and those in Quebec followed suit, the only exception being the Bank of British North America which had never reached the point of issuing notes in Upper or Lower Canada before suspension came into effect and still had none outstanding in either place.

Despite the improved economic climate across the border, that of Canada became worse as the year advanced. Directly responsible were the effects of the rebellion on public opinon outside the country, where the political disturbances of 1837 were regarded as a part of the revolutionary struggle for democratic institutions then sweeping over Europe, Great Britain, and even the United States. Thousands of emigrants who might have come to Canada remained at home or were deflected elsewhere, reducing Canadian immigration for 1838 to a mere 4,500 persons. As in 1837, the timber trade and continued military expenditures remained the mainstays of the economy, but these were insufficient to revive commercial activity. As always in world crises, the fringe economy of Canada forced its people to sweat it out alone.

Business during the summer months was generally uneventful but did produce one item of human interest. At the twenty-first annual general meeting, the shareholders approved the gift of two shares of Bank stock, valued at one hundred pounds, to the daughter of the Bank's first porter, Alexander McNiven, who had died the previous December. The gift had been made "in consideration of the faithful discharge of his station by the late Alexander

McNiven, for his length of service together with the destitute situation in which he left his orphan daughter." The practice of remunerating dependants of deserving employees has remained a policy of the Bank throughout its history.

By early autumn, 1838, it became known that the rebels were reorganizing in Vermont where so-called Hunters' Lodges had been established as bases for the invasion of Canada along the line of the Richelieu. The Governors of both Vermont and New York declared their states' neutrality and President Van Buren warned the public against interference, but preparations proceeded notwithstanding. The first skirmishes between the rebels and regular troops occurred early in November, and so-called battles were fought at Odelltown on November 9 and later at Beauharnois and Prescott, after which the rebellion rapidly subsided. Part of the rebel strategy featured a run on the banks which commenced on October 30. Because of the armed uprisings along the border, the Bank of Montreal was forced to cancel a specie shipment of $100,000 from New York, and when the Special Council was convened in extraordinary session on November 5 at the Château de Ramezay, the Bank immediately applied for relief.

A petition to the Governor and Council was hastily drafted, setting forth the hazards of bringing specie across the border and praying for authority to suspend specie payments. The Board's Minutes show that on November 6 the Deputy Commissary applied for a "considerable" advance against Treasury Bills on London; but this had to be refused while the matter of suspension was still in abeyance. However, suspension was authorized later that same day and on the seventh the Bank of Montreal placed its entire specie reserves of £120,000 at the disposal of the government. The second ordinance, like its predecessor, authorized suspension until June 1, 1839, and contained the same provisions.

3.

Rebellion had also broken out in Upper Canada, but on a lesser scale and with a smaller cost in human lives. After a single armed skirmish between Tories and Reformers near Toronto and a series of incidents on the Niagara frontier in December, 1837, the uprising had been easily suppressed. At the height of the trouble, however, anxiety for the security of the banks had caused the Commissary General to withdraw his accounts from even the Bank of Upper Canada, but the institution was still left with a monopoly of the provincial government's business. By January 1838, the bank reported £80,000 notes in circulation and £140,000 specie in its vaults. At this juncture, the Commissary General turned to the bank for funds to meet the unusual military expenditures, obtaining from it £50,000 in dollars and an offer to furnish notes to meet the department's outlays in the province. The offer was accepted and as a result the bank soon found itself in an extremely precarious position, with redeemable notes outstanding increased to £154,000 and its specie reserve decreased to £60,000.

In exchange for its advances the Bank of Upper Canada had received sterling bills on London which several months earlier had commanded premiums of up to eighteen and twenty per cent. By February, however, so marked had been the improvement in the balance-of-payments situation between London and New York, that sterling exchange had gone from a premium to a small discount in New York. In such circumstances the bank could not dispose of its London exchange, estimated at around £200,000, at the high premiums anticipated. Discovering that it had become more profitable to engage in domestic than in foreign operations, the bank now reversed the policy of 1837 and petitioned the Governor in Council for authority to suspend under the act passed the previous July. The petition was presented on March 6, 1838 – a time, it may be recalled, when many American banks and the banks of Lower Canada were looking forward to resuming specie payments.

Responsible for the curious timing of the about-face was the bank's desire to re-engage in commercial discounting by the issue of irredeemable notes. To justify the brash manoeuvre it was claimed that the disturbed condition of the frontier made it unsafe to bring specie from New York, a condition which actually existed only for a brief period in December. Notwithstanding the disingenuous character of the undertaking, the Executive promptly granted the petition, giving the provincial bank authority to suspend. Under the act passed the previous July, however, the note issue of a suspended bank could not exceed the amount of its paid-up capital; in the case of the Bank of Upper Canada, £200,000. The proscription proved only a minor hazard. On the last day of the legislative session a bill empowering a suspended bank to issue notes to twice the amount of its paid-up capital was rushed through the Assembly and Legislative Council. The act was to remain in force until the close of the next session of the legislature and promptly received assent although Sir Francis was already on recall.

News of these extraordinary proceedings was received with amazement by the financial advisers of the Colonial Office in London, but no rebuke was offered, possibly because of the somewhat strained relations provoked by earlier efforts to mould the course of banking in Upper Canada. However, when Head's successor, Sir George Arthur, arrived in Canada, he brought with him instructions to correct the situation. The banks of Lower Canada having resumed specie payments in May, Arthur addressed a circular on July 7 to the chartered banks of Upper Canada urging them to do likewise as soon as possible since there were no longer any valid reasons for suspension. The Commercial Bank was willing to resume if the Bank of Upper Canada would lead the way, but this the senior institution refused to do. With London credits amounting to £200,000 and £60,000 in specie, it could readily have acceded to the Lieutenant-Governor's wishes; instead the bank staunchly maintained that were it to resume specie payments the consequences would be too dire for contemplation. All loans would have to be called and dis- counting terminated, which would bring ruin to the country. The bank also claimed that the resumption of specie payments could only result in persons who were selling their possessions and moving to the States draining the province of its specie.

The arguments were entirely specious, but so great was the bank's political influence that it was able to have passed at the next session of the legislature an act authorizing the suspension of specie payments for another year and, quite as remarkable, to quash a recommendation of the Special Committee on Banking that chartered banks of the province be required to make a regular exchange of their notes, after the Suffolk clearing system in New England, and that balances be paid by sterling exchange on London. This recommenda- tion had been introduced at the behest of the Commercial and Gore banks which found themselves at the mercy of their powerful rival. Through poli- tical patronage, the senior bank had secured a virtual monopoly on sterling exchange, which it refused to sell to other banks or individuals except at an unreasonably high premium. Evidence presented to a special committee on banking at a later date reveals that following suspension on March 6, 1838, the Bank of Upper Canada had curtailed its discounts and used its note issue to purchase government exchange, while the Commercial and Gore banks had employed their capital almost entirely in promoting the trade of the province by making discounts to the public.

Shortt made this interesting observation: "There being much the same amount of the notes of each bank in circulation more Upper Canada notes

ARCH-RIVAL OF THE BANK OF MONTREAL

Founded in 1822, the Bank of Upper Canada soon came into conflict with its senior, the Bank of Montreal. Because of its political connections with the Family Compact, the York bank was able to have the Bank of Montreal barred from operating branches in the upper province.

Over the years there were frequent altercations between the two banks over note redemption. These resulted not so much from competitive antagonism as from the frustrating differences in currency valuation between the two provinces.

On many an occasion, the respective cashiers impatiently faced each other across a desk either in the building on St. James Street in Montreal or at the head office of the Bank of Upper Canada pictured here at the corner of Duke and George streets in York. The bank moved to this location in 1830 from its original site one block east, at the corner of Frederick Street.

were certain to fall into the hands of the Commercial Bank in the repayment of loans, than Commercial Bank notes into the hands of its rival; hence the balances at settlements would usually be against the Upper Canada Bank, and by requiring that balances should be met by exchange on London, the Commercial Bank would be obtaining an opening into its rival's close preserve."

Granted the stipulation asked for, the Commercial Bank was quite prepared to support the claim that the resumption of payments would speedily lead to the loss of specie and the bankruptcy of the provincial economy. Opposing the contention were the chief officers of the Bank of the People — the President, James Lesslie, and the Cashier, Francis Hincks, who had successfully managed the affairs of his bank throughout the crisis without resorting to suspension, and was besides one of the most experienced bankers in Canada. In his opinion, and in that of the press generally, the need for suspension had long since vanished, but in the event of its extension he felt that some restraint should be placed on the exorbitantly high exchange rates charged by the Bank of Upper Canada. Notwithstanding an unfavourable consensus, an act was passed in May 1839 authorizing suspension until November and thereafter at the discretion of the Lieutenant-Governor.

Ironically enough, the expenditures of the Commissary General on military account decreased greatly during the summer of 1839, bringing the premium on sterling exchange to the highest point in months. The Bank of Upper Canada then seized the opportunity to dispose of its sterling holdings at a satisfactory profit, and on November 1 voluntarily resumed specie payments. By December 5, 1839, the balances due from other banks and agents had dropped to £23,537 from £300,277 the previous March.

It is not surprising that the Bank of Montreal should have found itself seriously affected by the erratic and generally unpredictable behaviour of its up-country confrères. Prior to the collapse of 1837, it had had extensive credits outstanding in Upper Canada, and when disaster struck in May it had promptly gone to the assistance of the Bank of Upper Canada and the Commercial Bank to relieve them of the embarrassment caused by Bond Head's intervention in the specie crisis. Satisfactory relations continued until the Bank of Upper Canada suspended in March 1838, by which time it had a debit balance of £8,500 at the Bank of Montreal. The reason for this suspension, it will be remembered, was to enable the Bank of Upper Canada to switch its funds from the exchange market, where profit margins were narrowing, into domestic discounts. As it lent out its notes in this manner, more and more of them turned up for deposit at the Bank of Montreal because the balance of trade, as always, was in favour of the lower province. During the first five weeks of suspension by the Toronto bank, its debit balance at Montreal almost doubled to £16,952, and despite repeated requests, no offers were made to cover this account except on terms which the Board of the Montreal bank considered to be in contravention of the existing agreement. To resolve the increasingly brittle situation, Benjamin Holmes was ordered to "proceed forthwith to Toronto for the purpose of coming to a clear understanding as respects the continuance of the arrangement hitherto existing, or of making such other as may be consistent with the interests of this Institution, and which may enable it to continue to facilitate the Trade of the Country."

In compliance with these instructions, Holmes left for Toronto on April 14, 1838, and was absent from Montreal for the balance of the month, suggesting strained negotiations between himself and Thomas Ridout, the Cashier of the Bank of Upper Canada. On his return to Montreal, however, Holmes reported the settlement of the account and the intentions of Mr. Ridout in future of "maintaining amicable intercourse with the Bank."

The improvement was of short duration. On May 22, the Bank of Montreal, having determined to resume specie payments the next day, gave notice that it would no longer accept the Toronto bank's notes for deposit at par. A month later, on June 19, a letter was written to Ridout "to ascertain on what terms the Upper Canada Bank would give Exchange on London or New York, payable in their own Notes, for the purpose of accommodating the trade in respect to remittances made to this Province in Notes on non-specie paying Banks." No reply was forthcoming until August 3, when a letter from Ridout announced the intention of the Bank of Upper Canada to open its own agency in Montreal. Considering it "inconsistent with the interest of the Bank to continue as agents for bankers who cannot tender any reciprocity," the Board again dispatched Benjamin Holmes to Toronto with instructions to close out the account with the Bank of Upper Canada and to enter into an agreement with the Commercial Bank on advantageous terms.

Details of the agreement are lacking but the arrangements appear to have been moderately satisfactory for several months as the Bank of Montreal accepted the Commercial Bank's notes at a discount of $1\frac{1}{2}$ to 2 per cent and remitted its own paper to Upper Canada for collection through the bank's Kingston and Toronto offices. But despite the good intentions of the Commercial Bank, the chaotic exchange situation made its position extremely difficult and in December 1838 the Cashier, F. A. Harper, intimated the bank's "disinclination and inability" to keep its account covered by making good the collections sent to it by the Bank of Montreal. To relieve the situation, the latter institution opened negotiations with the Commissary General to transfer considerable funds to Toronto where they would be made available to the Commercial Bank as a means of securing the greatly needed exchange.

By the spring of 1839, it was apparent that business was on the way to recovery everywhere except in Upper Canada where the continuing monetary muddle made banking a problem of day-to-day expediency. The conclusion is borne out by an appeal by the Commercial Bank that the Bank of Montreal relinquish that part of the agreement which provided for exclusive agency representation in their respective territories. The Kingston bank wanted to establish its own agent in Montreal to sell exchange and, for that purpose, had apparently approached one of the officers of the Bank of Montreal to act for it. With admirable restraint the Board deemed that a conflict of interest might develop but not ungenerously acceded in principle to the Kingston bank's proposal. At the same meeting of the Board a copy of a petition of the City Bank of Montreal to the legislature of Upper Canada for the establishment of branches in the province was discussed, the Board deciding to submit a similar petition with the prayer that the same privilege be extended to all chartered banks of Lower Canada.

A bill to authorize incorporated banks to establish branches in Upper Canada was lost in committee and no more was heard about the matter until December. Meanwhile a new factor had been introduced into the complicated situation. In March, 1839, Sir John Colborne forwarded for the perusal of the Board of the Bank of Montreal a dispatch he had received from Sir George Arthur, Lieutenant-Governor of Upper Canada. The subject of the communiqué was Arthur's proposal that the Upper Canada banks resume specie payments and the Bank of Upper Canada's reasons for rejecting this suggestion. Among the latter, mention was made of the chaotic state of the provincial currencies and the burden this imposed on balancing payments between the provinces in times of monetary stringency.

The trouble lay in the different ratings given coins by the two provinces and in the fact that some coins were legal tender in one province and unacceptable in the other. French coins, for example, circulated legally in Lower Canada but not in Upper Canada, and the British crown was rated at 5s. 6d. currency in one province and 6s. in the other, both ratings being higher than the bullion value. The only standard coin in fact was the silver dollar, rated at 5s., but no one was compelled to pay in dollars. Whenever possible, payment in Lower Canada was made in over-rated French silver, and in Upper Canada, in over-rated British crowns, half-crowns or shillings. The Bank of Upper Canada urged that standard ratings be established by abolishing the French coins as legal tender and by the adoption of a common colonial silver coinage.

On the advice of the Bank of Montreal, the Administrator replied to Arthur, agreeing that the French coins were over-rated and that they should be gradually retired from circulation, but suggesting that in the meantime the French half-crown be rated at 2s. 6d., instead of 2s. 9d. as formerly. It was also urged that the Upper Canadian ratings of British crowns be lowered to the legal rate in Lower Canada. Concurrently, an ordinance was passed by the Special Council in Lower Canada to rate coins in proportion to their intrinsic value and a similar act was soon passed by the legislature of Upper Canada. Both measures were reserved for the approval of the Home Government and no further action was taken until after the arrival of a new Governor General, the Right Honourable C. Poulett Thomson, in October 1839. Meanwhile the currency remained in its customary state of disorder.

The twenty-second annual general meeting of the Bank of Montreal, held June 3, 1839, passed without incident, although the banks in Lower Canada had resumed specie payments two days earlier, when the period of legal suspension had ended. With a brighter future in prospect, the newly elected Board decided at its first meeting to recompense the staff for the past year of hardship. Throughout the previous year, duties on imports had had to be paid in specie which could only be obtained on the open market at an average premium of about eleven per cent. As a result of the consequent rise in the price of imported necessities, the Board voted a 12½ per cent, non-recurrent cost-of-living bonus for the staff, feeling that the general increase in salaries for which the employees had petitioned was unwarranted in the long run.

In spite of the fact that suspension in Upper Canada was to last until November, 1839, interprovincial bank co-ordination ran smoothly during the summer, but on the very eve of resumption trouble again appeared on the western horizon. At the end of October, F. A. Harper, the Cashier of the Commercial Bank, wrote to disclaim any liability on the part of his institution for losses arising from collections made by the Commercial's agents for the Bank of Montreal in Upper Canada. The situation was aggravated on November 8, when Harper remitted £12,500 in British silver to balance the Commercial account, computing the value on the over-rating established by the Upper Canada currency act of 1836. Not only was this manoeuvre in contravention of the 1838 agreement between the banks requiring that all balances be settled in "coin current by law in either province," but it also represented a loss to the Bank of Montreal of £1,250 currency because of the different ratings in the two provinces. A proposal to secure new agents in the upper province received some attention from the Board, but previous experience along these lines afforded little encouragement. When the Commercial Bank persistently refused to discharge their commitments on a fair basis, they were advised that "a departure from one article must be considered an abrogation of the whole." Tired of having to deal with inefficient and unreliable correspondents, the Board instructed Benjamin Holmes to request Charles A. Hagerman, the Attorney General of Upper Canada, to prepare a branch bill for submission at the next meeting of the legislature, and a retainer of £50 was subsequently sent for "the employment professionally" of Mr. Hagerman.

In order to strengthen their case, the Board, on December 6, approved an additional petition addressed to both houses of the Upper Canada legislature. It set forth the fact that the paid-up capital was then £452,500, and that "the Bank have almost necessarily become the medium of a considerable portion of the many transactions between the Provinces of Upper and Lower Canada and have been and are the means of greatly improving facilities of their commercial interchange." The petition also noted that, notwithstanding the differences in the legal value of gold and silver coins in the provinces, "if legislative protection were given to the incorporated banking institutions of one province, in their *bona fide* banking transactions in the other, such protection would moreover induce an extension of foreign as well as of provincial trade and would tend to that assimilation of feeling and habit which is so much to be desired by those who deprecate a severance of the connection with the parent state."

Other considerations made December 1839 a trying month. On November 27 had occurred the death in New York of Samuel Ward, a partner of Prime, Ward, King & Co. and, as an original shareholder of the Bank of Montreal, one of its oldest American friends. He had been in charge of the Canadian account, and, when New York newspapers in December printed allegations connecting Ward's name with an alleged conspiracy between New York and London houses against the Second Bank of the United States, the Bank of Montreal faced a difficult decision. It had already divided its New York agency business between Prime, Ward, King & Co. and Christmas, Livingston & Prime (who also acted for Rothschild) and the question arose as to what effect a possible scandal might have on the business of the former. Confusing the issue somewhat was the curious fact that the Bank of Montreal and Baring Brothers, chief correspondents of Prime, Ward, King & Co., had never been associated; in fact the London house was to become the Bank's rival in the financial field of Upper Canada. Notwithstanding an apparent desire to make new arrangements in New York, the Board of the Bank of Montreal voted to give Prime, Ward, King & Co. its unanimous support. The choice was to prove a wise one, as Christmas, Livingston & Prime went into bankruptcy just over a year later.

On the last day of the year a letter was received from Hagerman, advising that he could no longer serve the Bank's interest; having eloquently opposed the Governor-General's bill of union, Hagerman was now facing the consequences which resulted in his retirement from the post of Attorney General. However, the Board was able to turn with confidence to Thomas McKay, an old friend and one of Canada's foremost contractors, for further assistance in obtaining the agency charter. As a member of the Upper Canada Assembly, McKay was able to keep an eye on the bill until it had been passed by the House, but after it reached the Council it was not heard of again. Meanwhile the Bank of Montreal, largely through the persistent efforts of Peter McGill and T. B. Anderson, had been persuaded to prepare to open agencies in Upper Canada, irrespective of whatever legislative action might be taken. The services of Joseph Wenham, an experienced banker then occupying a responsible post with the Bank of Upper Canada, were secured for the purpose of exploring, on behalf of the Bank of Montreal, the steps to be taken to open agencies as soon as possible in Toronto and Kingston, and thereafter in other centres as circumstances might warrant.

Much obscurity has hitherto surrounded the details of the invasion of Upper Canada by the Bank of Montreal: Breckenridge and Shortt, for example, both place the date as 1838. It can now be stated with certainty that the *modus operandi* was not determined until after the employment of Joseph Wenham at the beginning of 1840. Thereafter, the seriousness of the Bank's purpose became apparent and even the Commercial Bank relented and agreed to settle its outstanding balances with the Bank of Montreal in acceptable currency rather than in over-rated British silver. However, the directors of the Bank of Montreal were not to be appeased.

During the spring of 1840, the lights in the board room on St. James Street burned long and often. After numerous discussions and negotiations with trusted friends and customers of the Bank, and after hearing the opinions of a fleet of lawyers, including those of the Hon. W. H. Draper, Hagerman's partner and the new Attorney General of Upper Canada, a plan was evolved to transfer the "privilege" of the Bank of the People (Toronto) to the Bank of Montreal. While Joseph Wenham acted as a field correspondent in Toronto and Kingston, the Board cleared up the final details and the Deed of Settlement with the Bank of the People was signed in Montreal on May 19, 1840. It called for a Bank of Montreal syndicate to purchase the entire £50,000 capital stock of the Bank of the People and for that institution to operate as the agency of the Bank of Montreal in Upper Canada. At the same time, it would continue to conduct its regular business, and late in June notices signed by Joseph Wenham and Benjamin Holmes were sent out to the Upper Canada news-papers, notifying the public that the Bank of the People had become the agent of the Bank of Montreal, and that the latter would henceforth hold itself responsible for all actions of the former, undertaking to redeem its notes in Montreal and Quebec at the prevailing discount rate of one per cent. At this point even the Family Compact bowed to the Bank of Montreal, and the President of the Bank of Upper Canada called on Joseph Wenham, offering to resume cordial relations and presenting a working agreement which was later ratified by the Board. The foothold of the Bank of Montreal in Upper Canada was now secure and throughout 1840-41 when all Canadian banks were being threatened with extinction by proposals emanating from the Lords of the Treasury in London, the Bank of the People began a process of expansion into such growing centres as Amherstburg, Cobourg, St. Catharines, and St. Thomas.

FIFTEEN

ON A NOTE
OF TRIUMPH

ON A NOTE OF TRIUMPH

I.

In Lord Durham's 1839 *Report on the Affairs of British North America* the
specific references to finance, banking, and currency are five in number and
contribute no more than five hundred words to the text. Durham, despite his
industrial family background, was essentially a political reformer and no
expert on economic matters. His report makes clear that he was not primarily
concerned with the financial straits in which the colonies found themselves,
or the inconveniences of their dual currencies. His view of these matters in
relation to Lower Canada is contained in a single paragraph:

> Setting on one side the management of the Crown Lands, and the
> revenue derived therefrom, which will be treated of fully in another part,
> it is not necessary that I should, on the present occasion, enter into any
> detailed account of the financial system of Lower Canada, my object
> being merely to point out the working of the general system of govern-
> ment as operating to produce the present condition of the Province. I

need not inquire whether its fiscal, monetary or commercial arrangements have been in accordance with the best principles of public economy. But I have reason to believe that improvements may be made in the mode of raising and expending the Provincial revenue. During my stay in Canada, the evils of the banking and monetary systems of the Province forced themselves on my attention. I am not inclined, however, to regard these evils as having been in anywise influential in causing the late disorders. I cannot regard them as indicative of any more mismanagement or error than are observable in the measures of the best governments with respect to questions of so much difficulty; and though the importance of finding some sufficient remedy for some of these disorders has, as I shall hereafter explain, very materially influenced my views of the general plan to be adopted for the government of this and the other North American Colonies, I regard the better regulation of the financial and monetary systems of the Province as a matter to be settled by the local Government, when established on a permanent basis.

His lordship's last recommendation was disregarded. Instead of leaving the regulation of the financial and currency systems to local government, the Imperial Government sought to impose its own views regardless of informed Canadian opinion. It was essential, of course, that the Home Government should take the lead in finance. Without such leadership and generous support at the time of union, the Province of Canada must have acknowledged its bankruptcy. In the related fields of currency and banking, however, Imperial paternalism had less fortunate results: little improvement was made in the chaotic currency, and the orderly evolution of Canadian banking along the lines of its historic development was placed in jeopardy. From the point of view of the Bank of Montreal particularly, the threatened changes were the more unacceptable since the system introduced by the Bank in 1817 had demonstrated its utility and adaptability over a quarter of a century and was better suited to its own commercial and economic environment than the banking systems of either Great Britain or the United States were to theirs.

To understand how this situation arose, it is necessary to consider the historical circumstances surrounding Durham's appointment; the influences to which he was exposed; the conduct of his mission and the political considerations which subverted his most enlightened recommendation – the immediate institution of responsible government. Most of these topics have been dealt with so exhaustively elsewhere that they need be referred to here only to establish their effects on banking and related subjects. But first some consideration must be given to the character of British colonial administration prior to the 1840's. Before that date, interest in the Canadian colonies was confined to several government departments each acting more or less independently: the Colonial Office, charged with administration under parliamentary directives; the War Office and the Board of Trade, both of which had acquired important vested interests in the colonies; the Post Office, for which they represented a source of revenue subject to Imperial patronage; and the Treasury Board, whose ardent concern had been largely confined to Upper Canada and dated only from the middle 1830's.

In theory, the Colonial Secretary was the cabinet officer through whom directives and communications were supposed to pass: in practice, and particularly in the presence of weak colonial secretaries, departments habitually acted on their own responsibility. Thus, from the 1760's on, the War Office had enjoyed sanctions which enabled it to conduct its military operations in Canada as it saw fit, and the Treasury Board, continuing policies applied earlier to the Thirteen Colonies, had obstructed every effort on the part of the Canadian provinces to regulate their currencies, although banking legislation, as noted, encountered little interference until the 1830's. However, this may be explained by the political influence in London of Edward Ellice, still a member of the London Committee which governed the affairs of the Hudson's Bay Company and leader of the lobby for Canadian commercial interests which had been a power in London since 1772. It was under such circumstances – and during the interregnum following the Rebellion – that the Treasury Board made its last assault on the banking and currency systems of Canada.

The seeds of rebellion were actually contained in the extraordinary concessions granted to the French-Canadian population by the articles of capitulation in 1760, but their germination can be linked directly to the failure of Lord Gosford's policy of "conciliation without concessions," instituted in 1835. Inspired by Papineau's Ninety-two Resolutions of 1834, Gosford's governorship alienated both the French-Canadian and British elements in the population and lighted the fires of armed insurrection.

To the majority of English Canadians, these rebellions were little more than riotous outbreaks engineered by renegade rabble-rousers; to the American press, on the other hand, the uprisings north of the border were seen as symbols of the same revolutionary spirit that had brought the United States into being two generations earlier. Papineau and Mackenzie were liberators fighting the ancient tyranny, and St. Eustache a place of martyrdom as heroic as Valley Forge. It was this version that first reached London at the beginning of the Christmas season in 1837. Brought by the New York-Liverpool packet, the news came as a surprise and shock to the government and public, but to no one more than the young uncrowned Queen Victoria. More than anything, perhaps, it was the emotional reaction of the eighteen-year-old sovereign to the story of St. Eustache that moved her friend, mentor, and prime minister, Lord Melbourne, to take the emergency action of suspending the constitution of Lower Canada. Although, as noted, the Act was proclaimed in Canada by Colborne on March 27, 1838, it had passed the British parliament on February 10. Thereafter, the colonial situation was accorded its usual priority at Westminster and it was not until March 31, seven weeks later, that "Our right trusty and right well-beloved Cousin and Councillor, John George, Earl of Durham," was commissioned Captain General and Governor-in-Chief of the British provinces in North America, with almost unlimited powers as Lord High Commissioner "for the adjustment of certain important questions depending in the said Provinces of Lower and Upper Canada respecting the form and future government of the said Provinces."

At forty-five years of age, Durham became one of the most brilliant, controversial and dynamic figures ever to occupy the Canadian stage, the central character of a fascinating historical novel still unwritten. The eldest son of a wealthy coal-owner, John George Lambton entered parliament in 1813 at the age of twenty-one and was elevated to the peerage as Baron Durham in 1828. He married the daughter of Lord Grey and from 1830 to 1833 served as Lord Privy Seal in his father-in-law's cabinet. The Reform Bill of 1832 was first drafted in his house, and his vigorous support of the measure won for this "king of the coal country" the nickname of Radical Jack. He broke with government policy on Ireland and resigned from the cabinet in 1833, when he was given an earldom. Two years later he was appointed British Ambassador to St. Petersburg, and on his return to London in 1837 became, as one of the ablest of the younger Whigs, a potent threat to the vacillating leadership of Melbourne. For this reason, perhaps, he was offered the governorship of Canada but refused the post as hardly worthy of his position, brains, and proven talents. He was persuaded to yield only by the Queen's personal solicitation.

Among Durham's distinctions was the introduction of modern techniques for the investigation of political disputes, a system now universally practised. To do this he assembled a staff of qualified researchers known for their analytical abilities and political acumen. Interestingly enough, Durham's private secretary was Edward Ellice the younger, a person with a rather special interest in Canadian affairs. Before leaving for Canada, Durham conferred with Robert Gillespie and Nathaniel Gould, persons high in the councils of the North American Colonial Association, and with George Moffatt and William Badgley, Canadian emissaries of the same association, who had come to London as special pleaders for the commercial interests. Their arrival coincided with Durham's appointment as Lord High Commissioner. Later developments suggest that his lordship was so strongly influenced by this group that he had come to firm conclusions about many aspects of Canadian affairs before ever leaving England.

Durham arrived in Canada with pomp and circumstance on May 29, 1838, and, after landing at Quebec, mounted a white charger to lead his retinue up the Rock to the Château St. Louis. Whether this was to impress the natives or to satisfy a whim of his cynical chief secretary, Charles Buller, is unknown. Two days later, he dismissed the twenty-two-man Special Council appointed by Sir John Colborne and substituted five members of his own choosing in their place. By dissociating his mission from the Château Clique, Durham gained the confidence of the French Canadians and, playing no favourites, also aroused the suspicions of die-hard Canadian loyalists by sending a mission to Washington to confer on the state of the border.

The first month of Durham's sojourn in Canada was devoted to the pressing problems that had arisen from the rebellion. His first important act, and the one that proved his undoing, occurred on June 28, the day of Queen Victoria's coronation, when he granted an amnesty to a number of political prisoners and banished eight others to Bermuda, on pain of death should they return. Early in July, Durham and his party left Quebec for Montreal on the palatial river steamboat *John Bull* which became the official residence during a first visit to the latter city. This, incidentally, was the *John Bull's* last season; it burned to the water's edge the following June, and several claims were made against the Bank of Montreal for bank-notes lost in the fire. None of the claims was allowed, but the Board's Minutes show that alleged losses of nearly £3,000 led to prolonged litigation.

Quitting Montreal after a brief stay, the Durham party proceeded by coach

HARBINGER OF CHANGE

Elevated to the peerage in 1828, John George Lambton came to the Canadas ten years later as Lord Durham "to set on foot various and extensive inquiries into the institutions and administration of those Provinces; and to devise such reforms in the system of their government as might repair the mischief which had already been done, and lay the foundations of order, tranquillity and improvement."

Although Durham spent only five months in the provinces, as High Commissioner and Governor-in-Chief, he was able to render to the British government one of the greatest state documents in colonial history.

and steamboat to Niagara for a four-day visit to Niagara Falls during which his lordship again roused Tory ire by toasting the President of the United States at a lavish goodwill dinner. Retorting to criticisms of the cost, Buller afterwards observed that "a million of money would have been a cheap price for the single glass of wine." Durham was also much criticized for a stop-over of only twenty-four hours at Toronto, where he talked with Sir George Arthur before returning to Montreal for discussions with Peter McGill and a committee recruited from among Montreal's leading merchants. Back in Quebec in September, he received the worst shock of his career: a newspaper report that Lord Brougham, an erstwhile cabinet colleague, had opposed the banishment of the rebels to Bermuda on the grounds that that colony was outside Durham's jurisdiction. When later dispatches not only confirmed this want of confidence but revealed that Melbourne had weakly acquiesced in it, Durham resigned and sailed for home on November 1 aboard a frigate appropriately named *Inconstant*.

The Durham Report, compiled on the voyage home to England, has been hailed by English-speaking Canadian historians as the greatest state document of colonial times, precursor of Dominion status, the British Commonwealth of Nations, and the Self-Determination of Peoples. French-Canadian historians have taken a less enthusiastic view, for no official document ever published conveyed such a wholesale condemnation of the way of life of an alien people. Nor was the Report received with unqualified approval by any contemporary group in Canada. Its analysis of the Canadian dilemma was brilliant and its central recommendation masterly, but it succeeded in angering Upper Canada Tories as well as French Canadians. The manner of the accomplishment was simplicity itself: the proposed union of the provinces under a single responsible government with complete autonomy in domestic affairs. Although the arrangement as eventually legislated provided for equal voting strength between Upper and Lower Canada, it was frankly loaded in favour of the English and was aimed toward the rapid assimilation and eventual submergence of the French enclave in British North America.

Much speculation has been devoted to the actual authorship of the Durham Report and the source of its inspiration. Viewed from an economic rather than a political angle, the conjunction of Gillespie, Gould, Moffatt, Badgley, McGill, and Ellice leads to the conclusion that Durham accepted the identical arguments for union put forward by the same London and Montreal commercial interests in 1822, and engrafted thereon his own advanced view of responsible government.

2.

The acclaim accorded the Durham Report has been largely inspired by its uncompromising advocacy of responsible government, although the document contains no ideas on the subject that had not been given more eloquent expression in the literature of the American Revolution. Furthermore, it signally failed to impress contemporary opinion, as it has so many historians, for its fine statement of the Canadian dilemma—"two nations warring in the bosom of a single state"—or for its exposition of the principles of colonial self-government within the framework of an imperial complex. Its greatest weakness is to be found in its scathing appraisal of French-Canadian culture and attainments, which made it the touchstone of French-Canadian nationalism. It seems probable, in fact, that the Report would never have been made public in its original form had it not been mysteriously "leaked" to *The Times* not long after the arrival of the *Inconstant* at Plymouth. Once public property, there was little that could be done to lessen its inflammatory quality. The report was tabled in the House of Commons on February 11, 1839, to become a bone of contention in Whig circles and, together with the Chartist and Anti-Corn-Law movements, one of the many causes of the collapse of Melbourne's divided ministry in May.

Lord John Russell, whose Ten Resolutions had fanned the embers of Canadian rebellion, succeeded Lord Glenelg as Colonial Secretary in a newly constituted third Melbourne ministry. His Union bill, submitted in June, was strongly reminiscent of the aborted Union Act of 1822 and, like it, lacked any provision for responsible government. In Canada the bill provoked the old irreconcilable reactions while establishing incongruous new alignments. In Upper Canada it was accepted by the reformers as a concession to their demands and denounced by the Family Compact as a betrayal of their loyalties and vested interests: in Lower Canada it was welcomed by the English commercial interests and repudiated by the French Canadians, the more radical among them seeing in it a cause for renewed rebellion.

Even in England, advanced liberal opinion found it impossible to reconcile responsible government with Imperial sovereignty—how could a governor general serve at one and the same time two masters, the Home Government and another elected in the united provinces? The problem appeared as insoluble as it had in the 1760's and 1770's. With Durham already stricken by the illness that was to cause his death in July 1840, and with no dedicated advocate to expound his views in Parliament, the Union bill was allowed to languish after its first reading. Yet it was apparent that the Canadian impasse must be resolved by union sooner or later and that a successor to Durham would have to be sent to Canada to prepare for the inevitable transition. The choice fell on Charles Poulett Thomson, a former member of the cabinet who, after refusing the post of Chancellor of the Exchequer, accepted the Canadian challenge and arrived in Quebec on October 19, 1839.

Known as Lord Sydenham after his elevation to the peerage in August 1840, Poulett Thomson was a successful business man who had won respect for his mastery of public finance and banking during a five-year tenure as President of the Board of Trade. He was closely connected with the Baltic timber trade and, with Sir Robert Peel, was a foremost advocate of banking and currency reform. With this background, and with his advanced liberal views, it was natural that he should have been received with misgivings by every segment of Canadian opinion. His Baltic lumber connections made him suspect to the commercial interests of Lower Canada, and his advocacy of free trade made him a threat to the agricultural interests of Upper Canada. To *les Canadiens,* who saw national extinction in union, and to many Canadians, who saw in union without responsible government a denial of their rights as British subjects, he was an object of hostility. Despite these initial prejudices, Sydenham became one of Canada's ablest Governors General. Like Durham, he had one of the best brains yet brought to bear on Canadian problems: unlike Durham, he was a master of political finesse and an economic realist to boot.

One of Thomson's first acts after his arrival in Canada was to summon the Special Council of Lower Canada and lay before it the broad outlines of union. Except for the opposition of the one-time radical leader, John Neilson, these were approved, with certain provisions: a permanent civil list; the improvement of the St. Lawrence at joint cost, and the protection of all rights granted previously to the citizens of both provinces.

Thomson next proceeded to Upper Canada where a legislative session was called for December 3, 1839. Arriving in Toronto, he found that conditions were even worse than he had suspected. Despite a good harvest, business generally had failed to respond to improvement elsewhere; the provincial debt had reached insupportable proportions and the currency was, as always, in

BENJAMIN HOLMES
ADDRESSES THE ASSEMBLY

The first parliament of the Province of Canada met on June 14, 1841, in a converted hospital in Kingston. The union of Upper and Lower Canada had been proclaimed the previous February, but few could have foreseen the tremendous economic impact of this legislative feat.

One of the main features of the Union was the consolidation of the debts of the Canadas and the granting of an Imperial guarantee for a loan of £1,500,000 on the London market. Such sums were unheard-of in Canada at that time, and the infusion of this capital bore the country aloft on a wave of prosperity and public improvements, to heights it had never before experienced.

Other financial matters also engaged the attention of the newly elected representatives, as the country had been wallowing in a marsh of economic torpidity since the specie crisis and rebellions of 1837. The Colonial Office and the Treasury in London had shown particular concern over the performance of the banks during this crisis, and, to complicate matters still more, Lord Sydenham had arrived with his own plan for a Provincial Bank. For its part, the Bank of Montreal had further provoked the Imperial mentors by going outside the provisions of its charter and purchasing the Bank of the People in Upper Canada, a move promptly condemned in a Treasury circular.

The seriousness of the whole situation can be seen here, vividly marked on the intent faces of the members of the Assembly, as Benjamin Holmes presents a petition for the renewal of the Bank's charter. Not only was the charter granted, but the prohibition respecting the acquisition of the Bank of the People was circumvented when the Bank received the right to open branches in the upper province – a privilege it had been denied since the early 1820's.

Painting by Jerry Lazare

375

a state of chaos. In the political arena, the Family Compact, implacably opposed to union, controlled both the Assembly and the Legislative Council; the Lieutenant-Governor, Sir George Arthur, had joined forces with the Tory oligarchy, believing that by so doing he was helping to preserve the British connection, and in the market place a sizable body of opinion favoured the creation of an independent republican state rather than union with Lower Canada.

Nevertheless, Thomson's personality and political skills were such that, in the short space of two weeks before the opening of the legislature, he won the approval of all but the most extreme elements to the principle of union. The achievement verged on the miraculous and was accomplished by persuading members of the several political factions that only through union could the province hope to find a way out of its economic morass. What was needed, he said, was "some great stroke . . . which shall turn men's thoughts from the channel in which they now run and give a fresh impetus to public works, immigration, and the practical improvement of the country's resources." The great stroke contemplated was a loan of £1,500,000 sterling, guaranteed by the Imperial Government, to pay off the crippling indebtedness incurred by Upper Canada, restore the provincial credit in England, and make possible the completion of the grand water transportation system without which an integrated Canadian economy could never be attained. Somewhat after the manner of the carrot and the donkey, the Imperial loan became the lure which enabled the Governor to attain the seemingly impossible goals he set himself.

Among those goals were the historically familiar political objectives: the acceptance of the principle of union; the introduction of new methods of administration; the reorganization of the Executive Council into a cabinet made up of responsible department heads; the settlement of the wretched Clergy Reserves controversy, the establishment of a school system, and the division of the province into municipal districts each of which would be responsible for the collection of local taxes and the conduct of local affairs. That many of these proposals should have become law, despite factious opposition and the poor state of Sydenham's own health, is an indication of his supreme qualities as a statesman, political leader and dedicated public servant; here, however, we are more concerned with the fiscal and financial plans with which he proposed to give his political measures substance.

Some features of a comprehensive plan for rehabilitating Canada's shattered finances may have been formulated before Thomson's departure from England, but others were developed on the basis of his Canadian observations. Essential to all else, of course, was the £1,500,000 loan to be raised on English credit, but this seems to have remained only a prospect until Thomson's dispatches of March 11 and June 27, 1840, convinced the Imperial authorities of its unavoidable necessity. Added later as enticements were promises of further Imperial expenditures for military defence, though not on the grandiose scale recommended previously by Colborne, and Imperial grants in aid of immigration so that newcomers from the British Isles would receive transportation and support from the time they landed in Canada until they had secured employment or were settled on the land. In the hope, perhaps, of stimulating industrial endeavours and at the same time alleviating some of the debt burden, it was proposed to double the import tariff on manufactured goods from 2½ to 5 per cent. But Thomson had brought with him to Canada a much bolder and more comprehensive scheme to place Canada's finances on a substantial basis and provide increased revenues for its continued growth. This was a proposal, based on ideas Thomson had distilled from contemporary British monetary debate, to establish a Provincial Bank of Issue which would recapture from the chartered banks the very profitable privilege of note issue.

At this juncture, it should be pointed out that a Select Committee on Banking and Currency of the House of Commons had been sitting in England since the financial crisis of 1836. In dispute were the two monetary theories that moulded banking practice in England and the United States during the nineteenth century; the one favouring laissez-faire banking in which competition between banks was counted on to control the circulation of notes, whether based on land or specie, the other a currency officially regulated so that convertibility of note issues into coin would be guaranteed under all circumstances. The leading exponent of the currency, as opposed to the laissez-faire, principle was Samuel Jones Loyd, later Lord Overstone, a foremost economic theorist and a close friend of Poulett Thomson; its leading parliamentary supporter Sir Robert Peel, the leader of the Conservative party. Although Loyd is regarded as the first exponent of the principle in a pamphlet published in 1837, it appears from a letter quoted later in this chapter that Poulett Thomson had advocated its adoption in the cabinet as early as 1833.

Peel's support of the currency principle found expression finally in the Bank Act of 1844, which separated the monetary and commercial functions of the Bank of England and laid the foundations of the present English banking system. By September 1839, however, at the time of Thomson's departure for

Canada, the Select Committee had asked some 9,270 questions of witnesses without coming to any definite conclusions.

In this connection, it may be recalled that Select Committees on Banking and Currency of the Assembly of Upper Canada had been sitting consecutively for more years than had that of the august House of Commons at Westminster. It is worth noting, too, that whereas the Committee in England had been engaged in an inquiry into the fundamentals of the English banking structure, those in Canada had been concerned only with modifications of a system that had proved itself generally satisfactory. At the time, in fact, the system established by the Bank of Montreal on Hamiltonian principles was better adapted to Canadian needs than was the existing English system to English needs. Yet, almost every writer on the subject has attributed to Canadian legislators and bankers of the period a congenital inferiority inherent in a colonial environment.

A Canadian Currency and Banking Committee was sitting during the crisis of 1837 and was instrumental in ameliorating the worst effects of Bond Head's refusal to sanction the suspension of specie payments. There occurred, however, largely as a result of the policies pursued by the Bank of Upper Canada, a progressive depletion of the coin in circulation and the working commercial capital of the province, and other steps became necessary.

As early as 1835, the Welland Canal Company had adopted the American practice of issuing its own interest-bearing paper, and in 1837 the City of Toronto had issued £6,000 in one-dollar notes, payable with interest in six months and negotiable for all debts owed the municipality. It was the success of this expedient – by 1839 the City of Toronto authorized the issue of a further £16,000 of notes printed from plates engraved in New York – that led a harassed legislature in November 1838, on the recommendation of the Select Committee, to authorize the Receiver General to issue twelve-month inconvertible treasury notes to the amount of £100,000. The bill was reserved by Sir George Arthur according to instructions from London and forwarded there for the consideration of the Lords of the Treasury and the Colonial Office. In 1839, a similar bill authorizing the issue of £250,000 of notes also failed to receive royal consent.

Monetary improvisation relieved the situation somewhat but the hard-money flight continued and the Select Committee recommended that new and more realistic ratings be given to the coins legally current in Upper Canada with a view to assimilating them with the new ratings established in 1839 by an ordinance of the Special Council of Lower Canada. This ordinance provided for the gradual retirement of the old French silver coinage and its replacement by coins of American, Mexican and English origin. While some inconsistencies existed in the revised ratings, a better solution of the currency muddle was provided than any advanced previously. On forwarding the enactments to the Colonial Office, both Colborne and Arthur urged that they be given royal assent pending the introduction of a provincial coinage. Sir George noted, inadvisably perhaps, that "It is intended by this measure to equalize the currency of this Province with that of the United States, to enable the banks to use money on the same terms as in that country."

Oddly enough, Thomson had sailed for Canada before the Treasury Board gave notice in the Official Gazette of its disallowance of both Canadian currency bills. In a dispatch to Thomson dated December 1839, but not received by him in Canada until January 1840, it was pointed out that the acts contravened an Imperial act passed in the reign of George III to prohibit Massachusetts and others of the Thirteen Colonies from managing their own currencies.

The reason for their disallowance is to be found in a Treasury Minute dated November 22, 1839. Despite earlier failures to impose sterling on Canada, it suggested that the currency of Canada be regulated exclusively by the Home Government through Orders in Council and Royal Proclamations, as was the case in the West Indies, the ratings to be determined with reference to the British pound sterling and, through it, to all other coins. A Board Minute of the Bank of Montreal for January 28, 1840, shows that the notice of disallowance was received on that date. The Bank had acquired £16,500 sterling at 15d. currency to the shilling, the legal rate in Upper Canada, in anticipation of approval of the bills equalizing the rates in the two provinces. It took steps forthwith to avoid incurring a loss by having to sell at the prevailing Lower Canada rate of 13d. to the shilling: the Board decided to continue redeeming the British shillings and sixpences "until such time as the full amount so issued shall have been returned to the Bank," but Holmes instructed the tellers "not to issue another piece of the above described coin."

For once Poulett Thomson's gifts of persuasion proved ineffective. When he communicated the views of Lord Russell to the commercial elite of Toronto, every shade of opinion was against him. The Toronto Board of Trade defiantly repudiated the attempt of the Imperial Government to interfere in the matter and in Lower Canada the Governor General encountered the same disposition, particularly from persons connected with the Bank of Montreal. Throughout the controversy over the pound sterling versus the dollar, the officers of that institution had been in favour of assimilating the two Canadian currencies to each other and both to that of the United States. Better than most other Canadians, they knew the costs and inconveniences of a monetary system still governed by an act passed to regulate the currency of the Commonwealth of Massachusetts seventy-five years before.

In the circumstances the Governor had no alternative but to beat a graceful retreat by proposing that the matter of currency reform be left in abeyance until after the union of the provinces, when he would present comprehensive measures in the legislature to deal with all fiscal, financial, banking, and monetary problems in their entirety. As the Union Act was not passed by the British House of Commons until July 1840, and was not implemented until June 1841, a hiatus of almost a year ensued during which the provinces were forced to labour under their ancient difficulties.

At this point in the tangled record an interesting question intrudes. Did Poulett Thomson discuss Canadian banking with Russell before leaving England to take up his gubernatorial duties? Durham's allusion to "the evils of the banking and monetary systems of the Province," injected without supporting evidence, suggests that Canadian banking was held in low esteem in London, as does Thomson's own despairing comment, later on, that "there is not a man in the legislature who understands these subjects at all." This being the consensus it would seem that corrective measures should have been considered while Thomson was still in England. However, it is difficult to reconcile this contention with the currency dispatches from Russell dated November and December, 1839, which followed Thomson to Canada, or a later dispatch of May 4, 1840, in which H.M. Principal Secretary of State for the Colonies forwarded a Treasury Circular requiring that certain restrictions be embodied in all future colonial bank charters. The suspicion arises, therefore, that the banking measures proposed by Thomson were put forward on his own initiative with a view to establishing the worth of the currency principle. A devout convert to that principle himself, he no doubt saw in Canada a splendid opportunity to prove its validity and by so doing not only strengthen the finances of the stricken province but aid in the conversion of his ambivalent English confrères.

3.

The officers and directors of the Bank of Montreal occupied a curious position during the period of stalemate that followed the passage of the Act of Union. Most of them, in their capacities as private citizens, had been strong partisans of union from the early 1820's; their views on this and related subjects had been adopted by Lord Durham, yet they appear to have played no part in the grand constitutional change-over. Notwithstanding their special interest in the proposed changes in the monetary and banking systems, they seem to have had no greater knowledge of the Governor's specific plans than had the ordinary citizen. They were never taken into his confidence; nor were their opinions invited as they had been by Durham. Whatever information they gleaned appears to have come to them by rumour, invariably disconcerting and sometimes alarming, despite the presence on the Special Council of the Honourable Peter McGill and the Honourable John Molson.

In such circumstances, it is not surprising that the directors should have entertained some misgivings about the future, although the Bank itself was in a strong position. With its paid-up capital of £500,000 and its successful invasion of Upper Canada through the Bank of the People, it had strengthened its position as the leading financial institution in the country and had, in fact, become one of the larger banks in North America. On the other hand, the life of the existing charter extended only to November 1, 1842; the Bank's several petitions for an extension had been ignored, although in June 1840 a minor amendment to the ordinance of 1838 was passed, permitting the president to receive a salary provided he relinquished all extramural business involvements. However, in the crucial matter of the currency bills, the Bank received no reports other than the message of January 28, 1840, telling of Thomson's announcement of their disallowance to the Assembly of Upper Canada. Far from wielding the sinister political influence commonly imputed to it, the Bank of Montreal appears to have carried no political weight whatever.

The date of the proclamation of the Act of Union was left to the Governor's discretion and it was not until February 5, 1841, that he announced that Union would become effective on February 10, the anniversary of the Queen's marriage, of the Treaty of Paris of 1763 ceding Canada to Britain, and of the granting of royal assent to the Act of 1838 suspending the constitution of Lower Canada – a rather incongruous series of events. Immediately after the proclamation, writs were issued for the election of representatives to the House of Assembly of the first Parliament of the Province of Canada. There followed in most ridings of the province, and more particularly in those around Montreal and Toronto, acrimonious struggles between various contending factions in which intimidation and incitement to violence played their traditional parts. An exception was the electoral district of Montreal, newly created by the Governor at the direction of the Colonial Office to ensure a safe majority for the predominantly English commercial interests of the city. A public meeting was held on the evening of March 11 in Rasco's Hotel, for the purpose of nominating candidates. As reported by the Montreal *Gazette*, an enthusiastic and orderly gathering of citizens was chaired by Adam Ferrie, a prominent merchant and later member of the Legislative Council, who strongly endorsed the near approach of Union and impressed upon his audience the need of electing representatives who would work for its success. When the meeting was thrown open to nominations, J. Dunscombe, who was to represent Beauharnois in the Assembly, proposed the names of Benjamin Holmes and George Moffatt. Holmes had been an employee of the Bank of Montreal from its formation, and Cashier from 1827; George Moffatt one of its most active directors from 1817 until 1835, when he resigned to devote his attention to the affairs of the British American Land Company and to engage his considerable talents in defence of the British connection. The *Gazette* editorialized on March 13 as follows:

> It is altogether unnecessary to dwell on the merits of our two candidates and the strong claims they have to be supported by every loyal citizen within the precincts of Montreal. . . . It is sufficient to say that they are worthy in every respect of representing such a metropolis in any situation whatsoever; that their election will reflect everlasting honor on our fellow citizens, and that while their interests and civil liberties can continue to be entrusted to the guardianship of such delegates as Holmes and Moffatt that they will never be compromised or betrayed. . . .

In letters to the *Gazette* both candidates pledged their unqualified support of British interest and British supremacy and asserted they would do all in their power to further Union.

The following morning, eleven of the thirteen directors of the Bank of Montreal attended a regular meeting of the Board. After disposing of routine matters the Cashier was asked to withdraw and the President brought up the subject of the previous night's political meeting. He expressed the opinion that "one of the first measures for the consideration of the Legislature would be the negotiation of the currency and other questions incidental to this." The next entry reads:

> It was moved by Mr. Brooke and seconded by Mr. Redpath that the experience and practical knowledge of the Cashier in matters of currency and finance may greatly aid in obtaining settlement of these important questions upon a basis favourable to the Banking Institutions of the Country, and consequently that his services as a Member of the House of Assembly during the ensuing session of the Legislature may so essentially contribute to the prosperity of the Bank as greatly to counterbalance the inconvenience of his temporary absence.
>
> Therefore Resolved that the full sanction of the Board be given to Mr. Holmes to comply with the wishes of the great body of Electors as expressed at the public meeting on the 11th instant.

The resolution was adopted by a vote of nine to two, only Vice-President Masson and William Lunn voting in the negative.

A second rally was held at St. Ann's Hall on the evening of March 22, when Holmes and Moffatt were declared elected by acclamation. The speeches of the successful candidates, which reiterated their pre-election pledges, were reported in the *Gazette*, whose editor commented on the happy outcome. Holmes spoke also in favour of public education, government aid to immigration, and the distribution of the waste lands of the province for that purpose. "With good schools, public improvements and union among ourselves, we shall have nothing to envy when we look across the forty-fifth parallel to a country where the laws are trampled under foot and where its citizens prate of liberty in the slave market."

During the remainder of the month, the directors' attention was devoted to problems arising from New York and Upper Canada operations but, on April 2, the question of the future was again raised by the President. It was then decided that a general meeting of the shareholders be called for May 17 to consider the following matters: the renewal of the charter; the advisability of increasing the capital by £250,000 to care for the increase of business in Upper Canada; a modification of the regulations governing the signing of bank-notes; and the establishment of the office of the President on a permanent stipendiary basis. In preparation for the shareholders' meeting, a special meeting of the directors was held on the evening of May 14, to approve a petition to the legislature and to consider the draft of an act "prepared in accordance with certain principles laid down as the basis for future bank charters in a circular from Lord John Russell dated 4th May, 1840 addressed to the Colonial Government." The President found many of the provisions of the circular objectionable, but which ones, and for what reasons, was not recorded in the Minutes. In conclusion, he remarked that he was "not prepared to say whether the present head of the government (Lord Sydenham) had made up his mind fully to insist upon these instructions should the Legislature take a different view of the subject." With the Bank's representation in mind, no doubt, he assured the Board that the matter would be subject to further inquiry.

On May 17 the shareholders unanimously approved the four proposals put before them, and on June 7 assembled again for the annual meeting. The year's business had shown signs of improvement. Immigration in 1840 had attained the pre-depression level of 32,000, and in Britain the second poor harvest in two years had kept the price of wheat above 60s. the quarter, permitting a large increase in Canadian grain exports. With the support of colonial preferences the timber trade also continued to expand, and the New Brunswick-Maine border dispute had maintained the British garrison above its normal strength, contributing its essential support to the Canadian economy. In view of the political situation, however, the directors had thought it preferable to keep the dividend to a rather modest six per cent, while fortifying the Bank against an unknown future by adding £16,284 to the Rest, thereby increasing it by 73 per cent. The President was voted the customary honorarium of £500, the staff thanked for the zealous discharge of its duties, and the outgoing Board reinstated without change. The next day the Honourable Peter McGill and the Honourable Joseph Masson were re-elected to their respective positions and all staff appointments were continued. In view of the Cashier's pending departure to take up his legislative duties, a committee was appointed to count the cash.

Benjamin Holmes left Montreal for Kingston four days later to attend the opening of the provincial parliament. On June 15 the Governor delivered the Speech from the Throne to a House that would give him a working majority so long as his powers of conciliation proved superior to the congeries of special interests ready to coalesce against him. At stake were, first, the acceptance of the Act of Union itself; second, the passage of various legislative reforms and, third, the approval of fiscal and financial innovations to provide the province with future revenues. Foremost among the last items was official

"SO SAGACIOUS AND INDEFATIGABLE"

Charles Edward Poulett Thomson, later Baron Sydenham, was not yet forty when he took up the task of converting Durham's recommendations into practical reforms. Joseph Howe was moved to write: "It is rare that a statesman so firm, so sagacious and indefatigable follows in the wake of a projector so bold."

Sydenham's formula for establishing a framework within which Canadians could govern themselves was, as he put it, to "take the moderate from both sides – reject the extremes – and govern as I think right." On proclaiming the union of Upper and Lower Canada, he warned the people: "In your hands now rests your own fate, and by the use which you make of the opportunity must it be decided."

assurance of the long-mooted Imperial guarantee of a loan of £1,500,000 sterling to restore the provincial credit and complete the arrested program of public works. Estimating the costs of a navigable ship channel from the Atlantic to Lake Huron at £1,470,000 sterling, Lord Sydenham said, "A very considerable amount of the capital required might be raised, without any charge whatever for interest, by the assumption by the province of the issue of paper payable on demand, which is now enjoyed by private banks or by individuals, without their being subjected to any charge whatever in return for the power thus granted them by the state." This, apparently, was Sydenham's first public statement concerning his cherished scheme for a provincial bank of issue based on the principles of the English currency school. Although he dwelt enthusiastically on the plan in his private correspondence and discussed it with such staunch supporters as Francis Hincks and W. H. Merritt, the Governor failed to elaborate further on the matter at the time. In the supercharged political atmosphere at the beginning of the session, he was evidently loath to invite public discussion of a proposal which might have proven highly controversial.

The opening weeks of the session, devoted largely to political manoeuvring and the alignment of forces, saw the Governor General introduce a precedent in colonial administration by becoming his own prime minister and head of the quasi-responsible government. By this means he hoped to facilitate the passage of those financial and organizational measures which he considered of paramount importance to the success of Union: consolidation of provincial finances, changes in the structure of government both on local and provincial levels, reform of the banking system, and expansion of public works. Following the establishment of rules for parliamentary procedure, various standing committees were appointed to draft legislation for the Assembly's consideration. Among these was one on currency, named at the request of Holmes, to consider "such measures as will most readily equalize the rates of exchange, and assimilate the currency throughout the Province."

The committee was originally made up of ten members under the chairmanship of Francis Hincks, former head of the Bank of the People and soon to become Inspector General of Accounts. It included John S. Cartwright, first president of the Commercial Bank of the Midland District, George Moffatt, and John Neilson, editor of the Quebec *Gazette* and leader of the French opposition to Union. Noticeably absent from the group was Benjamin Holmes, its progenitor, who, having completed his preliminary assignment, eased quietly into the background in classical bank fashion. However, when a similar committee on banking was appointed early in July, Holmes was named a member, as was W. H. Merritt. Because of the interlocking nature of their terms of reference and of their memberships, the two committees were combined on July 12, and dealt further with petitions concerning usury, bankruptcy and real-estate laws. Four reports in all were submitted, the last being tabled on August 27, 1841.

The extensive nature of the committee's two-month inquiry is revealed in Appendix O, *Journals of the Legislative Assembly of the Province of Canada, 1841*. The document contains the replies of twenty-seven persons connected with the colonial financial world to a series of eighteen questions submitted to them by the Select Committee. The purpose of the questionnaire was to obtain opinions on the prevailing state of the currency, the reforms needed, and whether the standard monetary unit of the province should be the British pound sterling or the American silver dollar; the witnesses were persons connected with the chartered banks as cashiers or branch managers, representatives of the Boards of Trade, the Commissary-General's Department and the Customs Service, and several private citizens. Associated with the Bank of Montreal were T. B. Anderson, a senior director and later president; Alexander Simpson, the Cashier of the Quebec Branch; Joseph Wenham, Cashier of the Bank of the People, Toronto, and John Patton, manager of its Kingston branch. Included in the committee's First Report were monthly statements of the Bank of Montreal from January 1, 1836 to July 15, 1841, showing the amount of cash in the vaults, discounts extended, and the exchanges bought and sold; the totals of exchange purchases and sales for that period were £2,592,834 and £1,775,779 respectively.

Among the replies received by the committee, there was general agreement as to the disruptive state of the currency and the reasons for it, but no consensus as to the cure, some respondents favouring the pound, some the dollar, and others a provincial currency conforming to the ratings established by the 1835 Assay Table of the United States Mint. While a majority of the replies were submitted in writing, several of those queried appeared before the committee in person. The following excerpts are representative of professional opinion in contrast to the extreme views inspired by British loyalty on the one hand and republican sentiments on the other. The witness is W. Walker, Esquire, Chairman of the Board of Trade of Quebec.

> Should it be decided that some change is to be made in our Currency, I would greatly prefer decimal Currency to British Sterling. . . . I think both gold and silver should be made the standard. . . . As before mentioned, the assimilation of our Currency would have the effect of preventing any great fluctuation in the rate of exchange between the different parts of the Province. . . . The present difference between our Colonial Currency and British Sterling being a mere matter of calculation, I cannot see why it [assimilation] ought to induce the introduction of British Capital. . . . The introduction of Sterling money and the assimilation of our circulating medium to the Old Country, would not, in my opinion, either facilitate the emigrant or induce a better understanding with the Mother Country.

The questionnaire displays much repetition which could only have been inspired by the Treasury dispatch that provoked it. This latter document sought for a second time to impose an Imperial sterling currency on Canada and the pioneer opinion poll appears to have been cunningly designed to refute the Lords of the Treasury with their own words. It did so by showing that the Board itself, by refusing royal assent to the bills assimilating the two Canadian currencies to each other, had perpetuated the very evils it sought to remedy. It can be seen from Walker's answers that the Canadians cared little about the effects of the condition of their currency on outside countries but were primarily concerned with domestic trade and the problems emanating from the unequal ratings. Among the land-holding and official classes of Upper Canada, it is true, a strong sentiment existed in favour of an imperial currency on the grounds that it would cement the bonds of Empire, promote immigration, and help to nullify American influences – the writer has seen the household account books of a grand dame of Montreal who insisted until her death in 1878 that her greengrocer and other purveyors render their semi-annual bills in the ancient Saxon reckoning – but even those who favoured sterling tender also favoured the retention of the silver dollar and half dollar for convenience, and public opinion generally regarded the attempt at Imperial interference as objectionable and ill-informed.

The Select Committee on Currency and Banking concluded its deliberations toward the end of July and on the 26th submitted its First Report to the Assembly. Upon receipt of the Report, the Assembly went into Committee of the Whole and a resolution was introduced, presumably by Benjamin

Holmes, recommending that the Canadian standard be the silver dollar, four of these dollars equalling £1 currency, and that all other coins be valued at their intrinsic values as determined by weight. Holmes was ordered to introduce a bill to this effect, which had already been prepared, and the bill was then read for the first time. When it reached the Council it was amended so that the pound sterling replaced the dollar as the standard and the value of the latter was raised from 5s. to 5s. 1d. The dollar was allowed, however, to retain its status as legal tender. The amended bill was passed reluctantly by the Assembly on September 3 but was reserved by the Governor General. The Imperial Government pondered over the enactment until March 11, 1842, when royal assent was at last granted. During this interval, the Canadian economy suffered feverishly as a result of not knowing which ratings would prevail, and the banks in Lower Canada attempted to unload their French coins, which were not mentioned in the Act and hence were in danger of becoming obsolete. When it did finally become law in Canada on April 27, 1842, the Act gave the country a uniform rating for its various coins and in so doing was a great relief to the common business man. However, its awkward ratings and the retention of Halifax currency did not endear it to those engaged in banking and exchange.

4.

The sittings of the Select Committee throughout July were principally concerned with the currency, but two other matters of paramount importance were also brought to its attention: Lord John Russell's Circular of May 4, 1840, setting forth restrictions to be incorporated in future bank charters; and Lord Sydenham's *Memorandum on the Paper Currency of Canada*, in which he disclosed, apparently for the first time, the complete details of his plan for a provincial bank of issue.

Sydenham's plan may be summarized as follows: the Provincial Bank would be established by legislative enactment and placed under the management of three commissioners; it would have the sole power of issuing paper on demand after March 1, 1843, a compensation for note circulation being paid to all banks whose charters extended beyond that date; the note issue would be initially limited to £1,000,000 currency in notes of one dollar and upwards, and would be backed by coin or bullion to the extent of twenty-five per cent; the chartered banks could deposit specie or government securities with the

Provincial Bank and receive its notes in return, being thus enabled to continue all their business except that of note issue. The sole function of the Provincial Bank would be that of a bank of issue, the net profits from which would be paid into the public account of the province; it would not accept deposits except from other banks, grant discounts, or deal in exchange. In short, it was to be in part a prototype of the reconstituted Bank of England, as soon to be formulated by Sydenham's colleague Peel in his Bank Act of 1844. The objects of the plan for Canada were threefold: 1) to obtain a paper currency assured as to convertibility and protected from injurious fluctuations; 2) to place at the disposal of the government the means of furthering the public works, and 3) to increase the revenues of the province through the profits from the note issue.

Just when Sydenham's *Memorandum* was transmitted to the Assembly is unknown, but it would appear to have been prior to July 11, for on that date he wrote to a friend in England, making these observations:

There is one of my Canadian measures on the anvil now in which you will feel an interest, and wish me success, I am sure. . . . I do not feel certain of getting it through; but if I can, I shall rejoice more than at any other work which I have been able to perform; for it will not only be good for this country, but will set an example to England, by which she may profit in a year or two when the Bank of England Charter is to be renewed. For it is the establishment of a perfectly sound paper currency by means of a single state bank of issue based upon the pure principle of the issue of paper against bullion or coin, to the exclusion of any other paper whatever, payable on demand; the principle, in short, for which I contended in the Cabinet in the first instance in 1833, and which Sam. Loyd has since so ably advocated in a pamphlet.

Circumstances at this moment are most favourable for the change; for the charters of nearly all the banks in both Provinces have either to be renewed this session or have only a few years to run. They are therefore at my mercy. This country, too, affords a greater field for the operations of such a bank than perhaps any other in the world. Owing to the wretched state of the paper issue in the United States, there can be little doubt that in two or three years the paper of our bank would be the chief circulation of all the States bordering on Canada, which would tax the Americans for our benefit to the extent of 60,000 *l.* or 70,000 *l.* a year.

*   *   *   *   *

I calculate the medium circulation of the Province at about 1,200,000 *l.* at present, for which a rest of one fourth would be ample; so that I at once get 900,000 *l.* to dispose of, or a clear gain of 40,000 *l.* to 50,000 *l.* a year, according to the value of money here. But I have not the least doubt that the extension of the circulation in the United States would, in a few years, more than double this profit. There will, however, be some deductions from this, as I must buy out the existing banks in order to carry out my scheme.

My chief difficulty is, that there is not a man in the legislature who understands these subjects at all, and to whom I can intrust my bill with any confidence. However, I get the members generally to come to me, and I give them lectures upon it; and thus, though there be little argument of much value employed in its discussion in the Assembly, I do not despair of carrying my point by the mere weight of authority, and the confidence which most of them place in me.

Sydenham's optimism and his enthusiasm in this matter must have been sources of great anxiety to the Canadian banks which, as he correctly pointed out, were dependent on the Assembly for renewal of their charters. Nevertheless, after Holmes transmitted the Governor's proposals to Montreal, some time elapsed before a special meeting of the Board of the Bank of Montreal was called, on July 31, "to take into consideration the government scheme for a Bank of Issue." Twelve of the thirteen directors attended, including the President and Vice-President, and "resolved to refuse assent to such a measure under the impression that as far as it is understood by the Bank it is fraught with the most injurious consequences as well to the stockholders as to the public at large."

It may be safely assumed that the Bank's objections to Lord Sydenham's proposal were transmitted to Benjamin Holmes in Kingston as quickly as could be, and that the Member for Montreal did his utmost to present them as effectively as possible. It could not have been an easy task. On all matters save banking, Holmes was one of the strongest supporters of Sydenham's liberal policies and regarded the Governor General highly, both as a statesman and as a man; and Francis Hincks, with whom Holmes had formed a strong personal friendship, not only approved the plan for a bank of issue but was chairman of the Select Committee on Currency and Banking; furthermore, to informed Canadians, there was nothing particularly novel or alarming about Sydenham's idea. As early as 1808, the establishment of state bank had been debated in the Assembly of Lower Canada; the successful Army Bills experiment during the War of 1812 had familiarized the public with government paper currency; and only a few years previously W. H. Merritt, then chairman of an earlier Select Committee on Currency and Banking, had introduced a state banking bill more sweeping than that proposed by Sydenham. In fact, government issue in Canada was eventually to be pioneered by the Bank of Montreal itself.

The main flaw in Sydenham's scheme was that it had been predicated on the weaknesses not of Canadian banking but of banking in England, where the system was currently under review and where one of the most serious problems was the number of bank failures that had taken place during the late depression. In marked contrast, Canada had experienced only two bank failures in twenty-odd years, the Bank of Canada in Montreal and the pretended Bank of Upper Canada in Kingston, and these under circumstances which cast no reflection on the banking system as a whole; nor had Canada ever suffered a lack of convertibility, except during the specie crisis. In Lower Canada, particularly, the bank-note circulation had never approached the three-to-one ratio prescribed in the original Articles of Association of the Montreal Bank. If there was a possible criticism of that institution it was that it had too strictly insisted on the liquidity of security taken against commercial discounts. Had the American system been adopted, it is possible that Canadian economic development might have proceeded more rapidly than it did; on the other hand, depositors and shareholders alike would have paid in cyclical disasters. If Canadian banking was inordinately conservative, it was also unprecedentedly safe.

As the principal parliamentary opponent of Sydenham's proposal, Benjamin Holmes had to overcome formidable obstacles. In this, however, he had considerable support; opposed to Sydenham's measure were all the chartered banks to whom the forfeiture of note issue would have meant the loss of a major function of their branches, a reduction in lending capacity, and a serious curtailment of profits. A considerable body of opinion, remembering the Family Compact and the Bank of Upper Canada, feared the effects of placing

EARLY BANKING MENTOR

If John Richardson was the father of Canadian banking, then Benjamin Holmes was the tutor who guided it through its youthful years. A member of the staff of the Bank of Montreal from its inception, first as discount clerk and later as cashier, Holmes worked ceaselessly to improve its services.

He was responsible for countless innovations and refinements in the technical operations of the Bank and kept a watchful eye on its all-important specie reserves. Since he was never a man noted for compromise, as many a customer and subordinate discovered, it is probably true to say that the Bank's early success was in large part the result of Holmes's forceful management.

financial control in the hands of the executive branch of government. There also remained the extreme elements in the Assembly, both French and English, who were adamant in their resistance to any legislation proposed by Lord Sydenham and supported by the Unionist coalition.

Having submitted its first report on July 26, the committee again reported to the House on August 13 to approve a petition of the Bank of Upper Canada that it be permitted to maintain its head office at Toronto rather than at "the seat of government" as required by its act of incorporation. Five days later a third report, dealing with the Usury Laws, was submitted, and on August 27, a fourth and final report.

The fourth report represents the first comprehensive official document on banks and banking to appear in Canada since the establishment of the Montreal Bank almost a quarter century before. This silver anniversary tribute to Canadian banking is of such interest and importance as to require inclusion in its entirety, together with a most interesting letter to Her Majesty the Queen:

FINAL REPORT of Select Committee on Currency and Banking.

THE Select Committee on Currency and Banking,–with an instruction to consider the expediency of one general system of Banking for the Province,–and to which were referred the several Bank Petitions, have the honor to make their final Report, as follows:–

Having examined the several Petitions from the Chartered Banks of this Province, praying for an extension of their Capitals–Your Committee have determined to recommend to Your Honorable House, that the prayer of these Petitions, and all other applications for Bank Charters, be complied with under the following restrictions, most of which have been recommended in a Despatch from Her Majesty's Principal Secretary of State for the Colonies:–

1st.   The amount of Capital of the Company to be fixed; and the whole of such fixed amount to be subscribed for within a limited period, not exceeding eighteen months from the date of the Charter or Act of Incorporation.

2d.   The Bank not to commence business until the whole of the Capital is subscribed, and a moiety at least of the subscription paid up.

3d.   The amount of the Capital to be paid up within a given time from the date of the Charter or Act of Incorporation, – such period, unless under particular circumstances, not to exceed two years.

4th.   The debts and engagements of the Company on promissory notes or otherwise, not to exceed at any time thrice the amount of the paid up Capital, with the addition of the amount of such Deposits as may be made with the Company's Establishment by individuals, in Specie or Government Paper.

5th.   All promissory notes of the Company, whether issued from the principal Establishment, or from the Branch Banks, are to bear date at the place of issue, and to be payable on demand in Specie at the place of date.

6th.   Suspension of Specie payments on demand at any of the Company's Establishments for a given number of days (not in any case exceeding 60) within any one year, either consecutively or at intervals, to forfeit the Charter.

7th.   The Company shall not hold shares in its own stock, nor make advances on the security of their shares.

8th.   The Company shall not advance money on security of Lands or Houses, or Ships, or on pledge of Merchandise, nor hold lands or houses, except for the transaction of its business, nor own ships, or be engaged in trade, except as dealers in Bullion or Bills of Exchange; but shall confine its transactions to discounting commercial paper and negotiable securities, and other legitimate banking business.

9th.   The dividends to shareholders are to be made out of profits only, and not out of Capital of the Company.

10th. The Company to make up and publish, periodical statements of its assets and liabilities (half yearly or yearly) shewing, under the heads specified in the annexed form, the average of the amount of its notes in circulation, and other liabilities at the termination of each week or month, during the period to which the Statement refers, and the average amount of specie or other assets that were available to meet the same. Copies of these Statements are to be submitted to the Provincial Government, and the Company be prepared, if called upon, to verify such statements by the production, as confidential documents, of the weekly or monthly balance sheets from which the same are compiled. And also to be prepared, upon requisition from the Lords Commissioners of Her

Majesty's Treasury, to furnish in like manner, such further information respecting the state or proceedings of its Banking Establishments as their Lordships may see fit to call for.

11th. No By-law of the Company shall be repugnant to the conditions of the Charter or Act of Incorporation, or the Statutes of this Province.

12th. As the insertion in Charters or Acts of Incorporation, of provisions relating to the detailed management of the business of the Corporation has, in several instances, been found to render the documents complicated and unintelligible, and has been productive of great inconvenience, it is desirable that such insertion should be avoided, and that the provisions of such Charters or Acts should be confined, as far as practicable, to the special powers and privileges to be conferred on the Company, and the conditions to be observed by the Company, and to such general regulations relating to the nomination and powers of the Directors, the institution of by-laws, or other proceedings of the Company, as may be necessary with a view to the public convenience and security.

13th. No Company to be allowed to issue its promissory notes payable on demand, to an amount greater than its paid up capital.

Form of Return referred to in Regulation No. 10

Return of the average amount of Liabilities and Assets of the Bank of
. . . . during the period from [1st January,] to [30th June,] 184–.

Promissory Notes in circulation, not bearing interest, - - - - - £

Bills of Exchange in circulation, not bearing interest, - - - - - £

Bills and Notes in circulation, bearing interest, - - - - - - - - £

Balances due to other Banks, - - - - - - - - - - - - - - - - £

Cash deposits, not bearing interest, - - - - - - - - - - - - - £

Cash deposits, bearing interest,   - - - - - - - - - - - - - - £

Total average Liabilities, - - - - - - £

Coin and Bullion,   - £

Landed or other property of the Corporation, - - - - - - - - £

Government Securities,   - - - - - - - - - - - - - - - - - - £

Promissory Notes or Bills of other Banks, - - - - - - - - - - - - £

Balances due from other Banks, - - - - - - - - - - - - - - - - £

Notes and Bills discounted, or other debts due to the Corporation, not included under the foregoing heads, - - - - - - - - £

Total average Assets, - - - - - - - - £

Your Committee are strongly of opinion that some uniform system of Banking should be adopted in the Province, and they would therefore recommend, that Private or Joint Stock Companies at present issuing paper in this Province without the sanction of the Legislature, should be prohibited from doing so, after the close of the next Session of Parliament. But Your Committee would at the same time recommend, that all Banking Institutions, recognized by the Laws of either section of this Province should receive Charters upon the same conditions as those now recommended to Your Honorable House.

In the course of their inquiries into the subjects referred to their consideration by Your Honorable House, it has come to the knowledge of Your Committee that a Royal Charter has been granted to a Company established in London, under the name and style of "The Bank of British North America," for the purpose of carrying on the business of Banking in the North American Colonies, with a capital of £1,000,000 sterling, and power to increase the same to the amount of £2,000,000.

Your Committee feel it an imperative duty to call the attention of Your Honorable House to this circumstance, believing that the exercise of the Royal Prerogative in this matter is contrary to the spirit and meaning of the Constitutional Act, which secures to the Provincial Legislature the entire management of the internal affairs of this Province.

In the confident hope that Your Honorable House will concur with them in this opinion, Your Committee have prepared an Address to Her Majesty on the subject, which accompanies this Report. They also submit sundry tabular Statements procured from the various Banking Institutions.

All which is respectfully submitted.

F. HINCKS,
Chairman.

To the Queen's Most Excellent Majesty.

Most Gracious Sovereign,

We, Your Majesty's most dutiful and loyal subjects, the Legislative Assembly of Canada, in Provincial Parliament assembled, beg leave most humbly to bring under the notice of Your Majesty a subject of the gravest importance to Your Majesty's faithful subjects in this Province. During the course of the present Session of Parliament we have learned with deep concern, that Your Majesty has been advised to grant a Royal Charter to a Company in the City of London, associated together for Banking purposes in the British North American Colonies, under the name and style of "The Bank of British North America,"–which Charter, besides conferring other privileges, authorizes the said Company to issue Bank Notes within this Province.

It becomes our solemn and bounden duty, on behalf of the people of Canada, whose Representatives we are, to protest against such an interference with their constitutional rights.

We beg leave most humbly to represent to Your Majesty, that the Statute of the Imperial Parliament, by virtue of which we are now assembled, was intended to confer upon the people of Canada the power of managing their own local affairs; and we had ventured to hope, from the tenor of the recent Despatches from Your Majesty's Secretary of State for the Colonies to Your Majesty's Representative in this Province, that non-interference in those affairs would be the principle on which Your Majesty's Councils would thenceforth be governed, in reference to the affairs of this Colony.

We are unwilling to weaken the force of our present remonstrance by pointing out to Your Majesty the inconvenience to which the Provincial Legislature may be exposed, and the loss which may be suffered by the inhabitants of this Province, owing to the exercise of the Royal Prerogative in this instance.

We respectfully and humbly pray Your Majesty's favourable consideration to this Address, believing that the constitutional rights of the Provincial Legislature, to control and manage the internal affairs of the Province, is a principle, to the maintenance of which the people of this important Colony are irrevocably pledged.

We beg to renew our assurances of entire devotion to Your Majesty's Person and Government.

The Final Report of the Select Committee on Currency and Banking embodied the principles which have since governed Canadian banking legislation and it must therefore be regarded as historically significant. However, it did not mark any real break with the past. On the contrary, the Report is remarkable for two other reasons: – 1) its endorsation, with unimportant modifications only, of the Canadian banking system introduced by the Bank of Montreal, and 2) its decisive repudiation of British tutelage in provincial banking matters. Not only did the Report of the Select Committee patently ignore Sydenham's revenue-producing bank scheme; it also rebuked the Mother of Parliaments for its invasion of Canada's newly acquired provincial rights. The fact that the Report contained many of the restrictions recommended in Lord John Russell's Treasury Circular in no way detracts from the sovereign character of the Canadian document – so many of the restrictions were already embodied in the acts incorporating Canada's chartered banks that one is given to wonder whether the Lords of the Treasury had ever troubled to study those documents in detail.

The Final Report was submitted to the Assembly on August 27 and referred to a Committee of the Whole House "to meet on Friday next," which would have been September 3. Apparently there was a postponement, for the next *Journal* reference is dated September 10, when the Report was debated and several amendments suggested. Although it was not mentioned in the Report, Sydenham's proposed bank of issue had been discussed at length by the committee, and, according to Hincks's *Reminiscences of his Public Life*, resolutions in favour of the bank had gained acceptance by his casting vote as chairman. However, when the matter came before the House on August 31, it was moved to be resolved "that it is inexpedient to take into further consideration, during the present Session, the establishment of a Provincial Bank of Issue, or the Issue, in any other way, of a paper currency on the faith of the Province." Either Sydenham had seriously miscalculated his "weight of authority" in the Assembly, or Holmes's extramural tutoring of his colleagues had been more effective than the Governor's lectures, for the resolution was carried by the House, 40–29. Sydenham's cherished plan was dismissed by a combination of French Canadians, Tories, and ultra Reformers; Hincks and Moffatt voting in the negative. Holmes thus accomplished his second mission for the Bank of Montreal.

Charged, by the Colonial Office, with bringing about legislative union without responsible government and, by the Lords of the Treasury, with making fundamental changes in the currency and banking systems of the North American colonies, Sydenham succeeded adroitly in doing neither. When his untimely death occurred, at the age of forty-two, the day after United Canada's first parliament was prorogued, the foundations of responsible government had been laid, the dollar had won ascendancy over the pound, and the Canadian banking system remained essentially unaltered. Seventy years before, another British statesman, Charles Townshend, had helped to precipitate revolution by attempting to interfere with the internal economy of earlier British American colonies. Differing only in degree was the Treasury Board's disallowance of the Canadian currency bills and its proposed restrictions on the chartered banks. Had Sydenham been a lesser man, had he been endowed with the inelasticity of a Gosford, the stupidity of a Head, or the arrogance of a Durham, Canadian history would have taken a different course. Thanks to his gift of compromise, a potentially dangerous controversy was settled unobtrusively by the democratic process.

Once the House was satisfied with the report of the Committee on Currency and Banking it was able to turn to the petitions for charter renewals and capital increases which had been submitted some two months earlier by the Bank of Montreal, the Quebec Bank and the City Bank. For some reason a similar petition of the Commercial Bank of the Midland District secured precedence and when passed by the legislature set the pattern for charters subsequently granted. An interesting feature of the Act, apparently inserted to offset the defeat of Sydenham's revenue note-issue, was the imposition of a one-per-cent tax to be levied on bank-note circulation, computed on the basis of monthly revenues as reported on May 15 and November 15. Penalties for perjury and failure to submit returns were included. The Act remained in force until 1849 and during the seven-year period produced revenues of £85,074, an annual average of £12,153 and much less than Sydenham had predicted for his Bank of Issue.

The bill to renew the charter of the Bank of Montreal was read for the third time on September 13 and passed by the Assembly. With the Legislative Council concurring, it was "presented for Her Majesty's assent and reserved for the signification of Her Majesty's pleasure thereon." It received the royal assent on March 11, 1842, and was proclaimed by Sir Charles Bagot, Sydenham's successor, on April 27 of the same year. A supplementary act, passed at the same time, authorized banks previously chartered in Upper Canada or Lower Canada to carry on their business throughout the Province of Canada.

The principal differences from the original charter were provision for the double liability of shareholders; the redemption of notes at the place of issue; the restriction of note issue below £1 to one-fifth of the paid-up capital, and the total issue of notes not to exceed the amount of the capital stock paid in. Another innovation was a restriction on discounts granted to directors or officers, to one-third of total loans, and the submission of more detailed returns than had been hitherto required. Omitted for the first time in a Bank of Montreal charter was the objectionable "death without benefit of clergy" penalty for theft and counterfeiting, a seven-year penalty at hard labour being substituted. The original charter, granted in 1822, contained twenty-one clauses; that of 1838, twenty-two, and that of 1841, forty-three. However, with the exception of the items noted above, there were no material changes, nor was the character of the Bank's operations altered in any way: instead, the right to practise its proven techniques in the upper province, now called Canada West, was also granted. The total effect of the renewed charter, in fact, was to re-confirm and give official endorsement to the Canadian system of commercial banking, as based on the principles instituted by the Montreal Bank in 1817.

The pertinent entry in the Resolve Book of the Board of the Bank of Montreal was recorded under date of September 18, 1841, and reads as follows:

> The Cashier having returned from Kingston, submitted to the Board a copy of the Bank Charter, which was passed in the Assembly on Monday last, granting an increase of capital to the extent required, making in all £750,000 Stock, and an extension of time to 1st June, 1862.

Written in a flowing Spencerian hand, the Minute is boldly inscribed as if on a note of triumph.

APPENDICES

APPENDIX A

ARTICLES

OF

ASSOCIATION

OF THE

MONTREAL BANK

To all to whom these Presents shall come;

Be it known and made manifest, that we the Subscribers, have formed an Association or limited Copartnership, and do hereby agree with each other, to conduct Banking Business in the manner hereinafter specified and described, by and under the name or style of

THE MONTREAL BANK

And we do hereby mutually covenant, declare and agree, that the following are and shall be the fundamental Articles of this our Association and Agreement with each other, by which we, and all Persons who at any time hereafter may transact Business with the said Company, shall be bound and regulated.

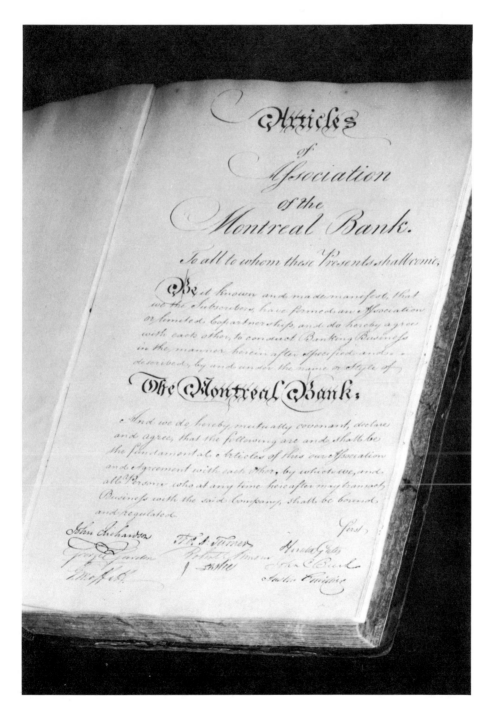

FIRST   The Capital Stock of the said Company shall not exceed Two Hundred and Fifty Thousand Pounds Current Money of this Province Divided into Five Thousand Shares of Fifty pounds each; and for the purpose of raising the said Capital Stock, a Book of Subscription shall be opened in this City after thirty days previous Notice in at least Four of the Provincial Newspapers, under the Superintendence of John Richardson, George Garden, George Moffatt, Thomas Andrew Turner, Robert Armour, James Leslie, Horatio Gates, John C. Bush, and Austin Cuvillier, or any three of them; and to continue open under their superintendence, until there shall have been an Election of Directors, as hereinafter provided, which Book shall be headed with the Present Articles of Copartnership or agreement, and shall continue open until the whole of the said Capital Stock shall have been subscribed. Every Person or Persons, Copartnership, Body Politic or Corporate, who may or shall become Members of this Association, may Subscribe for such and so many shares, as he, she, or they shall think fit, not however exceeding, in the first instance, twenty shares; and it is hereby agreed that the Shares respectively subscribed, shall be payable in Gold, or Silver Coin current in this Province, in the manner following, that is to say; Five per centum, as a deposit at the time of Subscribing; Ten per centum to the Directors, within ten days after they shall have been chosen in manner hereinafter provided; another payment not exceeding ten per centum, whenever they shall require it, at such time and place as they shall appoint for that purpose, giving thirty Days Previous Notice as aforesaid; and the remainder shall be payable in such instalments as a majority of the Directors shall agree upon; but no after instalment shall exceed Ten Per Centum upon the Capital Stock, for the payment of which, thirty Days notice, shall always be given.

SECOND   It is further mutually agreed upon, that whenever the Sum of Five Thousand Pounds shall have been actually deposited, or paid in on Account of the subscriptions to the said stock, notice thereof shall be given by the Persons under whose Superintendence the same shall have been received, in at least two of the Montreal Newspapers, and the said Persons shall at the same time, in like manner, notify the time and place of holding a meeting of the Subscribers, which shall be at the distance of not less than Thirty Days from the time of such notification for proceeding to the Election of the number of Directors hereinafter mentioned; and such Election shall then and there be made by a majority of shares voted for, in manner hereinafter prescribed in respect to the Annual Elections of Directors, and the Persons who shall then and there be chosen, shall be the first Directors, and shall be capable of serving until the expiration of the day fixed for making the Annual election: and the Directors so chosen, shall as soon thereafter, as circumstances can conveniently allow of, commence the Business and Operations of the said Bank, but no Bank Bills, or Bank Notes shall be issued, or put in circulation, nor any Bill or Note be discounted at the Bank until Twenty five thousand Pounds in Gold or Silver, shall be actually paid in, and received on Account of the Subscriptions to the said Capital Stock.

THIRD   For the good management of the Affairs of the said Association or Company, there shall be Thirteen Directors, who shall be Annually Elected by the Proprietors or holders of the said Capital Stock, at a General Meeting thereof to be Annually holden on the first Monday of June, at which Annual meeting the said Proprietors and Stockholders shall vote according to the Rule hereinafter Established, in respect to voting at General Meetings; And the Directors so Chosen by a Majority, in conformity to such Rule, shall be capable of serving as Directors for twelve months (unless any of them shall be removed for mal-administration before the expiration of that period by a General meeting of the Stockholders, or unless suspended, as hereinafter provided) and at their first meeting after such election, shall choose out of their number, a President and Vice-President, and their Places respectively, from time to time, fill up when Vacant by Death, resignation, absence from the Province or removal as abovesaid. In case of Death, resignation, absence from the Province for three months at a time, or the removal of a Director by the Stockholders, his place, in case of such removal, shall be filled up by the said Stockholders, and in the other cases, by the remaining Directors, or a majority of them, to serve, however, only until the succeeding General Meeting as abovesaid.

FOURTH   The Directors for the time being, shall have power to appoint such Officers, Clerks, and Servants under them, as shall be necessary for executing the Business of the said Company, and to allow them such compensation for their Services respectively, as shall be reasonable and proper; all which, together with the expenses of Building, House rent, and all other contingencies shall be defrayed out of the Funds of the said Company. The said Directors shall likewise be capable of exercising such other powers and authorities for the well regulating and ordering of the affairs of the said Company, as shall be prescribed by the Bye Laws and regulations thereof.

FIFTH   It is further covenanted and agreed upon by and between the parties to this agreement, that if the said Capital Stock of Two Hundred and fifty Thousand pounds is not Subscribed within three months after the said Book of Subscription shall have been opened, then and in such case it may be competent for any former Subscriber or Subscribers, to increase his, her, or their Subscriptions to forty shares; and if the aforesaid Capital Stock is not Subscribed within Four months after the said Book of Subscription shall have been opened, then, and in such case, the Deficiency may be Subscribed for by any Person or Persons, Body Politic or Corporate but they shall not be permitted respectively to hold more than

Fifty shares in the whole, unless the same be acquired by purchase after the said Bank shall have commenced its operation.

SIXTH   It is hereby expressly and explicitly declared to be the object and intention of the Persons who Associate themselves under the Style or Firm of THE MONTREAL BANK, that the joint stock or property of the said Company (exclusive of Dividends to be made in the manner hereinafter mentioned) shall alone be responsible for the Debts and engagements of the said Company. And that no person, who shall or may deal with this Company, or to whom they shall or may become in any wise indebted, shall on any pretence whatever, have recourse against the Separate Property of any present or future Member of this Company, or against their Persons, further than may be necessary to secure the faithful application of the Funds thereof, to the Purposes to which by these Presents they are liable. But all Persons accepting any Bond, Bill, Note, or other Contract of this Company, signed by the President, or Vice-President and countersigned or attested by the Cashier of the Company, for the time being, or dealing with it in any other manner whatsoever, thereby respectively give Credit to the said joint stock or Property of the said Company, and thereby respectively disavow having recourse, on any pretense whatever, to the Person or separate Property of any present or future Member of this Company, except as above mentioned. And all suits to be brought against this Company (if any shall be) shall be brought against the President for the time being: and in case of his Death or removal from Office, pending any suit against him, measures shall be taken at the Expense of the Company, for substituting his Successor in Office as a Defendant; so that Persons having demands upon the Company, may not be prejudiced or delayed by that event; or if the Person suing shall go on against the Person first named as Defendant (notwithstanding his Death or removal from Office) this Company shall take no advantage of such Proceeding on that account; and all recoveries had in manner aforesaid, shall be conclusive upon the Company, so far as to render the Company's said joint stock or property liable thereby, and no further; and the Company shall immediately pay the amount of such recovery out of their joint stock, but not otherwise. And in case of any Suit at Law, the President for the time being shall have full power in his own Name, and on behalf of the Company, to prosecute to Judgment and execution in the manner and form, as by the laws of this province it is provided; it being expressly understood and declared, that all Persons dealing with the said Company, agree to these terms, and are to be bound thereby.

SEVENTH   These Articles of Agreement shall be Published in at least one of the Newspapers Printed in the Cities of Quebec and Montreal for three months, and for the information of all Persons who may transact business with, or in any manner give Credit to this Company, every Bond, Bill, Note, or other Instrument or Contract, by the effect or terms of which the Company may be charged or held liable for the Payment of Money, shall especially declare, in such form as the Board of Directors shall prescribe, that payment shall be made out of the joint funds of this Company according to the present Articles of Association, and not otherwise; and a Copy of the Sixth Article of this Association, shall be inserted in the Bank Book of every Person depositing Money, or other valuable Property with the Company, for safe Custody, or a printed Copy shall be delivered to every such Person, before any such Deposit shall be received from him. And it is hereby expressly declared, that no Engagement can be legally made in the name of the said Company, unless it contain a limitation or restriction, to the effect above recited. And the Company hereby expressly disavow all responsibility, for any debt or Engagement which may be made in their Name, not containing a limitation or restriction to the effect aforesaid.

EIGHTH   The number of Votes to which each Stockholder or Stockholders, Co-partnership, Body Politic or Corporate, holding stock in the said Company, shall be entitled on every occasion when in conformity to the provisions and requirements of these articles, the votes thereof are to be given, shall be in the proportion following, that is to say; For one share, and not more than two, one Vote; for every two shares above two, and not exceeding Ten, one Vote, making five Votes for Ten Shares; for every four shares above Ten, and not exceeding thirty, one Vote, making Ten Votes for thirty shares; for every six shares above thirty, and not exceeding Sixty, one vote, making fifteen Votes for Sixty Shares; and for every eight shares above sixty, and not exceeding one Hundred, one vote, making twenty Votes for one Hundred. But no Person or Persons, Co-partnership, Body Politic or Corporate, shall be entitled to a greater number than twenty Votes, and all Stockholders resident within this Province, or elsewhere, may Vote by Proxy, if he, she, or they shall see fit, provided that such proxy be a Stockholder, and do produce a sufficient Authority from his constituent or constituents, for so representing and voting for him, her or them; provided also, that after the first election of Directors, no share or shares of the Capital Stock of the Company shall confer a right of Voting either in Person, or by Proxy, which shall not have been holden during Three Calendar Months at the least, prior to the Day of Election, or of the General Meeting, where the Votes of the Stockholders are to be given.

NINTH   None but a Stockholder, actually resident in the City of Montreal, and holding at least Ten Shares in the Capital Stock, and being a natural born Subject of His Majesty, or a Subject of His Majesty naturalized by Act of the British Parliament, or a Subject of His Majesty having become such by the conquest and cession of this Province, or any Person who shall have resided Seven years in the Province, and in any of the above cases, who shall have resided three years in this

City, one of which shall have immediately preceded the Day of Election, shall be capable of being Elected or chosen a Director of the said Bank, or shall serve as such.

TENTH   Nine of the Directors in Office shall be re-elected for the next succeeding twelve months, of which the President and Vice-President shall always be of the number.

ELEVENTH   No Director shall be entitled to any Salary or emolument, unless the same shall have been allowed to him by a General Meeting of the Stockholders; but the Stockholders may make such compensation to the President or Vice-President for their extraordinary attendance at the Bank, as shall appear to them to be reasonable and proper.

TWELFTH   Not less than Five Directors shall Constitute a Board, for the transaction of Business, whereof the President or Vice-President shall always be one, except in case of Sickness and necessary absence, in which case their places may be supplied by any other Director whom the President or Vice-President, so Sick or absent shall respectively by writing, under their hands appoint for that purpose. The President and Vice-President shall Vote at the Board as Directors, and in case of their being an equal number of Votes for and against any question before them, the President, and in his absence, the Vice-President, shall have a casting Voice.

THIRTEENTH   Any number of Stockholders, not less than fifty, who together shall be proprietors of Two Hundred and fifty shares, shall have power at any time, by themselves or their Proxies, to call a General Meeting of the Stockholders, for purposes relative to the said Association, giving at least six weeks Notice thereof, in at least one of the Newspapers published in this City, and specifying in such Notice the time and Place for such meeting with the object or objects thereof; and the Directors or any seven of them, shall have the like power at any time (upon observing the like formalities) to call a General meeting as abovesaid. And if the object for which any General meeting, called either by the Stockholders or Directors as abovesaid, shall be to consider of a proposal for the removal of the President, Vice-President, or other Director or Directors, for mal-administration, then and in such case, the Person or Persons so proposed to be removed, shall from the Day on which such Notice shall first be published, be suspended from the Execution of the Duties of his or their Office; and if he be the President, or Vice-President, his place shall be filled up by the remaining Directors, to serve during the time of such suspension.

FOURTEENTH   Every Cashier and Clerk of the Bank, before he enters upon the Duties of his Office, shall give bond, with two or more Sureties to the Satisfaction of the Directors; that is to say, every Cashier in a Sum not less than Five Thousand Pounds, with condition for his good and faithful behaviour; and every Clerk with like condition, and Sureties, in such Sum as the Directors shall consider adequate to the trust to be reposed in him.

FIFTEENTH   The Company shall not hold any Lands and Tenements, but such as may be necessary for the transaction and accommodation of the Business of the Bank, and for no other purpose: It shall nevertheless be competent for the Directors, on behalf of the Company, to take and hold Mortgages on property, by way of additional security for Debts contracted with the said Company in the course of its dealings; but on no account shall Money be lent upon mortgage, or upon Lands and other fixed property, nor such be purchased by the Company upon any pretext, except in the Special case above recited.

SIXTEENTH   The total amount of the Debts which the Company shall at any time owe, whether by Bond, Bill or Note, or other contract whatsoever, shall not exceed treble the amount of the Capital Stock actually paid in, (over and above a sum equal in amount to such money, as may be Deposited in the Bank for safe keeping) and [in] case of excess, the Directors, under whose administration it shall happen, shall be liable for the same, in their natural and Private Capacities, but it shall not exempt the Company or the Lands, tenements, Goods, or chattels thereof, from being also liable for such excess; such Directors, however, as shall have been absent when the said excess was contracted, or shall have entered their Protest against it, upon the Minutes of the Proceedings of the Board, may respectively exonerate and discharge themselves therefrom by pleading and Proving such absence, or showing such minutes.

SEVENTEENTH   The shares of the Capital Stock shall be Assignable and transferable according to such rules and forms, as may be established in that behalf, by the Board of Directors, but no Assignment or transfer shall be valid or effectual, unless such Assignment or transfer shall be entered or Registered in a Book or Books to be kept by the Directors for that purpose, nor until the Person or Persons making the same, shall previously discharge all Debts actually due by him, her, or them, to the said Company, which may exceed in amount the remaining Stock belonging to such Person or Persons; and in no case shall any fractional Part of a Share, or other than a Complete share or shares, be Assignable or transferable. And it is hereby further expressly agreed and declared, that any Stockholder, who shall transfer in manner aforesaid, all his Stock or Shares in this Company, to any other Person or Persons whatsoever, shall, *ipso facto*, cease to be a member of this Company, and that any Person or Persons whatever, who shall accept a transfer of any Stock or share in this Company, shall *ipso facto* become and be a member of this Company, according to these Articles of Association.

EIGHTEENTH   All Bills, Bonds, Notes and every contract and Engagement, on behalf of the Company, shall be signed by the President or Vice-President; and countersigned or attested by the Cashier of the Company; and the funds of the Company shall in no case be held responsible for any contract or Engagement whatever, unless the same shall be so signed and countersigned or attested as aforesaid.

NINETEENTH   The Books, Papers, correspondence, and funds of the Company, shall at all times be subject to the inspection of the Directors, but no Stockholder nor Director shall inspect the account of any Individual or Individuals, with the Company.

TWENTIETH   Half yearly Dividends shall be made of so much of the profits of the Company, as shall appear to the Directors advisable, and shall be payable at such place or places as the Directors shall appoint, of which they shall give Public Notice in at least two Newspapers Published in this City, at least thirty Days before; and the Directors shall every year, at the General Meeting, for election thereof, lay before the Stockholders, for their Information, an exact and particular Statement of the amount of the Debts due to, and by the Company, specifying the amount of Bank Notes then in circulation, and the amount of such Debts as in their opinion are bad, or doubtful; as also stating the surplus or Profit, if any remaining, after Deduction of losses and provisions for dividends, provided that the rendering of such statements shall not extend to give any right to the Stockholders nor Directors, to inspect the account of any Individual or Individuals with the Company.

TWENTY-FIRST   If there shall be a failure in payment of any part of the Sum or Shares subscribed by any Person or Persons, Co-partnership, Body Politic or Corporate, the party failing in paying the first instalment of ten per centum, succeeding the deposit of Five percentum hereinbefore required to be made at the time of Subscribing, shall respectively forfeit the said deposit to and for the use of the said Company, and the stock shall be sold at public sale, for the behoof of the Company, and on failure of paying the other instalments, or any of them, the party or parties failing therein, shall forfeit the original deposit of five per centum, and the dividend unpaid prior to the time for making such payment, and during the delay of the same.

TWENTY-SECOND   The said Company shall not directly or indirectly deal in anything, excepting Bills of Exchange, Gold or Silver Bullion, or in the Sale of Goods really and truly pledged for money lent, and not redeemed in due time, or in the Sale of Stock pledged for money lent, and not so redeemed, which said Goods and Stock so pledged, and not so redeemed, shall be sold by the said Company at Public

Sale, at any time not less than ten Days after the period for redemption; and if upon such Sale of Goods or Stock there shall be a surplus, after deducting the Expenses of Sale, over the payment of the money lent, such surplus shall be paid to the Proprietors thereof respectively.

TWENTY-THIRD   The Board of Directors are hereby fully empowered to make such other bye laws and regulations for the Government of the Affairs of the Company, and that of their Officers and Servants, as they, or a majority of them shall from time to time think expedient, not inconsistent with Laws, or these Articles of Association.

TWENTY-FOURTH   This Association shall continue until the first of January one Thousand eight Hundred and thirty-eight, and no longer; but the Proprietors of two thirds of the Capital Stock of the Company, may by their concurring Votes, at a General meeting to be called for that express purpose, revise or alter these Articles, or any of them, or dissolve the Company at any prior period provided that Notice of such meeting, and its object, shall be Published in all the Provincial Newspapers for six months previous to the time appointed for such meeting; and provided also, that no revision or alteration of these Articles shall subject any Stockholder or Stockholders to be bound beyond the amount of his, her or their Stock.

TWENTY-FIFTH   Immediately on any dissolution of this Association, effectual measures shall be taken by the Directors then existing for closing all the concerns of the Company, and for dividing the Capital and Profits which may remain among the Stockholders, in proportion to their respective interests.

IN WITNESS whereof we have Subscribed our names and firms to these Articles of Association of the Montreal Bank written upon this and the eighteen preceding pages, each page whereof is subscribed by John Richardson, George Garden, George Moffatt, Thomas Andrew Turner, Robert Armour, James Leslie, Horatio Gates, John C. Bush and Austin Cuvillier, which Subscription was opened on this twenty third day of June in the year of our Lord One Thousand Eight Hundred and Seventeen, and continued from Day to Day and subscribed at the Dates to which the Signatures have reference.

(*Signed*)

JOHN RICHARDSON	THOS. A. TURNER	
GEORGE GARDEN	ROBERT ARMOUR	
G. MOFFATT	J. LESLIE	JOHN C. BUSH
	HORATIO GATES	AUSTIN CUVILLIER

APPENDIX B

FIRST
BY-LAWS
OF THE
MONTREAL BANK

RULES *and* REGULATIONS *adopted by the President and Directors of the Montreal Bank for their Government and for prescribing the respective duties of the President, Cashier and Subordinate Officers of the Bank.*

FIRST   The Bank shall be opened and kept open for the transacting of business from Nine O'clock in the morning until Three O'clock in the afternoon from the first of May until the first November, and from the first November until the first of May, from Ten O'clock in the morning until Three O'clock in the afternoon, every day in the year, except on Sundays, the first of January, Epiphany, Annunciation, Ascension, Good Friday, His Majesty's Birthday, Corpus Christi or Fête Dieu, Saint Pierre and Saint Paul, Assumption, All Saints, Conception and Christmas Day, which days shall be considered as Holy Days, on which no business shall be transacted at the Bank, and the Cashier shall affix in some conspicuous place in the Bank a notice to that effect.

414

SECOND   There shall be a Common Seal to be provided by the
Board of Directors, and deposited in the Bank under the
control of the President. It shall be his duty pursuant to
the votes of the Board of Directors, to affix the same to
all conveyances, or other instruments where it may be
necessary, which shall be executed by him in his official
capacity on behalf of the Association.

THIRD   In all cases when a member of this Association may vote
by proxy, or when any transfer is made, or dividend
received, or other Act done by Attorney, such proxy shall
be held to produce his original authority or Letter of
Attorney, and deposit the same with the Cashier.

FOURTH   The Stock of every member of this Association shall be
considered to be pledged to the Company for any and all
monies, which such members may at any time owe the
Bank, and the Board of Directors may if they see cause,
refuse to make any transfer or pay any Dividend upon
such stock until such debt is fully discharged.

FIFTH   The Bank may take charge of the Cash of all such persons
as shall choose to place the same free of expense and
shall keep it subject to the order of the depositor, payable
at sight, and may also receive deposits of Ingots of Gold,
Bars of Silver, wrought plate, or other valuable articles of
small bulk, for safe keeping at the risk of the depositor.

SIXTH   The President or Vice-President shall preside at the meeting of the Board of Directors, and in their absence, or in
the absence of the person by them appointed to fill their
respective places, agreeable to the twelfth rule of the
Articles of Association, the Board shall choose a President
pro: tem:

SEVENTH   The duty of the Directors shall be divided into weekly
committees, viz: the President or Vice-President, whose
duty it will be to attend daily with one director, who
shall be styled the Director of the Week, and during the
recess of the Board shall manage such concerns of the
Bank as do not require the advice and interference of the

full Board, or a greater number of Directors: but in all cases notes which may have been acted upon by the Board shall not be altered by them. When a note may have been wholly omitted by accident, the weekly committee shall be authorized to give such directions concerning such note as they may think advisable. It shall be the duty of the Directors for the Week to report to the Board at their next meeting, all doings at the Bank in their Official Capacity.

EIGHTH   The days of discount shall be Tuesday and Friday of each week and the Directors shall assemble on those days at Ten O'clock precisely for the purpose of discounting, except if any of the Holy Days observed by the Bank should fall on those days, when the Directors shall meet on the succeeding day.

NINTH   A majority of votes shall determine all questions, except in cases of discount, when two of the Board voting in the negative, shall be sufficient to check the passing of a note, and all decisions shall be by Ballot.

TENTH   All Bills and Notes offered for discount shall be delivered in the Bank on Monday and Thursday in each week and laid before the Board of Directors by the Cashier on the succeeding Tuesday and Friday, at Ten O'clock together with a statement of the funds and situation of the Bank, on which days the discounts shall be settled, and such as are admitted shall be paid or placed to the Credit of the Applicant, on the day on which they are discounted, and may be drawn for at any time after One O'clock, and the Notes or Bills not discounted shall be returned at any time after One O'clock on the same day.

ELEVENTH   Discounts shall not be made for a longer time than sixty days, and the usual grace, unless by an unanimous vote of the Directors present at a meeting of the Board, and no discount shall be made, without two responsible names, but if property as shall be approved by the Board be deposited and pledged to an amount sufficient to secure the payment, with all damages, then one responsible name may be taken.

TWELFTH Notes of hand, Bills of Acceptance and all other negotiable Notes and Bills may be discounted without the endorsement of the applicant by an unanimous vote of the Directors present, and no renewal of the note shall be made without at least ten p. cent of the amount be paid, except by the unanimous vote of the Directors present.

THIRTEENTH The firm of a house in trade is not to be taken at the Bank, unless they shall in writing make known at the Bank the names of the Partners composing the same and the firm of a house to be considered as one name only.

FOURTEENTH Every person who opens an account and transacts business with this Bank, besides subscribing to the sixth clause of the fundamental Articles of this Association, as is therein provided, shall also subscribe his name in a Book to be kept for that purpose, to be called *the Book of Signatures*, and all persons who compose any house, keeping an account with this Bank, shall subscribe their names, and the signature of the firm in this Book, if residing in Montreal.

FIFTEENTH No credit shall be given on any pretense whatever to any person who may be at the time a Delinquent Debtor at the Bank, whether the delinquency be on paper discounted or left for collection, as promisor or endorser, and in order that the Board may be enabled to carry this regulation into exact operation, it shall be the duty of the Cashier to lay before the Board at each meeting for discount, the names of all delinquent debtors, designating those on discount and those on collection notes.

SIXTEENTH Discounts may be made on notes payable to the President and Directors of the Bank on such personal pledges, and other securities as the Board of Directors may deem expedient, consistently with the eleventh Article.

SEVENTEENTH All transfers for collateral security shall be made to the President and Directors of the Montreal Bank, and the President is hereby authorized to transfer such security on payment of the debt for which it is pledged.

EIGHTEENTH   Whenever a discounted note shall have remained delinquent it shall be the duty of the Cashier to enclose the
same to the solicitor of the Bank to be put in suit unless
otherwise ordered by the President or Vice-President and
Directors of the Week.

NINETEENTH   Persons leaving notes for collection shall be required to
have a memorandum of them at the same time and in
case of non-payment, or protest, the person lodging the
same shall pay the charges, before the notes are returned.
The Cashier shall put up a notice of this regulation in
some conspicuous place in the Bank.

TWENTIETH   A notice of the following tenor signed by the Cashier
shall be affixed in some conspicuous place in the Bank.

NOTICE

Whereas Notes and Bills may be left at the Bank for collection, it may sometimes happen that omissions in notifying the parties or other informalities or mistakes
respecting such Notes or Bills may take place, whereby
damage may accrue to the proprietors of them, or other
parties concerned, public notice is therefore hereby given,
that the Directors of this Institution, consider such Notes
and Bills as left wholly at the risk of the persons leaving
the same, and that the Bank will be responsible only for
monies actually received in payment thereof, but not for
any omissions, informalities, or mistakes whatever.

By Order of the Directors

(*Signed*) R. Griffin
Cashier.

TWENTY-FIRST   Notes and Bills left for collection must be lodged at the
Bank three days at least before they become due and none
under twenty-five pounds will be received.

TWENTY-SECOND   No individual or Co-partnership shall be responsible as
promisor or first endorser, or both to an amount exceeding Ten Thousand Pounds Currency, unless the surplus
be discounted on Collateral Security.

TWENTY-THIRD   No Director without special authority from the Board shall be permitted to inspect the Cash account of any person with this Bank.

TWENTY-FOURTH   It shall be the duty of the President and in his absence the Vice-President, to sign the Bills and Post Notes of the Bank, and to deliver them when signed to the Cashier, who shall give Duplicate Receipts therefor, one of which receipts to be taken in a Book especially to be kept by the President or Vice-President for that purpose, the other Receipt to be lodged with the Accountant for the time being. who on leaving his office in the Bank shall deliver said Receipts to his Successor unless otherwise directed by the Board of Directors.

TWENTY-FIFTH   It shall be the duty of the President or in his absence, the duty of the Vice-President, to inspect the vaults and other apartments of the Bank, once a week in company with the Director of the Week, to take an exact account of the Bank Bills, Post Notes, and money on hand, at least once in two months, or as much oftener, and at such times as the President or Vice-President may think proper to appoint, and the report of the President or Vice-President and of the said Director shall be recorded on the Books of the Bank and signed by them – to report fully and promptly to the Directors any circumstance affecting the interest of the Bank, which may come to his knowl-edge or which may be communicated to him by the Offi-cers of the Bank or any other persons: to examine Bonds given by the Officers of the Bank, to retain in his pos-session that given by the Cashier, and to deliver over the others to him for safe keeping – to cause a special meeting of the Directors whenever the circumstances of the Bank may in his opinion require it, and when this is the case to see that notice in writing be sent to each Director and more particularly it shall be his duty to cause the Books and Accounts of the Bank to be kept in a plain, regular and methodical manner.

TWENTY-SIXTH   It shall be the duty of the Cashier to cause the Officers, Clerks and Servants of the Bank, to attend to, and execute their respective duties, in conformity to such rules and regulations as may be prescribed by the Board of Directors; to take the general superintendence of the concerns of the Bank, and in case of actual delinquency, negligence or improper conduct, or in case of suspicion thereof of any person employed therein, to make an immediate and full confession, to the President, or Vice-President, of the knowledge he may possess or of the suspicions he may entertain respecting such persons; to present to the Directors at every meeting an exhibit of the state of the Bank, to Countersign at the Bank all Bills or Notes signed or to be signed by the President or Vice-President, or by order of the Board, to see that the Books and Accounts are kept in an orderly and methodical manner, under the direction of the President or Vice-President and never to suffer them to be behind the business of the day, to the end that whenever a clear and perfect exhibit of the state of the Bank shall be required, it may be speedily procured: daily to examine the Settlement of the Cash Accounts of the Bank, and whenever the actual amount disagrees with the Balance thereof, report the same to the President and Directors without delay. The Cashier shall have charge of all the Bills, Notes, Obligations, Money, Deposits and pledges; at the close of business of each day, he shall have the whole thereof in his possession and see that the same are safely deposited in the vaults of the Bank, one of the keys of which shall always remain in his possession. It shall be the duty of the Cashier, with the approbation of the President or Vice-President, to procure the necessary Books, Scales, Weights and Stationery for the use of the Bank. It shall also be the duty of the Cashier to record the votes and proceedings of the Board of Directors, promptly to furnish a Copy of all resolutions of the Board, to any of the Directors who may apply therefor, and whenever a committee is appointed, it shall be his duty to give notice in writing to the Chairman of the appointment, and its object if requested.

TWENTY-SEVENTH It shall be the duty of the first Teller to make all payments from the Bank, and to receive payments for Notes and Bills when due; he shall account daily, or oftener if required with the Cashier for all sums he may receive and in case of deficiency, he shall be responsible for the amount thereof. All checks on this Bank received by the Teller shall be delivered on the day of their receipt to the Accountant or Bookkeeper, to be by him entered, and if the Teller shall pay any checks drawn on this Bank, the person drawing the same not having the Amount thereof to his Credit in the Bank, he shall be charged with the Amount overdrawn, provided the same was without application to the Bookkeeper, but if the Bookkeeper shall have declared the check to be good, he shall be responsible for the sum overdrawn.

TWENTY-EIGHTH   It shall be the duty of the Second Teller to receive all Money, Bills, or checks brought to the Bank to be deposited and to enter the same to the Credit of the person depositing, or to the Credit of such person as the Depositor shall direct; also to receive payment of all Notes left for collection, and all Notes and Bills discounted, when the proprietors of the same shall request the Amount thereof to be passed to their Credit in the Bank. The Second Teller shall be held to account with the Cashier daily, or oftener if required for all his receipts or he shall account with the First Teller if directed to do so by the Cashier.

TWENTY-NINTH   The Bookkeepers shall keep the Accounts of the Bank in a conspicuous and methodical manner, they shall furnish statements from the Books whenever required so to do by the President, Directors or Cashier, they shall keep the Books regularly balanced and the Ledger in use shall always exhibit all the Accounts of the Bank. The Second Bookkeeper shall render all the assistance in his power to the First Bookkeeper, and in his absence shall take his place, together it shall be their duty to complete monthly to the end of each preceding month all the entries in the Check Book of the Depositors as speedily as possible; the First Bookkeeper shall make all entries from the Cash Book to the Ledger, and the same shall be entered before the preceding day. The Second Bookkeeper shall enter into the Cash Book the Receipts and Payments of the Tellers, the latter in alphabetical order, keeping the several payments to each person, as much as possible together, the amounts of each day to be entered and examined and to agree with those of the Tellers, before either of these leave the Bank. The Bookkeepers shall collect and assort the Checks each day and shall stamp a hole therein, and write on the cover, the day on which they were received, and at the end of the month, deliver the said checks, (after entering the same on the Check Books of the Depositors) to the respective persons by whom they were drawn. The Bookkeepers shall at all times, when checks are presented to them by any of the Tellers, declare whether the amount mentioned in the said checks is actually at the Credit of the Drawer, and if the Bookkeeper shall declare the Check to be good, and the person not having the amount thereof at his Credit at the Bank he shall be responsible for the sum overdrawn. In case of sickness, or other necessary absence of the Cashier, his duty shall devolve on the First Bookkeeper.

THIRTIETH   It shall be the duty of the Discount Clerk, to enter in a Blotter, all notes of hand, or Bills of Exchange offered for Discount, he shall cash the discount, shall record the same in a Record Book, and shall note on the back of the presentation or cover, the day of its being offered for discount, the number of the note, the date thereof, the number of the days it may have to run before it arrives to maturity, the amount thereof, by whom it is drawn, and endorsed, and by whom presented for discount. He shall keep an Account of all Notes, Bills and obligations paid at the Bank; he shall also keep a check book, on which shall be stated each discount, and as payments thereof are made, the same shall be by him entered in said Book, and when required by the Cashier, he shall exhibit the said accounts twice in each week, balanced, or demonstrate to him why they do not balance, he shall keep an account of all Bills, Notes, and obligations, which may be called for to be paid, and deliver the same to the Teller, and at the close of the business of each day shall compare his account of notes, etc. delivered, with the Teller's Account and receipts therefor, and if the same do not agree he shall immediately report the difference to the Cashier; he shall keep a Book in which shall be stated the amount due on every discount day from each individual to the Bank, either as promisor or endorser. It shall also be the duty of the Discount Clerk with the assistance of the Messenger to enter in a Book as soon as convenient after the same shall have been lodged at the Bank, all notes of hand, Bills of Exchange and obligations left for collection, with the times they may fall due.

THIRTY-FIRST   It shall be the duty of the Messenger to make out and deliver notifications to the several parties, on all notes of hand, Bills of Exchange, Bonds and obligations, as the same become due at the Bank. He shall also make collection of money when directed thereto. He shall be accountable for whatever may be entrusted to his charge and for all sums of money collected by him. He shall also be responsible to the Bank or to the parties concerned, as the case may be, for all losses arising from his negligence, errors or omissions in performing the duties assigned to him. He shall every day make out a list of the notes, Bonds and obligations that may be due on the succeeding day, which list he shall take with him when he delivers the notifications, and minute thereon, to whom and at what places the notifications were delivered, whether at the dwelling house of the parties, at their usual places of Business, at any place assigned by them for having their notifications left, or to the parties personally, and on his return to the Bank he shall sign the said list and deliver it to the Cashier who shall examine and regularly file the same. It shall likewise be the duty of the Messenger under the direction of the Discount Clerk, to take charge of the Notes and other Obligations left for Collection, to enter and file the same, to minute on the back or cover thereof, the names of the parties, the time when the same will fall due, and the interest due thereon.

THIRTY-SECOND   It shall be the duty of the Porter to keep the Bank house and appurtenances clean and in good order. He shall remain constantly at the Bank, while it may be open, either for Public or Private Business and shall not leave the same during the hours for Business but by permission of the Cashier. He shall make the fires and he shall light the lamps at the times he may be directed and before closing the Bank at night he shall examine every part of the building and appurtenances, and when the Bank is shut, he shall carry the Keys to the President or Vice-President and have the same again at the Bank timely in the morning if required.

THIRTY-THIRD   The Solicitor of the Bank shall have the Preference of the Law Business of the Bank, but he shall not receive any pay for such business, other than the usual Fees for the services he may render.

THIRTY-FOURTH   The writing up of the Depositors' Books, may be divided among the several officers of the Bank under such regulations as the Cashier may direct.

THIRTY-FIFTH   The present assignment of duties to the several officers of the Bank, shall not exclude the right of the Board to alter and increase the same at any time, as the interest of the Bank may in their opinion at any time require, and the respective officers thereof accept of their offices subject to this regulation. The Cashier and other officers of the Bank, shall be entitled to receive their Salaries, in quarterly payments, or oftener if they require it, for which they will receive an order from the Board.

THIRTY-SIXTH   In case of the absence of either of the respective officers from the Bank, in consequence of sickness or other unavoidable cause, it is their duty forthwith to acquaint the Cashier thereof, in order that arrangements may be made to supply their places, until they can again enter upon their respective offices.

THIRTY-SEVENTH   No officer or other person connected with the Bank shall directly or indirectly, in any way or manner whatever take or receive any perquisite, reward, or fee or emolument for any services done therein, other than the Salary allowed by the Bank, and it shall be the particular duty of the Cashier to see that this regulation is at all times carried into full effect, and to report any violation thereof to the Directors, as soon as he may obtain knowledge thereof.

THIRTY-EIGHTH   The President, Vice-President, Cashier and other officers of the Bank shall subscribe an Oath or affirmation to the following effect.

I, ... do swear (or affirm) that I will to the best of my knowledge and abilities perform the duties assigned to, and the trust reposed in me as .... of the Montreal Bank and keep secret the business thereof.

THIRTY-NINTH   The President, Vice-President, Directors and Cashier shall on or before the third day of November next make Solemn Oath, that they and each of them, will faithfully and strictly preserve inviolable secrecy of all the transactions of the Board of Directors at their meetings, either on special or general business, unless called upon to disclose the same in due course of Law, or to render an account of their proceedings to the Stockholders, or when the same may be otherwise necessary.

FORTIETH   The Stock of this Association shall be transferable at the Bank only by such Stockholder, or his legal representative in case of his death, or by his Attorney especially authorized for that purpose, and thereupon such Stockholder shall surrender and deliver up his Certificate, or receipt and execute a transfer in such form as the Directors shall prescribe and the President, Vice-President and Cashier shall thereupon issue a new Certificate to the person to whom the same is transferred, and in case such transfer shall not include the whole number of Shares specified in such Certificate or receipt, the original holders shall be entitled to a new Certificate for the number of Shares not so included and all persons holding such Certificates shall be entitled to an equal Dividend in proportion to their shares of the Profits of the Capital Stock, as well as all other privileges and immunities as Member and Stockholder in the Banking Company.

FORTY-FIRST   The Books and Accounts of the Bank shall be regularly Balanced on the third Mondays in the months of May and November in each year, at which time the half yearly dividend shall be declared and published as is directed by the fundamental Articles of the Association. The Books of transfers shall be shut for twenty days immediately preceding each of the days appointed for Balancing the Books of the Bank and declaring the half yearly dividend, and the Stockholders who shall stand in the Books of the Bank at the time the transfer shall be so suspended shall be entitled to receive such dividends of Profits then to be declared and paid and the same shall be paid to them or their Attorneys respectively.

FORTY-SECOND   The Board of Directors for the time being shall be a Committee to consider whether any, and if any, what alterations or amendments to the fundamental Articles of this Association, it is expedient for the Stockholders to adopt and to report thereon from time to time, at any meeting of the Stockholders.

(*Signed*)

	JOHN GRAY
GEORGE PLATT	THOS. A. TURNER
FREDK. W. ERMATINGER	GEORGE GARDEN
	HORATIO GATES
	G. MOFFATT
	J. LESLIE
	HIRAM NICHOLS
	JOHN MC TAVISH
	AUSTIN CUVILLIER
	ZABDIEL THAYER
	JOHN FORSYTH

APPENDIX C

BANK OF MONTREAL
PRESIDENTS
IN THE PERIOD COVERED
BY THIS VOLUME

The colonists who came together in 1817 to form Canada's first banking organization were largely the merchant-traders who built the commercial enterprises of Lower Canada. Typical of this pioneering group were the men who served as presidents of the Bank during its formative years.

First to hold this post was John Gray, an Englishman of whom little is known. He was a retired North West trader and lived at St. Catherines, "behind the mountain," on which he is reputed to have owned extensive property. No record of Gray's activities with the North West Company is available, but Civil Status Lists in the Old Court House of Montreal reveal that he married Mary Pullman on March 19, 1806, at which time he gave his age as "about forty years." He had two brothers in Montreal: Jonathan, who was the foremost notary of the city until his death in 1812, and Edward William, who was at one time Sheriff of Montreal.

JOHN GRAY

SAMUEL GERRARD

JOHN MOLSON

Succeeding John Gray in 1820 was Samuel Gerrard, who came to Canada from Ireland in 1787 at the age of twenty. Working his way up in Montreal's export-import business, he became a partner in Parker, Gerrard & Ogilvy, one of the firms engaged in the financing of the XY Company from 1797 to 1804; later, about 1811, Gerrard became a member of a new firm, Gerrard, Gillespie & Co., which took over the North West Company business of the former partnership. Never actually engaging directly in the fur trade, Gerrard found time to extend his services to several of Montreal's religious, educational and social organizations, and was also a Justice of the Peace.

Gerrard, who served as president of the Bank until 1826, died in Montreal on March 24, 1857, at the age of ninety.

The Bank's third President was John Molson, who served from 1826 to 1830. Probably the greatest entrepreneur of his time in Canada, John Molson came to Montreal from Lincolnshire, England, in 1782, at the age of eighteen. Four years later he established a brewery, which still flourishes under the direction of his descendants.

Up to the time of his coming to Canada, no barley was grown here. To get this vital ingredient for his brewing operation, Molson imported seed barley from England and gave it to the local farmers for nothing, with the promise that he would buy, at a certain price, all the barley they could raise and deliver to his works.

Molson's interests went far beyond brewing, however. He built the *Accommodation*, Canada's first steamboat. Robert Fulton's famous steamer the *Clermont* began operation on the Hudson in 1807; two years later the Molson vessel was launched on the St. Lawrence.

HORATIO GATES

PETER MCGILL

Under a special arrangement with the government, which gave him the exclusive right and privilege of constructing and navigating steamships within the province, Molson soon had several vessels plying between Montreal and Quebec.

Greatly interested in public causes, Molson was, with a number of others connected with the Bank, a member of the committee of citizens to superintend the erection of the Montreal General Hospital in 1821. He was a warden of the House of Industry, vice-president of the Montreal Fire Insurance Company in 1820, and a director of the Montreal Savings Bank.

Molson won a seat in the Legislative Assembly in 1816 and became a member of the Legislative Council in 1832.

In 1830, John Fleming* succeeded John Molson as president of the Bank and held the post for two years. Born in Aberdeenshire, Scotland, in 1786, he came to Canada at the age of seventeen and joined the mercantile firm of Hart, Logan & Co., of which he became the head in due time.

Fleming was a literary man of some distinction. He wrote a good deal and gathered one of the finest private libraries in the province. It consisted of some 11,000 volumes. His publications included *The Political Annals of Lower Canada, being a Review of the Political and Legislative History of that Province.*

To replace John Fleming, who died of cholera in 1832 at the age of forty-six, the directors chose Horatio Gates, who was, after John Richardson, perhaps the most important member of the group who founded the Bank. Without his highly successful efforts to obtain American investment capital, the new bank might never have got off the ground.

Born at Barre, Massachusetts, in 1777, the son of Captain Benjamin Gates who had served in the Army of the Continental Congress, Horatio Gates came to

* *No portrait available.*

Montreal early in his career and set up a mercantile firm that became one of the largest in the colonies.

Although Gates had active commercial interests on both sides of the border during the War of 1812, and was the subject of criticism on this account, he was, nevertheless, allowed to remain unmolested by the colonial authorities because of his valuable contribution to the common good, and he became a Canadian citizen in 1814. Some years later he was appointed a member of the Legislative Council of Lower Canada.

Like Fleming, Gates was a relatively young man when he died in 1834. He was succeeded by the great Peter McGill, who held the post of President longer than any that preceded or followed him. His term extended no less than twenty-six years, during which time he became recognized as one of the province's most worthy citizens.

Emigrating in 1809 from his native Scotland at the age of twenty, he engaged in business in Montreal, eventually forming his own company. In 1819 he became a director of the Bank. The son of John McCutcheon, he legally assumed the name of McGill in 1821 at the request of his uncle, the Honourable John McGill, whose estate he inherited in 1835.

McGill's interests were widespread. Beyond the management of his own firm and his duties as President of the Bank, he was concerned with the organization of Canada's first railway, the operation of the Lachine Canal and the development of one of the first steamboat companies in Canada.

In the same year as he became President of the Bank, McGill was made Chairman of the Champlain and St. Lawrence Railroad Company, which in 1836 began running from La Prairie to St. Johns on the Richelieu River, a distance of fourteen miles.

Aside from his interest in the Lachine Canal, McGill took a leading part in the development of steamboat transportation on the Ottawa River and Rideau Canal, through the organization in 1832 of the Ottawa Steamboat Company, of which he was President.

His community interests were no less varied. These included participation in government; he was appointed to the Legislative Council of Canada in 1841, and six years later he became Speaker of the Council, with a seat in the Executive Council.

Shortly after retiring from the Presidency of the Bank owing to ill health, the Honourable Peter McGill "passed away 28th September, 1860, full of years and honours at the age of seventy-one."

APPENDIX D

THE PHYN-ELLICE STORY

While seemingly extraneous to the history of the Bank of Montreal, the little-known dynasty or commercial complex of Phyns and Ellices and their numerous relations, associates, and affiliates were indubitably responsible for the founding of the institution; furthermore, and of more general historical interest, this complex played a greater role in the development of Canada's early commercial economy than has been accorded recognition. Hitherto, it has been generally accepted that the commercial beginnings that followed the British occupation in 1760 were undertaken by the somewhat heterogeneous and largely anonymous group of sutlers who accompanied Amherst's army to Montreal. Together with the two or three politically entrenched naval victualling firms who followed Wolfe up the St. Lawrence to Quebec, the same group has invariably been credited with the reorganization of the French fur trade and its remarkable extension into the valleys of the Mississippi and Missouri. The Phyn-Ellice record, first brought to light by R. H. Fleming in his monograph "Phyn, Ellice and Company of Schenectady,"

431

throws an entirely new light on the obscure origins of Canadian commercial enterprise. Far from being simply an outgrowth of haphazard though highly romantic and adventurous endeavour, Canadian commercial development can be traced back to a tightly organized and well financed effort made in response to North American influences rather than to localized colonial opportunity. It is to amplify the remote beginnings of both the Bank of Montreal and its causative environment that the following story has been included in these pages.

The Phyn-Ellice partnership was typical of most trading firms of its day in being primarily a family concern. It is probable that neither of the founding families had their roots in Scotland, but they were to be found in Aberdeenshire and Inverness-shire about the middle of the eighteenth century. By that time George Phyn and his friend William Ellice had both married into the Simpson family, George taking Janet as his wife and William taking Mary. The two couples had eleven children, of whom Alexander Ellice was to marry Anne Phyn, and George Phyn Jr. was to marry Catharine Ellice, thereby creating a further double tie both in the bloodline and in the business.

Although both families had substantial land holdings in Scotland, George Phyn and William Ellice began to look around for a fresh outlet for their capital and energy. Thus we find the first herald of the Phyn-Ellice commercial dynasty, John Duncan, arriving in America sometime in the early 1750's, apprenticed by George Phyn to a New York mercantile house. By 1760 he was associated with Captain Walter Rutherford, a New York merchant, and Rutherford's noted brother-in-law Peter Van Brugh Livingston, in a trading venture at Schenectady. No doubt Duncan was attracted to the place both by the many advantages it would offer as soon as the war then in progress was concluded and because of a desire to avoid conflict with the entrenched fur-trading monopoly at Albany. For nearly a century Schenectady had served as an advanced base of operations for independent trading with the Iroquois Confederacy, and once the war was over it would gain new importance as a staging base because of its proximity to the Stanwix portage to Lake Ontario.

It was due no doubt to Duncan's social and business connections with wealthy mercantile interests in New York that he was able in 1761 to obtain from General Amherst a grant of land on the Niagara portage, where he built a warehouse. This he stocked in July of the same year with goods to fulfil the contracts he had acquired from Sir William Johnson, Superintendent General of Indian Affairs, to supply presents for the Indians and provisions for the western posts. The grant of land was withdrawn later because of protests from other Albany merchants that it constituted a monopoly; but such was the advantage it gave Duncan that in 1762 he was able to place a resident partner, John Sterling, in Detroit, then a community of some two thousand persons, and thereby gain a foothold several years before rival Canadian groups were in a position to resume trading in the interior. So profitable were these operations that, on Duncan's advice, George Phyn sent one of his sons, James, to Schenectady in 1763. Thus began the transatlantic hegira of offspring that led Donald Creighton in *The Empire of the St. Lawrence* to describe George Phyn as "the unwitting patriarch of Canadian business" and was to result in the founding of the Bank of Montreal through the efforts of John Richardson. In 1766 the young Phyn was joined by his cousin Alexander Ellice, an advocate of the Scottish bar. Still in their mid twenties, the cousins provided capital for the expansion of Duncan's business and within a year bought out the founder's interest, at which time the firm became known as Phyn & Ellice.

At the time of its acquisition by the Phyn-Ellice partnership, John Duncan's business had become one of the most profitable in Schenectady. The importance of the town had further increased because it lay outside the area of military occupation controlled directly from Quebec, within which it was extremely difficult to obtain trading licences; it was through this town also that supplies for the Indian territory under Sir William Johnson's supervision were forwarded. Trade goods and supplies of various kinds were obtained from New York importing houses on credit, sorted and packaged at Schenectady, and forwarded in bateaux by lake and portage for delivery to the firm's agents or to independent traders at Detroit and Michilimackinac: in return, furs and other staples were collected at the posts and sent down the lakes to Schenectady where they were transported to New York for immediate sale or for reshipment to London. The Schenectady merchants held temporary monopoly over the exploitation of the old French fur-trading apparatus while the Canadian traders were not yet in a position either physically or politically, owing to the Seven Years' War, to re-establish the old French route up the Ottawa to Lake Huron and Michilimackinac. In fact it was not until 1767 that the first fur brigade left the latter post for Montreal.

In addition to the general trade, the firm seems to have enjoyed profitable contracts as suppliers to both the Indian Department and the Army Commissariat and to have received commercial paper from the west in the form of drafts drawn on government agencies, bills of exchange, and officers' remittances to families back in England. The volume of this business is uncertain but it appears to have been sufficiently profitable to enable John Duncan to retire on the strength of six years' profits, two of which must have been seriously depleted as a result of Pontiac's reign of terror and pillage.

At the outset of its career, the firm of Phyn & Ellice was faced with competition as outfitters and forwarders. Not only was the challenge of Quebec becoming more serious, but a change of regulations in 1768 transferred control of trade in the Indian territory to the provinces and, as a result, independent traders from Quebec were permitted to go out among the Indians, whereas formerly their activities had been confined to the military posts. The volume of trade rapidly increased, but so did the debauchery of the Indians as rum became the chief article of barter. The cousins met the situation boldly: John Porteous, a former associate of John Duncan, was made a partner to manage the company's business at Detroit and Michilimackinac; and Robert Ellice, a younger brother of Alexander, was brought from Scotland to Schenectady, also to be made a partner. The date of the arrival of yet another brother, James, is indefinite, but it is probable he arrived about this time. In 1768 also, James Phyn strengthened the firm's Schenectady connections by marrying a daughter of Dr. John Constable, an old acquaintance of Sir William Johnson. Following the marriage, the firm's headquarters were moved from "Bachelors' Hall" to more suitable surroundings, and there James brought his bride.

Despite the aggressive expansion of their business, Phyn, Ellice & Porteous found their competitive position gradually deteriorating for three principal reasons: the increase of Montreal activity at Michilimackinac; the difficulty of securing cargo space on the lakes following the granting of a forwarding monopoly to Alexander Grant, the chief of naval affairs on the Great Lakes; and the high cost and poor quality of British manufactured goods bought from New York importers, to whom the frontier trade assumed progressively less importance as the American economy expanded. It was to combat the first of these disadvantages that Porteous was taken into the partnership, while the second was met by the construction of a sloop at Detroit in association with other traders. Unfortunately, this was sold to Grant under an agreement which he failed to observe, but a second vessel of fifty tons burden, also built in association with Detroit clients, enabled the company to serve a larger number of customers in the Upper Country and to extend its operations through Lake Michigan to the Mississippi River. An effort to meet the third problem was made by establishing, for the first time, a direct contact overseas. This was with the firm of William and Alexander Forsyth, Scottish connections of the Phyn and Ellice families, to whom an order for 1769 was sent and along with it an invitation to "send us over a few of your boys or don't you choose they should become Americans?" Many Forsyth "boys" later migrated to Canada and became prominent merchants at Montreal, Kingston, Niagara Falls, and Detroit, correspondents of successive Phyn-Ellice partnerships, and active shareholders in the Bank of Montreal.

The year 1769 brought two major disasters. On arrival at New York, the goods shipped by Forsyth from Glasgow turned out to be more expensive than those which might have been obtained in London. Furthermore the non-importation agreements of American merchants, provoked by the Townshend Acts of 1767, had become effective, and no amount of influence could release the shipment after its arrival in New York. Unable to deliver the trade goods ordered for the Upper Country the previous autumn, Phyn, Ellice & Porteous suffered the loss of an entire year's business – a matter of some thousands of pounds – to Canadian rivals not affected by the American embargo. To prevent a repetition, Phyn, Ellice & Porteous, in the fall of 1769, sent a two-year supply order to the London firm of Neale &

Pigou with directions that should the Townshend Acts still be in force by the spring of 1770 (although repeal was confidently expected) the goods should be shipped via Quebec instead of New York. Although the acts were repealed on April 12, 1770, the shipment had already sailed for Quebec where James Phyn was on hand to meet it when it arrived on May 30. The goods were conveyed by him up the St. Lawrence and delivered to Alexander Ellice at Niagara for trans-shipment to John Porteous in Detroit.

Despite the successful use of the St. Lawrence route, and an increasing number of traders who were forsaking Schenectady for Montreal, Phyn and Ellice decided to remain where they had made their homes and resume importing via New York where their commercial connections were soundly established and where goods, particularly rum and tobacco, could be obtained more cheaply the year round. However, government patronage at Schenectady dropped sharply under the regime of Sir Guy Carleton, and so strong had become the Montreal competition that in 1772 we find Alexander Ellice in London, with a letter of introduction from Sir William Johnson, seeking an exclusive government contract to supply both the Indian Department and the western posts. While the contract was regarded as essential to the firm's future business, the argument given was that only by such means as a monopoly could the vicious debauchery and exploitation of the Indians be eliminated. Whatever merit the proposal may have had, it was embarked on without reckoning the political strength of the London merchants engaged in the Canadian trade and the mission proved a fiasco.

When Alexander returned to Schenectady with this news, James advocated a bold manoeuvre. Briefly, it called for Phyn, Ellice & Porteous to establish its own London office with James Phyn in charge to act as general agent both for the Schenectady partnership and for any other firms who wished to take advantage of Phyn's connections, experience, and knowledge of the colonies. This was not accomplished until 1774 because it became necessary to dissolve the partnership with Porteous in order to raise capital for the London venture. Assets were turned into cash, purchases curtailed, and new contracts concluded with up-country customers on the basis of the firm's future London position. To assist in this work still another member of the family connection arrived from Scotland, John Richardson, a grandson of George Phyn. By 1774 a sufficient liquid capital fund had been accumulated to enable James Phyn, his wife and their two sons to sail for England. They arrived in London in December and Phyn immediately opened a branch of Phyn, Ellice & Co., at the New York Coffee House, Cornhill. While several Quebec merchants had retired to London at an earlier date to represent the interests of their groups, Phyn, Ellice & Co. was probably the only English mercantile house established as a branch of a colonial enterprise.

Notwithstanding the immediate success of the London office, Phyn, Ellice & Co. in Schenectady suffered even worse setbacks in 1774-75 than they had in 1769.

The principal causes were the passage of the Quebec Act in 1774, which precluded the use of the old Mohawk route into Canada by restricting importation to certain customs offices, the most westerly of which was located at St. Johns, twenty miles southeast of Montreal; a new American embargo on British goods; and finally the American Revolution in 1775. Throughout this hiatus, Phyn, Ellice & Co. remained in Schenectady and profited temporarily from their dealings in exchange. In New York they were able to sell, at a high premium, bills drawn on James Phyn in London. The proceeds were then shipped to Isaac Todd, their representative in Montreal, who purchased, at a rate substantially below the New York premium, sterling bills on London which were then sent to James Phyn so that he could meet the New York drafts as they fell due. Thus perhaps were sown the first seeds of the idea for a full-fledged bank in Montreal.

While profitable both in cash and experience, the adventure in arbitrage was short-lived. In the spring of 1775 the Albany Committee of Safety, Protection and Correspondence received word that Phyn, Ellice & Co. were importing through Quebec. Thereafter it was only with the greatest difficulty that Alexander Ellice was able to secure a permit to travel to Niagara and thence to Canada on private business. Being opposed to the American cause, and having no intention of returning to Schenectady, he turned over the entire assets of the company to his brother James before leaving. Alexander spent the summer in the Upper Country and then journeyed to Quebec from whence he sailed for England in October, 1775. Both James and Robert Ellice were turned back at the Stanwix-Oswego portage in the spring of 1776, James to remain in Schenectady under close surveillance until 1779, when he was allowed to take an oath of allegiance to the State of New York; Robert to make his way to New York City, where he represented the firm's interests until September, 1778, when he sailed for Quebec.

To all intents and purposes, the Schenectady partnership was at an end and letters to this effect went out to their customers. Nevertheless, Alexander and William McComb continued as correspondents at Detroit for James Ellice who carried on the business at Schenectady and the operation of flour mills at Little Falls on the Mohawk River, erected in 1775 by Alexander Ellice.

After an active winter in London with James Phyn, during which he was smitten with the charms of James's sister, Anne, Alexander Ellice returned to Montreal in 1776 to re-establish the up-country business of supplying the needs of the old Schenectady customers. Such was the reputation of the firm and the loyalty of its customers that, in three years' time, the oldest of the Ellice brothers was able to return to London and marry Anne Phyn, leaving a flourishing Canadian business in the hands of Robert Ellice who had come up from New York to take over. The same year, a cousin, John Forsyth, was taken in as a partner in the Montreal firm and the name was now changed to Robert Ellice & Co.

Meanwhile, John Richardson, after serving as a clerk with Phyn, Ellice & Co. at

Schenectady and Detroit, became associated with John Porteous, the former partner, first in a privateering venture out of Boston, and later at Charleston, S.C.,
where Richardson shipped indigo, rice, tobacco and other products to Phyn, Ellice
& Co. in London. A trading venture followed in St. Augustine, Florida, but proved
less successful, and Richardson joined Porteous in New York where the latter was
supplying the British garrisons in New York and Philadelphia with goods shipped
by Phyn, Ellice & Co. from England. This business prospered until the declaration
of peace in 1783 when it was taken over by William Constable, James Phyn's
brother-in-law, after which it continued as a successful branch of the London firm
for many years. Richardson at this time apparently retained his connections with
both Porteous and Constable, and remained in New York until 1787, when he was
called on to become the Detroit representative of Robert Ellice & Co. of Montreal.
For upwards of ten years, therefore, John Richardson lived continuously in various
American cities where he made lasting connections and became intimately informed of all the financial aspects of the problems which beset the Continental
Congress. The knowledge and experience gained during this period were to stand
him in good stead at a later date.

During the War of American Independence, the Phyn-Ellice organization in
London expanded rapidly as a result of its American and West Indies business. It
was during this time that James Phyn procured the first of his series of ships named
Eweretta (other recorded spellings of which are *Euretta*, *Euretto*, *Everetta*, and
Ewretta). In 1781, the second was acquired through the purchase and rechristening
of the 350-ton *Latium*, and in 1792 a third, of 342 tons, was built for Phyn on the
Thames. It was this latter that made a name for herself in the fur trade, bringing
supplies across the Atlantic every spring for the Nor'Westers and taking back their
furs to be sold in London every autumn. At the war's close the firm was handling,
in addition to Canadian furs and skins, staples shipped to it from all parts of the
Atlantic seaboard from Newfoundland to the Caribbean. Such was the growth of
the concern by 1787 that John Inglis, a long-time employee and West Indies trader,
was taken into the partnership, as were James and Robert Ellice, the firm being
known as Phyn, Ellices & Inglis until James Ellice died later that year. Robert Ellice
died in 1790 and Alexander in 1805, at which time James Phyn retired, though he
did not die until 1821, and the direction of the business was taken over by John
Inglis and Edward Ellice, then aged twenty-four and the second of many children
born to Alexander and Anne Ellice.

The market in Canada, initially enlarged by the war, was kept buoyant by the
arrival in increasing numbers of United Empire Loyalists whose support, like that
of the Indian tribes, was for some years the responsibility of the government. At the
same time, the complete disruption of the Schenectady trade enabled Canadian
merchants to secure a monopoly of the western fur trade, a situation that was
prolonged for some twenty years after the peace of 1783 by Britain's continued

occupation of trading posts on American territory. Thus in 1784, when the second North West Company agreement was signed, Robert Ellice & Co. of Montreal were able to get the contract to supply the goods for two of the partners, McBeath and Pond, and in 1787 outfitted Gregory and McLeod, competitors of the North West Company. A year later, when McTavish, Frobisher & Co. became the exclusive agents for the Nor'Westers, half of the goods imported from England were supplied by Robert Ellice & Co. The ability to obtain so satisfactory a contract was based no doubt on the credit the London house was able to extend.

Despite the growing importance of the northwest trade, Robert Ellice embarked on expansion at Detroit. This perhaps was only natural, but nevertheless, it proved ill-advised. The firm's success had been based on the Ohio and Michigan trade and it was hoped, when conditions returned to normal, that trading could be resumed through Schenectady where the profits had been greatest and where the firm's assets were still secure in the hands of James Ellice, now an American citizen. This hope was never realized so far as the fur trade was concerned; in fact it was not until the War of 1812 that the Schenectady trade regained some of its former grandeur under John Jacob Astor. Following the Revolution, however, the Schenectady branch under James Ellice continued in business for many years.

Meanwhile the affairs of Robert Ellice & Co. at Detroit had reached such desperate straits that in 1787 John Richardson was sent there by the London partners to take charge. A year later, however, Robert Ellice fell ill and Richardson was ordered to Montreal to manage the entire Canadian business, which he took over, together with John Forsyth, when Ellice died in 1790. Thus, a new partnership, Forsyth, Richardson & Co., became another proliferation of this extraordinary family complex, since John Forsyth, born in Scotland in December 1762, was the sixth son of William Forsyth and Jean, a daughter of George Phyn.

On the basis of age and experience, it would seem that Richardson, then thirty-five, should have become the senior partner, since Forsyth was only twenty-eight. Why this did not come to pass is unknown, as are the respective interests of the the several partners: Phyn, Ellice & Inglis, John Forsyth and John Richardson, and at a later date Forsyth's brothers, James and Thomas. Two other brothers, George and Joseph, subsequently represented Forsyth, Richardson & Co. at Niagara and Kingston. This seems to indicate a predominant Forsyth interest which may explain John's preferential treatment; or it may simply have been that he was the continuing partner, long established in Montreal. In any case, all the documentary material available points to Richardson as the guiding genius of the firm.

Whatever the state of the firm's business at that time, improvements on several fronts were rapidly made. Thanks to the strong political influence in Quebec and London, a government contract was obtained to supply the sorely stricken Loyalists in Upper Canada. Soon after, it was possible to supply other rapidly growing settlements on the Lower Lakes with flour from the Ellice mills at Little Falls, and clothing, implements and other goods through their connections in Schenectady. With lines of supply originating at both Quebec and New York City, and with a long-established and highly reputed organization in Upper Canada, the firm quickly became the leading mercantile house in that region and maintained that position for many years. The brig *Nancy*, later destroyed during the War of 1812, was a venture of Forsyth, Richardson & Co., built to transport the company's goods from the Niagara portage to the Upper Lakes.

When American occupation and settlement finally made the Detroit area no longer attractive to Canadian commerce, Forsyth, Richardson & Co. liquidated their assets there and centred their activities at Michilimackinac, still the depot for the southwest trade beyond Lake Michigan and for the northwest trade beyond Lake Superior. There, in association with such old Schenectady customers as Todd, McGill & Co. and Grant, Campion & Co. (John Forsyth married Margaret Grant), Forsyth, Richardson & Co., carrying on the trend set by Robert Ellice, successfully challenged the growing strength of McTavish, Frobisher & Co. and, when the North West Company agreement of 1792 was concluded, were able to secure a share in the revamped enterprise. From then until 1798, when the firm broke away to form the New North West or XY Company, Forsyth, Richardson & Co. probably enjoyed a large share of the North West business as suppliers to McTavish, Frobisher & Co.

While important to the partnership, the northwest fur trade never became the exclusive interest of Forsyth, Richardson & Co. as it was and always remained for McTavish, Frobisher & Co. and their co-partners in the North West Company. Instead, as we have seen, the Montreal affiliate of Phyn, Ellice & Inglis conducted a general merchandise business which expanded very rapidly, especially in Upper Canada. The marked contrast in the business activities of Canada's two leading commercial organizations, Forsyth, Richardson & Co. and McTavish, Frobisher & Co., now becomes strikingly apparent: the first, with its English connection, was proliferated, the other monolithic. These differences were accentuated as population increased in Upper Canada with the influx of the "late Loyalists." There from the beginning, Forsyth, Richardson & Co. were the largest importers of general merchandise both from Britain and the United States and the largest exporters of staples to the same two markets. Engaged in such a trade, they had to deal with problems of credits, collections, remittances, exchanges and payments never encountered by the rival organization, engaged as it exclusively was in trade which was still conducted by the methods of primitive barter that had existed in North America before the coming of the white man. The diversity of Forsyth, Richardson & Co.'s business gave them a greater stake in Canada's growth and settlement, both of which were detrimental to those merchants interested solely in furs. Anything that could help expand agriculture and the domestic market for imports would be a boon to Forsyth, Richardson & Co., a menace to their North West rivals.

However, in spite of their attempts to found a bank in 1792 and their primary interests as suppliers, they became intricately involved in the various reorganizations which took place in the fur trade. They continued to hold a share in the XY Company until it was reunited with the North West Company in 1804. John Forsyth and John Richardson signed the merger agreement for John Inglis and Alexander Ellice, as well as for their own firm, thus giving both the London and Montreal houses an interest in the new company. They foresaw the approaching conflict between their North West Company and the Hudson's Bay Company and, taking advantage of the strength gained through amalgamation, Edward Ellice, in 1804, offered "103,000l. Navy 5l. per cents. for the whole Hudson's Bay Company." The transaction proved unfeasible but other attempts followed, including a plan by which Ellice, in conjunction with Simon McGillivray and Alexander Mackenzie, would buy stock control of the Hudson's Bay Company. This also failed, and as the pursuit of the retreating beaver was carried farther and farther westward, the monopoly enjoyed by the Hudson's Bay Company became more and more a source of hateful irritation to the North West Company. However, it was not until 1820, after armed robbery, kidnapping and outright warfare between the companies had brought both to the verge of bankruptcy, that the negotiations commenced which would unite the two great rivals. Andrew Wedderburn Colvile sat for the Hudson's Bay Company while the Nor'Westers were represented by William and Simon McGillivray and Edward Ellice, who now occupied a Whig seat in the British House of Commons, having been elected in 1818 as the member for Coventry. The records of the amalgamation procedures have never been made public, but considering the ravaged state of the North West Company and the dissension amongst its partners, Ellice and his confrères were able to secure an admirable settlement.

The original agreement gave the Nor'Westers half of the profits and a fair representation on the joint advisory board. However, subsequent revisions swung the balance of power in favour of the English company, and many of the old North West partners eventually died financially destitute. When the main supply route was switched to Hudson Bay, William McGillivray estimated that the loss to Montreal in wages, provisions and stores alone would amount to £40,000 annually. Losses of this nature caused much financial distress and heralded the unfortunate McGillivray bankruptcy, which fell heavily on the Bank of Montreal, causing a schism in its directorate. Some, however, such as Forsyth and Richardson, were able to discover new outlets for their entrepreneurial ability and thereby survive somewhat longer. They were of course closely connected with the Bank of Montreal, and in 1824, possibly as a result of Richardson's legislative efforts in promoting Canadian foreign trade, Forsyth, Richardson & Co. were awarded the contract as sole agents for the East India Company in Canada. They also continued their business in Upper Canada which had started with the United Empire Loyalist contracts, and their presence there was well rewarded when, in 1826, they were appointed financial agents of the Province of Upper Canada.

It is doubtful that their connection with the Bank of Montreal and their contacts in London did them any harm in their quest for this contract. In spite of the death of the original partners, John Richardson's in 1831 and John Forsyth's in 1837, the firm remained in business until May 17, 1847, when a notice appeared in the Montreal *Gazette* announcing the dissolution of the firms of Forsyth, Richardson & Co. of Montreal and Forsyth, Walker & Co. of Quebec. The winding-up procedures of the Montreal firm were to be under the direction of T. B. Anderson, its last president and a son-in-law of John Richardson. Anderson continued in business with new partners, but from this time on his energies were devoted primarily to the Bank of Montreal, of which he served as vice-president from 1847 to 1860 and as president from then until his resignation in 1869.

Meanwhile, in London, Edward Ellice, dubbed "the Bear," continued as a prominent figure in both the fur trade and politics. The only Nor'Wester to retain a say in the Hudson's Bay Company's management after 1824, when the vestigial advisory board was abolished, he remained until 1837 a member of the London Committee which directed the company's affairs. In 1825 he had assumed the unhappy and difficult task of administering the bankruptcy of Simon McGillivray which took him five full years, such was the mess of the books of McGillivrays, Thain & Co. During this period he gave up his seat in Parliament but returned in 1830 to serve first as Secretary of the Treasury and then as Secretary of War in the cabinet of Earl Grey, who was his brother-in-law by virtue of Ellice's marriage in 1808 to Lady Hannah Althea, younger daughter of the first Earl Grey.

It has been claimed that Ellice was the first merchant ever "to pass from the counting house to the cabinet." In view of his continuous support of all measures in the British parliament which would improve the commerce of the Canadas, it might also be said that he never really left the counting house. The impression is confirmed when we find him writing to his son, who had accompanied Lord Durham to Canada as an unpaid secretary, to advise him that "politics should never interfere with business." Since 1821, Ellice senior had been striving for the union of Upper and Lower Canada, hoping thereby to secure the ascendancy of the English commercial class. Frustrated in his attempts of 1821, 1828, and 1834, he plunged wholeheartedly into the task when his good friend and relative, Durham, was appointed Commissioner. He thoroughly briefed Durham as to his own views before the latter left for Canada, but later broke with him because Durham based his plan for union on socio-political principles rather than on the economic necessities with which Ellice was concerned. Angered when the Patriotes, in November 1838, seized his inherited estate at Beauharnois, which he valued at £50,000, Ellice rejoined the fray with renewed vigour. As party whip for the incumbent Whigs, he was in an excellent position to bring pressure to bear on the Colonial Secretary, Lord John Russell, who, it was said, "feared 'the Bear' even more than the most gifted leader of the opposition." Ellice also resorted to lobbying through the press, receiving a generous hearing in the *Morning Chronicle*, one of the proprietors of which was Simon McGillivray. However, these political manoeuvrings met with little success, and Ellice seems to have retired from the centre ring of the political arena, making only two more brief appearances: in 1848 as a member of a committee investigating the commercial crisis of 1847, and in 1855 as a member of Roebuck's committee to inquire into the administration of the Crimean War.

Although his official connection with the Hudson's Bay Company had terminated when he left the governing committee in 1837, Ellice remained enmeshed in their affairs for several years. By the agreement of 1824, he and the McGillivrays had been held responsible for any legal action against the North West Company based on happenings prior to 1821. To this end they had had to lay aside a fund of £50,000, and it was not until 1851 that Ellice managed to clear up all the suits. Even then the family interest in the trade did not cease, for his son, Edward, who had replaced his father on the governing committee, was appointed a Deputy Governor of the company in 1858. The Bear himself, however, remained England's most respected authority on North American affairs, consulted by both private and public interests. Although no longer the political power of old, he nevertheless continued to hold his seat in Parliament until he died in 1863, one century exactly after the arrival of James Phyn in America.

APPENDIX E

———————— ══⟪⟪⟪⟪⟪⟨⟩⟩⟩⟩⟩⟫══ ————————

COLONIAL

MONEY MATTERS

WHEN THE

BANK BEGAN

———————— ══⟪⟪⟪⟪⟪⟨⟩⟩⟩⟩⟩⟫══ ————————

Before the Montreal Bank issued Canada's first bank-notes upon its establishment in 1817, the currency situation in the colonies was deplorable. In consequence, most business was done by barter. Merchants were struggling with a hodge-podge of money from half a dozen different countries, as indicated on the following page by the selection of coins circulating in Canada during the early years of the nineteenth century.

"Our currency," said one outspoken colonist, "is like a Scotch haggis, made up of contradictions, of things good and bad, oatmeal, onions, hog's lard, butter, crumbs of bread, salt, pepper, garlic, leeks, parsley, &c &c."

The continuously changing values of these currencies made it impossible for merchants and traders to know from one day to the next where they stood financially. Indeed, it could be said that the chaotic currency situation was the most immediate reason for the founding of the Montreal Bank.

Methods of handling money a century and a half ago may seem to have been primitive by modern standards. Yet, exactness almost to a hair's weight was demanded by bankers of 1817, as revealed in the use of the sensitive little scale in the Bank's museum, illustrated here. It measures 5½ inches in length when folded down into its velvet-lined walnut case. With this scale, the bank-teller was able to judge whether, as often happened, someone had been "clipping" a coin for his personal benefit.

In contrast with this delicate device was the iron strong-box used by the Bank for the security and transport of money. This box, which was roughly a cubic foot in measure, weighed nearly a hundred pounds when empty. The transport of money in the Bank's early years was heavy business, and the movement of coin in substantial bulk from one town to another was quite common.

◀ Coins circulating in Canada in the early 1800's included those shown on the opposite page, from (A) United States; (B) United Kingdom; (C) Spain; (D) France; (E) Portugal; (F) Mexico.

FIRST CANADIAN MONEY   The three Montreal Bank notes reproduced on the opposite page are among the earliest issued by the Bank in denominations of one, two, five, ten, twenty, fifty, and one hundred dollars. These were, in effect, Canada's first bank-notes and their circulation proved a great boon to the merchants and traders of the colonies.

Canadian coinage did not come into being until nearly twenty years after the establishment of the Bank. When coins did appear in Lower Canada in 1836, the tokens, as they were called, were issued in one penny (deux sous) and halfpenny (un sou) denominations.

Bank tokens were instituted by the Bank of Montreal, but they were promptly made available for issue by the other banks.

By 1838 the Bank of Montreal had tokens peculiar to itself, carrying an impression, on the obverse, of the Bank's head-office building, while the reverse showed the coat of arms of the City of Montreal as some earlier tokens had done. Several issues, dating from 1838 to 1844, showed side and front views of the building.

Examples of these tokens appear below. The two on the left are the "bouquet sous" of the earliest mintage of 1836-37, while the four on the right are of the later designs peculiar to the Bank of Montreal, from 1838 to 1844.

BIBLIOGRAPHY

The archives of the Bank of Montreal have, of course, been the most important source of material for this history. However, extensive use has also been made of the Public Archives of Canada, at Ottawa, especially in referring to government correspondence and documents, several early pamphlets, and numerous collections of personal papers and records of the colonial period. Most of the vital statistics have been taken from Census of Canada publications and the 32nd General Report of the Immigration Commission. Legislative information has been derived from the *Journals* of the respective Assemblies and Councils, as well as from reports of parliamentary debates in contemporary newspapers. The most generally consulted of the latter were the *Canadian Courant*, *Le Canadien*, the Kingston *Chronicle*, the Montreal *Gazette*, the Quebec (Official) *Gazette*, the Montreal *Herald*, the Quebec *Mercury*, *La Minerve*, *Le Spectateur Canadien*, and the Montreal *Transcript*, all of which the Canadian Library Association has made available through its microfilming program and catalogue.

Of many published works consulted, the following proved particularly useful:

ANDRÉADÈS, A.   *A History of the Bank of England*
Translated by Christabel Meredith
London: P. S. King & Son, Ltd., 1909.

BORTHWICK, REV. J. D.   *History and Biographical Gazetteer of Montreal to the Year 1892*
Montreal: John Lovell & Son, 1892.

BREBNER, J. BARTLET   *Canada: A Modern History*
Ann Arbor, Michigan: The University of Michigan Press, 1960.

~   *North Atlantic Triangle*
New Haven: Yale University Press, 1945.

BRECKENRIDGE, R. M.   *The Canadian Banking System, 1817-1890*
New York: Macmillan & Company, 1895.

~   *The History of Banking in Canada*
(National Monetary Commission,
61st Congress 2nd Session, Senate Document 332)
Washington, D.C.: Government Printing Office, 1910.

BRYANT, ARTHUR   *The Age of Elegance, 1812-1822*
London: Collins, 1950.

CAMPBELL, MARJORIE WILKINS   *The North West Company*
Toronto: The Macmillan Company of Canada Limited, 1957.

CAMPBELL, REV. ROBERT   *A History of the Scotch Presbyterian Church, St. Gabriel Street, Montreal*
Montreal: W. Drysdale & Co., 1887.

CLAPHAM, SIR JOHN   *The Bank of England*, vol. II
Cambridge: Cambridge University Press, 1944.

CREIGHTON, DONALD   *The Empire of the St. Lawrence*
Toronto: The Macmillan Company of Canada Limited, 1956.

DENISON, MERRILL   *The Barley and the Stream*
Toronto: McClelland and Stewart Limited, 1955.

DOIGE, THOMAS   *An Alphabetical List of the Merchants, Traders and Housekeepers residing in Montreal*
Montreal: James Lane, 1819.

DURHAM, JOHN GEORGE, LORD — *Report on the Affairs of British North America*
ed. Sir C. P. Lucas. 3 vols
Oxford: The Clarendon Press, 1912.

EASTERBROOK, W. T. & AITKEN, HUGH G. J. — *Canadian Economic History*
Toronto: The Macmillan Company of Canada Limited, 1956.

FLEMING, R. H. — "Phyn, Ellice and Company of Schenectady"
Contributions to Canadian Economics, vol. IV, 1932
Toronto: University of Toronto Press, 1932.

FULFORD, ROGER — *Glyn's, 1753-1953, Six Generations in Lombard Street*
London: Macmillan & Co. Ltd., 1953.

GLAZEBROOK, G. P. DE T. — *A History of Transportation in Canada*
New Haven: Yale University Press, 1938.

GUILLET, EDWIN C. — *Early Life in Upper Canada*
Toronto: The Ontario Publishing Co., Limited, 1933.

~ *The Great Migration*
Toronto: Thomas Nelson and Sons, 1937.

HAMMOND, BRAY — *Banks and Politics in America
from the Revolution to the Civil War*
Princeton, N.J.: Princeton University Press, 1957.

HIDY, RALPH W. — *The House of Baring in American Trade and Finance*
Cambridge, Mass.: Harvard University Press, 1949.

HINCKS, SIR FRANCIS — *Reminiscences of his Public Life*
Montreal: William Drysdale & Co., 1884.

HODGETTS, J. E. — *Pioneer Public Service*
Toronto: University of Toronto Press, 1955.

INNIS, H. A. — *The Fur Trade in Canada*
Toronto: University of Toronto Press, 1956.

JAMIESON, A. B. — *Chartered Banking in Canada*
Toronto: The Ryerson Press, 1959.

KINCHEN, OSCAR A. — *Lord Russell's Canadian Policy*
Lubbock, Texas: The Texas Tech. Press, 1945.

LOWER, A. R. M. — *Colony to Nation*
Toronto: Longmans, Green & Company, 1946.

MACKINTOSH, W. A.   "Canada and Vermont," *Canadian Historical Review*,
vol. VIII, 1927. Toronto: University of Toronto Press, 1927.

MC IVOR, R. CRAIG   *Canadian Monetary, Banking and Fiscal Development*
Toronto: The Macmillan Company of Canada Limited,
1958.

PRESSNELL, L. S.   *Country Banking in the Industrial Revolution*
Oxford: The Clarendon Press, 1956.

REDLICH, FRITZ   *The Molding of American Banking: Men and Ideas*
2 vols. New York: Hafner Publishing Company Inc., 1951.

RICH, E. E.   *History of the Hudson's Bay Company*, vol. II
London: The Hudson's Bay Record Society, 1959.

ROSS, VICTOR   *A History of the Canadian Bank of Commerce*
2 vols. Toronto: Oxford University Press, 1920 and 1922.

SANDHAM, ALFRED   *Ville Marie, or, Sketches of Montreal, Past and Present*
Montreal: George Bishop & Co., 1870.

SCROPE, G. POULETT   *Memoir of the Life of the Right Honourable Charles
Lord Sydenham*
London: John Murray, 1844.

SHORTT, ADAM   "The Early History of Canadian Banking"
Journal of The Canadian Bankers' Association, IV-V.

~ "Canadian Currency and Exchange under French Rule"
J.C.B.A., V-VI.

~ "The History of Canadian Currency, Banking and
Exchange," *J.C.B.A.*, VII-XIV.

~ "Hon. John McGill and the First Problems of Domestic
Exchange in Upper Canada," *J.C.B.A.*, XXIX.

~ "Hon. John Richardson, Merchant, Financier and
Statesman," *J.C.B.A.*, XXIX.

~ "Hon. William Allan, Merchant and Banker"
J.C.B.A., XXX.

~ "Austin Cuvillier, Merchant, Legislator and Banker"
J.C.B.A., XXX.

~ "Horatio Gates, Wholesale Merchant, Banker and
Legislator," *J.C.B.A.*, XXX.

SHORTT, ADAM "Hon. George Moffatt, Merchant, Statesman and Banker"
J.C.B.A., XXXII.

~ *The Life of Lord Sydenham* ("Makers of Canada," XV)
Toronto: Morang & Co., 1908.

~ (ed.) *Documents Relating to Canadian Currency,
Exchange and Finance during the French Period*
2 vols. Ottawa: F. A. Acland, 1925.

SHORTT, ADAM, (gen'l eds.) *Canada and its Provinces*, vols. I-V
& DOUGHTY, A. G. Toronto: Glasgow, Brook & Company, 1914.

STACEY, C. P. *Canada and the British Army* (Rev. ed.)
Toronto: University of Toronto Press in association
with The Royal Commonwealth Society, 1963.

TERRILL, F. W. *A Chronology of Montreal and of Canada
from A.D. 1752 to A.D. 1893*
Montreal: John Lovell & Son, 1893.

TUCKER, GILBERT N. *The Canadian Commercial Revolution, 1845-1851*
New Haven: Yale University Press, 1936.

WADE, MASON *The French Canadians, 1760-1945*
Toronto: The Macmillan Company of Canada Limited,
1955.

WALLACE, W. STEWART *The Pedlars from Quebec and other Papers on
the Nor'Westers*
Toronto: The Ryerson Press, 1954.

~ *Documents Relating to the North West Company*
Toronto: The Champlain Society, 1934.

ACKNOWLEDGEMENTS

The publishers are much indebted to numerous organizations and private persons for assistance in the gathering of illustrative matter and related historical data for this volume and gratefully acknowledge their invaluable help and co-operation.

Among the archives, museums and libraries extending help are the following: Albany Institute of History and Art; Bank of Canada (Money Museum); Château de Ramezay; City of Montreal (City Planning Board); Glenbow Foundation; Lachine Historical Society; Manitoba Provincial Library; McGill University (McCord Museum); New Brunswick Museum; Province of Quebec (Ministry of Cultural Affairs); Provincial Archives of British Columbia; Public Archives of Canada; Royal Canadian Geographical Society; Toronto Public Library; University of Michigan (William L. Clements Library); University of Toronto (Royal Ontario Museum, Sigmund Samuel Canadiana Collection); Vermont Historical Society.

Commercial corporations which have kindly supplied material are Canada Steamship Lines Limited (Canadiana Collection) and the Hudson's Bay Company.

Private individuals who have contributed to the undertaking, either through the loan of old pictures and engravings or through advice and research assistance in one form or another, include Mr. Anthony Clegg, Mr. Edgar Andrew Collard, Mrs. I. B. M. Dobell, Commander Allan H. Easton, Mr. John King, Mr. Lawrence M. Lande, Mr. Hyman Lipson, Mr. Louis Mendelson, Mr. Stanley Pearce, Professor G. F. G. Stanley, Mr. Robert Verity and Mr. W. J. G. Wadsworth.

The publishers are indebted to the Montreal General Hospital for permission to reproduce the portrait of the Honourable John Richardson, chief benefactor of the hospital in its early years.

453

INDEX

454

Ellice, William, (App. D) 432

Ellice & Co., Robert, 33; (App. D) 436, 437, 438

Ellice, Kinnear & Co., 314

Erie and Ontario Railroad, 235

Erie Canal, 53, 110, 111, 181, 199, 247

Ermatinger, Charles Oakes, 268

Ermatinger, Frederick W., 85-86, 100, 132, 236, 237, 248
    and reform of B of M management, 215, 216, 225-33

Essex Bank (Salem, Mass.), 60

Eweretta, 31, 32; (App. D) 437

failures:
    bank, 96, 158, 204, 206-7, 219, 246, 270, 281, 325, 328, 392
    business, 91-92, 221, 225, 306, 328, 348

Family Compact, 181, 303, 307, 345
    and Bank of Upper Canada, 116, 154-58, 266, 283, 301, 357, 364, 392
    and Union of Upper and Lower Canada, 373, 376

Farmers' Bank, 310, 346

Federalist party (U.S.), 60

Fenians, 183, 184

Ferrie, Adam, 382

fiat money, 202

"Fifty-four forty or fight", 183

Fils de la Liberté, 351

Finlay, James, 248

Finlay, John, 55

First Bank of the United States (1791-1811), 26, 57-59, 60, 71, 83, 108, 184
    demise of, 59, 64, 94, 185
    as model for Canadian banking, 62, 129, 140

Flaxman, John, 121

Fleming, John (President 1830-32), 4, 198, 224, 290; (App. C) 429, 430
    as B of M president, 288, 289, 323
    as B of M vice-president, 236, 266
    and McGillivray bankruptcy, 238, 239, 243
    and reform of B of M management, 216, 224-34

Fleming, R. H., "Phyn, Ellice and Company of Schenectady", (App. D) 431

Forbes plan for a provincial currency, 281-82

Forges du St. Maurice, 6, 27

Forsyth, George, 92, 314; (App. D) 438

Forsyth, James, (App. D) 438

Forsyth, John (Vice-President 1825-26), 30, 31, 55, 71, 102, 188; (App. D) 436, 438, 439, 440, 441
    as B of M director, 85, 86, 92, 104, 171
    as B of M vice-president, 215
    and McGillivray bankruptcy, 212, 239, 243
    and reform of B of M management, 208, 215, 220, 225-34

Forsyth, Joseph, (App. D) 438

Forsyth, Thomas, (App. D) 438

Forsyth, William, (App. D) 438

Forsyth, William & Alexander, (App. D) 434

Forsyth, Richardson & Co., 30, 77, 102, 162, 169, 192; (App. D) 438, 439-40, 441
    agents for East India Co., 198, 222, 229; (App. D) 440
    and Canada Banking Company, 25, 26, 28, 31
    financial agents for Upper Canada, 222, 288
    and Montreal Bank, 92, 104, 117
    and XY Company, 33, 43, 63-64

Forsyth, Walker & Co., (App. D) 441

Fort Edward, 38

Fort Frontenac, 132

Fort Kaministikwia, 175

Fort Lennox, 347

Fort William, 67, 166, 167, 172, 173, 175, 210

Franklin, F., 101

Fraser, John, 34

Fredericton (N.B.), 317, 318

free banks and banking, 258-59, 278, 281, 307, 308

free trade, 196, 197, 327, 374

Freer, Noah, 150-51

French and Indian War, 29

French Revolution, 37

Frobisher, B. & J., 33

Frontenac (steamship), 169

Froste, Robert, 229, 233, 234

Frothingham, John, 332

Fulton Robert, 98, 224; (App. C) 428

fur trade, 4, 12, 17, 22, 23, 24, 29-36, 37, 164-74, 175, 213, App. D, 431-42 *passim*
    and B of M, 171, 221
    decline of, 42-43, 63
    exports, 33, 36, 38, 39, 63, 210-11

Furniss, Albert, 318

Gallatin, Albert, 59, 185

Galt, John, 282

Garden, George (Vice-President 1818-19, 1819-22), 104, 119, 163, 171, 188, 193

THE AUTHOR

Merrill Denison was born in Detroit, Michigan, in 1893. His mother was Canadian and he spent most of his early life in Ontario, later studying architecture at the universities of Toronto and Pennsylvania, and in New York and Paris. He joined the American Field Service in 1916 and served with the French and American armies during the remainder of World War I, after which he practised his profession briefly in Boston and New York.

Returning to Canada in 1921, he became the Art Director of Hart House Theatre at the University of Toronto and while there wrote the first of a series of realistic comedies, later published under the title of *The Unheroic North*, which established him as a leading Canadian playwright. Upon his mother's death in 1921 he took on the management of the family estate at Bon Echo, Ontario, until 1929, after which he devoted his energies exclusively to writing.

As author of "The Romance of Canada," a series of historical plays broadcast in 1931-32 by the Canadian National Railways and produced by Tyrone Guthrie, Mr. Denison became one of the pioneers of radio drama. He specialized in this field after moving to New York, where he wrote "Great Moments in American History", "The Forum of Liberty", "America's Hour", and many other radio series. During World War II he was a consultant for the Wartime Information Board and the United Nations Information Office, and served as a correspondent for the B.B.C. During the New York phase of his career he remained a frequent contributor to Canadian and American magazines, with an ever-widening interest in business history.

Mr. Denison's published works include *The Unheroic North, Advancing America, Klondike Mike—an Alaskan Odyssey, Harvest Triumphant—the Story of Massey-Harris, The Barley and the Stream—the Molson Story, The Power to Go—the History of the American Automobile Industry*, and *The People's Power—the Story of Ontario Hydro*.

DESIGN / *Frank Newfeld*

LAYOUT / *John Elphick* • CHAPTER TITLE ILLUSTRATIONS / *Laurence Hyde*

TYPE / The text is set in Pilgrim, a type face designed by Eric Gill in 1936. Based on a classical Roman model (Trajan's Column) as was Perpetua, it was originally called Bunyon and was designed for use in select and limited editions. Pilgrim appeared in Linotype in 1953.

PRINTING & BINDING / Lithographed in six colours by The Southam Printing Company Limited on 70-lb. specially opacified Lucerne Text; bound in C.I.L. PX7 pyroxylin cloth and foil stamped in three colours, by the T. H. Best Printing Company Limited.

ENDPAPERS / Photographic reproductions of "Agriculture" and "Navigation," two of four Coade plaques that were set in the façade of the Bank's Head Office building erected on Place d'Armes in 1819.